Mass Media
and
American Politics

Mass Media
and
American Politics

THIRD EDITION

Doris A. Graber
University of Illinois at Chicago

A Division of Congressional Quarterly Inc.
1414 22nd Street N.W., Washington, D.C. 20037

Printed in the United States of America

Third Printing

Library of Congress Cataloging-in-Publication Data

Graber, Doris A.
  Mass media and American politics.

  Includes index.
  1. Mass media—Social aspects—United States.
2. Mass media—Political aspects—United States.
I. Title.
HN90.M3G7   1989   320.973'028   88-16127
ISBN 0-87187-475-X

To
Jack, Jim, Lee, Susan, Tom—
my very special students

CONTENTS

Tables and Figures   xi

Preface   xiii

1 Media Power and Government Control   1

Political Importance of Mass Media   3
Functions of Mass Media   5
Effects of Mass Media   12
Government Control of Mass Media:
    Assumptions and Methods   20
Summary   29

2 Ownership, Regulation, and Guidance of Media   35

Control and Ownership: Public, Semipublic, and Private   36
Patterns of Private Ownership   41
Curbs on Private Control of the Media   50
Control by Media Personnel   59
Summary   68

3 News Making and News Reporting   75

Models of the News-Making Process   76
The Gatekeepers   77
Effects of Gatekeeping   94
Appraising the News-Making Process   102
Summary   104

4 Press Freedom and the Law   111

Access to the Media   112
Access to Information   123
Individual Rights vs. the Public's Right to Know   131
Summary   140

5 **Media Impact on Attitudes and Behavior**   147

Differential Effects of Print and Broadcast News   148
The Role of Media in Political Socialization   149
Differences in Media Use and Socialization   155
Choosing Media Stories   159
Learning Processes   164
Learning Effects: Knowledge and Attitudes   167
Learning Effects: Behavior   176
Summary   182

6 **Elections in the Television Age**   193

The State of Research   194
The Consequences of Media Politics   196
Media Content   206
Media Effects   222
Summary   227

7 **The Struggle for Control: News from the White House, Congress, and the Courts**   235

The Adversary Relationship   235
The Media and the Executive Branch   237
The Media and Congress   254
The Media and the Courts   265
Summary   270

8 **The Media as Policy Makers**   277

Manipulative Journalism in Perspective   278
Muckraking Models   280
Beyond Muckraking: Power Plays and Surrenders   285
Agenda Building   287
Documentaries and Docudramas   295
Methods: Fair and Foul   297
Summary   299

9 **Crisis Coverage**   305

The Nature of Crisis Conditions   305
Four Crises   306
Media Response and Role   309
Summary   323

10 Foreign Affairs Coverage **327**

The Foreign News Slice in the News Pie 328
Making Foreign News 329
Appraising Foreign News Making 351
Impact on Public Opinion 353
Exporting News 354
Summary 357

11 Trends in Media Policy **365**

Dissatisfaction with the Media 366
The Impact of New Technologies 373
The Shape of the Future 382
Summary 387

Index **393**

TABLES AND FIGURES

Tables

2-1   Selected Characteristics of Journalists   61
2-2   Issue Positions of General Public and Journalists   64
2-3   Most Frequently Used Newspapers and Magazines   66

3-1   Sources of Front-Page News Stories   79
3-2   Comparative Frequency of Mention of Selected
         Index Crimes by Chicago Police Official Records
         and by *Chicago Tribune*, 1976   85
3-3   Frequency of Mention of News Topics   88
3-4   Network Coverage of State News, Yearly Average,
         July 1985-June 1987   90

5-1   Rankings of Top Twenty-five Content Categories
         and Average Ratings Across Ten Markets   161
5-2   Reasons for Attention or Inattention to News Stories   162
5-3   Recall of Specific Information on Unemployment
         and Inflation   170
5-4   Television News Comprehension Scores   171
5-5   Network Television News Characteristics   175

6-1   Distribution of Coverage Areas in the 1983 Chicago
         Mayoral Primary and General Elections   208
6-2   Source Orientation in the 1983 Chicago Mayoral
         Primary and General Elections   211
6-3   Candidate Evaluations in Post-Labor Day
         Network Television News, 1984   214
6-4   Newspaper Issue Coverage in the Last Month of the
         1968, 1972, 1976, and 1980 Presidential Campaigns   217
6-5   Issue Mention by Presidential and
         Vice-Presidential Candidates During
         the 1980 General Election   218

6-6   Median Number of Local Newspaper Paragraphs
      Mentioning Selected Themes in Fourteen Tight
      Congressional Races, September 27-
      November 7, 1978   221
6-7   Presidential Qualities Mentioned by the Public
      and by Newspapers, 1976   223
6-8   Comparison of Percentage of Mention of Issues
      and Events by Newspapers, Television, and
      Survey Responses, 1976   225

7-1   Evening Network News Coverage of the Three
      Branches of Government, July 1986-June 1987   237
7-2   Tone of CBS News Coverage of the President,
      January 1968-January 1985   243
7-3   Issue Focus of Evening Network News Coverage of
      the President and Congress, July 1986-June 1987   256
7-4   An Evaluation of Press Coverage of Congress   263

8-1   Source Orientation Regarding Nuclear Energy
      Stories, 1970-1983   291

9-1   Principal Sources of Disaster Information   309

10-1 Distribution of Foreign Correspondents   332
10-2 Foreign Language Fluency of American Reporters   333
10-3 Agree/Disagree on "U.S. Adds to Third
      World Poverty"   334
10-4 Network Coverage of Major Regions, 1972-1975
      and 1976-1979   342

11-1 Ownership of Top Fifty Cable Systems   379

Figures

2-1   Diverse Holdings of General Electric Company   43

11-1 The Cable TV Explosion   378

PREFACE

American mass media have changed significantly since 1984 when the second edition of *Mass Media and American Politics* was published. The primary reasons are business mergers involving the electronic media and newspaper chains; the deregulation policies of the Reagan administration, as reflected in the Federal Communication Commission's rules; and the growth of new media technologies such as cable and satellite television transmission. To describe and analyze the extent of these major changes and their impact on politics and political news, a new edition of the book was needed. This new edition describes these changes and their impact on politics and political news. It also incorporates important advances in the study of media effects and in-depth analyses of media content in previously unexplored areas of politics. Many of the new data come from my own ongoing research on the impact of television news on politics. Throughout the book political events and research findings have been updated, and fresh examples have replaced old accounts.

Although much has changed, the basic features of the interrelation between mass media and American politics have remained the same, testimony to the maturity of the relationship. Therefore, the organizational structure of the book has been retained. While the book discusses all of the mass media, the primary emphasis remains on news produced by television and newspapers, the chief sources of current information for people in public and private life. Magazines, radio, and personal conversation play a distinctly subordinate role. I chose this emphasis so that I could explore each topic in reasonable depth but still keep the book modest in size.

The major reasons for writing the book initially are as valid in 1988 as they were in 1980 when the first edition was published. The influence of mass media on contemporary American politics remains pervasive and profound. The need still exists for a college level, up-to-date introductory text that analyzes the essential connection between media and politics from a primarily political perspective.

In the past most research focused on the relationship between media and politics during elections, a pattern that continues, although it has become less pronounced. As the references in the text and in the suggested readings at the end of each chapter indicate, the scope of research has broadened considerably since 1980. However, most of these recent studies are specialized, focusing on single segments of the total picture. A text was needed that explored and highlighted other areas and provided an overview of the entire field. *Mass Media and American Politics,* third edition, serves that purpose.

Chapters 1, 2, and 3 examine the mass media as institutions in the American political system. These chapters show how the media are both molded by and reflect that system and how they affect its performance and the interplay among public and private institutions. Media structures, personnel and operations, and the impact they have on media content are explained and assessed. The next two chapters analyze the effects of news on individuals. Chapter 4 describes the legal rights of ordinary citizens, public officials, and newspeople to obtain and publish information and to be protected from damaging publicity. The wealth of new information about political learning and opinion formation is explored in Chapter 5, along with new theories about media-induced asocial and prosocial behavior. Much of this material is based on my own research and on research undertaken jointly with Professor Maxwell E. McCombs, currently at the University of Texas at Austin, and Professor David H. Weaver, currently at Indiana University.

The forceful influence of the media in a variety of political situations is the subject of Chapters 6 through 10. These situations include media coverage of elections (Chapter 6); the interplay between the media and major political institutions such as the presidency, Congress, and the courts (Chapter 7); investigative reporting and its effects on public policy (Chapter 8); the role of the media in natural and manmade crises (Chapter 9); and the steadily growing part that media play in the conduct of foreign policy (Chapter 10). The book concludes with a discussion of emerging policy trends and the new technologies and political forces shaping them (Chapter 11).

Besides the relentless march of events that dictated a number of changes, the shape of the new edition owes much to colleagues and students who have commented on the book and to the scholars whose research has provided new insights. Their contributions are deeply appreciated. Special thanks are due to Edie N. Goldenberg of the University of Michigan and William C. Adams of George Washington University for reading the original manuscript with exceptional care and making very constructive suggestions. I am also indebted to my research assistants, Michelle Rydz, Issa Nour, and especially Thomas Burke. They tracked down many elusive references and data and contributed to the new research presented in the book. The third edition also benefited immensely from the writing skills and careful editing of Barbara de Boinville and the final polishing by Kerry Kern. Joanne Daniels, director of CQ Press, and the team she heads provided invaluable support that greatly eased the many chores entailed in book production. The concern and friendship of the CQ crew has been a real morale booster.

The time required to write a book, or to complete an extensive revision, usually is taken from the category labeled "family time." When it is willingly and even cheerfully surrendered by those who hold claim to it, research and writing progress with a minimum of emotional strain. Family time donated to a book is a generous, treasured gift. I am grateful to my family for this indispensable contribution to my work and for the love and understanding that it represents.

Doris A. Graber

CHAPTER 1

Media Power
and Government Control

In the summer of 1987, the American public watched television with rapt attention as congressional committees tried to unravel the mysteries of international arms deals, hostage ransoms, and secret missions to a hostile country. Apparently, American policy had been planned and carried out surreptitiously by a few members of the president's National Security Council staff. They had sought the release of American hostages by selling arms to Iran and had then diverted the profits to an antigovernment faction in Nicaragua. Congress and the State and Defense departments had not been kept informed of these actions, as required by law.

At stake was the political reputation of an incumbent president, the image of Congress as a zealous guardian of the public interest, and the political future of several high-level public officials. The media drew parallels between the affair and the Watergate scandal and the Vietnam War disaster that had damaged the Nixon and Johnson presidencies so severely.

When the hearings were over, the political impact of the investigation was quite different from what the investigating committees had anticipated. President Ronald Reagan was far less damaged than his critics had hoped and television had permitted the key actor in the drama—Lt. Col. Oliver L. North—to become the darling of the public rather than the villain that the committee leadership had wished to portray. Some disappointed committee members, with the wisdom of hindsight, even suggested that television experts should have been hired by the legislators to advise them how to use the medium to best advantage. What had gone wrong?

Part of the problem sprang from the impressions created by staging the event for the television cameras. The seating arrangements placed the members of the committees on raised tiers above the witnesses. "On television, it gave the appearance of dozens of inquisitors glaring down at a single witness, a situation guaranteed to inspire sympathy for the witness." [1]

Another unexpected factor was the uncanny ability of Colonel North to project a favorable image on television. The boyish-looking colonel, wearing a marine uniform decorated with six rows of ribbons topped by parachute wings, looked like an all-American hero, a man of character and vigor whose word could be trusted. By contrast, the chief counsel for the House of Representatives, John W. Nields, Jr., whose thinning blond hair curled over his collar, looked like an aging version of the discredited college-student protestors of the 1960s. When Nields began the interrogation with sharp questioning, and North responded with seeming openness and patriotic compassion, the sympathies of the public went to North. A *New York Times*/CBS News poll immediately following the last day of North's testimony showed only 14 percent of the public harboring negative feelings about the colonel. Seventy-three percent called him "a real patriot."

Journalistic commentary did an about-face. Comments about North had been mostly negative prior to his appearance on television. News anchor Tom Brokaw, for example, had called him "a soldier of fortune more or less who conducted things with a 'Mission Impossible' theme." After the hearings, commentary turned predominantly favorable. *New York Times* columnist R. W. Apple, Jr., called North's testimony "a bravura performance rooted in the American tradition. Underdog, true believer, one man against the crowd . . . , the lonesome cowboy . . . , the honest man facing down the politicians. . . . Pensive, passionate, sanctimonious, sincere, impatient, articulate, aggressive, cocky, contrite—he was all of those things and more." [2] In the end, a man who began the week as a pariah ended up at the top of the political popularity heap.

Committee members agreed that the public enthusiasm generated by Colonel North's testimony affected the investigation and politics in general. Public opinion polls showed a sizable decline in the number of people who considered the Iran-contra affair, or "Irangate," as serious as Watergate. More people approved of American aid to dissident Nicaraguans. Afraid of public anger if North were pressured too extensively, committee members had refrained from asking him several questions that could have been highly damaging, including questions about the illegal shredding of important documents. In the wake of North's superb television performance, it became doubtful that plans for criminal prosecution of the colonel could be carried forth without a public uproar. "Olliemania" even inspired some supporters to urge Colonel North to run for the presidency.[3]

Political Importance of Mass Media

The impact of television on the politics of the Iran-contra affair is but one example of how mass media, in combination with other political factors, can influence American politics. News stories often play a crucial part in shaping the perceptions of reality of millions of people in all walks of life. News stories take Americans to the battlefields of the world in Central America or the Middle East. They give them ringside seats for walks on the moon or oil explorations beneath the sea. They provide the nation with shared political experiences, such as watching presidential election debates or congressional investigations, that then form a basis for public opinions and for uniting people for political actions.[4]

The media often serve as attitude and behavior models. In the process of image creation, the media indicate which views and behaviors are acceptable and even praiseworthy in a given society and which are unacceptable or outside the mainstream. Audiences can learn how to conduct themselves in ordinary social and work situations, how to cope with personal crises, and how to evaluate major social institutions like the medical profession or the police. Media stories also indicate what is deemed important or unimportant by America's dominant groups, what conforms to prevailing standards of justice and morality, and how various events are related to each other.[5] In the process the media present a set of cultural values that their audiences are likely to accept in whole or in part as typical of American society. The media thus help to integrate and homogenize American society.[6]

Attention to the mass media is all-pervasive among twentieth-century Americans. The average high school graduate nowadays has spent more time in front of a television set than in school, much of it during preschool and elementary school days. Even in school much learning about current events is based on information provided by the media. As adults, Americans spend nearly half of their leisure time watching television, listening to the radio, or reading newspapers and magazines. Averaged out over an entire week, this amounts to more than seven hours of exposure per day to some form of mass media news or entertainment. Television occupies three-fourths of this time. With access to cable and satellite television, as well as video recorders, these figures are rising. Despite considerable dissatisfaction with the quality of television programs, television is the primary source of news and entertainment for the average American. It is also the most trusted.

Reprinted by permission: Tribune Media Services.

On a typical evening 98 million people, nearly half the country's population, are watching television between 8:00 and 9:00 p.m. If a "special" is broadcast, as many as 75 million to 80 million people may watch it.[7] In 1984 the debate between presidential candidates Walter Mondale and Ronald Reagan was watched by 120 million Americans, not to mention millions of foreign viewers. The ability to attract such vast audiences of ordinary people, as well as political elites, constitutes a major ingredient in the power of the mass media. Mass media provide a nationwide forum for the individuals and groups that they choose to cover. The messages disseminated by the mass media deal with important aspects of the nation's political and social life. People rely on mass media for this information and generally deem it credible.

In terms of social norms, the mass media are powerful because the American public believes that a free press should keep it informed about the wrongdoings of government. Media images are especially potent when they involve aspects of life that people experience only through the media, rather than directly in their own neighborhoods. The personal and professional lives of politicians, revolutions in distant lands, frenzied trading at stock exchanges, heart transplants, and space shuttle landings are not generally experienced firsthand. Rather, popular perceptions of these activities are shaped largely by the images portrayed in news and fictional stories in print and electronic media. For example, prime time television exaggerates the likelihood of becoming a victim of crime. Heavy viewers, therefore, fear crime more and take more protective measures than do light viewers.[8]

Politically relevant information is often conveyed through stories that are not explicitly concerned with politics. Many entertainment shows on television, for example, picture social institutions, such as the police or the schools, in ways that convey esteem or heap scorn on them. They also express social judgments about various types of people. For instance, in the past television often depicted blacks and women as socially inferior and limited in abilities. This type of coverage conveys messages that audiences may accept at face value. They may believe that social conditions and judgments shown on television as widely accepted are socially sanctioned and therefore ought to be maintained.

Not only are the media the chief source of nearly every American's views of the world, but they are also the fastest way to disperse information throughout the entire society. News of the assassination of President John F. Kennedy and the attempt on the life of President Reagan spread with incredible speed. In both cases better than 90 percent of the American people heard the news within ninety minutes of the event, either directly from radio or television or secondhand from other people who had received mass media messages.[9]

Functions of Mass Media

What major functions do the mass media perform? Three functions mentioned by political scientist Harold Lasswell are (1) surveillance of the world to report ongoing events, (2) interpretation of the meaning of events, and (3) socialization of individuals into their cultural settings.[10] To these three, a fourth function should be added: deliberate manipulation of the political process. The manner in which these four functions are performed affects the lives of individuals, groups, and social organizations, as well as the course of domestic and international politics. Let us look at each of them in turn.

Surveillance

Surveillance involves two major tasks. For the political community at large, "public" surveillance throws the spotlight of publicity on selected people, organizations, and events. This publicity may then make them matters of concern to politicians and to the general public. It may determine which political demands are exposed and which are kept hidden. It also may force politicians to respond to situations on which their views would not otherwise have been aired. For individual citizens in their private capacities, "private" surveillance informs them about current events. While it may lead to political activities, its primary functions are gratification of personal needs and quieting of anxieties. The media, as Marshall McLuhan has observed, are "sense extensions" for individuals who cannot directly witness most of the events of interest to them and their communities.[11]

Public Surveillance. Because it arouses civic concerns and stimulates action, public surveillance is politically significant. Newspeople determine what is "news"—which political happenings will be covered and which will be ignored. Their choices affect who and what will have a good chance to become the focus for political discussion and action.[12] Without media attention the people and events covered by the news might have no influence, or reduced influence, on decision makers. Conditions that may be tolerated while they remain obscure may quickly become intolerable in the glare of publicity. This is why politicians, who seek to garner or avoid publicity, time and structure events with media coverage in mind.

The following example illustrates the power of publicity to produce public action. On June 19, 1979, a controversial Chicago medical clinic, described by the Chicago *Tribune* as the Midwest's largest prescription mill, closed its doors for good. The reason was a series of reports published in the paper about the activities of the clinic. In the wake of revelations that the clinic was dispensing vast quantities of dangerous sedatives and other pills under the guise of treating patients for stress and weight problems, six clinic doctors quit hastily, forcing suspension of operations. Following the newspaper stories, a suit was brought by the Cook County state's attorney charging the clinic with violation of the Illinois Medical Practices Act. The American, Illinois, and Chicago medical associations took action to ensure better protection of the public from prescription mills staffed by unethical physicians. Because the Chicago clinic had branches in Miami and Atlanta, officials at those locations, alerted by the *Tribune* reports, began comparable investigations.[13]

In the summer of 1979, many other prescription mills were operating in Chicago and throughout the nation. Had the media publicized them prominently, action might have been taken to close them too. Without public surveillance through the media, they continued to function. Of course, not all media publicity is beneficial. In many instances misperceptions and scares created by media stories have undermined confidence in good policies, good people, and good products. The human and economic costs have been vast.[14]

Fear of publicity can be as powerful a force in shaping action as actual exposure. Politicians and business leaders know what damage an unfavorable story can do and act accordingly, either to hide the story or to atone for their misdeeds by public confessions of guilt and regrets. Thus, when marijuana use became an issue in 1987 in the failed Supreme Court nomination of Justice Douglas Ginsburg, a parade of officials openly confessed to similar sins or vowed publicly that they had never indulged. Major effects of public surveillance may arise indirectly from impressions created by news stories. If media stories dwell on crime and corruption in the inner city, residents may move to the suburbs, leaving the inner city deserted and even less safe and depriving it of tax revenues. Speculation that international conflicts or oil embargoes are in the offing may scare investors and produce fluctuations in domestic and international stock markets and commodity exchanges. Serious economic (and hence political) consequences may ensue.

The media not only bring matters to public attention; they also can doom people and events to obscurity by inattention. Lack of coverage may spring from the necessity to limit publication because the information supply exceeds the media's capacity to transmit it. Newspapers have only limited amounts of space available for news; time constraints on television and radio newscasts are even more stringent. The media also ignore matters that do not seem newsworthy by accepted journalistic criteria or that fail to catch their attention. Conscious attempts to suppress information for ideological or political reasons are another, less frequent reason for lack of coverage.

For many years left-wing social critics have faulted mainstream American journalists for using their news selection power to strengthen white middle-class values and suppress socialist viewpoints. They claim that these choices are made deliberately to perpetuate capitalist exploitation of the masses, in line with the ideological preferences of media owners. Critics also claim that the media have intentionally suppressed the facts about dangerous products, such as alcohol and tobacco, and about the socially harmful activities of large corporations, which may be responsible for water and air pollution or unsafe consumer goods.[15] Right-wing critics complain that the media give undue attention to the views of the enemies of the established social and political order in hopes of undermining it. Each camp can cite a long list of stories to support its contentions.[16]

Media people deny these charges. They disdain political motives in news selection and defend their choices on the basis of general criteria of newsworthiness (treated more fully in Chapter 3). Like the social critics, they can muster a lot of evidence from news stories to support their claims. At the heart of controversies over the ideological bias of the media lie two basic questions that cannot be answered conclusively. The first concerns people's motivations. How can one prove what motivates journalists to act in certain ways? And is it fair to ascribe motivations to them in the face of their denials? The second question relates to story effects. To what degree can media stories produce the goals owners and news professionals are allegedly seeking?

Besides calling attention to matters of potential public concern, the media also provide cues to the public about the degree of importance of an issue. Important stories are covered prominently—on the front page with big headlines and pictures or as a major television or radio feature. Less important matters are buried in the back pages or given very brief exposure on television or radio.[17] However, nearly all coverage, even though it is brief and comparatively inconspicuous, lends an aura of significance to publicized subjects.

Through the sheer fact of coverage the media can confer status on individuals and organizations. They "function essentially as agencies of social legitimation—as forces, that is, which reaffirm those ultimate value standards and beliefs, which in turn uphold the social and political status quo."[18]

Television made black civil rights leaders and their causes household names. Martin Luther King, Jr., and Jesse Jackson became national figures. A political candidate whose efforts to win an election are widely publicized, a social crusader whose goals become front-page news, or a convicted murderer or terrorist who wins a hearing on radio or television often becomes an instant celebrity. Their unpublicized counterparts remain obscure and bereft of political influence.

Because the attention of the media is crucial for political success, actors on the political scene deliberately create situations likely to receive media coverage. Daniel Boorstin has labeled events arranged primarily to stimulate media coverage "pseudo-events."[19] They may range from news conferences called by public figures even when there is no news to announce to physical assaults on people and property designed to dramatize grievances.

Decisions about what to publish and thereby put on the agenda for public discussion and possible action are not completely up to the discretion of media personnel. Some things cannot be ignored because of their extraordinary significance or because they have become widely known already or because of competitive pressures. For example, news about prominent persons and major domestic or international events must be reported.[20] But beyond the unavoidable events, there remains an extremely wide range of persons and events for which coverage is optional.

The power of the media to set the civic agenda is a matter of concern because it is not controlled by a system of formal checks and balances as is power at various levels of government. It is not subject to periodic review through the electoral process. If media emphases or claims are incorrect, remedies are few. Citizens can be protected from false advertising of consumer goods through "truth in advertising" laws, but there is no way in which they can be protected from false political claims or improper news selection by media personnel without impairing the crucial rights to free speech and a free press. Media critic Jay Blumler expresses the dilemma well:

> Media power is not supposed to be shared: That's an infringement of editorial autonomy. It is not supposed to be controlled: That's censorship. It's not even supposed to be influenced: That's news management! But why should media personnel be exempt from Lord Acton's dictum that all power corrupts and absolute power corrupts absolutely? And if they are not exempt, who exactly is best fitted to guard the press guardians, as it were?[21]

Private Surveillance. Average citizens may not think much about the broader political impact of the news they read, hear, and watch. They use the media instead to keep in touch with what they deem personally important. The media are their eyes and ears to the world, their means of surveillance, which tell them about economic conditions, weather, sports, jobs, fashions, social and cultural events, health and science, and the public and private lives of famous people.

Being able to stay informed makes people feel secure, whether or not they remember what they read or hear or see. Even though the news may be bad, at least they feel that there will be no unsettling surprises. News reassures them that the political system continues to operate in the face of constant crises and frequent mistakes. Reassurance is very important for people's peace of mind. It tends to keep them politically quiescent because there is no need to act if political leaders seem to be doing their jobs. In turn, this has significant consequences for the stability of the political system and the ability of government to function.[22] For good or ill, the public's quiescence helps to maintain the political and economic status quo.

Other significant private functions that the mass media fulfill for many people are entertainment, companionship, tension relief, and a way to pass the time with minimal physical or mental exertion. The mass media can satisfy these important personal needs conveniently and cheaply. Through the media, people who otherwise might be frustrated and dissatisfied can participate vicariously in current political happenings, in sports and musical events, in the lives of famous people, and in the lives of families and communities featured in the news.[23]

Interpretation

Media not only survey the events of the day and make them the focus of public and private attention, but they also interpret their meanings, put them into context, and speculate about their consequences. Most incidents lend themselves to a variety of interpretations, depending on the values and experiences of the interpreter. The kind of interpretation that is chosen affects the political consequences of media reports. For example, since 1962 the way in which the media interpret the legal and social significance of abortions has changed considerably. Abortion used to be interpreted almost universally as murder. The emphasis was on the abortionist as the villain and the pregnant woman as an accomplice in the heinous crime. Now abortion is often cast into the frame of women's rights. Many believe the pregnant woman has the right, with certain limitations, to protect her physical and mental health or the welfare of an infant likely to be born to a life of physical and mental suffering. The key situation that brought about the switch in media interpretation, and eased the change in public attitudes toward abortion, involved a television personality, Sherri Finkbine, who had taken thalidomide during her pregnancy before the drug's ill-effects on infants were known. Fearing a severely malformed baby, she underwent an abortion in 1962.

Instead of reporting the action as murder, as had been the custom, news media throughout the country defended Sherri Finkbine's action. To steer clear of the negative connotations of the word *abortion*, journalists used a new vocabulary to put the act into a different light. They talked of "surgery to prevent a malformed baby," of "avoiding the possibility of mothering a drug-deformed child," and of the necessity of inducing a miscarriage to spare a child from loathing "its own image and crying out against those who might have spared it this suffering." [24]

Numerous circumstances influenced the type of interpretation that the Finkbine story received, but the primary factor was the reporters' or editors' decision, made independently or in response to pressures from the community or the news organization itself, to stress a particular image and to choose available informants and facts accordingly. Such journalistic choices play a large role in determining the political consequences of various situations.

By suggesting the causes and relationships of various events, the media may shape opinions even without telling their audiences what to believe or think about. For example, linking civil strife in El Salvador to the activities of Soviet and Cuban Communist agents ensured that the American public would view the situation with considerable alarm. Linking the hostilities to poverty and social oppression would put them into a far less threatening light. No explicit media warnings would be required to produce these diverse reactions.

There are countless ways in which news presentations can predetermine the conclusions that people are likely to draw, as political scientists Lance Bennett and Murray Edelman point out:

> We [journalists] can attribute any social problem to official policies, the machinations of those who benefit from it, or the pathology of those who suffer from it. We can trace it back to class or racial inequalities, to

ideologics such as nationalism or patriotism, or to resistance to the regime. We can root the problem in God, in its historic genesis, in the accidental or systematic conjuncture of events, in rationality, in irrationality, or in a combination of these or other origins. In choosing any such ultimate cause we are also depicting a setting, an appropriate course of action, and sets of virtuous and evil characters, and doing so in a way that will appeal to some part of the public that sees its own sentiments or interests reflected in that choice of a social scene.[25]

The items that media personnel select to illustrate a point or to characterize a political actor need not be intrinsically important to be influential in shaping opinions and evaluations. During the 1988 presidential election, the *Miami Herald* reported that a young woman had spent the night at the home of Gary Hart, then the front-runner among Democratic candidates, while his wife was absent. Although the story shed little light on Hart's political capabilities, five days after it was published nationwide Hart abandoned the race. Contrary to expectations, he reversed the decision several months later, but the story and his temporary withdrawal severely damaged his chances for winning the presidential nomination.

Socialization

The third major mass media function mentioned by Lasswell is political socialization (discussed more fully in Chapter 5). It involves the learning of basic values and orientations that prepare individuals to fit into their cultural milieu. Prior to the 1970s, socialization studies largely ignored the mass media because it was thought that parents and the schools were the primary agents. Studies conducted in the 1970s finally established that the media play a crucial role in political socialization.[26] The bulk of information that young people acquire about the nature of their political world comes from the mass media. It reaches them either directly through exposure to the electronic and print media or indirectly through exposure to the media of their families, teachers, acquaintances, and peers. Mass media information presents to the young specific facts as well as general values. It teaches them which elements produce power, success, and dominance in society, and it provides them with models for behavior.[27] Young people make heavy use of such information to develop their opinions because they lack established attitudes and behavior patterns.

Public opinion polls show that most of the new orientations and opinions that adults acquire during their lifetime also are based on information supplied by the mass media. People do not necessarily adopt the precise attitudes and opinions that may be suggested by the media. Rather, mass media information provides the ingredients that people use to adjust their existing attitudes and opinions to keep pace with a changing world. The mass media must be credited, therefore, with a sizable share of continuing adult political socialization and resocialization. Examples of resocialization—the restructuring of established basic attitudes—are the shifts in sexual morality and racial attitudes that the American public has undergone since mid-century and the changing views on relations with mainland China and with the United Nations.[28]

Manipulation

In the post-Watergate era direct manipulation of the political process by the media has once again become very common, after decades of neutral reporting when most American journalists acted primarily as chroniclers of information provided by others. Major print and electronic media now operate their own investigative units. Feature articles and television shows devoted exclusively to revealing the results of investigations have become highly popular. "Sixty Minutes," the CBS weekly collection of minidocumentaries, has reached and maintained top audience ratings for many years.

The purpose of these modern shows, like that of their predecessors early in the century, is to *muckrake*. The term comes from a special rake designed to collect manure. President Theodore Roosevelt was the first to apply it to journalists who conducted their own investigations into corruption and wrongdoing to stimulate governmental action to clean up the "dirt" they had exposed. Muckraking today may have several different goals.[29] The journalist's primary purpose may be to write stories that expose misconduct in government and produce reforms. Alternatively, the chief purpose may be to present sensational information that attracts large media audiences and enhances profits. The investigations by *Washington Post* reporters that led to President Richard Nixon's resignation in the wake of the Watergate scandal were in the muckracking tradition. That story and others involving manipulation can be found in Chapter 8.

Effects of Mass Media

The public believes that the media have an important impact on the conduct of politics and on public thinking. Politicians act and behave on the basis of the same assumption. But many studies conducted by social scientists fail to show substantial impact. Why is there such a discrepancy between many social science appraisals of mass media effects and the general impression, reflected by public policies, that the mass media are extremely influential?

There are three major reasons. To begin with, many studies, particularly during the 1950s and 1960s, have taken a narrow approach to media effects. Second, theories about the ways in which people use newspapers, television, radio, and other mass media have enhanced the belief in "minimal effects" because these theories suggest that people are disinclined to learn from the media. Finally, social scientists have encountered great difficulties in measuring effects because media stimuli make their impact as part of a complex combination of social stimuli.

Early Studies

Focus on Vote Choices. Eager for neat, readily quantifiable research designs, American social scientists began to study the effects of the mass media primarily in one narrow area: vote change as a result of media coverage of presidential elections. Among these early studies, several are considered classics. The first is *The People's Choice* by Paul Lazarsfeld, Bernard Berelson, and Hazel Gaudet of Columbia University. It reported how people made their voting choices in Erie County, Pennsylvania, in the 1940 presidential election. Sequels followed in short order. The best known are *Voting: A Study of Opinion Formation in a Presidential Campaign,* by Columbia researchers Bernard Berelson, Paul Lazarsfeld, and William McPhee; *The Voter Decides,* by University of Michigan researchers Angus Campbell, Gerald Gurin, and Warren E. Miller; and the Michigan group's *The American Voter,* by Angus Campbell, Philip E. Converse, Warren E. Miller, and Donald Stokes.[30]

The early voting studies were based on the assumption that media influence could be ascertained by measuring its impact on voting choices. A well-publicized campaign presumably changed votes. If it did not, this indicated that the media lacked influence. Subsequent studies have shown that this reasoning is incorrect. There may be measurable media influence even when vote choice remains stable. Besides, media effects vary, depending on the office at stake and the historical period. At the time of the early voting studies, change of vote choice was quite uncommon in presidential elections because people's choices hinged heavily on their allegiance to one of the two major parties. Predictably, only a few people changed their voting intentions as a result of media coverage. In recent years party allegiance has weakened substantially among many voters, and the opportunities for media influence on vote choice have been far greater.

Had the investigators concentrated on other settings, such as judicial or nonpartisan elections (for which few voting cues outside the media are available), they might also have discovered greater media-induced attitude change. Substantial media influence might have been discovered even in presidential elections if changes in people's trust and affection or knowledge about the candidates and the election had been explored. The early studies largely ignored these other types of media influences because they did not result in easily measurable behavior and attitude changes. Yet such changes constitute important media influences that are crucial components of a variety of political behaviors, quite aside from voting decisions.

The early voting studies focused almost exclusively on the individual citizen and failed to trace the linkages between effects on individuals and effects on the social groups to which they belong and through which they influence political events. Farm workers in California might not change their votes after hearing a candidate charge that illegal Mexican immigrants were taking jobs from American workers and depressing wage scales. But they might well use their union to testify against legislation permitting illegal immigrants to remain in the United States. They might even participate in violence against farmers who hire large numbers of alien workers. In turn, these activities might affect U.S.-Mexican relations and harm the worldwide image of the United States. Yet the early studies of media effects totally ignored such impacts on the entire political system and its component parts.

The findings that media effects were minimal were so pervasive in early research that, after an initial flurry in the 1940s and 1950s, social science research into mass media effects fell to a low ebb. Social scientists did not want to waste their time studying inconsequential effects. Despite seemingly solid evidence of media impotence, they did not care to swim against the stream of established knowledge. Consequently, in study after study dealing with political socialization and learning, the mass media were hardly mentioned as an important factor.

Learning Theories. The early findings were all the more believable because they tied in well with theories of persuasion. Mass media messages presumably miss their mark because they are impersonal. They are not tailored to the needs of specific individuals, as are the messages of parents, teachers, and friends. They do not permit immediate feedback, which then allows the sender to adjust the message to make it more suitable for the receiver. Furthermore, there is no compulsion to listen to mass media messages and no need to answer. Hence it is easy to ignore them.

Although there is a lot of truth to these claims, they fail to consider that television can simulate intimate personal settings. Audiences frequently interact with the television image as if it were actually present in front of them. They may look upon television commentators and actors as personal friends or enemies. Children often imitate people and situations seen on television, making them a part of their direct personal experiences.

Further support for the "minimal effects" findings came from various cognitive consistency theories. They postulate that average individuals dislike being presented with information that is incompatible with cherished beliefs. To avoid this painful experience and the neces-

minimal effects)

sity to change established beliefs, people expose themselves very selectively to the media. Social scientists have evidence that people are indeed selective in their use of the media and search for information that reinforces what they already believe and know. But, as will be discussed more fully in Chapter 5, the phenomenon is quite limited.

Recent Research

When researchers resumed their investigations of mass media effects in the wake of persistent evidence of strong media impact, they cast their net more broadly. Researchers began to look beyond media effects on voting to other effects during elections and in situations involving other types of political events. In this vein, researchers examined media impact on factual learning, on opinion formation, and on the satisfaction of a variety of human needs. They have also looked beyond the individual to effects on political systems and subsystems, a search that promises to be highly rewarding. But despite improvements in research designs and techniques, research into mass media effects has remained hampered by serious measurement problems.

Measuring Complex Effects. Mass media effects are difficult to measure, both at the level of the individual and at the societal level, because they are highly complex and elusive. The most common measuring device at the individual level—self-assessment of impact elicited during a poll—is notoriously unreliable. Researchers lack tools to measure the substance of human thinking objectively. Even when thoughts lead to overt behavior, they cannot accurately judge the nature of the thought. Moreover, actions spring from a variety of motivations among which media impact may play only a small part.

Assessing mass media impact is especially difficult because mass media audiences already possess a fund of knowledge and attitudes that they bring to bear on new information. Since researchers rarely know precisely what this information is, or the rules by which it is combined with incoming information, they cannot pinpoint the exact contribution that particular mass media stories have made to an individual's cognitions, feelings, and actions. To complicate matters further, the impact of the mass media varies depending on the subject matter. For instance, media impact apparently is greater on people's perceptions of civil rights policies and the conduct of the Vietnam War than on their views about energy policy.[31]

Assessments of television's role in spurring opposition to the Vietnam War illustrate the problems faced in proving media impact. A number of analysts ascribe the public's growing dissatisfaction with U.S. involvement in Vietnam in the late 1960s and early 1970s to media treatment of the war.[32] Television for the first time brought an ongoing war into American living rooms. In vivid color it showed the dead and wounded, blazing villages, and the faces of horrified children. Starting with the Tet offensive in 1968, which called into question optimistic reports about the impending victorious conclusion of the war, there was a constant barrage of antiwar stories.[33] Demands to get out of the war were featured, but little attention was paid to requests to escalate the fighting. It is easy to demonstrate the thrust of coverage and to document the growth of the antiwar sentiment. It is well-nigh impossible to establish the precise contribution that media coverage made to changing the public's view by picturing the war as an unnecessary, rather than a necessary, evil.

Similarly, it is difficult to prove that sharp curtailment of media coverage of Vietnam, after U.S. forces had been withdrawn in 1973, prevented a turnaround in policy and public sentiment. Americans in and out of government learned very little about what happened in Vietnam and the adjacent countries in the wake of the Communist takeover. For instance, atrocity stories coming from Cambodia, which the French press published because of that country's earlier ties to Cambodia, were given very little play in the American press. But one cannot be sure that ample coverage of the atrocities in the American press would have made Americans regret the withdrawal of U.S. troops from Southeast Asia.

Ignoring Unanticipated Effects. Measurement of media effects has also suffered because unanticipated effects are frequently ignored. If the anticipated effects fail to materialize, the researcher may claim that there are no effects. For example, when ABC television broadcast a highly publicized television drama about the horrors of nuclear war, it was widely either hoped or feared that many of the 80 million viewers would become more concerned about nuclear war. Their expectations that defense against nuclear war is possible would be dashed, and they would be more likely to join antinuclear groups and lobbies. None of these effects materialized. Accordingly, surprised observers of the impact of the broadcast reported that it had fallen flat. Most researchers, however, failed to notice several totally unexpected important effects. The percentage of people who had previously criticized President Reagan for pursuing policies likely to lead to war dropped sharply from 57 percent before the broadcast to 43 percent afterwards. In political terms, this amounted to decreased opposition to the military policies of the Reagan administration. At the same time, the broadcast also made people more conciliatory toward the Soviet Union and more supportive of general arms limitation agreements between the super powers.[34]

A Case Study: The Demise of the Neutron Bomb. On June 6, 1977, the *Washington Post* published a front-page story about a new nuclear weapon. The information had been disclosed during a congressional appropriations committee hearing where funding for ongoing nuclear weapons research was under consideration. According to the story, the new weapon, a neutron bomb, "cuts down on blast and heat and thus total destruction, leaving buildings and tanks standing. But the great quantities of neutrons it releases kill people." The idea of enhanced radiation bombs was not really new. Research and development had been conducted for twenty years. The objective was creation of a minimally destructive nuclear weapon to be used by Europeans on their own territory to repel invading armies. The U.S. Defense Department viewed the neutron bomb largely as an antitank weapon that would kill invading tank crews while sparing people and property in surrounding areas.[35]

Over the next ten months, the *Post* story caused consternation among executive branch officials, senators, Western European leaders, and political activists. Concern with media coverage and how to influence it became paramount, to the exclusion of concerns about the merits or faults of the weapon. As National Security Adviser Zbigniew Brzezinski commented quite accurately, "The *Post* article touched off a political explosion that reverberated throughout the United States and Europe."[36]

Most importantly, the article forced high-level public officials to take action. President Gerald Ford's decision to authorize funding for the weapon had never received official approval from the Carter administration. In the wake of the *Post* article, President Jimmy Carter ordered a delay in production. Sen. Mark Hatfield of Oregon hurriedly introduced an amendment to the appropriation bill to ban further funding for neutron weapons. The expected fight in the Senate then permitted the *Post* to justify follow-up stories and to publish anti-neutron bomb editorials. Gradually, other media began to pick up the story. On June 17, NBC ran a film clip showing the gruesome effects of neutron radiation on monkeys. ABC ran the clip a week later, and NBC then repeated it on the "Today" show. Meanwhile lurid *Post* front-page stories continued to unearth additional disquieting facts about the effects of neutron radiation, and other papers picked up the coverage. Little attention was paid to the Defense Department's explanations of the purpose and effects of neutron bombs.

Early in July the Defense Department began a low-key media campaign on behalf of the weapon to head off the Hatfield amendment barring funds. Reporters were invited for background briefings, and top Defense Department officials made the rounds of news talk shows. President Carter asked for continued funding during a televised press conference. The next day the Senate defeated the Hatfield amendment but voted that funding for the bomb should be suspended until the president certified that the national interest required constructing the bomb.

Meanwhile anti-neutron bomb forces in Europe had begun to mobilize and antibomb stories and articles began to proliferate. The Soviet Union added its voice in a massive antibomb propaganda campaign. Most allied leaders in Western Europe favored deployment of the bomb, believing that it held promise of repelling a Soviet invasion without nuclear escalation and without the devastation of much of Europe. But, scared by media-whipped opposition, they wanted to deflect the anger of antibomb forces from themselves onto President Carter by claiming that the United States was pushing the bomb. The Carter administration would not cooperate. Equally concerned about the consequences of antibomb media coverage, it wanted to deflect opposition by claiming that the European allies were urging deployment of the bomb. To resolve the impasse, the Carter administration embarked on an information campaign to build public support for the bomb. When opposition continued, however, the president changed his mind and in April 1978 abandoned the project. National Security Adviser Brzezinski explained that Carter feared he would be stigmatized as leading "the administration which introduced bombs that kill people but leave buildings intact." The image created by the *Post* article had come to roost.[37]

The demise of the bomb had been blamed on the press, beginning with the initial *Washington Post* story and continuing with subsequent news stories by the *Post* and other media in the United States and Europe. Without such coverage, appropriations for the bomb might have continued, and it might have been deployed quietly, without vociferous public opposition. Neither the Carter administration, the Senate, nor the European allies had expressed concern over the production and deployment of neutron weapons before 1977. Even after the stories broke, government leaders in Europe and the United States considered the bomb a worthwhile weapon. Its abandonment made Carter seem weak and caused major strains in the North Atlantic Treaty Organization (NATO).

The role of the *Post* and other media is not as clear-cut as it may seem, however. Actual deployment of the bomb, as distinct from its development, perhaps could not have been kept quiet since the bomb represented an important new type of weapon. It also seems doubtful that the well-organized antinuclear movement in the United States and Europe would have accepted the new weapon without attempts to stir public opposition. Ever eager to condemn NATO military efforts in Europe, the Soviet Union with its vast propaganda machine certainly would have stirred up protests that could have stopped production and deployment. Finally, a more determined president, more adept at public relations aspects of public policy, might have been able to control the debate over the bomb by preparing a more favorable image for it before the press could talk of "killer warheads" that destroyed people but left buildings intact.

It is impossible to prove conclusively how crucial the media were in the neutron bomb case. It is equally impossible to prove that the media played no role or merely a minor role. Inability to prove mass media impact beyond a doubt has made social scientists shy away from assessing media influence on many important political events. In fact, social scientists often go to the other extreme and deny that effects exist simply because these effects defy measurement. This is unfortunate since many effects that cannot be measured precisely can be observed in the field and studied in the laboratory.

Statistical versus Political Significance. Social scientists also have been rather rigid in interpreting the significance of media influence when it has been found. They have falsely equated statistical significance with political significance, despite the fact that media impact on a small number of individuals can have great political consequences.

For example, during an election only 1 or 2 percent of the voters may change their voting decision because of media stories. That is a very small, statistically negligible effect. Politically, however, it may be a major impact because many important elections, including several presidential elections, have been decided by a margin of 2 percent of the voters. If 2 percent of the vote had gone to the losing candidate in the 1976 presidential race, Ford would have stayed in the White House, and Carter would have remained a peanut farmer. Two percent of the voters sounds like a small number, but it runs into thousands, and even hundreds of thousands, when translated into actual numbers.

On an even smaller scale, if a broadcast of details of a race riot attracts a few listeners to the riot site and stimulates some to participate, the situation may escalate beyond control. Similarly, the impact of a single news story may change the course of history if it induces one assassin to kill a world leader or convinces one world leader to make an important political decision.

Influencing Elites. Another major problem with social science research on mass media effects is that it has concentrated on measuring the effects on ordinary individuals, rather than on political elites. The average individual, despite contrary democratic fictions, is politically fairly unimportant. Mass media impact on a handful of political decision makers usually is vastly more significant than similar impact on ordinary individuals. In addition, the impact on decision makers is likely to be far more profound because mass media information relates more directly to their immediate concerns. They may pay close attention to stories in which the public is not interested and which it often fails to understand.

A case in point is a brief column that appeared in the *Washington Post* in the summer of 1983. In it a Carter cabinet member complained that there had been little public reaction to reports that a campaign briefing book prepared for President Carter had fallen into the hands of the Reagan campaign staff. The information in the book allegedly had been used to brief Reagan for his debate with Carter, in violation of campaign ethics and, possibly, national security. The column caught the attention of one member of the congressional subcommittee with jurisdiction over the Ethics in Government Act. He, in turn, called it to the attention of the subcommittee chairman, Rep. Donald J. Albosta, a Michigan Democrat. The upshot was a major congressional investigation into the entire affair. Initially the story produced no noticeable political waves, even though it had reached a worldwide audience, but it caught the eye of two politicians who were in a position to act.[38]

In light of what we have discussed thus far, it seems totally unrealistic to deny that the media are important in setting the stage for ongoing political developments, in shaping the views and behaviors of political elites and other selected groups, and in influencing the general public's perception of political life. As Theodore White put it hyperbolically:

> The power of the press in America is a primordial one. It sets the agenda of public discussion; and this sweeping political power is unrestrained by any law. It determines what people will talk and think about—an authority that in other nations is reserved for tyrants, priests, parties and mandarins.
>
> No major act of the American Congress, no foreign adventure, no act of diplomacy, no great social reform can succeed in the United States unless the press prepares the public mind.[39]

Even if one takes a totally negative position, arguing that the media are nothing but a conduit of information over which they have no control, one cannot deny that people throughout the world of politics consider the media to be powerful and behave accordingly. This importance, which is an effect of media coverage, is reflected in efforts by governments everywhere, in authoritarian as well as democratic societies, to control the flow of information produced by the media lest it subvert the prevailing political system.

Government Control of Mass Media: Assumptions and Methods

Attempts by governments to control and manipulate the media are universal because governments worldwide believe media are important political forces. This belief is based on the assumption that institutions that control public information can shape public knowledge and behavior and thereby determine the support or opposition of citizens and officials to the government and its policies. Through control over mass information institutions and the stories they produce, governments everywhere seek to preserve the political system as a whole as well as to regulate the media and other social institutions that depend on media publicity. Although control occurs in all societies, its extent, nature, and purposes vary.

Several major reasons account for these variations. Political ideology is one of them. In countries where free expression of opinion is a paramount value and where dissent is respected, the media tend to be comparatively unrestrained. The right of the press to criticize government also flourishes when the accepted ideology grants that governments are fallible and often corrupt and that average citizens are capable of forming valuable opinions about the conduct of government. Finally, freedom of the press, even when it becomes a thorn in the side of the government, is more easily tolerated where governments are well established and politically and economically secure. In Third World nations, for instance, where governments are unstable and resources limited, it may be difficult to tolerate press behavior that is apt to topple the government or retard its plans for economic development.

Nowhere are the media totally free from formal and informal government and social controls, even in times of peace. On the whole, authoritarian countries control more extensively and more rigidly than do nonauthoritarian ones, but all systems represent specific points on a continuum of control. There are also gradations of control within nations, depending on the current regime and political setting, regional and local variations, and the nature of news. Common types of control systems used in authoritarian and nonauthoritarian societies will be described without specifying any particular country.[40]

Authoritarian control systems are of two types: those that are nonideological and simply represent a desire by the ruling classes to tightly control media output so that it does not interfere with the conduct of government and those that are based on a totalitarian ideology, such as communism. The latter type actively uses and controls the media to support ideological goals. Examples of nonideological authoritarian control can be found in states ruled by military governments, such as Chile or Ethiopia. Examples of control based on communism are found in the Soviet Union and the People's Republic of China.

There are also two types of *nonauthoritarian approaches to control,* although they are not linked to differences in political ideology. Rather, these types are linked to differences in philosophies about the role that the media ought to carve for themselves in countries where they enjoy a great deal of freedom. The two types of nonauthoritarian approaches have been labeled *libertarian* and *social responsibility.* When journalists in democratic societies subscribe to the libertarian philosophy, they feel free to report whatever they wish as long as public tastes are satisfied. By contrast, when social responsibility philosophies prevail, newspeople expect to contribute to the betterment of society, spurring media audiences to behave in socially responsible ways. Journalists in the United States and Western Europe furnish examples of both of these philosophies. Often libertarian and social responsibility journalism occur simultaneously, or they may alternate during successive historical periods.[41]

In today's world, authoritarian systems of media control prevail in the majority of countries. Authoritarian countries would like to impose such systems universally by controlling international aspects of news reporting everywhere. In sessions of the United Nations Educational, Scientific and Cultural Organization (UNESCO), they have opposed freedom of reporting about their countries even when the stories are gathered by journalists from democratic societies for their own media. The argument has been made that only news that supports the established regime should be permitted and that all newspeople should be subject to supervision by officials of the country whose affairs they report. This story is told more fully in Chapter 10.

Role of Media in Authoritarian Regimes

What are the basic assumptions that underlie authoritarian and nonauthoritarian philosophies of media operation, and what types of governmental structures and practices have been invented to implement these philosophies?

Communist and other authoritarian systems operate on the assumption that the government knows and represents the best interests of the people. Therefore, the mass media must not interfere with the operations of the government or endanger its survival. The press may point out minor deficiencies or corruption of low-level officials and suggest adjustments in line with prevailing policies, but beyond that it is considered inappropriate to criticize the basic system or its rulers. The policy of *glasnost,* or openness, initiated by the Soviet leadership in 1987, has increased the emphasis on critical stories, but the scope of permissible criticism has remained narrow.

In most authoritarian political systems the mass media must take positions that firmly support the government. News must engender support for major policies, such as economic development or literacy campaigns. It must echo official stands about who the country's domestic and international friends and enemies are. But the media are free to choose the stories they wish to publish, as long as the offerings do not hurt the state or interfere with public policies.

In totalitarian societies the role of the media is more stringently defined. The likely political and social effects of a story—rather than its general significance, novelty, or audience appeal—determine what will be published and what will be buried in silence. For instance, the Soviet media report comparatively few stories about accidents, disasters, and crimes because these matters are believed to be devoid of value in teaching citizens proper conduct. Events reflecting favorably on politics in capitalist countries are usually ignored because information about them would undermine the negative official images presented of the non-Communist world.

Newspeople are encouraged to select stories that contain socially useful information and are apt to strengthen the people's allegiance to the Communist system. According to Lenin, the press must be a propagandist, agitator, and organizer for the revolutionary aims of Communist societies. It must be closely integrated with other instruments of state power, serving the public by publishing stories that will unify people around the approved ideas of life and politics.

Even entertainment programs must serve political purposes. Thus music and drama performances, and even cartoon shorts in movie theaters, must carry appropriate social messages or have historical significance. Many kinds of Western music, modern art, and sexually explicit theater are banned, particularly if performances and exhibits will reach large audiences. For entertainment that is deemed to have social merit, funding is available even if the audience is small. The government supports such entertainment financially because it serves the important public purpose of shaping people's minds in support of the system.

Role of Media in Nonauthoritarian Regimes

The basic assumptions underlying mass media control in democratic countries contrast sharply with those of authoritarian societies. In democracies, governments are viewed as fallible servants of the people. They are deemed to be potentially corrupt, stupid, or abusive of citizens. Consequently, they must be constantly watched and, if they misbehave, criticized.

The media are regarded as objective reporters of good and evil who scrutinize the passing scene on behalf of a public that can and must appraise the performance of its officials. Journalists serve as the watchdog fourth branch of government, which monitors excesses and misbehavior of the executive, legislative, and judicial branches. Through playing an adversary role, journalists provide the feedback that democratic systems need to remain on course. If, as the result of their scrutiny, governments fall and public officials are ousted, this is as it should be.

Broadly stated, this is the theory behind the role of media in democratic societies. The practice is less clear-cut. In the United States, for example, neither newspeople nor government officials are completely at ease with the media's watchdog role. The media usually support the political system and rarely question its fundamental tenets. They limit their criticism to what they perceive as perversions of fundamental social and political values or noteworthy examples of corruption and waste. Their links to the existing power structures are strong because they depend heavily on the high and mighty as their sources of news. Newspeople may even share information with government agencies, including policing bodies such as the Federal Bureau of Investigation and the Central Intelligence Agency. At times, reporters in a democratic society withhold important news at the request of the government to spare it or particular officials from embarrassment or interference. This happened in the United States when the *New York Times* withheld news about the forthcoming Bay of Pigs invasion of Cuba in 1961.[42] Government officials, in an effort to keep their images untarnished by media attacks, may use rewards and punishments to keep the media watchdog in line. These tactics are described more fully in Chapter 7.

The chief obligation of the mass media in free societies is to provide the general public with information and entertainment. According to the libertarian philosophy, anything that happens that seems interesting or important for media audiences may become news. It should be reported quickly, accurately, and without any attempt to convey a particular point of view. Subjects with the widest audience appeal should be stressed, even if that means sex and violence stories and entertainment rather than serious information. The fact that this emphasis also serves the market orientation of the media is an extra benefit.

Although audiences may learn important things from the media, teaching is not the media's chief task. Nor is it their task to question the truth, accuracy, or merits of the information supplied to them by their selected sources. Rather, it is left to the news audience to decide what to believe and what to question.

In contrast to libertarians, adherents to social responsibility tenets believe that news and entertainment presented by the mass media should reflect social consciousness. Media personnel should be participants in the political process, not merely reporters of the passing scene. As guardians of the public welfare, they should foster political action when necessary. If reporters think, for instance, that pollution or racial segregation are prevalent social evils, they should publicize these matters to make them news, even when nothing new has happened. Likewise, undesirable viewpoints and questionable accusations should be denied exposure, however sensational they may be. If reporters believe that the government is hiding information that should be made public, they should try to discover the facts and publish them.

The type of journalism advocated by social responsibility journalists and the type of journalism advocated by totalitarian journalists have philosophical resemblances. Adherents of both approaches advocate using the media to support the basic ideals of their societies and to shape people into more perfect social beings. They are convinced that their goals are good and would not be achieved in a media system dominated by the whims of media owners or audiences.

But the similarities should not be exaggerated. Social advocacy in nonauthoritarian systems lacks the fervor, clout, and single-mindedness it has in systems where media control is monopolized by the government. Social responsibility journalism rarely speaks with a single uncontested voice throughout the entire society. Nevertheless, it frightens and antagonizes many news professionals and news audiences. If one agrees that the media should be used to influence social thought and behavior for "good" purposes, it becomes difficult to determine which purposes deserve to be included in that category. Critics of social responsibility journalism point out that journalists do not have a public mandate to act as arbiters of social values and policies in a society without a single vision of truth and goodness. Newspeople lack the legitimacy that in a democracy comes only from being elected by the public or appointed by duly elected officials.

Whatever the merits or faults of these arguments may be, at the present time social responsibility journalism is popular with a sizable proportion of the news profession.[43] Pulitzer prizes and other honors go to journalists who have successfully exposed questionable practices in the interest of social improvement. The most prominent "villains" targeted for exposure are usually big government and big business.[44]

Control Methods: Authoritarian Regimes

Four types of controls of the press are widely used: legal, normative, structural, and economic.[45] Accordingly, all governments have laws to prevent serious press misbehavior, and all societies have social norms that members dare not defy. The way media organizations are structured and operated shapes their product, as does the ampleness and source of their economic support.

The combination of methods by which governments control the media varies and so do the major objectives of control. Authoritarian societies seek to restrict access to mass communications to voices friendly to the regime and to ensure that news stories remain supportive of most government policies. By contrast, nonauthoritarian regimes rarely make formal attempts to deny foes of the regime access to the media. However, they often try to avert publicity that endangers the national defense or violates widely held social norms.

In many authoritarian societies control over media content is established by limiting entry into the media business. For example, the government may grant newspaper franchises only to select people who support the government in all its endeavors. Often such franchises bestow monopoly control. Control through franchising media entrepreneurs is quite common for electronic media, even in democratic countries, because the government assigns broadcast channels. But democratic countries use this power less frequently to shut out political opponents. Newspapers generally do not require licenses in democratic societies. In the United States, for instance, anyone who has sufficient money may start a newspaper or newsletter. No permits are necessary.

Other methods used primarily by authoritarian countries to control publications are subsidies to favorite publishers or favoritism in the allocation of tightly controlled paper stocks for printing newspapers and magazines. Newspaper publishers whose activities displease the government may find themselves out of business because they cannot obtain paper. These types of economic controls may be imposed quite openly through formal rationing and subsidy schemes, or they may be imposed informally. The government may merely inform a disliked publisher that paper stocks are insufficient to supply that particular enterprise.

Media also may be controlled through manipulating access to news. For instance, the government may release information only to favored publications, putting less favored ones effectively out of business. While such practices are common in authoritarian societies, they occasionally happen on a smaller scale in more open societies. Angered by press coverage of his presidency, President Nixon at one point barred *Washington Post* reporters from his press plane.[46]

In addition to controlling the news business through franchises and restraints on access to news, authoritarian governments often limit what may be published. This may be done routinely or selectively. In some countries nothing can be printed or broadcast until it has been approved by the government censor, who can suppress any story that the government deems objectionable. At times deletions are made after papers or magazines have been prepared for printing or already printed. This leaves tantalizing white spaces or missing pages. Television and radio scripts are often written or edited directly by government officials and must be broadcast without editorial changes.

Authoritarian societies frequently use treason and sedition laws to control media output. Treason and sedition are usually defined broadly in these countries so that anything that is critical of the government is potentially treasonable or seditious. People judged guilty of these crimes may be removed from the media business, sentenced to prison, or even executed. Such severe punishments are extremely strong deterrents to publishing stories that attack the government. Accordingly, disobedience is rare. Most publishers in totalitarian societies avoid difficulties with the official censor and with treason and sedition laws by refraining from using material that is likely to be objectionable. Government censorship then becomes replaced largely by self-censorship, easing the job of the official censor considerably.

When authoritarian regimes are totalitarian, media control is simplified because the government owns and operates all mass media and fully controls their output. Additionally, totalitarian countries frequently block out all unapproved communications from abroad. This includes jamming of foreign broadcasts and prohibiting the import of foreign printed materials. The strictness with which these controls are applied waxes and wanes, depending on the country's relations with other powers. But even during friendly interludes, totalitarian regimes rigidly control any information from abroad that might undermine their political system. They view such censorship as an intellectual quarantine that must be imposed to keep evil influences from undermining a beneficial political system.

Control Methods: Nonauthoritarian Regimes

In democratic societies official control of the content of mass media is deemed largely unnecessary. Entry to the mass media business is open to people representing a wide spectrum of political views. In the United States the First Amendment to the Constitution, which provides that "Congress shall make no law . . . abridging the freedom of speech, or of the press," has given the media an exceptionally strong basis for resisting government controls. The courts have ruled, however, that the protection is not absolute and must give way on occasion to social rights that the courts consider to be superior.

Competition among papers, magazines, and television and radio stations presumably generates a variety of viewpoints. If some media attack the government, other media will support it. Positive and negative as well as right and wrong information will somehow balance out. The underlying, intriguing, but questionable assumption is that the audience will be able to extract the truth from these conflicting reports. Unfortunately, average citizens generally do not have time to expose themselves to a wide array of different media. When confronted with clashing opinions, they find it difficult to determine their merits. Anyone who has listened to the promises and claims made by contending politicians knows how hard it is to evaluate them. Confusion and resigned disinterest, rather than enlightenment, are the likely outcomes.

Even in societies with basically open communication systems, some controls, such as laws and court decisions and informal social pressures, guard against excesses by the media. In the United States the courts have generally ruled that these controls may be enforced only after the bounds of proper publication have been exceeded. Courts have been very loathe to impose "prior restraint" by granting injunctions that would stop publication of information on the grounds that it would cause irreparable harm. But informal social and political pressures and the fear of indictments after publication have restrained presentation of potentially dangerous stories.

Controls in nonauthoritarian societies generally fall into four categories: guarding state survival through treason and sedition laws, shielding sensitive governmental proceedings, protecting individual reputations and privacy, and safeguarding the prevailing moral standards of the community. All societies have treason and sedition laws that prohibit publication of information that must be kept secret to protect the country against foreign and domestic enemies who endanger its national survival. The big problem is to determine the point at which secrecy is so essential that freedom to publish must give way. In democratic societies media and the government are in perennial disagreement about the exact location of this point. Governments lean toward protection; the media lean toward disclosure.

There is little argument that treason and sedition are beyond the boundaries of unrestricted publication, even in an open society. More controversial are curbs on publication of government secrets—so-called "classified information." Governments try to establish controls over the publication of material that may be harmful to themselves or to individuals. For instance, confidential reports about the performance of government agencies, records of bidding on public jobs, and conversations during closed meetings are generally shielded from publicity. Finally, most governments also have laws protecting the reputations of individuals or groups and laws against obscenity. The merits of these controls on publication are discussed more fully in Chapter 4.

Defining the limits of government restraint on information raises difficult questions for democratic societies. Does any degree of official censorship open the way for the destruction of free expression? What guidelines are available to determine how far censorship should go? What types of material, if any, can harm children? Or adults? Should prejudicial statements be prohibited on the ground that they damage the self-image of minorities? The answers are controversial and problematic.

In addition to formal control of potentially "dangerous" news in authoritarian and nonauthoritarian societies, many informal restraints exist. As we shall see in Chapter 7, all governmental units, and often many of their subdivisions, have their own information control systems by which they determine what news to release, how to present it, and what news to cover up.

The limitations on the freedom of publication even in nonauthoritarian societies raise questions about the actual freedom enjoyed by the media compared with their counterparts in authoritarian societies. Is there really a difference, for example, in the independence of government-operated television networks in France and in the Soviet Union? The answer is a resounding "yes." The degree of restraint varies so sharply that the systems are fundamentally different. In totalitarian societies the media are essentially an arm of government whose main purpose is to support the regime in power. In democratic societies the media are usually free to oppose the regime, to weaken it, and even to topple it. While they rarely carry their power to the latter extreme, the potential exists. It is this potential that makes the media in nonauthoritarian societies a genuine restraint on governmental abuses of power and a potent shaper of governmental action.

Summary

The mass media are an important influence on politics because they regularly and rapidly present politically crucial information to huge audiences. These audiences include political elites and decision makers, as well as large numbers of average citizens whose political activities, however sporadic, are shaped by information from the mass media.

The mass media are more than passive transmission agents for available information. Decisions made by media personnel determine what information becomes available to media audiences and what remains unavailable. By putting stories into perspective and interpreting them, media personnel assign meaning to the information and indicate the values by which it ought to be judged. News shaping is unavoidable because space is limited and because facts do not speak for themselves. Hence the media select and shape much of the raw material needed by political elites and the general public for thinking about the political world and planning political action. At times, newspeople even generate political action directly through their own investigations or indirectly through their capacity to stimulate pseudo-events.

Although many social scientists have remained somewhat skeptical about claims of large-scale media impact on politics, governments everywhere are keenly aware of the political importance of the media. Governments therefore have developed philosophies about the political role to be played by the media in their societies and about the proper ways to control the impact of the media on government activities. These philosophies have been implemented by constitutional and legal rules as well as by a host of informal arrangements. In this chapter we have briefly described how the basic philosophies, constitutional arrangements, and legal provisions differ in authoritarian and nonauthoritarian regimes.

Notes

1. Stephen Engelberg with David E. Rosenbaum, "What the Iran-Contra Committees Wish They Had Done Differently," *New York Times,* November 20, 1987. The names of the committees that jointly conducted the questioning were the House Select Committee to Investigate Covert Arms Transactions with Iran and the Senate Select Committee on Secret Military Assistance to Iran and the Nicaraguan Opposition.
2. R. W. Apple, Jr., "The Colonel Stands His Ground," *New York Times,* July 12, 1987, sec. 4.
3. In March 1988 Oliver North and the three other principals in the Iran-contra affair were indicted on charges of conspiring to defraud the United States and thwart congressional inquiries. Special Prosecutor Lawrence Walsh indicated that he had not yet completed his investigation of North; how Walsh's findings will affect the colonel's public image remains to be seen.
4. For a brief overview of current knowledge about mass media effects, see Leo W. Jeffres, *Mass Media Processes and Effects* (Prospect Heights, Ill.: Waveland Press, 1986), chaps. 6-9.
5. The clues that mass media stories supply to the culture of their societies are discussed by George Gerbner, "Toward 'Cultural Indicators': The Analysis of Mass Mediated Public Message Systems," in *The Analysis of Communication Content,* ed. George Gerbner, Ole R. Holsti, Klaus Krippendorff, William J. Paisley, and Philip J. Stone (New York: Wiley, 1969), 123-132.
6. John M. Phelan, *Mediaworld: Programming the Public* (New York: Seabury Press, 1977).
7. A good though somewhat dated source for media statistics is Christopher H. Sterling and Timothy R. Haight, eds., *The Mass Media: Aspen Institute Guide to Communication Industry Trends* (New York: Praeger, 1982). Also see Warren K. Agee, Phillip H. Ault, and Edwin Emergy, *Main Currents in Mass Communications* (New York: Harper and Row, 1986). For politicians, close attention is a professional requirement. Michael Gurevitch and Jay G. Blumler, "Linkages Between the Mass Media and Politics: A Model for the Analysis of Political Communications Systems," in *Mass Communication and Society,* ed. James Curran, Michael Gurevitch, and Janet Woolacott (Beverly Hills, Calif.: Sage, 1979), 274.
8. George Gerbner, Larry Gross, Michael Morgan, and Nancy Signorielli, "Charting the Mainstream: Television's Contributions to Political Orientation," *Journal of Communication* 32 (1982): 106-107.
9. Walter Gantz, "The Diffusion of News About the Attempted Reagan Assassination," *Journal of Communication,* 33 (Winter 1983): 56-65.
10. Harold D. Lasswell, "The Structure and Function of Communication in Society," in *Mass Communications,* ed. Wilbur Schramm (Urbana: University of Illinois Press, 1969), 103.
11. Marshall McLuhan, *Understanding Media: The Extensions of Man* (New York: McGraw-Hill, 1965).
12. Chapter 3 gives a more detailed definition of news. Evidence that the media set the agenda for national issues is presented in Donald L. Shaw and Maxwell McCombs, *The Emergence of American Political Issues: The Agenda-Setting Function of the Press* (St. Paul, Minn.: West Publishing, 1977), and in sources cited there. See also the essays in Sidney Kraus and Richard M. Perloff, eds., *Mass Media and Political Thought* (Beverly Hills,

Calif.: Sage, 1985); John P. Robinson and Mark R. Levy, *The Main Source: Learning from Television News* (Beverly Hills, Calif.: Sage, 1986); and Gladys Engel Lang and Kurt Lang, *The Battle for Public Opinion* (New York: Columbia University Press, 1983).

13. William Gaines and Eileen Ogintz, " 'Prescription Mill' Closes as Heat's Put on Pill Centers," *Chicago Tribune,* June 20, 1979.

14. For an outline of the various types of media influences, see Colin Seymour-Ure, *The Political Impact of Mass Media* (London: Constable, 1974), 21.

15. Examples of such criticism can be found in W. Lance Bennett, *News: The Politics of Illusion,* 2d ed. (New York: Longman, 1988); and Michael Parenti, *Inventing Reality: The Politics of the Mass Media* (New York: St. Martin's Press, 1986).

16. An example of a conservative Washington-based media analysis group is Accuracy in Media (AIM). It publishes periodic reports of its media investigations. For claims that journalists in the elite media are ultraliberal, see S. Robert Lichter, Stanley Rothman, and Linda S. Lichter, *The Media Elite* (New York: Adler and Adler, 1986).

17. Maxwell E. McCombs and John B. Mauro, "Predicting Newspaper Readership from Content Characteristics," *Journalism Quarterly* 54 (Spring 1977): 3-7.

18. Jay G. Blumler, "Purposes of Mass Communications Research: A Transatlantic Perspective," *Journalism Quarterly* 55 (Summer 1978): 22.

19. Daniel Boorstin, *The Image: A Guide to Pseudo-Events* (New York: Atheneum, 1971).

20. Criteria of what constitutes "news" are discussed fully by Bernard Roshco, *Newsmaking* (Chicago: University of Chicago Press, 1975), chap. 3.

21. Blumler, "Purposes of Mass Communications Research," 228.

22. The results of reassuring publicity are discussed by Murray Edelman, *The Symbolic Uses of Politics* (Urbana: University of Illinois Press, 1964), 38-43.

23. George Comstock, Steven Chaffee, Natan Katzman, Maxwell McCombs, and Donald Roberts, *Television and Human Behavior* (New York: Columbia University Press, 1978), 423-451.

24. Marvin N. Olasky and Susan Northway Olasky, "The Crossover in Newspaper Coverage of Abortion from Murder to Liberation," *Journalism Quarterly* 63 (1986): 31-37.

25. W. Lance Bennett and Murray Edelman, "Toward a New Political Narrative," *Journal of Communication* 35 (1985):156-171.

26. The early writings include David Easton and Jack Dennis, *Children in the Political System: Origins of Political Legitimacy* (New York: McGraw-Hill, 1969); Fred I. Greenstein, *Children and Politics* (New Haven: Yale University Press, 1965); Richard Dawson and Kenneth Prewitt, *Political Socialization* (Boston: Little, Brown, 1969); and Robert D. Hess and Judith Torney, *The Development of Political Attitudes in Children* (Chicago: Aldine, 1967). Examples of the studies in the 1970s are Sidney Kraus and Dennis Davis, *The Effects of Mass Communication on Political Behavior* (University Park, Pa.: Pennsylvania State University Press, 1976); Steven H. Chaffee "Mass Communication in Political Socialization," in Stanley Renshon, ed., *Handbook of Political Socialization* (New York: Free Press, 1977). Also see Ellen Wartella, ed., *Children Communicating: Media and Development of Thought, Speech and Understanding* (Beverly Hills, Calif.: Sage, 1979).

27. In *Mediaworld* Phelan contends that the mass media have replaced more

traditional social groups as the source of behavior models and as a demonstrator of the ideals of society.

28. Evidence that the public links attitude changes to mass media information comes from successive public opinion polls. See Benjamin I. Page, Robert Y. Shapiro, and Glenn R. Dempsey, "What Moves Public Opinion? *American Political Science Review* 81 (March 1987): 23-43. Also see Shanto Iyengar and Donald Kinder, *News that Matters: Television and American Opinion* (Chicago: University of Chicago Press, 1987); and Doris A. Graber, *Processing the News: How People Tame the Information Tide,* 2d ed. (New York: Longman, 1988).

29. Fay Lomax Cook, Tom R. Tyler, Edward G. Goetz, Margaret T. Gordon, David Protess, Donna R. Leff, and Harvey L. Molotch, "Media and Agenda Setting: Effects on the Public, Interest Group Leaders, Policy Makers, and Policy," *Public Opinion Quarterly* 47 (1983): 16-35.

30. Paul Lazarsfeld, Bernard Berelson, and Hazel Gaudet, *The People's Choice* (New York: Columbia University Press, 1944); Bernard Berelson, Paul Lazarsfeld, and William McPhee, *Voting: A Study of Opinion Formation in a Presidential Campaign* (Chicago: University of Chicago Press, 1954); Angus Campbell, Gerald Gurin, and Warren E. Miller, *The Voter Decides* (Evanston, Ill.: Row, Peterson, 1954); and Angus Campbell, Philip E. Converse, Warren E. Miller, and Donald Stokes, *The American Voter* (New York: Wiley, 1960).

31. Edmund B. Lambeth, "Perceived Influence of the Press on Energy Policy Making," *Journalism Quarterly* 55 (Spring 1978): 11-18.

32. David Halberstam, *The Powers That Be* (New York: Knopf, 1979), 483-515. See also Michael Arlen, *Living-Room War* (New York: Viking, 1969).

33. Peter Braestrup, *Big Story* (New York: Doubleday Anchor, 1978).

34. William C. Adams, Dennis J. Smith, Allison Salzman, Ralph Crossen, Scott Hiber, Tom Naccarato, William Vantine, and Nine Weisbroth, "Before and After *The Day After:* The Unexpected Results of a Televised Drama," *Political Communication and Persuasion* 3 (1986): 191-213. See also Stanley Feldman and Lee Sigelman, "The Political Impact of Prime-Time Television: 'The Day After,' " *Journal of Politics* 47 (May 1985): 556-578.

35. This story of the neutron bomb is based on the account in Martin Linsky, *Impact: How the Press Affects Federal Policymaking* (New York: Norton, 1986), 21-39.

36. Ibid., 22.

37. Ibid., 32.

38. *New York Times,* July 13, 1983.

39. Theodore White, *The Making of the President, 1972* (New York: Bantam, 1973), 327.

40. The discussion is modeled on Fred Siebert, Theodore Peterson, and Wilbur Schramm, *Four Theories of the Press* (Urbana: University of Illinois Press, 1963).

41. For a brief account of media history in the United States, see Bernard Roshco, *Newsmaking* (Chicago: University of Chicago Press, 1975), 23-57.

42. James Aronson, *The Press and the Cold War* (Indianapolis: Bobbs-Merrill, 1970), 165-169.

43. A study of North American journalists in the early 1970s showed that only 35 percent believed in neutral reporting. See John Johnstone, Edward Slawski, and William Bowman, *The Newspeople* (Urbana: University of Illinois Press, 1976), 117-123. For a somewhat different perception see

David H. Weaver and G. Cleveland Wilhoit, *The American Journalist: A Portrait of U.S. News People and Their Work* (Bloomington, Ind.: Indiana University Press, 1986).

44. See, for example, Bernard Rubin, *Media, Politics, Democracy* (New York: Oxford University Press, 1977); and Erik Barnouw, *The Sponsor: Notes on a Modern Potentate* (New York: Oxford University Press, 1978).

45. Gurevitch and Blumler, "Linkages," 283.

46. This and many similar incidents are reported in William E. Porter, *Assault on the Media: The Nixon Years* (Ann Arbor: University of Michigan Press, 1976).

Readings

Agee, Warren K., Phillip H. Ault, and Edwin Emery. *Main Currents in Mass Communications.* New York: Harper and Row, 1986.

Graber, Doris A., ed. *Media Power in Politics.* Washington, D.C.: CQ Press, 1984.

Jeffres, Leo W. *Mass Media Processes and Effects.* Prospect Heights, Ill.: Waveland Press, 1986.

Leonard, Thomas C. *The Power of the Press: The Birth of American Political Reporting.* New York: Oxford University Press, 1986.

Nimmo, Dan, and James E. Combs. *Mediated Political Realities.* 2d ed. New York: Longman, 1988.

Ranney, Austin. *Channels of Power: The Impact of Television on American Politics.* New York: Basic Books, 1983.

Tuchman, Gaye. *Making News: A Study in the Construction of Reality.* New York: Free Press, 1978.

CHAPTER 2

Ownership, Regulation, and Guidance of Media

The French government owned and operated all television stations in France until 1986, when it approved creation of two commercial stations. The government awarded the licenses for the new stations to companies favorable to incumbent president François Mitterrand's Socialist party. The three existing government channels were already operated by Socialist party sympathizers. Opposition parties cried foul, claiming that control of the commercial stations by Socialists would vastly enhance their political power. Even if the Socialists lost the 1987 elections, their control of all major television outlets would make it difficult for the victorious party to carry out its programs.

When a conservative government assumed power after the elections, it promptly rescinded the licenses granted to Socialist sympathizers and awarded them to conservatives. It also replaced the Socialist directors of the three government stations with supporters of the new administration.

The struggle over control of French television is a modern version of the classic battle for control of the information communicated to political elites and the general public. Concern about who will wield media power has been a central issue in American politics since colonial days. It has become particularly important in the twentieth century because of the public policy issues raised by new technological developments and forms of business concentration. The pros and cons of public and private control will be weighed in this chapter, along with arguments for and against big business influence in the media industry. The impact of internal and external pressures on the industry, including those arising from the nature of its personnel and from citizen lobby groups, is also assessed. The public policy issues involved in media control are so complex, so intertwined with political predispositions and preferences, that no approach stands out as clearly "best." It therefore is no wonder that attempts to legislate have produced clashes of views, litigation, and little agreement on what the laws should be.

Control and Ownership: Public, Semipublic, and Private

Control and ownership of the media take a number of forms, each of which affects the nature of media output. The authoritarian pattern of total government control and its effects have already been discussed. As noted, some nonauthoritarian countries also control and own media, particularly radio and television, but their control over content is much looser, and their penalties for violations are much lighter.

Forms of Control: Pros and Cons

One reason for concern about media control and ownership is expressed in the old adage, "He who pays the piper calls the tune." If you fear government and its policies, you are likely to disapprove of direct operation of the media by government. You will be leery about extensive government regulation of privately operated media. But if you are afraid of the business ethics of private individuals and corporations, you would not want media control in private hands or directly influenced by large corporate enterprises.

Public policy issues raised by the debate over the merits of public versus private ownership of television illustrate the pros and cons. When governments own and operate major television channels, programming tends to reflect governmental policies closely, even in democratic countries. France, Israel, and Sweden are examples. However, Britain's experiences with operating radio and television through the British Broadcasting Corporation (BBC) show that governments, if they wish, can keep programming reasonably free from direct political interference. Big business control of television, if divided among various large corporations, is likely to bring more conflicting interests into play than would government control. For instance, a conglomerate heavily involved in export industries will not share the same views on tariffs as a conglomerate interested primarily in domestic manufacturing. Even within conglomerates, the interests of various components may clash, thus moderating the stands of the general management and lessening the chances that specific business interests will dominate programming.

Although there is more chance for diversity of political outlooks when business rather than government controls programming, the pressures springing from profit considerations are well-nigh irresistible under business control. Media offerings must be structured so that they yield financial returns to the owners of media enterprises. Governments are free from such pressures because they can use tax money to finance whatever programs they deem to be in the public interest. They must consider intragovernment power struggles, but they do not need to concern themselves with the size of their audiences. Private owners do because their income depends on small fees from audiences or on large fees from advertisers and other sponsors. The latter want to attract large numbers of viewers, particularly those in the eighteen- to forty-nine-year age group, who hold the bulk of purchasing power. Mass appeal, rather than any social or cultural concerns, becomes the primary goal.

Given the pros and cons of government and business control, which is the better system? The answer depends on one's assessment of the motivations of the public and private sectors and one's beliefs about the proper role of the media. Today, when distrust of government is high and people view "big media" as a counterfoil to "big government," private control is the option preferred by most Americans. In terms of programming, the choice of this option means that the bulk of television fare will be geared to simple, emotion-laden programming that attracts large, diverse audiences. It also means shying away from controversial or troublesome issues that may antagonize and deplete media audiences and subsequently diminish advertising revenues.

Although such programming draws the wrath of many people, particularly intellectual elites, one can argue that their disdain constitutes intellectual snobbery. Who is to say that the mass public's tastes are inferior to those of elites? The argument that people would choose educational programs over fluffy entertainment, if they had the chance, also can be refuted easily. Proof is plentiful that the mass public does indeed prefer light entertainment to more serious programs.[1] In print news, for example, magazines featuring sex or violence far outsell journals that treat political and social issues seriously. In fact, scholarly political journals frequently require subsidies to remain in print. Huge crowds are willing to pay heavily in time and money to see movies featuring heinous crimes and explicit sex. The most popular pay television channels show what is euphemistically called "adult entertainment," while channels devoted to highbrow culture languish and often perish.

Related to the concerns about domination of the media by government or private business interests is the fear of undue concentration of power. Diversity of ownership presumably encourages the expression of a great variety of views, which, to many Americans, is the essence of democracy. There must be a wide open marketplace into which ideas and opinions flow freely. But there is no agreement on exactly how diverse ownership must be to ensure this adequate flow of information

Drawing by Ziegler; © 1987 by The New Yorker Magazine, Inc.

and the opportunity for freedom of expression.[2] The American public appears to be more concerned about the concentration of media ownership in comparatively few hands than about control of media by private enterprise. Social reformers, on the other hand, are more concerned about business control, claiming that it caters to the lowest levels of taste.

Public Control

In the United States outright government ownership and control over media have been comparatively limited. However, they are growing as more and more local governments become involved in owning cable television systems or operating channels on privately owned systems. Government ownership raises serious unresolved questions about the limitations, if any, to be placed on the government's rights to use these outlets to further its partisan political purposes.[3]

The federal government is most heavily involved in broadcasting. Abroad it controls broadcasts to American military posts and owns various types of foreign propaganda outlets. Some of the programs put out by propaganda agencies such as the Voice of America are barred from broadcast on the domestic airwaves because members of Congress have been reluctant to expose American audiences to deliberate propaganda.

A substantial proportion of radio broadcast space, ranging from 50 percent in the pre-Carter years to 25 percent currently, is outside the control of ordinary regulatory agencies. It belongs to the federal government, which uses it for radio services supplied by the executive branch. Another 40 percent of the space is shared by the government and private interests, leaving only 35 percent for the exclusive use of the private sector.[4] Altogether, foreign and domestic federal broadcasts equal the volume of commercial broadcasts produced in the United States.

Semipublic Control

Media operation by semipublic institutions is another control option. The public broadcasting system is one example. It represents a mixture of public and private financing and programming, and public and private operation of radio and television stations. Created through the Public Broadcasting Act of 1967, the public broadcasting system supports educational and public service television stations whose programs do not generally attract large audiences. These stations usually cannot find enough commercial sponsors to pay for their shows.

Roughly one-fourth of American television stations participate in the public broadcasting system. In 1987 members included 394 noncommercial television stations and 296 noncommercial FM radio stations linked together as National Public Radio (NPR).[5] The administrative arrangements for the public broadcasting system, regulated now under the Public Telecommunications Act of 1978, have been complex. A Corporation for Public Broadcasting (CPB), staffed by political appointees, has handled the general administration, but it has been kept separate from the programming side of the operation to insulate public broadcasting from political pressures. A separate Public Broadcasting Service (PBS) has produced television programs, often in collaboration with state-supported foreign broadcast systems, like Britain's BBC, or France's Antenne Deux, or Japan's NHK.

The attempt to keep the Corporation for Public Broadcasting from influencing programming has failed. The corporation does not tell public television stations what specific programs they should feature. Instead, it has guided programming by paying for some types of programs and refusing to pay for others. This has constituted effective purse-string control of programming by government. In the field of radio, NPR was created both to produce and distribute programs. Since cost considerations made it impossible to include all noncommercial radio stations, only the largest, best-organized ones were included. Some 350 stations currently qualify and are eligible for CPB funding grants and participation in NPR programs.[6]

Private foundations, which are usually backed by big business enterprises and large corporations, have poured money into the public broadcasting system. Currently, they contribute more than twice as much money as the government.[7] Like government, this has given them influence over programming. In recent years many prime-time programs distributed by public broadcasting have been partially financed by corporations. To further ease the financial woes of public television, the Federal Communications Commission (FCC) during the Reagan years permitted the Public Broadcasting Service to engage in some commercial broadcasting of economic news and to accept a limited amount of advertising. The general public also has influenced public broadcasting through donations and community advisory boards. Nevertheless, inadequate financing is an enduring problem. A proposal to finance CPB through a tax on the sale of all television and radio stations received congressional support in 1987, primarily because it was viewed as a way to reduce government spending for public broadcasting. Since the powerful broadcast industry strongly opposes such a tax, its passage is doubtful.

Public television is distinguished from commercial television primarily by an emphasis on experimental programs, cultural offerings like classical music and ballet, academic lectures and documentaries, selected sports broadcasts, and minority-oriented shows. The nature and quality of programming varies widely because public television represents a decentralized bevy of local stations. The audience for public television, except for its children's programs (which represent a third of public television's programming time) has been small. On an average day or evening only 7 percent of the television audience tunes in to public television or public radio.[8] Even minority groups, for whom a number of public broadcast programs are presumably tailored, prefer the entertainment provided by commercial stations. Because of the limited appeal of public broadcasting and pressures to reduce public expenditures (totaling $200 to 300 million in federal funds and covering 20 percent of CPB's annual budget), there have been demands to disband the system completely and reallocate its frequencies to commercial channels.[9] Some of its programs might then be shown on commercial stations with federal subsidies.[10]

Supporters of the system contend that audience size should not be a criterion in judging its merits. Rather, the system should be viewed as a provider of needed special services that are neglected by commercial television precisely because they lack mass appeal or are commercially unattractive. Innovations pioneered by public broadcasting have spread to commercial broadcasting. It played a leading role in developing the system of captions for the hearing-impaired. Public radio and public television also were among the first to move to satellite distribution systems that made it possible to deliver multiple national program services to communities.[11]

Since its inception, and particularly since public funding has increased beyond the minute initial amounts, the public broadcasting system has been subjected to considerable political pressures. For example, President Richard Nixon tried to make the system more responsive to government wishes by shifting some control over local programming from Washington, D.C., to the more pliable local managers. As expected, this change led to more traditional programming. Such maneuvers demonstrate that dependence on public funds, even when these funds constitute only one-quarter to one-third of total funding, may mean subservience to government control, despite barriers to direct government influence.

The ultimate fate of public broadcasting is in doubt. As one communication expert has noted:

> It is likely that legislative and regulatory provisions regarding public broadcasting will continue to be influenced more substantially by the struggles among much larger political and economic forces than by the most careful analysis of the needs of the enterprise. There is considerable conflict among these external agendas, and to various degrees they all detract from a discussion of how the long-term broader public interest might be realized through public broadcasting.[12]

Private Control

Public ownership of the mass media as well as semipublic control, as exemplified by the Corporation for Public Broadcasting and National Public Radio, have been discussed. To round out the picture, one needs to consider the many arrangements in which control is in private hands, subject to the laws and regulations of different governmental agencies. Private control arrangements range from individual ownership, where one person owns a newspaper or radio or television station, to ownership by huge corporate conglomerates.

Patterns of Private Ownership

The facts about media control patterns are relatively simple to explain, but there is much disagreement about their consequences. The overarching feature of media control in the United States is that it is predominantly in private hands. Owners include small and large business interests, labor groups, religious and ethnic organizations, and many other types of interests represented in American society.

Business Configurations

The general trend in America toward diversified enterprises also characterizes the media business. Of course, there are *independents*, individuals or corporations that run a single media venture and nothing else. The publisher who owns one newspaper or one radio or television station is an example. However, their numbers are declining, except for the tiniest enterprises.

Multiple owners have become increasingly common. These are individuals or corporations who own several media of the same type—mostly radio or television stations, or newspapers. Since there are fewer than two thousand daily newspapers in the entire United States, fewer than five thousand AM and four thousand FM commercial radio stations, and fewer than eight hundred VHF and six hundred UHF commercial television stations, one might question whether a chain of twenty or thirty of these media ought to be controlled by a single owner.[13] Nevertheless, this has been the trend.

Even more common than the trend toward multiple owners has been the trend toward *crossmedia ownership,* ownership by an individual or corporation of several types of media, such as newspapers *and* television stations or newspapers *and* radio stations. This ownership pattern is worrisome when one owner controls all media in the same location. For instance, the same person might own a town's newspaper and television and radio station, effectively monopolizing local information sources.

A fourth pattern encompasses *conglomerates,* individuals or corporations who own media enterprises along with other types of businesses. The General Electric Company (GE) is an example. Figure 2-1 illustrates the diversity of GE's interests. Those who are wary about the public-mindedness of large corporations fear that their nonmedia business interests may color their news policies. If, for instance, there is a soundly based demand to reduce the defense establishment, or to oppose construction of a missile system, the management of a conglomerate such as GE, which holds many defense contracts, may not examine these questions open-mindedly.

In major urban centers most media are owned by individuals or corporations that fall into the multiple-owner, crossmedia, and conglomerate classifications. For instance, the *Chicago Tribune* is owned by the Tribune Company, which owns nearly two dozen media enterprises and more than a dozen companies outside the media field.[14] The major television stations in Chicago are owned by the national television networks and the Tribune conglomerate. Similarly, the major Chicago radio stations are owned by ABC, CBS, and NBC, the Tribune, Westinghouse, and other conglomerates. The radio stations that remain under single ownership are mostly very small with comparatively weak signals. By 1983 only 14 percent of all VHF and 32 percent of all UHF radio stations in the one hundred largest markets nationwide remained under control by independents. For television stations in the one hundred largest markets, the figure was 21 percent.[15]

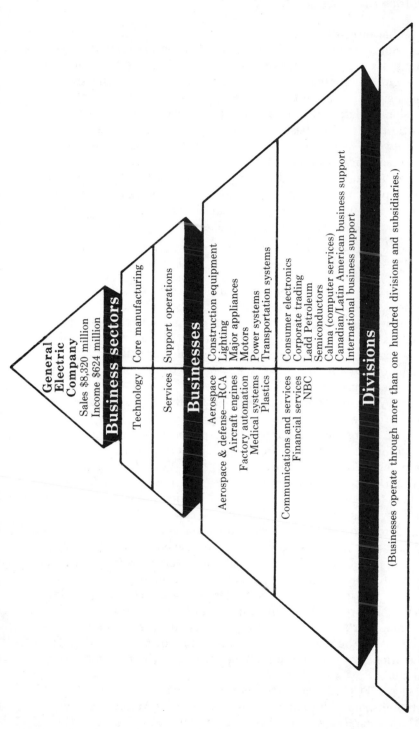

General Electric Company
Sales $8,320 million
Income $624 million

Business sectors

Technology
Services

Core manufacturing
Support operations

Businesses

Aerospace
Aerospace & defense—RCA
Aircraft engines
Factory automation
Medical systems
Plastics

Communications and services
Financial services
NBC

Construction equipment
Lighting
Major appliances
Motors
Power systems
Transportation systems

Consumer electronics
Corporate trading
Ladd Petroleum
Semiconductors
Calma (computer services)
Canadian/Latin American business support
International business support

Divisions

(Businesses operate through more than one hundred divisions and subsidiaries.)

Figure 2-1 The Diverse Holdings of General Electric Company

Sources: Standard and Poor's Corp., *Corporation Records*, September 1987; General Electric, *Annual Report*, 1986; and Dun and Bradstreet, *America's Corporate Families*, 1987.

The number of media outlets controlled by individuals or corporations varies widely. In 1987 Cox Broadcasting Corporation owned eight radio stations, six television stations, thirty-seven cable television systems, and eight newspapers; the New York Times Company owned twenty-nine newspapers, one radio station, five television stations, one cable television outlet, and nine other types of communication enterprises. Capital Cities/ABC, besides owning the American Broadcasting Company Network, owned a cable television network, seven television stations, nineteen radio stations, and nine daily and forty weekly newspapers as well as magazines and other publications.[16] But one cannot judge the sweep of control exercised by any group merely by looking at the number of its outlets. Three additional factors need to be considered: *market size, competition within the market,* and *prestige of each media institution.*

Market Size

For purposes of assessing mass media performance and regulating electronic media, the country is generally divided into "markets" rather than states or regions. A market is the area in which a particular media enterprise attracts a substantial audience. For instance, each television station has a signal that can be clearly received by people living within a certain radius of the station. All of the people within that radius who can receive the signal are considered to be within the market. This means that they can be expected to respond to advertising for products and services provided by program sponsors.

Altogether, there are four hundred newspaper markets in the country and two hundred-seventy broadcast markets. Their size varies widely. In major metropolitan areas such as New York, Chicago, or Los Angeles, a market with a fifty-mile radius may have a population of several million people. The same radius for a station in Wyoming might cover more cows than people.

The Federal Communications Commission considers market size only partially in its regulations designed to prevent concentration of ownership. To ensure that people throughout America are exposed to a wide variety of media voices, FCC regulations stipulate top limits for the numbers of stations that can be under the same ownership. Additional restrictions are imposed on multiple and crossmedia ownership within the same market. But there are no limits on the size of audiences that may be within the reach of a particular media owner, as long as the television stations cover no more than 25 percent of the nation's television households.

In 1984 the FCC increased the number of media enterprises that one owner may hold. The current limit is twelve AM radio stations, twelve FM radio stations, and twelve television stations. All of these may be very high frequency.[17] This means that an owner can be in thirty-six different markets (a few more for minority owners), each reaching the homes of millions of people, as long as the 25 percent television market share limit is honored. At present, four out of every five television stations in the one hundred most densely populated markets, which serve nearly 90 percent of the nation's households, belong to multiple-owner groups.

Newspapers can enter an unlimited number of markets. Consequently, newspaper chains can expand at will, up to the limits allowed by antitrust and antimonopoly laws.[18] By 1985 more than 68 percent of America's daily papers, boasting 78 percent of total circulation, were controlled by national and regional chains.[19] There are more than 160 such chains, but the majority control fewer than ten papers. However, the 26 groups that owned ten or more papers controlled 55 percent of all chain-owned papers. In terms of circulation, Gannett was the leader in 1987 with nearly 6 million copies per day. It owned the country's first national newspaper, *USA Today,* launched in 1982 (1,417,077 daily circulation). Second in line, behind Gannett, was Knight-Ridder (3,493,000 daily circulation), followed by Newhouse (3,100,000), Dow Jones (2,601,000), the Tribune Company (2,600,000), and the Times Mirror Company (1,093,000).[20] In terms of numbers of papers under its control, Gannett also was first, with ninety-three daily papers. Knight-Ridder was fourth with thirty-four papers, Newhouse eighth with twenty-six papers, Dow Jones ninth with twenty-three papers, and the Tribune Company and the Times Mirror Company both trailed with nine papers. While these figures are constantly changing as papers are bought and sold, the relative rankings remain stable.

By 1985, the ten largest chains accounted for nearly half of the total daily newspaper circulation (63 million copies) in the United States. This means that one-third of the papers read in the United States on any given day transmit news screened by personnel from only ten large business enterprises. The proportion of circulation controlled by chain-owned papers has been growing over the decades, but not by leaps and bounds. Although individual papers within chains generally enjoy editorial-page autonomy, they tend to be more uniform in political endorsements than are independently owned papers.[21]

Influence is even more concentrated for television. Instead of ten companies controlling one-third of the market, three huge conglomerate-owned networks—NBC, CBS, and ABC—dominate more than a third of the television households in the nation. Altogether, the three networks own sixteen television stations.[22] In addition, their parent companies—the Columbia Broadcasting System, Capital Cities/ABC, and General Electric Company—own other media enterprises such as recording companies, publishing houses, movie theaters, and radio and television equipment and supply companies, as well as unrelated ventures such as real estate firms, car rental companies, food supply houses, and home furnishing manufacturers.[23]

The networks produce a limited number of television and radio entertainment programs for their own use. The bulk of entertainment programming comes from other sources. Because production of programs is not regulated by government, this part of their business is not directly under FCC control.[24] However, the broadcast stations that each network owns are within the regulatory reach of the FCC, as are the "affiliates"—stations that regularly subscribe to the programs produced by a network.

The network-owned television stations are in the largest media markets. This means New York, Chicago, and Los Angeles for all three networks, supplemented variously by Philadelphia, Washington, D.C., St. Louis, Detroit, and San Francisco. In addition to producing and buying programming for its wholly owned stations, each network also supplies approximately 65 percent of the programming for its affiliates. Even nonaffiliated stations make extensive use of network-selected programs following their initial runs. Because the vast majority of commercial stations are network affiliated, much of televised information reaching American households is subject to choices and decisions made by network personnel. In addition, networks control radio outlets domestically as well as radio and television stations abroad. To keep these figures in proper perspective, one must keep in mind that the three networks compete vigorously with each other for public favor and that they do not dominate programming completely for affiliates. One must also consider that nearly 33 million households were served by cable television by 1986, and nearly 31 million households owned video cassette recorders (VCRs) that permitted them to supplement over-the-air television fare.[25]

The capstone to the picture of narrowly held control over information outlets is supplied by the wire service companies. A huge share of the news stories appearing in nearly every paper in the country, and featured on television or radio news, comes from the wires of the Associated Press (AP) and United Press International (UPI). The roots of these two organizations go back to 1848, when six New York newspapers formed a cooperative association to share the cost of collecting foreign news. Out of this initial effort grew large organizations that employ reporters scattered throughout the world to collect and report news. News stories and bulletins are then transmitted electronically to subscriber papers and radio and television stations. Ninety-nine percent of news sources in the United States that disseminate news daily are served by either AP, UPI, or both. Associated Press has the lion's share of the market, while financially ailing UPI has been losing ground. A handful of other wire services, such as those operated by the *New York Times,* the *Los Angeles Times,* and the *Chicago Tribune,* serve their own papers, along with a more limited clientele of subscribers.

News stories and bulletins supplied by the wire services are either used verbatim or rewritten by their clients. Depending on the resources available to a particular news organization for gathering and writing its own news, the proportion of wire service stories used directly or in rewritten form may vary from less than 10 percent to 80 percent or more of all stories. For many newspapers, a look at the mix of stories carried by wire services on any particular day will accurately foretell the mix of stories carried by the paper.[26] Wire service stories tend to predominate for foreign news and even for national news for smaller papers and stations that cannot afford their own correspondents. This means that a large share of news production in the United States is dominated by two giant news-producing companies. However, none of the situations of limited competition that have been discussed involves monopoly controls. Even in one-newspaper towns, there is usually some inter-media competition from television and radio stations. Unfortunately, while carriers differ, the messages they present are likely to be very similar.[27]

Intramarket Competition

To preserve competition within each market, FCC rules now prohibit multiple and crossmedia ownership within the same market. However, this rule does not affect most radio and television combinations existing prior to 1970 or newspaper and broadcast media combinations existing before 1975. To reduce dominance by the networks, the FCC also mandates that in markets with more than three television or radio broadcast stations at least one of every three stations must be reserved for owners who are not affiliated with any network.

Despite efforts to increase intramarket competition, limited competition (oligopoly) conditions prevail in the majority of markets. Electronic media are generally owned in pairs, limiting the total number of media owners in the community. Intramarket newspaper competition has also become rare. Ninety-eight percent of all American cities have only one daily newspaper.[28] Newspaper competition is rare outside the largest cities. Suburban dailies, which flourish in a few major cities, do not substantially alter the situation because their coverage of major news stories is usually limited.[29] In addition to a monopoly over local print news, newspaper owners frequently own a local television or radio station as well. However, the FCC has forced newspapers to relinquish broadcast properties whenever the combination enjoys a total monopoly within the market.

Prestige Leadership

Another reason for homogeneity in news supply is the consensus among journalists about the nature of news and the elements of good reporting. There are widely accepted standards of professionalism in journalism, just as there are in law or medicine or engineering. As part of this system of norms, certain members and products are widely accepted as models whose influence reaches far beyond their own organization. Critics call this the "jackal syndrome" or "pack journalism." [30] In the political news field the *New York Times* is the lion whom the jackals follow. In television Dan Rather or Tom Brokaw are models for the profession. Other news professionals watch what information these sources present, how they present it, and what interpretations they give to it, and they then adjust their own presentations accordingly. [31] The upshot is that the multiplication of voices in the media marketplace has contributed relatively little to meaningful diversity in news. The newcomers quickly join the old chorus and hum the prevailing tunes.

Small Business versus Big Business Control

The steady trend toward consolidation in the media industry has left control of information increasingly in the hands of a limited number of very large organizations. Because concentration has generally stopped short of infringing antitrust and antimonopoly laws, these laws have been of little help in halting or reversing it. [32] As will be pointed out in Chapter 3, economic factors are largely responsible for consolidation. Production of television programs and worldwide news gathering are very expensive. Only large, well-financed organizations, which are able to spread the costs over many customers, can provide the lavish media fare to which the American public has become accustomed. [33]

Even when there is no infringement of antitrust and antimonopoly laws, is it sound public policy to allow the rapid pace of consolidation of media enterprises to continue? Is there a danger that centralized control, besides bringing undesirable uniformity, also will lead to neglect of local needs? Does the absence of newspaper competition in American cities prevent diverse viewpoints from being presented to the public? The evidence lends little substance to these fears. [34] Neither does it sustain claims that the media giants routinely suppress diversity among the news outlets under their control, squelch antibusiness news, and stress antilabor, pro-Republican, and jingoistic stories. It is true that many important stories are not published, including some that would be poor publicity for big business, but there is no hard evidence that the choices that are necessary to cope with an oversupply of news conform predominantly to a conservative political orientation. [35] In fact, many prominently featured broadcasts, movies, and magazine and newspaper articles in recent years have carried stories critical of conservative policies in general and of the business community in particular.

The charge that media owners pressure media personnel into supporting the existing political system also is not borne out. American journalists in large organizations, like their colleagues in small, independently owned enterprises, are interested in appealing to their audiences, and therefore their stories usually reflect the values of mainstream American society, regardless of the journalists' personal political orientations.[36]

What about the argument that small, individually owned enterprises would produce better programming, more suited to local needs? One way to test this assertion is to compare the amount of news and other public service programs offered by various types of television stations. By and large, news and public service programming has been more plentiful on stations owned by big business and by conglomerates than on stations owned by individuals.[37] Network stations do best of all. Similarly, radio stations and newspapers that have the best public service coverage, as judged by professional journalists, generally are controlled by large business enterprises or are part of a large network.

The contention that individually owned, small enterprises provide poorer public service than their larger, group-owned cousins is open to question. The measures of public service programming used by the FCC and most media studies are primarily quantitative. They gauge how much broadcasting time is spent on certain kinds of programs, but they do not analyze the quality of the programming. Small stations may make up in quality what they lack in quantity.

It is quite plausible, however, that big business control actually does mean qualitatively superior programs. Large enterprises are able to absorb the losses that are often incurred in the production of documentaries and public service programs. They have more money than do small enterprises to spend on talented people, research, investigations, and on costly entertainment shows. For example, in the fall of 1983, ABC could present a lengthy documentary on the dangers of nuclear warfare, limiting commercial interruptions, even though it meant losing money.

High costs explain why television programs produced in the United States fail to recapture their initial investment.[38] By 1987 hour-long episodes of prime-time programs often cost more than $1 million. Even the news is lavishly produced. Networks use multiple crews to cover simple events like presidential news conferences. As many as ten crews have been sent abroad to report on fighting in Lebanon. On an average, each story broadcast on the NBC nightly news costs $63,000. Top-rated news anchors command multi-million-dollar salaries, with Dan Rather leading the pack at CBS ($2.5 million), followed by Tom Brokaw at NBC ($1.8 million), and Barbara Walters and Peter Jennings at ABC (approximately $1 million). All in all, the costs of news production have been staggering.[39]

On balance it seems that some of the arguments made against big business control of media are exaggerated. So are some of the arguments in favor of control by small enterprises. When FCC rules have forced small stations to spend time on non-network programs, the results generally have been poor. Unable to afford costly original programs produced locally, these stations have filled their non-network hours with cheap canned movies or syndicated quiz or talent shows. The arguments concerning the respective merits of big and small media enterprises cannot be settled definitively until more thorough comparisons of the quality of programs have been made. In the meantime it is important to recognize that current policies designed to reduce media concentration and encourage local programming rest on questionable assumptions and have failed to meet their objectives.

Curbs on Private Control of the Media

FCC Regulations

Even though the media business is largely in private hands in the United States, the federal government regulates some aspects of media management. The chief control agency is the FCC, a bipartisan body appointed by the president and confirmed by the Senate. It was a seven-member body until the summer of 1984, when its size was reduced to five commissioners to save money. In 1986 the appointment term was shortened from seven to five years, ensuring a faster turnover of commission personnel and greater control by the president. In theory, the commission is an independent regulatory body. In practice, congressional purse strings, public and industry pressures, and presidential control over appointment of new members, including naming the chairman, have gravely curtailed its freedom of operation. The commission's independence is also weakened because its rulings can be appealed to the courts and have been overturned on a number of occasions. Conflicting political pressures from outside the agency as well as internal political pressures influence FCC policy making. As the authors of *The Politics of Broadcast Regulation* note:

> The broadcast policy-making system is usually modest in its goals, flexible in policy choices, sensitive to feedback, and prone to dealing with immediate problems through steps and options that are only incrementally different from existing policies. ... A consequence of these characteristics is a reactive rather than an innovative system sluggish to respond to change in its environment, particularly to technological change that probably will be very rapid in the next decade or so. Clearly there are problems with this kind of policy-making system.[40]

Given the vagueness of its mandate under the Communications Act of 1934 to "serve the public interest, convenience, and necessity," the FCC has found it difficult to identify the objectives that should guide its regulatory powers. It has had to determine what social, economic, and technical goals the communications industry should achieve. It also has had to deal with conflicts over the adoption of various technologies and with the philosophical issue of regulation versus deregulation. On balance, the FCC's record of setting goals and enforcing its rules has earned it the reputation of being a benign and ineffective watchdog over the public interest at best and an industry-kept, pressure-group-dominated lapdog at worst.

The FCC's primary area of responsibility is control over the electronic media. The print media are essentially uncontrolled except for antitrust and monopoly laws that the Justice Department uses to curtail print media monopolies. However, economically weak newspapers have been permitted to combine their business and production facilities, free from these restraints, as long as their news and editorial operations are separate. By 1987 twenty-one agreements for combining the business aspects of newspapers were in effect. It remains uncertain to what degree, if any, print media will be subject to the same controls as electronic media when they use electronic transmission, such as teletext or satellite transmission of newspaper copy.

FCC control takes four forms: (1) rules limiting the number of stations owned or controlled by a single organization, (2) examination of the goals and performance of stations as part of periodic licensing, (3) rules mandating public service and local interest programs, and (4) rules to guarantee fair treatment to individuals and to protect their rights. While none of these rules deal directly with content, all of them increase the chances that content will be diverse and of civic importance.

Rules Limiting Station Ownership. As explained earlier, to prevent high concentrations of media ownership and ensure diversity of information sources, the FCC limits the number of stations that television and radio owners may control. It does not limit the number of households that may be within the range of any one group of owners, aside from the 25 percent market share limit for television. Consequently, while most groups reach only a small percentage of the nation's homes, the thirteen largest groups each command an audience in excess of 5 million households, with three to six people each.[41] This gives each owner a chance to dominate the radio or television information supply of up to 30 million people, nearly one-sixth of the nation.

Since 1970 the FCC has had a one-to-a-customer rule that prohibits any party from acquiring more than one AM and FM radio station or more than one television station in the same market. This rule now also applies to cable systems. The rule has diversified station ownership, but it has not required the breakup of existing groups that violate the one-to-a-customer rule. Similar rules restrict newspaper-television, newspaper-radio, or newspaper-cable combinations. About one-third of all groups with television interests still have newspaper properties. Many of these multimedia combinations were formed at the urging of the FCC, which once thought that this type of arrangement would lead to better news services. In anticipation of rules forcing the divestiture of properties in the same market, several owners have arranged swaps of properties. For instance, late in 1977 the *Washington Post* and *Detroit News* arranged to exchange television stations so that the *Post* would own a Detroit station and the *News* a Washington station.

Station owners are very eager to retain their licenses because station ownership has been enormously profitable. In 1980 the average television station was four times more profitable than the average Fortune 500 company, and the average network-owned station was six times more profitable.[42] Moreover, no investment is initially required to get a license from the government. Licenses of profitable stations can be sold for a high price since the demand exceeds supply.

This picture of steady profitability changed in the late 1980s. Television news units were especially hard hit. They were forced to slash budgets and lay off several thousand employees. Partial deregulation of the television industry, the rise of new networks, such as media mogul Ted Turner's cable news network, and the development of new technologies generated fierce competition. Independent television stations multiplied, as did cable systems, television satellites, video recorders, and similar services such as teletext and microfiche. Affiliates reduced their reliance on network programming by producing their own news shows or importing satellite programs. Network audience share dropped from 91 percent in 1977 to 68 percent in 1987, producing a drop in advertising rates. Advertising revenues also declined because the pool of large advertisers shrank in the wake of business mergers.[43] The networks themselves caught the merger fever. ABC merged with Capital Cities Communications, NBC was acquired by General Electric, and CBS barely fought off acquisition at great financial cost.

Today the FCC rarely uses its major power to lessen ownership concentration—refusal to renew a television license at the end of five years or a radio license after seven years. In the past shock waves pulsed through the media industry when the FCC refused a license. The landmark case involved Boston television station WHDH-TV, which was owned by a local newspaper company that also operated two local radio stations and held a controlling interest in a cable television company. Even though the station had performed well, the FCC in 1969 awarded the license to a competitor, Boston Broadcasting Inc., controlled by a citizens' group. This was the first time that a license was granted to a competing applicant on grounds involving the media concentration issue. Sen. John O. Pastore, then chairman of the Senate Communications Subcommittee, expressed fear that license withdrawal might henceforth be used capriciously for political reasons. His efforts finally led to new FCC rules that nearly guarantee license renewal to stations that perform their job satisfactorily.

In the past the FCC rarely encouraged new communications media in order to increase competition and diversity. It initially discouraged innovations such as FM broadcasting, VHF and UHF telecasting, and cable television. This attitude has changed in recent years, and the commission now encourages new entrants into the marketplace. For instance, it has fostered direct satellite broadcasting, pay television, and low-power television stations for small markets.

Licensing as Performance Control. What is satisfactory performance? Television and radio must "serve the public interest, convenience, and necessity," but beyond requiring broadcasters to ascertain the community needs and interests by talking with community leaders, there are no guides for interpreting these rules. Even the requirement to keep in touch with community leaders was dropped in June 1984. This leaves the media and the FCC great leeway in determining what qualifies as good programming. The FCC has looked at the mix of programs, the proportion of public service offerings, and the inclusion of programs geared to selected groups. It has not scrutinized the subject matter of broadcasts in detail.

This hands-off attitude has applied to both program inclusions and exclusions. For instance, the FCC declined a viewer's request to order stations to provide information about Russian and Chinese political and military activities in North Korea. The viewer had argued that the American public needed this information to put into perspective reports about U.S. military activities in Southeast Asia. Similarly, despite concerted public lobbying the FCC has not ordered the networks to delay programming unsuitable for children until late evening and to reserve the early evening broadcast hours for "family" shows. However, the FCC did let it be known that it would not prevent the industry from instituting such a plan on its own. The industry did so for a while, but has now abandoned the effort.

Through its licensing of news outlets, the FCC has tried to ensure the new licensees will meet the information needs of socioeconomic groups different from those already served by existing stations in a given area. When there are several qualified applicants for new broadcasting stations, the FCC is authorized to use a lottery to make the award. Recent court decisions have challenged the legality of weighting the lottery in favor of women, minorities, labor unions, and community organizations that are underrepresented in the ownership of telecommunications facilities.[44] Once a license has been granted, the owners hold it for good and may even sell it with little government intervention. For stations that fulfill the requirements of public service broadcasting, do not engage in discriminatory or fraudulent practices, and receive few or no complaints about poor programming, renewal has become automatic.

Since the 1970s numerous civic groups have entered renewal hearings to protest the type of programming offered or omitted by a particular station. As a result of such pressures, the FCC has reluctantly withdrawn licenses from a few stations over the years. These withdrawals have made broadcasters more careful than in the past to avoid public opposition.

Compared with regulatory agencies in other countries, even in Western Europe, Canada, and Australia, the FCC controls the electronic media with a very light hand. It could, if it wished, rigorously define what constitutes "programming in the public interest." [45] It could enforce its rulings more strictly and verify station performance records at license renewal time. The threat of license withdrawal for rule violations could be used as a much more powerful deterrent to misbehavior and as a much stronger lever to guide programming. Part of the problem is that the FCC staff, which numbers fewer than 1,900 people, is much too small to cope with all the duties assigned to the agency. In fact, it is chronically behind schedule, even for routine matters such as publication of its annual reports.

Public Service and Local Programming. In the past the FCC stipulated the minimum time that ought to be devoted to public service programs. Under the 5-5-10 rule, which is no longer enforced, 5 percent of programming had to be devoted to local affairs, 5 percent to news and public affairs, and 10 percent to nonentertainment programs. Beyond checking a television station's log to ascertain that it recorded the minimum amount of public service programming (the requirement had already been dropped for commercial radio broadcasts), the FCC did not examine the nature and quality of programs labeled "public service." Most stations' logs exceeded the stipulated amount.[46]

To ensure that stations leave some time for programs of interest to local communities, the FCC requires that one prime-time hour between 7:00 and 11:00 p.m. is set aside for non-network programs. However, the "prime-time access rule" permits stations to fill all or part of the local programming slot with network news or public affairs programs, documentaries, or children's shows. The intent of the rule thus can be readily circumvented as long as the program choice was made by the local station. Obviously, the rule has not worked very well to promote genuinely local programming. As discussed earlier, most stations find it too costly to produce original programs. When they do, they prefer covering national and international news rather than local events that are less glamorous. Whenever groups of stations produce programs jointly, the strictly local focus also suffers.[47]

Fair Treatment Rules. The FCC has also made rules about access to the airways for candidates for political office and for people who have been the subject of media attacks. These types of controls are discussed in Chapter 4.

The Decontrol Debate

The difference in treatment between the unregulated print media and the regulated electronic media has become highly controversial in recent years. Critics deny that broadcast restrictions are still justified on the grounds that the number of broadcast channels is severely limited.[48] In light of new technical developments, such as cable television and communications satellites, the number of broadcasts within reach of average Americans has vastly expanded. Whereas competition has been rising among broadcasters, it has been falling among daily newspapers. Average Americans are generally limited to one local newspaper. The high cost of starting a paper and a finite advertising pool discourage would-be competitors. One can argue, therefore, that television and radio are far more competitive than the unregulated newspaper business and should be freed from all controls.

Such arguments have been quite prominent in the debates surrounding efforts to revise the Communications Act of 1934. In 1978 Lionel Van Deerlin of California, the chairman of the House Communications Subcommittee, proposed to remove nearly all restrictions on the operation of radio and television stations. FCC rules to ensure fair treatment would give way to marketplace competition as the chief regulatory mechanism. Stations would still be expected to provide news, public affairs programs, and locally produced programs throughout the broadcast day, but without specific performance rules.

The use of licensing as a tool to force broadcasters to conform to government policies also was to be restricted under the proposed legislation. Licensees were to pay fees based on the value of advertising accounts in the station's market. This income was intended to support public television, subsidize minority ownership of stations, provide rural telecommunications development, and defray the costs of telecommunications regulations. Public broadcast stations, whose programs would be federally financed, were to be prohibited from accepting any private funding, thus freeing them from all commercial pressures.

Opponents of extensive deregulation argued that the age of electronic plenty was still a far-off vision. Moreover, multiplying channels available for broadcasting did not automatically mean more diversity. Most channels were likely to use the traditional sources of programs to fill air time, as was already happening in cable systems where cable operators drew heavily on materials produced by other broadcasters.[49] Finally, it was argued that the impact of television on public life in America was so profound that the public interest required continued controls.

The 1978 proposals and subsequent, scaled-down revisions failed in the face of vigorous opposition by industry lobbies, public interest groups, and representatives of public television. Even though full-scale attempts to rewrite the Communications Act of 1934 are doomed to rough legislative sailing, the trends toward deregulation that they have exhibited have been strong enough to find expression recently in the rules and regulations issued by the FCC. For instance, radio has been deregulated so that stations can now choose their own programming formats and are no longer required to include a specified proportion of public service programs.[50] Cable television also has been freed from most of the rules once imposed by the FCC. And rules barring network acquisition of cable stations have been relaxed.

Control by Industry Associations and Advertiser Pressures

Industry lobbies are another means of controlling the mass media. Radio and television interests, especially the networks and their affiliated stations, are active lobbyists. Most belong to the National Association of Broadcasters (NAB), a powerful Washington lobby despite the diversity and often clashing interests of its members. The NAB has a membership of 5,400 radio and television stations. It has a staff of 140 people and an active Political Action Committee.[51] The networks have additional lobbying agents in Washington who are in continuous contact with the FCC. These lobbies are particularly concerned about guarding the freedom networks now enjoy in programming.

Besides the NAB, there are a number of other trade associations and publications, such as *Broadcasting* magazine, whose staffs engage in lobbying, often at crosspurposes to each other. For newspapers the American Newspaper Publishers Association (ANPA) is one of the most prominent. These organizations try to influence appointments to the FCC and guide public policies that affect new technologies that may threaten established systems or practices. For instance, the network lobbies for many years tried to stifle cable television and to acquire control over domestic satellites.

To forestall regulation by outside bodies, the industry developed mechanisms for self-control. The NAB has had a radio code since 1929 and a television code since 1952 that set forth rules on program content and form. Both codes have been modernized periodically. The industry-wide codes are now superseded by individual codes in major broadcast enterprises and codes adopted by the Council of Better Business Bureaus. Scholars, too, have set forth codes of journalism ethics, most of which are quite vague, such as the five principles advocated by Edmund Lambeth. Ethical behavior, he contends, requires telling the truth and heeding humaneness, above all. It also requires striving for fairness, striving for independence from power holders, and acting as responsible trustees for the public's interests.[52] What these principles mean in practice is left for decision in specific cases.

The impact of industry-wide codes has always been limited. NAB codes, for example, applied only to NAB member stations that chose to subscribe to them. In 1977, a typical year, 25 percent of all TV stations were not NAB members, and nearly one-half of the members did not subscribe to the codes.[53] Penalties for code violations were minimal. The worst penalty was withdrawal of a station's right to list itself as a subscriber to the code. Therefore, the code exerted only a limited amount of moral pressure on the industry. It did serve to blunt demands by pressure groups for government intervention to set and enforce standards.

Somewhat stronger pressures on program content arose in the 1970s from advertisers who actually withdrew their commercials from programs they considered to be obscene or excessively violent. Sears Roebuck was one of the earliest and largest advertisers to do so. Other companies, such as Procter and Gamble, the top television advertiser in the nation, retained consultants to seek out acceptable programs for their advertisements and avoid unacceptable ones. With thirty-second advertisements on top-rated shows yielding in excess of $400,000 in 1987, threats of withdrawal constituted tremendous economic pressures. In the wake of such pressures from advertisers, the number of programs featuring violence, particularly during prime-time hours, dropped temporarily.

There is deep concern, however, that advertisers, spurred by pressure groups, could become unofficial censors. For instance, General Motors' sponsorship of an Eastertime program on the life of Jesus was cancelled because evangelical groups objected to the content. There were crippling withdrawals of advertising from a CBS documentary on gun control, opposed by the gun control lobby, and from a series of interviews featuring ex-president Nixon, which aroused the ire of Nixon foes. In 1986 a number of public television stations refused to air a public television program on border disputes involving Israel because of strong objections by major Jewish groups. The television networks, although not shy about saturating the airwaves with uninhibited sex in television dramas, have refused advertising designed to instruct viewers about the use of condoms for protection against unwanted pregnancies and the acquired immune deficiency syndrome (AIDS). Again, religious groups are the unofficial censor. On the political front, "Amerika," a serial drama depicting life in the United States ten years after a Soviet takeover, aroused objections from so many groups in 1987, including the Soviet Union's government, that it was cancelled. Protests over the cancellation then led to its reinstatement, though in a watered-down version.

Citizen Lobby Control

Citizens' efforts to affect the quality of broadcasting began in earnest in 1966 when the Office of Communication of the United Church of Christ, a public interest lobby, challenged the renewal of a TV license for a Jackson, Mississippi, station, WLBT-TV, because the station had discriminated against black viewers.[54] Blacks then constituted 45 percent of the Jackson population. The challenge failed, but it was the beginning of efforts by many other citizen groups to use pressure tactics to challenge license renewals.

A major victory was finally won in 1975 when the FCC refused to renew licenses of eight educational television stations in Alabama and failed to grant a construction permit for a ninth station because citizen groups had charged racial discrimination in employment at these stations. There also had been complaints that programs that dealt with affairs of the black community had been unduly excluded.[55] Since then, numerous stations have yielded to pressure for increased minority employment and programming rather than face protracted legal action.

The National Citizens' Committee for Broadcasting (NCCB), headed by former FCC commissioner Nicholas Johnson, became widely known for sharp attacks on the shallowness of broadcasting and the weakness of governmental control. Besides watching and criticizing national media policy, the committee also aided the surveillance activities of local groups. It has now been absorbed into the broadcast media monitoring group of the Ralph Nader consumer protection organization. Other prominent national citizens' lobby groups include Accuracy in Media (AIM), a well-financed conservative media-monitoring organization; the Coalition for Better Television (CBTV), representing fundamentalist religious groups; Citizens for the American Way (CAW), a liberal media organization intent on blocking conservative lobbies; Action for Children's Television (ACT); the National Black Media Coalition (NBMC); and the National Latino Media Coalition (NLMC).

Despite the substantial impact of such groups on FCC rule making and licensing procedures, the 1980s saw a decline in citizens' national lobbying efforts.[56] One reason was the difficulty of sustaining citizen interest over long periods of time; another was lack of financial support and loss of leadership. The broadcast lobby defeated efforts to obtain public funding for citizens' groups, and foundation support dried up. Many groups were also discouraged by reversals in the high courts of substantial victories won in the low courts. Some of the energies of citizen groups have been redirected into lobbying at the local level to ensure that the emerging cable system serves the interests of various publics.

In addition to the more than sixty organizations concerned exclusively with media reform, other organizations, such as the Parent Teacher Association, the National Organization for Women, and the American Medical Association, have lobbied on a variety of media issues. These include concern about stereotyping, access to media coverage and to media employment and ownership, advertising on children's programs, and enforcement of FCC program regulations. The groups' tactics include monitoring media content, publicizing their findings, and directly pressuring broadcasters, advertisers, media audiences, and government control agencies. Protest by PTA members has pressured advertisers, who, in turn, have succeeded in reducing the number of violent programs shown in the early evening hours. Legal maneuvers have ranged from challenges of license renewals to damage suits for the harmful effects of media content.[57]

It is difficult to assess the precise influence of these organizations, either individually or collectively, because many of their goals overlap with other forces that affect media policy. The causes for which they have worked have prospered, however, over the years, and part of the credit undoubtedly belongs to them. Yet these groups, if they remain active, have a long road to travel before they can match the clout and resources enjoyed by the broadcast lobby and by public officials involved in media control.[58]

Control by Media Personnel

Thus far the influence over media output of government, media owners, associations, and audiences has been discussed. It is also important to consider the influence of the people who actually produce the news and entertainment programs: reporters, writers, editors, and producers. They control the specific stories that become news. As William Small puts it: "This is the rubbing point, the actual confrontation with what is happening. It is also the point of greatest influence." [59] What determines their choices and thus shapes the flow of news and entertainment?

The question can be answered from three perspectives. *Personality theory* can be used to explain newspeople's professional behavior in terms of personality and social background factors. A second approach is *organization theory*. Because newspeople operate within news production organizations, their behavior can be explained by examining organizational pressures and goals. Lastly, one can seek clues to the influence of media personnel in *role theory*. Depending on the professional role conceptions that media personnel adopt, the stories will vary. For instance, journalists who see themselves as impartial reporters of the news will behave differently from those who see themselves as partisan reformers.

Background and Personality Factors

Factors known to influence occupational performance include social background and traits that are idiosyncratic to particular individuals. Examples of background factors are level of education, race, and sex. Their precise impact on professional orientations remains a matter of heated scientific and political controversy. Idiosyncratic factors, which include artistic tastes, emotional outlook, and intellectual interests, explain why newspeople who come from similar backgrounds will nonetheless prefer different stories or will give a different emphasis to the same news story or entertainment plot. Personality factors and organizational logic intertwine, with the latter setting the broad boundaries of what is acceptable news.

What are some of the personality and background factors that influence the substance and shape of news? Data collected by G. Cleveland Wilhoit and David H. Weaver for their study *The American Journalist* are helpful in answering this question. Other studies support these findings, which are based on telephone interviews with 1,001 randomly selected newspeople in the United States.[60] The sample was divided into journalists working in "prominent" news organizations—major networks, big city newspapers, and wire service organizations—and journalists working in small towns and relatively little-known news enterprises. Each group was further divided into supervisory (42 percent) and nonsupervisory (58 percent) personnel.

Wilhoit and Weaver found that the social profile of newspeople closely resembled the profile of other professionals in the United States. Ninety-five percent were white, 66 percent were male, 60 percent were Protestants, and 70 percent had graduated from college. Sixty percent had taken some college-level journalism courses. The vast majority (93 percent) had been brought up in a church-going family and claimed to derive their journalistic ethics from their upbringing (72 percent) or from their job environment (88 percent).

In 1982, the year of the survey, only 5 percent of the executives in the prominent media were black, as Table 2-1 indicates. At the staff level, blacks constituted 3 percent. In the less prominent organizations,

Table 2-1 Selected Characteristics of Journalists (in percentages)

Characteristic	Prominent organizations		Nonprominent organizations	
	Executives	*Staffers*	*Executives*	*Staffers*
Female	28	23	28	41
Black	5	3	2	4
College graduate	64	56	50	58
Democrats	33	51	38	40
Republicans	9	4	22	20
Independents	58	44	38	39
Other	—	1	2	1
Left orientation [a]	31	33	22	25
Middle roaders	57	55	57	59
Right orientation	12	12	21	17

Source: Adapted from G. Cleveland Wilhoit and David H. Weaver, *The American Journalist: A Portrait of U.S. News People and Their Work* (Bloomington: Indiana University Press, 1986), 12-64.

Note: In prominent organizations, $N = 58$ for executives and 78 for staffers; in nonprominent organizations, $N = 413$ for executives and 450 for staffers.

[a] Designations are self-identifications and include people claiming the orientation or claiming to lean toward it.

2 percent of the executives and 4 percent of the staffers were black, and most of them worked for organizations serving the black community. At a time when blacks, Hispanics, and Asian-Americans constituted nearly 14 percent of the population, they owned less than 1 percent of radio and television stations. This was true despite federal efforts to increase minority representation on the assumption that a heterogeneous country is best served when media owners and staffs mirror the nation's diversity. If demographically distinct groups are uniquely qualified to assess their own needs, then racial, ethnic, and cultural underrepresentation in the media is undesirable.

Likewise, if balanced presentation of information requires that media organizations have women staffers in proportion to their numbers in the population, the media do not measure up, even though conditions have vastly improved in recent years. In the prominent organizations women made up 28 percent of the executives and 23 percent of the staff. In the nonprominent media 28 percent of the executives and 41 percent of the staffers were women. Newspeople are also generally younger, more urbanized, and have greater job mobility than the general population.

What effect do demographic characteristics have on the news product? The evidence is inconclusive. It also may be debatable whether adequate coverage of the nation's problems requires media organizations that are a microcosm of the larger society. Nevertheless, there appear to be certain connections between the product and the demographic characteristics of the personnel. For example, most general media emphasize established white middle-class groups and values and neglect minorities and poor people and their concerns. They also stress urban rather than rural affairs and supply heavy doses of primarily male-dominated sports. These patterns suggest that news output reflects reporters' backgrounds and interests.[61] An alternative explanation is that the patterns cater to the tastes of the kinds of audiences that advertisers find most attractive.

Like other professionals, newspeople have far more formal education than the general population. In the group working for prominent organizations, 64 percent of the executives and 56 percent of the staffers were college graduates, as were 50 percent of the executives and 58 percent of the staffers in the less prominent organizations. Newspeople without college degrees usually had received no professional training as journalists and so were less likely to have been exposed to social responsibility norms so prevalent on American college campuses. When asked about their professional goals, they were more likely to stress neutral reporting of facts, rather than interpretation and social advocacy. In fact, education appears to be the single most important background characteristic that shapes newspeople's general philosophy of reporting. People with more schooling are likely to be more liberal and have a keener sense of social responsibility.[62]

Only a very small percentage of the working press in prominent news organizations were Republicans. Among executives, 33 percent were Democrats, 58 percent were Independents, and 9 percent were Republicans. Among the staffers, 51 percent were Democrats, 44 percent were Independents, and 4 percent were Republicans. The rest had other affiliations. Comparable figures for the general population were 44 percent Democrats, 30 percent Independents, and 24 percent Republicans.[63] The many who called themselves "Independents" were more likely to identify with Democrats than Republicans.

These data on party affiliation show that owners of prominent media hire Democrats and liberal Independents to operate their media properties although they themselves usually share the Republican leanings of the big business community.[64] The political orientations of the personnel are reflected in the overall tone of the prominent media. Economic and social liberalism prevails, as does a preference for an internationalist foreign policy, caution about military intervention, and some suspicion about the ethics of established large institutions, particularly big business and big government. However, in deference to the greater conservatism of media audiences, reporters restrain their liberalism somewhat.[65] Media personnel also treat the major parties fairly in most election campaign coverage. Such evenhandedness is encouraged by anticipation of scrutiny and criticism on that score. Media bias has rarely been investigated outside the election context. Hence the extent to which biased reporting is a problem in prominent media is not fully known.[66]

Among the nonprominent media, the patterns of party affiliation and political leanings were far more representative of political patterns throughout the United States. Among the executives, 38 percent were Democrats, 22 percent were Republicans, and 38 percent were Independents. Among the staffers, 40 percent were Democrats, 40 percent were Independents, and 20 percent were Republicans. A circular effect seems to be at work: people in small towns perpetuate their more conservative outlook because their media, taking their cues from the audience, are comparatively conservative. However, the strength of Republican influence is less than it appears on the surface because the majority of Independents lean toward the Democrats, as noted earlier.

Table 2-2 presents the results of a nationwide survey by the *Los Angeles Times* in which newspeople and members of the general public were asked about their political views. While the two groups agreed fairly closely on many issues, journalists were nearly always more liberal when they disagreed. The widest gaps occurred for social issues.

When newspeople were asked about their general political orientations, 22 percent claimed to be left or left-leaning and 18 percent right or right-leaning. Fifty-eight percent saw themselves as middle-of-the-road. Obviously, these political orientations are muted by organizational pressures. In fact, by newspeople's evaluation, 30 percent of the media for which they are working are right or right-leaning, only 12 percent are left or left-leaning, and 57 percent are characterized as middle-of-the-road.[67]

In recent decades journalists as a group, like the general public as a whole, apparently have become more conservative. However, these trends are less noticeable among the leaders of the profession, judging from surveys of media elites at the *New York Times*, the *Washington Post*, the *Wall Street Journal*, *Time*, *Newsweek*, *U.S. News & World Report*, the three major networks, and public television. These media elites, who have a disproportionately large influence on political elites, remain liberals with cosmopolitan, antibourgeois orientations. Fifty-four percent see themselves as left-of-center, compared with 19 percent who lean to the right. In their judgment seven out of every eight of their colleagues lean to the left.[68]

On the idiosyncratic level, a person who enters the journalism profession, compared with personnel in other business enterprises, is generally more idealistic and more humanistic and prefers nonroutine

Table 2-2   Issue Positions of General Public and Journalists (in percentages)

Issue	Public	Journalists
Pro business	33	27
Pro labor	32	31
Business regulation		
Pro	22	49
Anti	50	41
Government aid to poor		
Pro	83	95
Anti	11	3
Income leveling laws		
Pro	55	50
Anti	23	39
South Africa disinvestment		
Pro	31	62
Anti	27	29
Verified nuclear freeze		
Pro	66	84
Anti	22	13
CIA Nicaraguan contra aid		
Pro	19	17
Anti	44	76
Defense budget		
Raise	38	15
Maintain	51	80
Abortion rights		
Pro	49	82
Anti	44	14
School prayer		
Pro	74	25
Anti	19	67
Affirmative action		
Pro	56	81
Anti	21	14
Death penalty for murder		
Pro	75	47
Anti	17	47
Hiring homosexuals		
Pro	55	89
Anti	31	7
Hand gun controls		
Tighten	50	78
Maintain	41	19

Source: Adapted from William Schneider and I. A. Lewis, "Views on the News," *Public Opinion* 8 (August/September 1985): 7.

Note: N = 2,992 for public, 2,703 for newspeople, drawn from 621 newspapers. Figures exclude "neutral" and "don't know" responses.

work.[69] Social psychologists have discovered that such people tend to be on the left end of the political spectrum, with a sense of mission about reforming the injustices of society. They are opposed to regimentation and fiercely protective of their personal and professional independence.

Reporters' unique life experiences are also important in shaping their views of the world. It matters what personal contacts they are able to make. Washington-based reporters, for instance, may be able to use friendships with well-connected government officials to get important scoops. But, as a result of close personal ties with these officials, they may become captives of their sources' perspectives on the world.

Organizational Factors

Colleagues and settings strongly influence newspeople. Every news organization has its own internal power structure that develops from the interaction of owners, journalists, news sources, audiences, advertisers, and government authorities. In most news organizations today, the internal power structure is slightly left of middle America, yet predominantly supportive of the basic tenets of the current political and social system.

When asked how much their editors try to censor or influence their reports, three out of four newspeople indicate that explicit directives are rare. However, when top executives do exercise control, it usually involves politically crucial matters. More than half of the reporters concede that higher-ups select story assignments for them, and two-thirds say they are required to submit their stories to editorial scrutiny.[70] Thus the crucial phases of initiation of stories and final acceptance are subject to organizational controls. Although editorial censorship is rare, the possibility exists and serves to tether reporters to organizational norms.

Organizational pressures begin to operate even before the job starts. Most people join news organizations and remain with them only if they share the organization's basic philosophy. To win approval, professional recognition, and advancement, reporters learn very fast which types of stories are acceptable and which are likely to be squelched. They behave accordingly. This is particularly true if morale is high within the organization and if, as is generally the case, newspeople feel that their organization is producing a good product (85 percent do).

Relationships with colleagues are particularly important within the large, prominent news enterprises, where newspeople receive their main social and professional support from coworkers, rather than from the community at large. The opposite holds true in small towns, where newspeople often interact quite freely with community leaders and receive their support.

Which news organizations are regarded most highly by the journalism community? If use of a medium is a gauge of respect, then, as Table 2-3 indicates, *Time* magazine, *Newsweek,* and the *New*

Table 2-3   Most Frequently Used Newspapers and Magazines
(percent of journalist readers)

Publications	Readers	Publications	Readers
Time	52	*Washington Post*	15
Newsweek	48	*Atlantic Monthly*	10
New York Times	33	*New Yorker*	10
Wall Street Journal	25	*National Geographic*	9
U.S. News & World Report	16	*USA Today*	9
Regional/city magazines	16	*Boston Globe*	9
Sports Illustrated	16	*Chicago Tribune*	9

Source: Adapted from G. Cleveland Wilhoit and David H. Weaver, *The American Journalist: A Portrait of U.S. News People and Their Work* (Bloomington: Indiana University Press, 1986), 34, 37.

Note: N = 994 journalists for newspapers, 939 journalists for magazines.

York Times rank highest. They captured the attention of one-third to one-half of the journalists. The fourteen most widely used publications included six newspapers and eight magazines. In addition, journalists watch television, but they value it far less highly than they do print media. Fifty-three percent watch the local news, and 34 percent watch the national news regularly during the week.[71] Overall, 17 percent rank the media as doing a very good job, 78 percent give them a fairly good rating, and 4 percent think they do a bad job.[72]

All of the highly rated, influential news organizations give ample coverage to news and usually shy away from sensational treatment. Most of them have headquarters along the northeastern seaboard. This distribution supports the frequently heard claim that American journalism is intellectually dominated by the Eastern press, which accounts for roughly 8 percent of the news profession. These are the "generative" media that produce the news that "derivative" media distribute. These are the media staffed by elite journalists whose social perspectives are left-liberal in contrast to the views characterized as "middle America."[73] The heavy reliance by newspeople throughout the country on these eastern "elite" news sources is one reason why patterns of American news coverage are broadly similar throughout the country. Regardless of regional and local differences that shape social and political views, Americans share most of their news. This provides a basis for nationwide public opinions that bear, to a marked degree, the imprint of the pacesetter media.

Despite the substantial evidence of media influence on American politics, most newspeople refuse to take responsibility for the impact on the public of their choice and cast of news stories. These self-appointed watchdogs of government and other social institutions insist routinely and appropriately that government and business must take responsibility for the intended and unintended consequences of their actions, yet they refuse to do the same. Instead, journalists commonly argue that journalism is a craft and not a profession. Those doing the crafting, they claim, are little more than conveyors of bits of information created by others for which these others are solely responsible.

Role Models

Although editors and reporters take many cues about story importance and interpretation from the eastern elite media, they shape their basic news policies according to their own views about the role that media should play in society. The effects of the social responsibility role compared with libertarian stances have already been considered. News products also vary depending on whether newspeople see themselves largely as objective observers who must present facts and diverse views voiced by others or as interpreters who must supply meanings and evaluations. In the United States and Great Britain, journalists value the role of "objective" reporter highly. Explicit expressions of reporters' opinions are kept out of news stories and relegated to editorial and feature pages. In France and Germany, by contrast, all news tends to be editorialized.[74] The style is akin to that used by American weekly news magazines like *Time* and *Newsweek*.

Obviously, journalists' perceptions of their proper role shape news and are politically significant. They also often lead to organizational conflict. This was graphically demonstrated in 1978 when the Australian publisher Rupert Murdoch bought several American publications, including the *New York Post,* the *Village Voice,* the *New West* magazine, and the *New York* magazine. The staffs of these organizations brought suit to stop the sale because they were unhappy about the role model Murdoch had adopted for his other publications—namely, to entertain and shock the public. The courts declined to interfere, saying that the choice of a role model is an editorial function.[75] A number of key staff people then resigned, unwilling to work for a publication that followed a role model they disliked.

Readers who live in large cities or subscribe to out-of-town papers often can select the types of papers they want. They may choose a paper like the *Wall Street Journal,* which tailors its news to the tastes of businesspeople, or like the *New York Times,* which emphasizes broad general coverage. Most people, however, cannot pick and choose news sources representing particular role models so easily. They have only a single print source readily available and a few radio and television stations. They are, therefore, limited to the role models represented by these sources.

Summary

In this chapter we have examined the most common types of ownership and control of the media. The national government owns and operates vast overseas radio and television enterprises. At home it partially controls a far-flung system of public television and radio broadcasting that provides an alternative to commercial programming.

For the average American these government-controlled systems are peripheral, compared with privately owned print and electronic media enterprises. The major political problem in the private sector is concentration of ownership of media and concentrated control over news and entertainment programs. There has been great concern that the American public is ill-served because much of the media output is controlled by large business conglomerates, and newspaper competition is limited in most cities. Comparatively few, potentially biased minds thus shape the news and entertainment supply that undergirds public perceptions of political issues.

We have looked into the structure of the media business and government regulations designed to avert the potential dangers of concentration. We also have tried to evaluate the impact of the existing system on the form and slant of news and entertainment. Many prevailing views about the interrelation between media structures and functions appear to be wrong. Business ownership has not led to programming dominated by business perspectives. It has not shielded big business from harsh criticism. Coverage of local news has not withered, and large, rather than small, enterprises have excelled in providing news and entertainment. Since fears about the ill effects of the current structure seem misdirected, further research is needed to provide a sounder basis for public policies intended to ensure that American media serve the public interest.

Media operations and products are shaped not only by who owns them, but also by industry lobby groups and citizens' lobbies. The roles played by members of the media establishment are influential as well. Because media output is influenced by the people who collect information and produce stories, by the organizations that shape their approaches to their tasks, and by the conceptions of media roles that prevail among them, these facets of the control picture have been examined. They show clearly discernible patterns and trends that are reflected in media products. Given the diversity of influences that are brought into play when news and entertainment are produced, it is as yet impossible to assess the precise impact that each of these influences has on media content in general or even on a particular story. In the next chapter we will focus more closely on the actual news production process for additional clues to the mystery of the mix of influences shaping the news.

Notes

1. Examples of highly rated light entertainment are the "Cosby Show" and "Family Ties" (comedies), "Dallas" (a quasi-soap opera), "Miami Vice" (a crime show), and "60 Minutes," the popular investigative series that shares many qualities with popular detective shows. In addition, there are the ever-popular sports events such as the Superbowl, entertainment industry awards presentations, and competitions such as the Miss America pageant.
2. Ben H. Bagdikian, "The U.S. Media: Supermarket or Assembly Line," *Journal of Communication* 35 (Summer 1985): 97-109. For a negative view of the "marketplace of ideas" concept, see Benjamin Ginsberg, *The Captive Public: How Mass Opinion Promotes State Power* (New York: Basic Books, 1986), 98-148.
3. "Despite the expressed insulation of public broadcasters from federal editorial domination, case law specifically allows broadcast program decisions to be dictated by political officials when the state is licensee. Therefore, potential conflict exists between First Amendment and political interests." William Hanks and Lemuel Schofield, "Limitations on the State as Editor in State-Owned Broadcast Stations," *Journalism Quarterly* 63 (Winter 1986): 798.
4. Erwin G. Krasnow, Lawrence D. Longley, and Herbert A. Terry, *The Politics of Broadcast Regulation*, 3d ed. (New York: St. Martin's Press, 1982), 23, 74.
5. Kenneth R. Clark, "CPB, PBS Agree to Call for Less Disagreement," *Chicago Tribune*, January 11, 1987.
6. Benjamin M. Compaine, Christopher H. Sterling, Thomas Guback, and J. Kendrick Noble, Jr., *Who Owns the Media: Concentration and Ownership in the Mass Communications Industry*, 2d ed. (White Plains, N.Y.: Knowledge Industry, 1982), 342; and National Public Radio: *Annual Report*, 1986.
7. S. L. Harrison, *Washington Monthly*, January 1986, 33.
8. The composition of this audience is analyzed in George Comstock, Steven Chaffee, Natan Katzman, Maxwell McCombs, and Donald Roberts, *Television and Human Behavior* (New York: Columbia University Press, 1978), 116-121. Also see Ronald F. Frank and Marshall G. Greenberg, *Audiences for Public Television* (Beverly Hills, Calif.: Sage, 1982).
9. During budget negotiations, President Reagan vetoed congressional appropriations for CPB amounting to $761 million in the first year and $615 million in the second year of the 1987-89 period. Instead, the administration proposed $255 million for CPB for the entire period. *Congressional Quarterly Almanac, 1986* (Washington, D.C.: Congressional Quarterly, 1986), 288.
10. For example, see Bruce M. Owen, *Economics and Freedom of Expression: Media Structure and the First Amendment* (Cambridge, Mass.: Ballinger, 1975).
11. Willard D. Rowland, Jr., "The Federal Regulatory and Policymaking Process," *Journal of Communication* 30 (Summer 1980): 141. Education-based audience differences are discussed in W. Russell Neuman, "Television and American Culture: The Mass Medium and the Pluralist Audience," *Public Opinion Quarterly* 46 (Winter 1982): 478-481.
12. Rowland, "The Federal Regulatory and Policymaking Process," 149.
13. *American Statistical Index*, press release 9282-4, June 30, 1986. Also see Phillip H. Ault, "Mass Ownership Takes over the Media," in *Main Currents*

in Mass Communications, ed. Warren K. Agee, Phillip H. Ault, and Edwin Emery (New York: Harper and Row, 1986), 168-173.

14. Besides media holdings, Tribune enterprises encompass the fields of energy, mining, trucking, paper, finance, and a major league baseball team. Dun and Bradstreet, *America's Corporate Families,* 1987, vol. 1, 1,277; see also Standard and Poor's Corp., *Corporation Records,* December 1987, 2852.

15. Herbert H. Howard, "An Update on TV Ownership Patterns," *Journalism Quarterly* 60 (Fall 1983): 395-400.

16. *Directory of Corporate Affiliations* (Wilmette, Ill.: National Register Publishing, 1987), 310; Dun and Bradstreet, *America's Corporate Families,* 1987, vol. 1, 6196; Standard and Poor's Corp., *Corporation Records,* October and November, 1987.

17. AM (amplitude modulation) stations and VHF (very high frequency) stations reach the largest audiences. The newer FM (frequency modulation) and UHF (ultra high frequency) stations use different parts of the airwaves and reach fewer people. Their signals cannot be received by radio and television sets designed only for AM and VHF reception.

18. Antitrust regulations become operative when the eight largest firms in a particular type of business control more than 50 percent of the market, and the twenty largest firms control 75 percent or more of the market.

19. Ault, "Mass Ownership," 168ff.

20. See Ault, "Mass Ownership"; Standard and Poor's Corp., September 1987, 2808, 2852, 5875, 6395, 9261; and *Fortune,* August 1987, 63.

21. Daniel B. Wackman, Donald M. Gillmor, Cecilie Gaziano, and Everette E. Dennis, "Chain Newspaper Autonomy as Reflected in Presidential Campaign Endorsements," *Journalism Quarterly* 52 (Fall 1975): 411-420.

22. Compaine et al., *Who Owns the Media,* 329.

23. Capital Cities/ABC interests include motion pictures, advertising, insurance, marketing, and tourism. For CBS, it is production and sale of musical instruments, toys, warehousing, consulting, packaging, and audio-video products. The various holdings of NBC's parent company, General Electric, are diagrammed in Figure 2-1. Standard and Poor's Corp., *Corporation Records,* November 1987, 5775, 8676, 8849.

24. They are subject to operational regulations, however. For instance, one network may not operate a second network covering the same market. The amount of programming that may be produced is also limited.

25. Standard and Poor's Corp., *Industry Surveys,* vol. 2, 1987.

26. Maxwell E. McCombs and Donald L. Shaw, "Structuring the 'Unseen Environment,'" *Journal of Communication* (Spring 1976): 18-22.

27. Benjamin M. Compaine, "The Expanding Base of Media Competition," *Journal of Communication* 35 (1985): 81-96; and Nancy Signorielli, "Selective Viewing: A Limited Possibility," *Journal of Communication* 36 (Summer 1986): 64-76.

28. Compaine et al., *Who Owns the Media,* 36-37.

29. In 1983 there were ninety professional, business, and special service dailies, twenty-seven foreign language dailies, and 7,497 less-than-daily-frequency newspapers in the United States. *IMS Directory of Publications* (Fort Washington, Pa.: 1983).

30. J. Herbert Altschull, "The Journalist and Instant History: An Example of the Jackal Syndrome," *Journalism Quarterly* 50 (Autumn 1973): 389-396.

31. For example, see J. Herbert Altschull, "Khrushchev and the Berlin 'Ultimatum': The Jackal Syndrome and the Cold War," *Journalism Quarterly* 54 (Fall 1977): 545-551.

32. David C. Coulson, "Antitrust Law and the Media: Making the Newspapers Safe for Democracy," *Journalism Quarterly* 57 (Spring 1980): 79-85; Ben H. Bagdikian, "Conglomeration, Concentration, and the Media," *Journal of Communication* 30 (Spring 1980): 59-64; and James N. Rosse, "The Decline of Direct Newspaper Competition," *Journal of Communication* 30 (Spring 1980): 65-71.

33. A brief comparison of media systems throughout the world is presented in Jeremy Tunstall, *The Media Are American: Anglo-American Media in the World* (New York: Columbia University Press, 1977). Also see Michael Rice with James A. Cooney, eds., *Reporting U.S.-European Relations: Four Nations, Four Newspapers* (New York: Pergamon, 1982).

34. Compaine, "Media Competition," 88; Robert M. Entman, "Newspaper Competition and First Amendment Ideals: Does Monopoly Matter?" *Journal of Communication* 35 (1985): 147-165; and Stephen Lacy, "The Effects of Intracity Competition on Daily Newspaper Content," *Journalism Quarterly* 64 (Summer/Autumn 1987): 281-290.

35. For a contrary view, see Erik Barnouw, *The Sponsor: Notes on a Modern Potentate* (New York: Oxford University Press, 1978).

36. A scientific appraisal of the effects of owners on media output is presented in Frank Wolf, *Television Programming for News and Public Affairs: A Quantitative Analysis of Networks and Stations* (New York: Praeger, 1972). Also see S. Robert Lichter, Stanley Rothman, and Linda S. Lichter, *The Media Elite: America's New "Powerbrokers"* (New York: Adler and Adler, 1986).

37. Gary A. Hale and Richard C. Vincent, "Locally Produced Programming on Independent Television Stations," *Journalism Quarterly* 63 (Autumn 1986): 562-568.

38. Don R. Le Duc, "Deregulation and the Dream of Diversity," *Journal of Communication* 32 (Autumn 1982): 174.

39. Kenneth R. Clark, "Network Woes," *Chicago Tribune Magazine*, May 17, 1987, 28.

40. Krasnow, Longley, and Terry, *The Politics of Broadcast Regulation*, 284.

41. Compaine et al., *Who Owns the Media*, 329.

42. Ibid., computed from pp. 33 and 397.

43. Clark, "Network Woes," 22-42.

44. Krasnow, Longley, and Terry, *The Politics of Broadcast Regulation*, 93.

45. Ibid., 18.

46. Many contradictory bills have been introduced in Congress to deal with news and public service programming requirements. Most of them die early in the game. *Congressional Quarterly Weekly Report* is an excellent source for tracking these legislative developments.

47. Nancy R. Csaplar, "Local Television: The Limits of Prime-Time Access," *Journal of Communication* 33 (Spring 1983): 124-131.

48. See Owen, *Economics and Freedom of Expression*.

49. Because the practice is so widespread, a Copyright Royalty Tribunal has been set up to administer payments made by cable systems to the owners of the various programs used by cable. Le Duc, "Deregulation and the Dream of Diversity," 171.

50. Krasnow, Longley, and Terry, *The Politics of Broadcast Regulation*, 23.

51. *Encyclopedia of Associations* (Detroit, Mich.: Gale Research Co., 1988), vol. 1, 76.

52. Edmund B. Lambeth, *Committed Journalism: An Ethic for the Profession* (Bloomington: Indiana University Press, 1986). See also Bruce A. Linton,

"Self-Regulation in Broadcasting Revisited," *Journalism Quarterly* 64 (Summer/Autumn 1987): 483-490.

53. Joel Persky, "Self Regulation of Broadcasting—Does It Exist?" *Journal of Communication* 27 (Spring 1977): 200-210.
54. *Office of Communication of the United Church of Christ v. FCC*, 359 F.2d 994 (D.C. Cir., 1966).
55. Krasnow, Longley, and Terry, *The Politics of Broadcast Regulation*, 54-62.
56. Ibid., 56-57.
57. These activities are summarized in Anne W. Branscomb and Maria Savage, "The Broadcast Reform Movement at the Crossroads," *Journal of Communication* 28 (Autumn 1978): 25-34.
58. Forrest P. Chisman, "Public Interest and FCC Policy Making," *Journal of Communication* 27 (Winter 1977): 77-84.
59. William Small, *To Kill a Messenger* (New York: Hastings House, 1970), 280.
60. G. Cleveland Wilhoit and David H. Weaver, *The American Journalist: A Portrait of U.S. News People and Their Work* (Bloomington: Indiana University Press, 1986). Some of the data presented here are not included in the published study. For an example of other supportive studies, see S. Robert Lichter and Stanley Rothman, "Media and Business Elites," *Public Opinion* 4 (November 1981): 42-60.
61. Herbert J. Gans, *Deciding What's News: A Study of CBS Evening News, NBC Nightly News, Newsweek and Time* (New York: Pantheon, 1979), 39-69, 116-145, 182-213.
62. John Johnstone, Edward J. Slawski, and William T. Bowman, "The Professional Values of American Newsmen," *Public Opinion Quarterly* 36 (Winter 1972-1973): 522-540.
63. Center for Political Studies, University of Michigan, 1982 surveys.
64. For a comprehensive analysis of media elites and a comparison with other elites, see Lichter, Rothman, and Lichter, *The Media Elite*.
65. Gans, *Deciding What's News*, 39-69, 182-213. Frank J. Sorauf, "Campaign Money and the Press: Three Soundings," *Political Science Quarterly* 102 (Spring 1987): 25-42, demonstrates the neo-progressive outlook of the press using coverage of campaign finance news as a test case.
66. C. Richard Hofstetter, *Bias in the News: Network Television Coverage of the 1972 Election Campaign* (Columbus: Ohio State University Press, 1976), 187-207.
67. Wilhoit and Weaver, *The American Journalist*, 25-32.
68. Lichter and Rothman, "Media and Business Elites," 42-60; also Stanley Rothman and S. Robert Lichter, "Media and Business Elites: Two Classes in Conflict," *Public Interest* 69 (1982): 111-125.
69. John Hohenberg, *The Professional Journalist*, 4th ed. (New York: Holt, Rinehart and Winston, 1978); and Idowu Sobowale, "The Social-Psychological Predictors of Commitment to Journalism" (Paper presented at the Midwest Association for Public Opinion Research, Chicago, Ill., 1978).
70. John Johnstone, Edward Slawski, and William Bowman, *The Newspeople* (Urbana, Ill.: University of Illinois Press, 1976), 86. Twenty percent of the journalists in the Wilhoit and Weaver study believe in neutral reporting. However, 49 percent subscribe to both neutral and participant philosophies. These philosophies thus do not appear to be mutually exclusive.
71. Wilhoit and Weaver, *The American Journalist*, 32-38.
72. William Schneider and I. A. Lewis, "Views on the News," *Public Opinion* 8 (August/September 1985): 6-11, 58-59.
73. Thomas E. Patterson and Ronald P. Abeles, "Mass Communications Re-

search and the 1976 Presidential Election," *Items* 2 (June 1975): 13-18.
74. See, for example, Rice and Cooney, *Reporting U.S.-European Relations.*
75. Charles Whelton, "Getting Bought: Notes from the Overground," *Village Voice*, May 2, 1977, 51.

Readings

Besen, Stanley M., Thomas G. Krattenmaker, A. Richard Metzger, Jr., and John R. Woodbury. *Misregulating Television: Network Dominance and the FCC.* Chicago: University of Chicago Press, 1985.

Ettema, James S., and D. Charles Whitney, eds. *Individuals in Mass Media Organizations: Creativity and Constraint.* Beverly Hills, Calif.: Sage, 1982.

Head, Sydney W., and Christopher H. Sterling. *Broadcasting in America: A Survey of Electronic Media.* 5th ed. Boston: Houghton Mifflin, 1987.

Krasnow, Erwin G., Lawrence D. Longley, and Herbert A. Terry. *The Politics of Broadcast Regulation.* 3d ed. New York: St. Martin's Press, 1982.

Lichter, S. Robert, Stanley Rothman, and Linda S. Lichter, *The Media Elite: America's New Powerbrokers.* New York: Adler and Adler, 1986.

Snow, Marcellus S., ed. *Marketplace for Telecommunications: Regulation and Deregulation in Industrialized Democracies.* New York: Longman, 1986.

Wilhoit, G. Cleveland, and David H. Weaver. *The American Journalist: A Portrait of U.S. News People and Their Work.* Bloomington: Indiana University Press, 1986.

CHAPTER 3

News Making
and News Reporting

On a cold January afternoon during the 1984 presidential campaign, eight major Democratic contenders gathered for a debate at Dartmouth College. The three-hour confrontation was intended as a test of the intellectual and political strength of each candidate. Americans could then judge which man provided the best alternative to incumbent president Ronald Reagan. People in 10 million American households watched the proceedings, evidence of substantial public interest. The wide-ranging debate covered foreign policy in Lebanon and Central America, the nuclear freeze issue and the role of conventional arms, economic issues such as inflation, unemployment, and poverty, and social policies affecting education and health care. Here is how the *Chicago Tribune* highlighted this significant story on its front page the next day:

> Walter Mondale and John Glenn engaged in a short but spirited shouting match Sunday, perhaps to the benefit of one of the other Democratic presidential candidates sharing the stage with them.
>
> Near the end of the year's first debate among all eight Democratic contenders, Glenn started the fireworks by calling Mondale's economic policies "vague gobbledygook of nothing." Glenn said he was "disgusted and tired of all the vague promises" Mondale had made.
>
> By the time Glenn finished claiming that Mondale's proposals would add billions of dollars to the federal budget and that the former vice president was indiscriminate with his campaign promises, Mondale was on his feet, waving his arms and saying, "Point of personal privilege, Mr. Chairman."
>
> Mondale claimed that Glenn was using "voodoo numbers" in his attack and defended his policies, while Glenn, off to his right, muttered that Mondale was using "third-grade arithmetic."

When the candidates finished, former Florida Gov. Reubin Askew said, "You're both right." After the laughter died down, Askew explained, "They're both right in what they had to say about each other." [1]

The fractious exchange between candidates Glenn and Mondale became the *Tribune*'s major theme, although it had taken up only a tiny portion of the three-hour debate, which otherwise had been polite and calm. A very brief résumé of the important topics aired in the debate was relegated to back pages in the paper.

Emphasis on trivial aspects of the news at the expense of more substantive subject matter characterizes televised news as well. An analysis of network coverage of the 1987 Iran/contra congressional hearings showed that only 9 percent of the nightly news stories about that event dealt with substantive policy issues.[2] The television networks spent more time on the rescue of a toddler from an abandoned well in Texas than on the confirmation hearings of a candidate for the U.S. Supreme Court. Semifinal tennis matches have been televised even when it meant cutting time set aside for newscasts covering a papal visit to the United States. Live interviews with heads of states have been interrupted to present routine commercials.

What is wrong with these priorities? What stories should the news media cover? What stories do they cover, and why? In the first two chapters we have discussed important factors that have a bearing on these questions. In this chapter we will describe the news-making process in detail, its effects on the products brought forth by the mass media, and the political consequences.

Models of the News-Making Process

Scholars have identified four models of the news-making process: *the mirror model, the professional model, the organizational model,* and *the political model.* Each represents a judgment of what the major forces behind news making are or ought to be, and each profoundly affects the nature of news and its political impact.

Proponents of the mirror model contend that news is and should be a reflection of reality. Newspeople observe the world around them and report what they see as accurately and objectively as possible. "We don't make the news, we merely report it," proponents of this view claim. The implication is that newspeople are nothing more than conduits for information produced by others. They reflect whatever comes to their attention; they do not shape it in any way.

Critics of the mirror model point out that this conception of news making is unrealistic. Millions of significant events take place daily, forcing journalists to make choices about the general categories and specific stories to be published. Events that are publicized inevitably loom larger than life, reshaping the picture that the real world presents. Events that are ignored routinely vanish into nothingness. Even films and photographs distort reality. A small group of demonstrators may look like an invading army when cameras zoom in on them.

In the professional model, news making is viewed as an endeavor of highly skilled professionals who put together an interesting collage of events selected for importance, attractiveness to media audiences, and balance among the various elements of the news offering. For economic reasons, audience appeal is the most important consideration. This, in a sense, makes the audience the ultimate judge of which stories may pass scrutiny and which will be ignored.[3]

The organizational model is based on organizational theory. Its proponents contend that news selection emerges from the pressures inherent in organizational processes and goals. Pressures springing from interpersonal relations and professional norms within the news organization are important, as are constraints arising from technical news production processes, cost-benefit considerations, profit orientations, and legal regulations such as the Federal Communication Commission's rules.

Finally, the political model rests on the assumption that news everywhere is a product of the ideological biases of individual newspeople, as well as of the pressures of the political environment in which the news organization operates. When the prevailing political environment is capitalist democracy modified by social welfare orientations, as is true in the United States, this ideological base sets the tone for the world view implicit in most fact and fiction stories. Supporters of the prevailing system are pictured as good guys, opponents as bad guys. High-status people and institutions are covered by the media; those who are outside the dominant system or remote from the centers of power are generally ignored.

None of these models, by itself, can explain the news-making process because the process reflects all of them in varying degrees. Since the influences that shape news making fluctuate, one needs to examine individual news-making situations carefully to account for the factors at work. Organizational pressures, for instance, vary depending on the interactions of people within the organization. Audience tastes change or are differently interpreted. Perceptions of "facts" differ, depending on reporters' dispositions. Moreover, the precise mix of factors that explains news making in any particular instance depends to a large degree on chance factors and on the current needs of a particular news medium.

The Gatekeepers

The relatively few people who select news are often called "gatekeepers" because they tightly control admission to the publicity arena.

Gatekeepers include wire service and other reporters who initially choose stories, the editors who assign the reporters and accept or reject what they submit, disc jockeys at radio stations who present five-minute news breaks, and television program executives. On the average newspaper or news weekly fewer than twenty-five people are involved. On the three major networks the combined editorial personnel responsible for choosing news number fewer than fifty people.

These few, particularly those who make news choices for nationwide audiences, wield a tremendous amount of political power. In public opinion polls that rank the influence of various American institutions on public life, the news media routinely rank high among the top ten. When pollsters asked a national sample of Americans which telephone call the president should answer first if a topnotch editor, business leader, church figure, and educational leader called simultaneously, most chose the newspaper editor.[4] As we saw in Chapter 1, news stories influence what issues ordinary people as well as political elites will think about. Of course, media gatekeepers are not entirely free in their story choices. Coverage of certain stories, such as wars, assassinations, and airline hijackings, is almost mandatory. But others can be included or omitted at will. On an average night somewhat more than half of the stories on each network represent unique choices; the rest are covered by all or nearly all of the networks.[5]

Those who make news choices select the sources through whose eyes the public views the world. As Table 3-1 shows, government officials are the main source of the vast majority of political stories reported by the wire services and national and local media. This gives the officials whose views are presented an excellent chance to influence the slant of the news. However, when highly controversial issues are at stake, gatekeepers usually turn to unofficial sources as well.[6]

Basing the news on a narrow spectrum of sources can lead to biased reporting. A study of stories dealing with the controversial consequences of marijuana use and the need for laws to protect public health and safety revealed that the views of top scientists specializing in marijuana studies were rarely aired. Reporters gave widest publicity instead to the views of "celebrity" authorities in tangentially related fields and to administrative officials in government agencies such as the National Institute of Mental Health, the Food and Drug Administration, and the Department of Health and Human Services. Consequently, the issue was portrayed almost exclusively from the perspective of health administrators with scant attention to the views of drug-use specialists.[7] Reporters' choices of sources also have led to one-sided presentations in stories about genetic engineering (recombinant DNA) research, the swine-flu vaccination program, and the development of an artificial heart.[8]

Table 3-1 Sources of Front-Page News Stories (in percentages)

Source	*Times/Post* staff stories	Local press staff stories	Wire services staff stories	Total stories
Government				
U.S.	32	16	36	31
State	5	15	6	7
Local	6	17	5	7
Foreign	11	—	13	10
Group-linked person	25	36	19	24
Private person	4	6	4	4
Foreigner	4	—	7	5
Other	12	9	11	11

Source: Adapted from Jane Delano Brown, Carl R. Bybee, Stanley T. Wearden, and Dulcie Murdock Straughan, "Invisible Power: Newspaper News Sources and the Limits of Diversity," *Journalism Quarterly* 64 (Spring 1987), 49. Reprinted by permission of the Association for Education in Journalism and Mass Communication, publishers of *Journalism Quarterly.*

Note: Based on content analysis of news stories attributed to staff or wire service writers and published in the *New York Times, Washington Post,* and four local papers in North Carolina from 1979 to 1980. $N = 2,363$ for *Times/Post* stories, 804 for local press stories, and 2,048 for wire service stories, for a total of 5,215 stories. "Group-linked" persons are identified as members of a group but are not necessarily official spokespersons.

A study of sources used for stories about welfare reform, consumer issues, the environment, and nuclear energy concluded that journalists favor sources that reflect their own inclinations.

> On welfare reform, liberal sources predominate over conservative ones. On consumer issues they look to Ralph Nader, the public interest movement, and liberal activist groups. On pollution and the environment, they select activist environmental groups and, once again, liberal leaders. On nuclear energy, anti-nuclear sources are the most popular. . . . Journalists by no means depend exclusively on liberal viewpoints. They cite a mixture of public and private, partisan and non-partisan, liberal and conservative sources. But the liberal side consistently outweighs the conservative.[9]

Sources who have gained recognition as "experts" through media publicity tend to be used over and over again. Newspeople may neglect other, less publicized sources.

A few, highly respected national newscasters also are extraordinarily influential. By singling out news events for positive or negative commentary, they may sway public and official opinions. If anchors Peter Jennings, Tom Brokaw, or Dan Rather declare that income tax cuts will benefit the rich, or that an American military presence in the Middle East will risk war, popular support for these policies may plunge.[10] A sixty-second verbal barrage on the evening news or a few embarrassing questions can destroy programs, politicians, and the reputations of major organizations. Political leaders fear this media power, and usually they are unable to blunt it or repair the damage.[11]

Because Americans like to view their media as effective guardians of the public interest, the positive consequences of news story choices are usually stressed. Negative or questionable consequences should not be overlooked, however. Peter Braestrup, chief of the Saigon bureau of the *Washington Post* during the Vietnam War, claims that unwise story choices and interpretations about the conduct of the war misled the public and government officials. After an exhaustive study of news reports and commentary about the 1968 Tet offensive of the North Vietnamese, Braestrup concluded that poor story selections led to policies that changed the course of the war. Walter Cronkite and other commentators had used available information to piece together a picture of defeat for the South Vietnamese and American forces when the information really indicated a defeat for the North Vietnamese. These erroneous interpretations heightened existing antiwar pressures. They contributed to the collapse of public support for the war, produced a speedup of troop withdrawal, and encouraged President Lyndon B. Johnson's decision to abandon a second-term race.[12] Opinions may differ about the wisdom of the end result, but the great weight that is sometimes given to misleading media interpretations is indisputable.

General Factors in News Selection

What becomes news depends, in part, on the background, training, personality, and professional socialization of news personnel. In the United States this means, by and large, upwardly mobile, well-educated white males whose political views are liberal and who subscribe in ever larger numbers to the tenets of social responsibility journalism (discussed in Chapter 2). It does not generally mean women and minorities, although their numbers have been rising in the wake of affirmative action policies. It most certainly does not mean people who routinely beat the drums for established political leaders or their policies. Although most journalists support basic American values, they are a cantankerous breed, forever looking for ways to challenge the wisdom and behavior of political elites.

News personnel operate within the broad political context of their societies in general and their circulation communities in particular. Most of them have internalized these contexts so that they become their frames of reference. After comparing newspaper versions of the same story in different papers, George Gerbner, dean of the Annenberg School of Communications, concluded that there is "no fundamentally non-ideological, apolitical, non-partisan news gathering and reporting system."[13] If a reporter's political context demands favorable images of racial minorities, news and entertainment will reflect this outlook most of the time. If adverse criticism of minorities is encouraged, the same stories used elsewhere to praise minorities will be used to defame them.[14]

News selection also hinges on the intraorganizational norms and professional role conceptions of newspeople. Pressures of internal and external competition influence them as well. Within each news organization reporters and editors compete for time and space and prominence of position for their stories. News organizations also compete with each other for audience attention, for advertisers, and, in the case of the networks, for affiliates. If one station or network has a very popular program, others often will copy the format and try to place an equally attractive program into a parallel time slot to capture its competitor's audiences and advertisers. Likewise, papers may feel compelled to carry stories simply because another medium in the same market has carried it. Story choices made by the *Washington Post,* the *New York Times,* or *Christian Science Monitor* become models to be followed.

Political pressures also leave their mark. Media personnel depend on political leaders for much of their information and are therefore subject to manipulation by these sources. Vulnerability springs from intensive, frequent contacts and the desire to keep relationships cordial. For instance, when journalists were asked about their relationship with Gov. Nelson Rockefeller of New York, they agreed that he "co-opted the press in varying degrees and thus avoided ... critical detachment or impassionate analysis." Newspeople admittedly were under his spell because "Rockefeller made himself and state political news interesting to reporters and their editors and then to the public. Not only did he skillfully work to make news ... but he orchestrated it superbly and, whenever he could, tried to accommodate the professional necessities of newswriters."[15] The ability to use the media to political advantage without antagonizing newspeople is the mark of the astute politician. Reporters can rarely resist such pressures for fear of alienating powerful and important news sources.

Economic pressures are even more potent than political pressures in molding news and entertainment. Newspapers and magazines need sufficient income to cover their production costs. Except for those that are subsidized by individual or group sponsors, publications must raise this income from subscription rates, from advertisers, or from a combination of these sources. Most costs for television and radio programming are covered solely by advertising income. Therefore, media offerings must appeal to large numbers of potential customers for the products that advertisers sell. This means that programs and stories must be directed either to general audiences in the prime consumption years of life (roughly twenty-five to forty-five) or to selected special audiences who are key targets for particular advertiser appeals. For instance, toothpaste, laundry detergent, and breakfast cereals are best marketed to the huge nationwide audiences who watch the regular nighttime situation comedies or detective stories; personal computers, fancy foreign sports cars, or raft trips down the Amazon are most likely to find customers among a select few. Advertisers for these latter products are attracted to upscale circulation journals such as *National Geographic* or *Psychology Today* or to specialized television documentaries.

Because the bulk of programming is directed to the general public, television and radio must maintain a smooth flow of appealing programs throughout the prime evening hours. Many people watch television indiscriminately. As long as the program is unobjectionable, they will remain with the station. In fact, viewers preselect fewer than half of the shows they watch.[16] If boring or controversial programs come on, a sizable part of the audience will defect to another station and remain tuned to it for the rest of the evening. Such considerations deter producers in prime time from mixing serious audience-losing programs with light entertainment. Fears of losing the audience for an entire evening also are major reasons for opposition to expanding the nightly network news to a full hour.

The need to keep audiences watching a particular station even affects the format of news and public service programs. Newscasters are selected for their physical attractiveness. Informal banter is encouraged, and nearly every newscast contains some fascinating bits of trivia or a touching, yet inconsequential, human interest story. Media people occasionally underestimate the tastes of the public for serious presentations, as shown by the popularity of "The Day After," a documentary drama about the ravages of nuclear war, and by the massive attention given to presidential news conferences and addresses. But these are the exceptions rather than the rule. H. L. Mencken was probably right when he said that "nobody ever went broke by underestimating the public's taste." As one station manager reminded his staff somewhat condescendingly:

> Remember that the vast majority of our viewers hold blue-collar jobs. The vast majority of our viewers never went to college. The vast majority of our viewers have never been on an airplane. The vast majority of our viewers have never seen a copy of the *New York Times*. The vast majority of our viewers do not read the same books and magazines that you read. . . . In fact, many of them never read anything.[17]

What is publishable news is a decision that hinges on shared attitudes of newspeople and their audiences, and on the nature of their social and political settings. There is no magical quality that makes something "news." What is publishable in one setting for one medium is not necessarily appropriate for another. Newsworthiness of individual

Houston
Houston Chronicle

THE PERSIAN GULF!
THE PERSIAN GULF!
THE NATION'S STANDING ON
THE BRINK OF A PRO FOOTBALL
STRIKE, AN' ALL YOU HEAR
ABOUT IS THE PERSIAN
GULF!

Courtesy of C. P. Houston and the *Houston Chronicle.*

stories will vary from country to country, audience to audience, and time to time. Thus in 1903, when Orville and Wilbur Wright invited the press to Kitty Hawk, North Carolina, to cover their attempts to fly an airplane, not a single reporter came. Only seven American newspapers considered the first controlled and sustained flight newsworthy enough to print stories about it, and only two papers gave the feat front-page play. Seventy-six years later all facets of aviation fascinated the public. Flocks of reporters came to see a lone pilot, using human foot power, pedal across the English Channel in a light-weight aircraft called the *Gossamer Albatross.* The story received worldwide press and television coverage.

Criteria for Choosing Specific Stories

In addition to deciding what, in general, is publishable news, gate-keepers must choose particular news items to include in their mix of offerings. The motto of the *New York Times,* "All the News That's Fit to Print," is an impossible myth; there is far more publishable news available to the paper than it can possibly use. Gatekeepers also must decide how they want to cover each item. For instance, at the height of the Vietnam War, ABC camera crews were ordered to concentrate on bloody battle scenes. This led to a story emphasis on the military. Later on the focus shifted to internal corruption in Vietnam, black-marketeering, political opposition, and the treatment of ex-Viet Cong—a change that prepared the home front for withdrawal of American troops.[18]

The criteria newspeople use in story selection relate to audience appeal rather than to the political significance of the story, its educational value, its broad social purposes, or the newspeople's own political views. This emphasis, and the economic necessities that mandate it, needs to be kept in mind when the totality of media output is evaluated. It explains why the amount and kind of coverage of important issues are not commensurate with their significance in the real world at the time of publication. For instance, a single heinous crime may focus attention on crime stories and lead to an upswing in their number and prominence—giving the appearance of a crime wave at a time when crime rates actually may be going down. A crystallizing event, such as the surgeon general's report on smoking and health, may call attention to a long-standing problem that has not changed in substance. By the same token, a noteworthy event that has received a lot of coverage in the past may be dropped from peak attention because the audience is getting bored, even though the significance of the story may be increasing.[19]

A ten-year comparison of media stories with statistics on escalation of the Vietnam War, crime rates, and urban riots revealed that the peak year for riots was 1968; the peak year for riot stories was 1967. In 1967 the ratio of riots to riot stories was 4 to 1; in 1968 it was 12 to 1. With riots no longer anything "special," the ratio went to 16 to 1 in 1969 and 65 to 1 in 1970.[20] Similarly, a twelve-year scan of terrorism stories shown on network television revealed "a cumulative pattern of coverage that bears scant relationship to actual trends of terrorism over time."[21] As shown in Table 3-2, the discrepancy between the frequency of a newsworthy event and its coverage is especially well illustrated by crime news reporting.

Five criteria are used most often for choosing news stories. First, stories must have a *strong impact* on readers or listeners. A major earthquake in China would receive less coverage than a minor tremor in California because of its lesser impact on American news audiences. People want to read about things relevant to their own lives. Stories about health hazards, consumer fraud, or a poor family winning a million-dollar lottery prize influence people more than do unfamiliar happenings with which they cannot identify. To make stories attractive, newspeople commonly present them as anecdotes that show their effect on average people. Inflation news becomes the story of the housewife at the supermarket; foreign competition becomes the story of laid-off workers in a local textile plant. In the process of personalization, the main points of the story are often lost, and the news becomes trivialized.

The second element of newsworthiness is *natural or man-made violence, conflict, disaster,* or *scandal.* Wars, murders, strikes, earth-

Table 3-2 Comparative Frequency of Mention of Selected Index Crimes by Chicago Police Official Records and by *Chicago Tribune,* 1976

Crime	Police crime mention		*Tribune* crime mention	
	N	*Percent*	N	*Percent*
Murder	820	0.2	689	26.2
Rape	1,172	0.4	88	3.4
Robbery	17,489	5.7	283	10.8
Assault	11,001	3.6	152	5.8
Burglary	38,369	12.4	56	2.1
Theft	111,008	36.0	90	3.4
Auto theft	32,421	10.5	19	0.7
Total	212,280	68.8	1,377	52.4

Source: Doris A. Graber, *Crime News and the Public* (New York: Praeger, 1980), 40.

Note: Chicago Tribune coverage dates start and end one week later than do police crime report dates. Police dates are January 8, 1976, to January 5, 1977. *Tribune* data include crimes outside the Chicago area and therefore are not strictly comparable to Chicago police data. All differences between police and media data are significant at the .01 level, using chi square.

quakes, accidents, or sex scandals involving prominent people—these are the kinds of things that excite audiences. In fact, inexpensive mass newspapers became viable business ventures in the United States only when the publishers of the *New York Sun* discovered in 1833 that papers filled with breezy crime and sex stories far outsold their more staid competitors. Mass sales permitted sharp price reductions and allowed the "penny press" to be born.

People also remember violent behavior better than nonviolent fare. For instance, in 1978 the most widely followed and remembered news event in the United States was the murder of nine hundred members of an American religious sect in Guyana. Ninety-eight percent of the respondents to a Gallup poll knew of the event—a number matched only by those who remembered the attack on Pearl Harbor in 1941 and those who recalled the dropping of atomic bombs on Hiroshima and Nagasaki in 1945.

A third element of newsworthiness is *familiarity.* News is attractive if it pertains to well-known people or involves familiar situations of concern to many. The public's keen interest in celebrities is demonstrated by the amazing amount of detail that people can retain about the powerful and famous. More than two decades after the assassination of President John F. Kennedy in 1963, many Americans still remember details of the funeral ceremony, as well as where they were when they heard the news. The sense of personal grief and loss has lingered, bridging the gap between the average person's private and public worlds. People value the feeling of personal intimacy that comes from knowing details of a famous person's life.[22]

The fourth element of newsworthiness, particularly important for newspapers and local television, is that an event must be *close to home*. This heavy preference for local news rests on the assumption that people are most interested in what happens near them. Local media flourish because local events are their exclusive province, free from competition by national television and national print media. In fact, roughly 75 percent of the space in local media is used for local stories.[23] Because national television news must concentrate on matters of interest to viewers throughout the entire country, it cannot depict events close to everyone's home. The public receives so much news from Washington and a few major metropolitan areas that these cities and their newsmakers have become familiar to the nation. This, in a sense, makes them "local" events in what media analyst Marshall McLuhan has called the "global village" created by television.

Lastly, news should be *timely* and *novel*. It must be something that has just occurred and is out of the ordinary, either in the sense that it does not happen all the time, like the regular departure of airplanes or the daily opening of grocery stores, or in the sense that it is not part of the lives of ordinary persons.

Among these five basic criteria, *conflict, proximity,* and *timeliness* are most important, judging from a survey of television and newspaper editors who were given sixty-four fictitious stories by a team of researchers and then asked which they would use and their reasons for using them.[24] Conspicuously absent from their choice criteria was the story's overall significance. Significance does play a part, however, when a major event is communicated, such as the outcome of a national election, the death of a well-known leader, or a calamitous natural disaster. Nevertheless, most stories are selected primarily to satisfy the five criteria mentioned earlier.

Gathering the News

News organizations establish regular listening posts, or "beats," in those places where events of interest to the public are most likely to occur. In the United States, beats at the centers of government cover political executives, legislative bodies, court systems, and international organizations. Places where deviant behavior is most apt to be reported, such as police stations and hospitals, are monitored. Fluctuations in economic trends are recorded at stock and commodity markets and at institutions designed to check the pulse of the nation's business. Some beats are functionally defined, such as the "health" or "education" beat.

Reporters assigned to them generally cover a wider array of institutions on a less regular schedule than is true of the more usual beats.

Stories emanating from the traditional beats at the national level, such as the White House, Congress, the Pentagon, and the Justice Department, have an excellent chance of publication, either because of their intrinsic significance or because reporters stationed there have filed stories that have cost money and effort to produce. In the *New York Times* or *Washington Post,* for instance, stories from regularly covered beats outnumber other stories two to one and capture the bulk of front-page headlines.[25]

All major media tend to monitor the same places. Consequently, news patterns are stable and uniform throughout the country. On the nightly news the leading story is shared by at least two of the major networks 91 percent of the time. It is featured on the third network in only a slightly less prominent position.[26] As Table 3-3 documents, the media are "rivals in conformity." [27] The table is based on daily content analysis of three Chicago newspapers and five nightly news telecasts, two of them local to Chicago. It shows the proportionate frequency of mention of various news topics and presents striking evidence that the same kinds of stories and story types, although not necessarily identical stories, are reported by newspapers, local television, and national television. The same holds true for other media appealing to similar clienteles in other cities throughout the country.[28] Predictably, the greatest variations occur when local news is covered. Media that feature a lot of stories from their localities will show substantial variations in content in the categories that encompass such stories.

News, as media scholar Leon Sigal has put it, is always "the standardized exceptional." [29] Each day's or week's news is like a familiar play with slight changes in the scenes and dialogue and with frequent replacements in the cast of minor players although not of major actors. News is exceptional in the sense that it does not portray ordinary events, like eating breakfast or washing clothes or taking the bus to work. It is standardized in the sense that it deals with the same types of topics in familiar ways and produces standardized patterns of news and entertainment throughout the country. Repeated coverage of the same familiar scenes conveys to the public the feeling that all is going according to expectations and that, even when the news is bad, there is little to worry about. It has all happened before, and people have managed to cope.

News organizations, including the giants in the business, cannot afford to have full teams of reporters and camera crews dispersed across the country. They generally station teams in only half a dozen cities where the equipment, support staff, and news personnel are good. Locations are not selected with an eye to covering all parts of the nation equally well or to providing diverse settings.

Table 3-3 Frequency of Mention of News Topics (in percentages)

Topic	Chicago Tribune	Sun Times	Daily News	CBS local	NBC local	ABC national	CBS national	NBC national
Government/politics								
National government	39.3	36.8	37.3	25.2	23.1	43.0	44.1	43.6
Elections	8.5	10.6	12.4	8.3	7.4	17.0	16.3	16.7
State government	2.0	1.5	.9	3.3	2.6	.6	1.0	.9
City government	2.1	.3	1.3	5.2	3.8	.8	.5	.5
Miscellaneous	.7	.7	.0	1.1	1.2	.8	.6	.4
Total	52.6	49.9	51.9	43.1	38.1	62.2	62.5	62.1
Economic issues								
Economy status	2.7	2.2	2.6	1.3	1.2	1.8	1.8	2.1
Business/labor	6.6	6.8	5.3	8.0	12.1	8.4	7.3	7.5
Environment/ transportation	3.6	4.3	1.9	11.1	10.8	3.8	4.3	4.4
Medicine/health	2.8	2.5	1.7	4.0	5.5	2.3	3.0	3.5
Total	15.7	15.8	11.5	24.4	29.6	16.3	16.4	17.5
Social issues								
Deprived groups	3.0	3.1	4.1	2.6	2.4	2.9	3.1	2.6
Education/media/religion	4.9	2.3	3.0	4.9	4.7	3.0	3.2	2.7
Leadership style	1.3	1.6	1.5	.2	.2	.9	.7	.7
Disaster/accidents	2.5	2.0	2.6	4.6	5.9	3.5	3.0	3.6
Police/security	5.3	7.6	8.3	4.0	3.7	1.6	1.7	1.6
Corruption/terrorism	4.5	6.0	6.0	4.9	3.9	3.3	3.5	3.4
Individual crimes	8.4	10.8	10.3	9.5	10.1	4.4	4.3	5.0
Miscellaneous	1.9	.7	.6	1.6	1.4	1.9	1.5	1.6
Total	31.8	34.1	36.4	32.3	32.3	21.5	21.0	21.2

Source: Author's research.

Note: Excluded are stories about daily living, sports, art, and entertainment. $N = 29,648$ for *Chicago Tribune*, 548 for *Sun Times*, 466 for *Daily News*, 6,155 for CBS local, 10,346 for NBC local, 7,372 for ABC national, 7,653 for CBS national, and 6,984 for NBC national.

Table 3-4 shows the percentage of network news stories devoted to individual American states in broadcasts monitored from July 1985 to June 1987. The table also reports the number of electoral votes cast by each state in the 1988 election as a rough measure of that state's population and political significance. Coverage of news about the states is extremely uneven. Twenty-four states were covered by fewer than twenty-five stories annually, with Delaware, Kansas, North Dakota, Rhode Island, and Vermont receiving fewer than ten stories during that time. Such sparse coverage denies their news and their problems a national audience. Overall, the forty-one states covered by fewer than fifty stories annually represent 60 percent of the country in electoral votes, but receive only 44 percent of the state news coverage. At the other end of the spectrum, California (averaging 308 stories) and New York (averaging 232 stories) combined received nearly as much coverage as the thirty lowest ranking states. If Florida and Texas are added, the four front-runners in coverage receive a disproportionately high 39 percent of the state news coverage, when one weighs their importance by their 25 percent share of electoral votes.

Ninety percent of picture coverage comes from the cities in which camera crews are regularly stationed—Washington, D.C. (where 50 percent of all news originates), and usually New York, Cleveland, Boston, Chicago, and Los Angeles.[30] Of course, special events will be covered anywhere in the country. Every network reports presidential nominating conventions, wherever they are held, and routinely follows presidential travels, whether the destination is tiny Plains, Georgia, former president Jimmy Carter's home town, or the Great Wall of China. In 1987 more than 250 reporters journeyed to Oakdale, Louisiana, which has a population of only 7,100, and stayed for more than a week until the twenty-six hostages taken during a prison riot were safely released. Aside from a few exceptional happenings, events in remote sites are most likely to be covered if they involve prominent people and are scheduled in advance so that plans can be made to have media crews available.

Prior planning is also important for more accessible events. Time is needed to allocate camera crews, move them into position, and process and edit pictures. The necessity of planning ahead leads to an emphasis on the predictable, such as formal visits by dignitaries, legislative hear ings, or executive press conferences. The news output reflects this preference for formally scheduled events. The development of portable camera equipment producing videotapes that can be broadcast with little further processing has greatly eased this problem. "Spot news" can now be filmed and broadcast rapidly. This is only one example of the profound impact of technological developments on the content of the news.

Table 3-4   Network Coverage of State News, Yearly Average, July
1985-June 1987

Number of stories	States		Percentage of combined electoral vote	Percentage of television stories
0-24	Alaska	Nebraska	26	16
	Arkansas	New Hampshire		
	Connecticut	New Mexico		
	Delaware	North Dakota		
	Idaho	Rhode Island		
	Indiana	South Carolina		
	Kansas	South Dakota		
	Kentucky	Utah		
	Maine	Vermont		
	Maryland	West Virginia		
	Mississippi	Wisconsin		
	Montana	Wyoming		
25-49	Alabama	New Jersey	34	29
	Arizona	North Carolina		
	Hawaii	Ohio		
	Iowa	Oklahoma		
	Louisiana	Oregon		
	Michigan	Tennessee		
	Minnesota	Virginia		
	Missouri	Washington		
	Nevada			
50-103	Colorado		15	17
	Georgia			
	Illinois			
	Massachusetts			
	Pennsylvania			
163-180	Florida		9	15
	Texas			
232-308	California		16	24
	New York			

Source: Data compiled by the author from the Vanderbilt Television News Archive Index,
July 1985 through June 1987.

Note: $N = 4,578$. Stories from Washington, D.C., that cover national events are excluded.

News Production Constraints

Many news selection criteria reflect the need to process news rapidly and to publish it quickly. Time pressures explain the emphasis on pseudo-events—events created for easy reporting by the media or for the media. Pseudo-events constitute almost 70 percent of all television news stories.[31] For example, politicians frequently plan pictorially attractive happenings, like bridge dedications or county fair visits, to accommodate newspaper or broadcast deadlines. When newspeople need a quick story about a revolution in Central America or youth gang violence, they arrange interviews with familiar leaders, whose remarks, knowledgeable or not, then instantly become *the* Central America or *the* youth gang story.

Once stories reach media news offices, selections must be made extremely rapidly. Ben Bagdikian, a former *Washington Post* editor who studied gatekeeping at eight newspapers, found that stories usually are sifted and chosen on the spot. They are not assembled and carefully balanced with an eye to the overall effects. Here is how Bagdikian described the scene in a typical newspaper office.

> The news editor arrives at 6 A.M. to find an overnight accumulation of fifty thousand words, most of it regional and national news from the wire services, some of it from the paper's reporters in outlying bureaus, who transmitted it by teletype the night before.
> In addition to making decisions on incoming wire stories, this particular news editor makes decisions on local stories handed him by the city editor and the state editor. He also is handed the output of two wire-photo machines that during the day produce ninety-six photographs from which he selects sixteen.[32]

In the course of the day, the news editor chooses additional items for publication by scanning wire service as well as locally originated news. The editor examines about 110,000 words of wire news daily, equivalent to the size of an average book, and 5,000 words of news from the local staff. The editor also must select photographs, consult with city editors about story assignments, and decide what to place on page one in light of the changing news scene.

Bagdikian reports that the typical newspaper gatekeeper was able to scan and discard individual stories in one or two seconds. His study of the reasons stories are rejected revealed that only 2.5 percent were turned down because the editor did not care for the substance of the story or objected to its ideological slant. Twenty-six percent were rejected because of lack of space. The remaining 71.5 percent were rejected because they were judged to lack some or all of the elements of newsworthiness discussed earlier. The published newspaper usually contains the same proportions of different types of news as the original pool from which the stories were selected.[33]

Rejection rates varied for different types of stories. Overall, 89 percent of all wire service news was rejected. So were 93 percent of human interest stories, 92 percent of crime news, 74 percent of farm news, and 69 percent of science news. Even though much of the human interest information was rejected, it still constituted the largest single news category—23 percent of total news. By contrast, science news took 5 percent of total space and farm stories 6 percent.[34]

Bagdikian reports that for stories that were accepted, fast gate-keepers could skim through the entire story and even make minor changes in only four seconds. The average reading time was six seconds. At such speeds, judgments are almost instantaneous. There is no time to reflect or to weigh the merits of one story over another. Stories are judged more by how they balance previously selected stories than by their intrinsic importance. If the gatekeeper has ideological preferences, these are served instinctively, if at all, rather than deliberately.

Because the flood tide of information continues throughout the day, the gatekeeper accepts very few stories in the early hours of each shift. Closer to the deadline, when news has to go to press, the pace of story selection quickens. When the deadline arrives, a news story must be extraordinarily important to replace stories that have already been accepted or are already in press. Ordinarily, stories left over at the end of the day will not be used on the next day because newer stories will have replaced them. Accordingly, a late-breaking story, unless it is very unusual or significant, has little chance for publication. What becomes news thus depends heavily on when it happens. West Coast afternoon stories are frequent casualties because they generally happen too late to be incorporated into the network evening news, which is run on an East Coast schedule.

Public relations managers know the deadlines of important publications, such as the *New York Times, Wall Street Journal, Time, Newsweek,* and network television news. They schedule events and news releases so that stories arrive in gatekeepers' offices precisely when needed. If their releases are attractively presented and meet newsworthiness criteria, journalists find it hard to resist using them. This is especially true for smaller publications that lack adequate resources to produce their own stories.[35] News providers, eager to gain publicity for their causes, thus can influence the news production process. If news sources want to stifle publicity, they can announce the news just past the deadlines, preferably on weekends when few newscasts are scheduled. For instance, the Nixon administration fired the special Watergate prosecutor on the weekend. This became known as the "Saturday night massacre." Nixon's hope that the timing would minimize publicity was only partially fulfilled.

Publications with less frequent deadlines, such as weekly news magazines, have a lot more time to decide what to publish. News magazine staffs also have more resources than most daily papers to dig out background information and present stories in a context that helps readers to evaluate them. These magazines are ideal for people who want quick, interpretive news that concentrates on a limited number of events.

Television news staffs have even less time than newspapers to investigate most stories and far less time to provide background and interpretation. When background or investigative stories do appear on television, they frequently originate in the print media. The problem of insufficient time pertains not only to preparing stories but also to presenting them. The average news story on television and radio takes about a minute, just enough time to announce that an event has taken place and present a fact or two about it. Complex stories may have to be scratched entirely if they cannot be drastically condensed.

Print media have space problems as well, but they are less severe than time constraints faced by electronic media. The average newspaper reserves 55 percent of its space for advertising. Out of its 45 percent "newshole," generally 27 percent goes for straight news stories, the remainder for features of various types. Some papers reserve a standardized amount of space for news; others expand or contract the newshole depending on the flow of news and advertising. But whether the paper is a slim eight-page version or five to ten times that size, there is rarely enough space to cover stories as fully as reporters and editors would like.[36]

Besides the need to condense a news story into a brief capsule, television reporters also want stories with visual appeal. Unfortunately, what is visually appealing may not be important. For instance, during political campaigns, motorcades, rallies, hecklers, and cheering crowds make good pictures. Candidates delivering speeches are visually dull by comparison. Television cameras therefore concentrate on the colorful scenes rather than on the speechmaker. If these happenings are flashed on the screen in competition with the speech, they often distract from what the candidate is saying. Events that make dull pictures may have to be omitted.

Because picture production is expensive for television as well as for print, picture stories selected early are likely to be kept even if more important stories break later. Financial considerations, as well as personnel reasons, favor information originated by the staff. News organizations prefer stories by employees already on their payroll to wire service stories by unknown reporters or stories from outside sources for which additional fees must be paid. News executives also have personal relationships with their own staffs and do not want to disappoint them by rejecting their stories.

Effects of Gatekeeping

The gatekeeping influences that have been discussed give a distinctive character to the American news product. There are many exceptions, of course, when one looks at individual programs or stories. There are also noticeable differences in emphasis among the conservative rural press, more moderate papers in small- and middle-sized towns, and the liberal press in major metropolitan centers. For instance, a study of the women's page/lifestyle section of American daily newspapers showed that news about the women's movement and women's careers constituted 20 percent of the coverage in this section in rural papers and nearly double that amount in papers in metropolitan areas.[37] Despite these variations, several shared attributes of American news stand out. They will be discussed under four headings: people in the news, actions in the news, general characteristics of the news, and support for the establishment.[38]

People in the News

The gatekeeping process winnows the group of newsworthy people to a very small cadre of familiar and unfamiliar figures. Herbert Gans's study of news magazines and network television news showed that familiar people appear in three out of every four news stories. Most are political figures. Fewer than fifty politicians are in the news regularly. The list is headed by the incumbent president. Other people receive coverage primarily for unusual or remarkable activities, but incumbent presidents are covered regardless of what they do. News about presidential candidates ranks next; in presidential election years it often outnumbers stories about the president.[39]

A third well-covered group consists of major federal officials, such as political leaders in the House and Senate, the heads of major congressional committees, and cabinet members in active departments. In the post-Watergate period major White House staff members are part of the circle. The Supreme Court is in the news only intermittently, generally when important decisions are announced. Agency heads rarely make the news except when they announce new policies or feud with the president. Some people, however, are regularly in the news regardless of their current political status merely because their names are household words. Members of the Kennedy clan are a prime example.

Below the federal level, the activities of governors and mayors from large states and cities are newsworthy if they involve major public policy issues or if the incumbent is unusual because of race, sex, or prior newsworthy activities. Notorious individuals also receive frequent news attention if their deeds have involved well-known people. Presidential assassins, mass murderers, or members of extremist political groups fall into this category. Ample coverage also goes to targets of congressional investigations and politicians indicted for wrongdoings in office.

Among the many powerful people rarely covered in the news are economic leaders (such as the heads of large corporations), financiers, and leaders of organized business (such as the National Association of Manufacturers or the U.S. Chamber of Commerce). A few colorful labor leaders, such as George Meany and James Hoffa, have been news figures, but this was probably due more to their personalities than to their jobs. Important military leaders also remain obscure unless they conduct major military operations. Political party leaders surface during elections but remain in the shadows at other times. Political activists, such as civil rights leaders or the heads of minority parties, and consumer activists, such as Ralph Nader, come and go from the news scene, depending on the amount of visible conflict they are able to produce. The same holds true for the heads of voluntary associations, such as antiabortion groups or church leaders.

Most people never make the news because their activities are not unusual enough to command media attention. Ordinary people have their best chance for publicity if they protest or riot or strike, particularly against the government. The next best chance goes to victims of disasters, personal tragedy, and crime, and to the actors who brought about their plight. The grisly nature of crimes, disasters, or other human tragedies, rather than the identity of the people involved, determines their newsworthiness. Ordinary people also make the news if their lifestyles or social activities become highly unusual or if their behavior diverges greatly from the norm for persons of their age, sex, and status. Finally, ordinary people make the news in large numbers as nameless members of groups whose statistical profile is reported or whose opinions have been tapped through polls or elections.

Action in the News

The range of activities reported in the news is quite limited— conflicts and disagreements among government officials (particularly friction between the president and Congress about economic or foreign policies), violent and nonviolent protest (much of it about government activities), crime, scandals and investigations, and impending or actual disasters. When the nation is involved in war, a large number of war stories are reported.

Stories about government policies also provide frequent story material. These generally deal with policy decision making rather than policy execution. Government personnel changes, including campaigns for office, are another news focus. Finally, two aspects of normal social change receive substantial coverage from time to time: major national ceremonies, like inaugurations or moon landings, and important social, cultural, or technological developments, like the participation of women in the space exploration program or advances in the fight against cancer.

General Characteristics of the News

These criteria for newsworthiness and the constraints on news production shape American news and its impact, regardless of the particular subject under discussion. Three features stand out. American news stresses novel and entertaining events, familiar people and situations, and conflict and violence. Social problems are ordinarily neglected.

Novelty and Entertainment. The demand for stories that are new and exciting often means that sensational and novel occurrences drown out news of more lasting significance. For instance, eight times as much space and time are devoted to sports news as to news about local community problems such as school finance or housing.[40] Dramatic events, such as airline hijackings or serial murders, preempt more significant happenings. Preoccupation with a single striking event, such as the stock market crash of October 19, 1987, can shortchange coverage of other news, such as a punitive American airstrike against Iranian targets. Speculations about a religious broadcaster's strong prospects in the 1988 Iowa presidential caucuses drowned out a Soviet leader's announcement of plans to withdraw from the long and bloody Afghanistan war.

The emphasis on entertainment also leads to stress on trivial aspects of serious stories. As noted earlier, complex issues are presented as simple human interest dramas. Inflation is likely to become a story about John Doe, working-class homeowner, who is struggling to pay his mortgage. Such personalized stories do not explain the larger issues involved in inflation. But, judging from attention patterns, they are far more likely to be noticed than learned discussions by economic experts.

The search for novelty and entertainment also produces news that focuses on the present and ignores the past. The here and now is what counts most. This leads to fragmented and discontinuous news. It is aired as it is received, so that the background needed to place a story into its context is often missing. Clarifications are usually buried in the back pages. On television, snippets of news may be presented together to drive home an easily understandable theme, such as "Washington is in a mess" or "the inner city is decaying." The theme may come through, but the individual news item is blurred.

Fragmentation makes it difficult for audiences to piece together a coherent narrative of events. More background and interpretation would help, but it would also increase the chance for subjective interpretation by news commentators. A few papers, such as the *Christian*

Science Monitor, cover fewer stories and present them in more detail. People who carefully read *Monitor* stories acquire a better background for understanding social issues, but they miss out on other news for which there is no space. They may also get skewed information if newspeople misinterpret the significance of complex events.

Familiarity and Similarity. The demand for stories about familiar people and events close to home explains the circular nature of such coverage. Familiar people and situations are covered minutely, which makes them even more familiar and therefore even more worthy of publicity. The reverse is also true. During the 1988 presidential election campaign, Gov. Mario Cuomo of New York, whose rousing oratory had made news during the 1984 Democratic National Convention, became a potential candidate in many people's minds even though he never entered the race officially. Meanwhile, official entrants, such as Democrat Bruce Babbitt and Republican Jack Kemp, received less media attention and remained unfamiliar. They were forced to abandon the quest.

Familiar people may become objects of prying curiosity. The details of their private lives may take up an inordinately large amount of time and space in the mass media. This happened when Mayor Richard Daley of Chicago died in 1976. The media provided a minute-by-minute account of his last moments. The public was kept informed about his blood pressure, the emergency medical procedures being performed, and the manner in which his family was told about his death. For several days much of the news in the Chicago area was taken up by these minutiae, to the exclusion of more salient stories. The important story, obscured initially, was that the mayor's death had launched a major power struggle for control of Chicago's politics.

Another significant consequence of the criteria of newsworthiness is that American news is very parochial compared with news in other countries. This neglect of news about foreign people and cultures leaves Americans deficient in their understanding of international affairs, a subject explored more fully in Chapter 10. Again, the pattern is circular. For instance, if events in Peru are rarely covered, stories about Peru will require a lot more background to make sense to Americans. This may take more time and space than the media are willing to give to any story, except during a crisis. Therefore, foreign coverage in American media is usually about people to whom Americans feel culturally close and whose policies are somewhat familiar, like the English, the Canadians, and people of Northern European countries. Foreign news concentrates on situations that are easy to report, which often means violent events like revolutions, major disasters, and the like. This type of coverage conveys the faulty impression that most foreign countries are always in serious disarray.

Conflict and Violence. The heavy news emphasis on conflict and bad news, which is most prevalent in big city media, has three major consequences.[41] The first and perhaps most far-reaching consequence is the dangerous distortion of reality that emphasis on negative news events may create. Crime coverage provides examples. Media stories rarely mention that many neighborhoods are relatively free of crime. Instead they convey the impression to many people that the whole city, and particularly inner city areas, are dangerous jungles. This impression may become a self-fulfilling prophecy. In the wake of crime publicity, many people avoid the inner city. They even shun comparatively safe neighborhoods after a single, highly publicized crime. The empty streets then make crime more likely.

Studies of people's perceptions of the incidence of crime and the actual chances that they will be attacked indicate that their fears are geared to media realities. In the world of television drama, the average character has a 30 to 64 percent chance of being involved in violence; in the real world the average person's chance of becoming a crime victim is a small fraction of that number.[42] Similarly, heavy media emphasis on air crashes and scant coverage of automobile accidents have left the public with distorted notions of the relative dangers of these modes of transportation.

Emphasis on conflict may cause some people to believe that violence is an acceptable way to settle disputes. Others argue that by bringing conflict into the open, media may promote its resolution, but clearly they may also make it worse.[43] This often happens when media dramatize a conflict by highlighting its more sensational aspects and oversimplifying it, picturing it as a confrontation between two clearly defined sides. It is the hawks against the doves in war, the victors or losers in a legislative battle, the Communists versus anti-Communists in a struggle abroad. Even when a situation is not actually confrontational, the media may present it as a feud or a fight. Yet divergent viewpoints expressed by parties, or unions, or members of a legislature may not mean that they are locked in battle.

Average people, when presented with clashing claims, often feel confused and find it extremely difficult to determine where the truth lies. They have neither the facts nor the time to explore the issues. They are also left with the disquieting sense that conflict and turmoil reign nearly everywhere. This impression is likely to affect people's feelings toward society in general. They may contract "videomalaise," characterized by lack of trust, cynicism, and fear.[44] Many social scientists believe that such feelings undermine support for government, destroy faith in leaders, produce political apathy, and generally sap the vigor of the democratic process.

Finally, the popularity of violence stories has encouraged groups who seek media coverage to behave violently or sensationally to enhance their chances for publicity. One example comes from a lengthy strike by a union of Chicano workers against a Texas furniture company. During the first year, the nonviolent strike received very little publicity. To attract media coverage the leaders decided to stage noisy marches to the Capitol on the first and second anniversaries of the strike. Moderate language in appeals to the company and city authorities was replaced by fighting words. City councilors were called "rednecks" and challenged to stop the union's marches. These inflammatory accusations created a confrontation, brought city police to the scene, and heightened tensions. Celebrities, including Sens. Edmund Muskie of Maine and Birch Bayh of Indiana and farm labor leader Cesar Chavez, were invited to enter the fray. These maneuvers broke the year-long dearth of media coverage. No longer peaceful, the strike finally received ample publicity. In turn, this created sufficient pressure to bring about a settlement.[45]

A taste for conflict is not the same as a taste for controversy, however. Fear of offending members of the mass audience, wire service subscribers, or affiliated station managers often keeps stories dealing with controversial subjects like abortion or corruption in the church out of the media, especially network television. If those stories are reported, the treatment is ordinarily bland, carefully hedged, and rarely provocative. In fact, the world that television presents to the viewer generally lags behind the real world in its recognition of controversial social changes. The civil rights struggle, women's fight for equality, and changing sexual mores were widespread long before they became common on the television screen or received serious attention in the print media. Compared with television, newspapers can afford to be more daring because normally there is no other daily paper in the same market. Moreover, the nature of the medium makes it easier for the audience to ignore stories they find offensive or distasteful.

Neglect of Social Problems. Despite the ascendancy of social responsibility journalism, the constraints of news production still force the media to neglect serious social problems, such as alcoholism, drug addiction, environmental pollution, and care of the elderly and disabled. The pattern changes after a dramatic event, such as a rash of deaths in nursing homes or a big welfare fraud case. If a reporter investigates and finds that six elderly people starved to death because of neglect, the spotlighted incident may then lead to a series of reports on food in retirement homes. The shocking deaths provide the element of novelty. After that novelty has worn off, interest dims and media attention flags, even if the problem remains unsolved.

Another reason why social problems are neglected is that most media staffs are inadequately trained to cover them. Proper appraisal of the administration of nursing homes or prisons or pollution control programs requires technical knowledge. Specialized reporters with expertise in areas such as urban affairs, science, or finance are available, as yet, only in large news organizations. Moreover, a science reporter can hardly be expected to be an expert in all fields of science. Nor can a reporter skilled in urban problems be expected simultaneously to master the intricacies of a major city's budget, its transportation system, and its services to juveniles. Because most news organizations throughout the country lack the trained staffs needed to discuss major social problems constructively, politicians and all kinds of "experts" can easily challenge the merits of unpalatable media stories.

Judging from media use patterns, most of the public is not very interested in most social problems or the hazards of unhealthful lifestyles. For those who are interested and might be in a position to combat social problems, lack of adequate media coverage makes it more difficult to rouse public support and become newsworthy in the process.

Support for the Establishment

The gatekeeping process also yields news that basically supports political and social institutions in America. Although the media regularly expose the misbehavior and inefficiencies of government officials, for the most part they display a favorable attitude toward political leaders and the American political system. Misconduct and poor policies are treated as deviations from the norms, thereby implicitly reaffirming the merit of prevailing norms. Assumptions that underscore the legitimacy of the current political system are routinely embedded in news stories. For instance, when police protect a factory from violence by workers, it is assumed that they are the legitimate guardians of public order engaged in an appropriate government activity. The possibility that workers should own the factories and have a right to wrest them from the control of capitalists is never raised. Similarly, stories discussing the plight of homeless children tacitly assume that they ought to be living in conventional family units. The fact that other arrangements might be preferable is largely ignored.[46]

American political symbols and rituals, such as the presidency, the courts, elections, and patriotic celebrations, are treated with a high degree of respect by the media, enhancing their legitimacy. By contrast, news stories cast a negative light on anti-establishment behavior, such as protest demonstrations that disrupt normal activities, inflammatory speeches by militants, or looting during a riot. Obscenity and profanity in public places usually are edited out of news events. When they are featured, they generate floods of complaints about disrespect, prying and poor taste. This puts dampers on such exposés, at least temporarily.

Explicit and implicit support for the established system, as well a sugar-coating of political reality, sometimes help and sometimes hurt the public interest. They hurt if faults in the established system and prevailing political ideologies are allowed to persist when publicity might lead to correction. The fear of publicity can also have a salutary effect on errant public figures. There are, however, situations in which shielding the shortcomings of the political system and even individual misconduct may be helpful. For instance, at times of national or international crisis, when the nation's prestige is an important political asset, detrimental stories can severely weaken the country. Similarly, the ability of elected leaders to govern effectively can be seriously damaged by disclosures of flaws in their personal lives, such as extramarital ventures.

Generalized support for the establishment and the status quo is not unique to the media, of course.[47] Most institutions within any particular political system go along with it if they wish to prosper. People on their staffs have been socialized to believe in the merits of their political structures. Moreover, financial concerns make it essential for the media to cater to advertisers and audiences who firmly support the American political system. Staff members whose personal ideologies differ usually conform with established norms to avoid conflict with their bosses, advertisers, or affiliated stations.[48] People are socialized throughout life to support their country and its policies. They want to believe that their government is competent, honest, and working hard to solve the nation's major problems. They often resent exposés that call into question this comfortable sense of security. Media support for the establishment thus helps to maintain respect for it and perpetuate it.

Establishment support is further strengthened by the media's reliance on government information and press releases. As pointed out earlier, in the United States the bulk of news, particularly news pertaining to activities beyond the local community, comes from officials and agencies of the government.[49] Official viewpoints are likely to be particularly dominant when reporters must preserve access to their special beats, like the Pentagon or Justice Department, or when story production requires government assistance in collecting or gaining access to data. For instance, when military personnel are needed to transport correspondents to war zones, or when film producers want demonstrations of moon-flight research, the resulting stories are apt to support official views.[50]

Government officials and agencies are also used routinely to verify information. Reporters generally equate official position and rank of sources with accuracy. The higher the official level and rank the better. The assumption that government sources, such as police departments, or Department of Agriculture spokespersons, or presidential press aides, are reliable is, of course, debatable, especially since the particular thrust given to a story may put agencies into a good or bad light. Many private groups have complained that nearly exclusive reliance on government sources deprives them of the chance to publicize their own, more accurate versions of stories and that it results in one-sided reporting, tilted toward support of the establishment.

Appraising the News-Making Process

Do newspeople do a good job in selecting the types of news and entertainment categories they cover? Do they allot appropriate amounts of time and space to each of these categories? Do they fill them with good individual stories? The answers depend on the standards that the analyst is applying. If one contends that news can and should be a mirror of society, faithfully reproducing a miniature version of life, the news-making process leaves much to be desired. With their emphasis on the exceptional rather than the ordinary, on a few regular beats rather than a wide range of news sources, and on conflict and bad news rather than the ordinariness of daily life, the media picture a world that is far from reality. Reality becomes further distorted because the process of shaping news events into interesting, cohesive stories often gives these events totally new meanings and significance. This is why critics claim that the news creates reality rather than reports it.[51]

If one adopts the classical albeit debatable American notion that the media should be the eyes and ears of intelligent and aware citizens who are interested primarily in news of major social and political significance to their community and country, one will again find fault with the gatekeeping process. Obviously, much space and time are given to trivia, and many interesting developments are ignored or reported so briefly that their meaning is lost. Often the human interest appeal of a story or its sensational aspects are distracting the audience from recognizing the story's real significance.[52]

To find fault is easy; to suggest realistic remedies is far more difficult. Few critics would agree on what is noteworthy enough to deserve publication. Gradations and ranks in significance depend on the observer's world view and political orientation. Much of the published criticism of the media consists of polemical works that take the media to task for omitting the critic's areas of special concern. But one person's intellectual meat is another's poison. Conservatives would like to see more stories about the misdeeds of America's enemies and about waste and abuse in social service programs. Liberals complain that the media legitimize big business and the military and neglect social reforms and radical perspectives. Frequently, there is the additional charge that political bias dictates the choices made about inclusion and exclusion of media fare and about story focus and tone. These charges have been particularly common when the media have featured controversial public policy issues, such as the dangers of atomic energy generation or the merits of a new weapons system, or when political campaigns or demonstrations were covered.

A number of content analyses of such events definitely refute the charges of political bias, if bias is defined as deliberately lopsided coverage or intentional slanting of news. These analyses show instead that most newspeople try to cover a balanced array of issues in a neutral manner and do include contrasting viewpoints.[53] Most studies of bias have involved situations, such as elections, in which bias charges could be anticipated. Media personnel therefore may have taken exceptional care to cover elections evenhandedly. But even in more general realms, such as the coverage of American business enterprises, there may be more evenhandedness than one might expect from the frequent charges of both pro- and antibusiness bias in the media. A team of investigators sampled more than two thousand households nationwide to analyze the public's perceptions of bias in business news coverage. It discovered that 61 percent of the respondents considered business news biased. But half thought the bias was probusiness, while the other half thought it was antibusiness.[54]

When coverage is unbalanced, as happens often, the reasons generally spring from the news-making process itself rather than from politically or ideologically motivated slanting. For instance, when Alexander Haig bowed out of the presidential race in 1988 and endorsed Sen. Robert Dole, three networks led with the story. The reason for this media prominence was a snow storm in New Hampshire that forced cancellation of most other campaign events on that day. Geography also affects the news-making process. Events happening in Chicago are reported more fully nationwide than are similar events in Denver because the networks have a permanently leased wire from Chicago to New York but not from Denver to New York. The New Hampshire presidential primary receives disproportionately ample coverage because it happens to be the first one in a presidential election year.

Inevitably, the stories that are publicized represent a small, unsystematic sample of the news of the day. In this sense every issue of a newspaper or every television newscast is a "biased sample" of current events. Published stories often generate follow-up coverage, heightening the bias effect. Attempts to be evenhanded may lead to similar coverage for events of dissimilar importance, thereby introducing bias.

News can be evaluated not only as a mirror of society or as a reflection of socially and politically significant events, but also from the standpoint of audience preference. By and large the media gatekeepers appear to be doing well by that standard. A 1983 study showed that on a scale of 0 to 100, Americans rated the appeal of television shows at 73.

More than 90 percent of all shows received ratings of 50 or above.[55] People like the products of the mass media industry well enough to consume them on a scale unheard of in the past. Three out of every four adults say they read newspapers regularly; nearly all homes have radio and television and use them extensively. In the average household the radio is turned on for three hours a day and television for seven. Millions of viewers, by their own free choice, have switched from other pretelevision age sources of diversion to watching shows condemned as "trash" by social critics and often even by the viewers themselves. These same people ignore shows and newspaper stories with the critics' seal of approval.

If viewed simultaneously from all three perspectives, the media overall have developed a balanced approach. Most newspapers and broadcast enterprises try to mirror at least a portion of the world. Most of the large news organizations also see it as their function to present some serious political and social information and analysis. At the same time, most cater to the audience's appetite for easily digested entertainment and diversion. The end product cannot fully satisfy everyone.

Summary

What is news depends on what a particular society deems socially significant and/or personally satisfying to media audiences. The prevailing political and social ideology therefore determines what type of information will be gathered and the range of meanings that will be given to it. News collection is structured through the beat system to produce the desired information.

Beyond the larger framework, which is rooted in America's current political ideology, overt political considerations rarely play a major part in news selection. Instead, the profit motive and technical constraints of news production become paramount selection criteria. These criteria impose more stringent constraints on television than on print media because television deals with larger, more heterogeneous audiences and requires pictures to match word stories. Unlike newspapers, which rarely have competition in the local market, television must compete for attention with several other electronic outlets.

The end products of these various constraints on news making are news media that generally support the American political system, but emphasize its shortcomings and conflicts because journalists see themselves as watchdogs of public honesty and because conflict is exciting. News is geared primarily to attract and entertain rather than to educate the audience about politically significant events. The pressures to report news rapidly while it is happening often lead to presentation of disjointed fragments and disparate commentary. This leaves the audience with the impossible task of weaving the fragments into a meaningful tapestry of interrelated events.

If judged in terms of the information needs of the ideal citizen in the ideal democracy, the end product of the gatekeeping process is inadequate. This is especially true of television, which provides little more than a headline service for news and which mirrors the world like the curved mirrors at the county fair. Reality is reflected, but it seems badly out of shape and proportion.

Most of us, however, only faintly resemble the ideal citizen, and most of us look to the media for entertainment rather than for enlightenment. From this perspective a different appraisal suggests itself. By and large, American mass media serve the general public about as well as that public wants to be served in practice rather than in theory. Entertainment is interspersed with a smattering of serious information. Breadth of coverage is preferred over narrow depth. In times of acute crisis, as we shall see in Chapter 9, the media can and do follow a different pattern. Serious news displaces entertainment, and the broad sweep of events turns into a narrow, in-depth focus on the crisis. But short of acute crisis, superficiality prevails most of the time.

Notes

1. Jon Margolis and Lea Donosky, "Mondale, Glenn Set Off Fireworks During Debate," *Chicago Tribune,* January 16, 1984; see also Howell Raines, "Debate Among Democrats Draws Sharpest Exchanges of Campaign," *New York Times,* January 16, 1984.
2. "No Time for Policy," *Media Monitor* (August 1987): 2.
3. Audience surveys can assess the popularity of specific newspaper stories or television programs. Major rating services, such as A. C. Nielsen and the American Research Bureau (ARB), use electronic devices to monitor television shows being watched and the demographic composition of the audience. For both radio and television, advertising rates are based on audience size. A 1 percent increase in audience size can mean many millions of additional advertising income. Industry representatives strongly resisted the new "people meter" measuring device, introduced by Nielsen in 1987, because it produced significant changes in audience ratings when compared with the older methods. Newspaper rates are based on paid circulation, which is monitored by an independent agency, the Audit Bureau of Circulations. Audiences are rarely asked if they would prefer different programs to existing fare. Qualitative appraisals are available but are not currently used.
4. "Mr. President, Ben Bradley Calling," *Public Opinion* 9 (September/October 1986): 40.
5. Gerald C. Stone and Elinor Grusin, "Network TV as the Bad News Bearer," *Journalism Quarterly* 61 (Autumn 1984): 517-523; and Joseph R. Dominick, "Business Coverage in Network Newscasts," *Journalism Quarterly* 58 (Spring 1981): 179-185. See also Norman R. Luttbeg, "News Consensus: Do

U.S. Newspapers Mirror Society's Happenings?" *Journalism Quarterly* 60 (Autumn 1983): 484-488, 578.

6. Jane Delano Brown, Carl R. Bybee, Stanley T. Wearden, and Dulcie Murdock Straughan, "Invisible Power: Newspaper News Sources and the Limits of Diversity," *Journalism Quarterly* 64 (Spring 1987): 45-54; and Sharon Dunwoody and Steven Shields, "Accounting for Patterns of Selection of Topics in Statehouse Reporting," *Journalism Quarterly* 63 (Autumn 1986): 488-496.

7. R. Gordon Shepherd, "Selectivity of Sources: Reporting the Marijuana Controversy," *Journal of Communication* 31 (Spring 1981): 129-137. Also see Sharon Dunwoody and Michael Ryan, "The Credible Scientific Source," *Journalism Quarterly* 64 (Spring 1987): 21-27; and Stanley Rothman and S. Robert Lichter, "Elite Ideology and Risk Perception in Nuclear Energy Policy," *American Political Science Review* 81 (June 1987): 383-404.

8. Nancy Pfund and Laura Hofstadter, "Biomedical Innovation and the Press," *Journal of Communication* 31 (Spring 1981): 138-154.

9. S. Robert Lichter, Stanley Rothman, and Linda S. Lichter, *The Media Elite* (New York: Adler and Adler, 1986): 62. The study is reported on pp. 54-71.

10. The impact of news stories attributed to highly credible sources is described in Benjamin I. Page, Robert Y. Shapiro, and Glenn R. Dempsey, "What Moves Public Opinion?" *American Journal of Political Science* 81 (March 1987): 23-43.

11. Barbara Matusow, *The Evening Stars: The Rise of the Network News Anchors* (Boston: Houghton Mifflin, 1983).

12. Peter Braestrup, *Big Story* (Garden City, N.Y.: Anchor Books, 1978).

13. George Gerbner, "Ideological Perspective and Political Tendencies in News Reporting," *Journalism Quarterly* 41 (August 1964): 495-508.

14. For a discussion of the social systems framework for mass communications analysis, see James S. Ettema, "The Organizational Context of Creativity," in *Individuals in Mass Media Organizations: Creativity and Constraint*, ed. James S. Ettema and D. Charles Whitney (Beverly Hills, Calif.: Sage, 1982), 91-106.

15. David Morgan, *The Capitol Press Corps: Newsmen and the Governing of New York State* (Westport, Conn.: Greenwood Press, 1978), 44-47.

16. Ron Powers, *The Newscasters* (New York: St. Martin's Press, 1977), 30.

17. Quoted in ibid., 79. The evidence on whether editors and reporters assess their audiences' tastes properly is mixed. Ralph K. Martin, Garrett J. O'Keefe, and Oguz B. Nayman, in "Opinion Agreement and Accuracy Between Editors and Their Readers," *Journalism Quarterly* 49 (Autumn 1972): 460-468, say they do. Leo Bogart, in "Changing News Interests and the Mass Media," *Public Opinion Quarterly* 23 (Winter 1968-1969): 560-574, holds to the contrary.

18. Edward Jay Epstein, *News from Nowhere* (New York: Vintage Books, 1974), 17-18.

19. G. Ray Funkhouser, "Trends in Media Coverage of the Issues of the '60's," *Journalism Quarterly* 50 (Fall 1973): 533-538.

20. Ibid.

21. Michael X. Delli Carpini and Bruce A. Williams, "Television and Terrorism: Patterns of Presentation and Occurrence, 1969 to 1980," *Western Political Quarterly* 40 (March 1987): 45-64.

22. Somewhat similar feelings are harbored even toward the casts of soap operas. People whose lives are confined largely to their homes often adopt

soap opera stars as part of their family. They avidly follow the trials and tribulations of these people and may even try to model themselves after them.

23. A study of 149 small and large newspapers reports the following news space allocations: local, 75 percent; sports, 6 percent; national, 4 percent; women's issues, 4 percent; international, 3 percent; editorial, 3 percent; state, 3 percent; financial, 2 percent. The measurements refer to space in column inches of total newshole. Dan Drew and G. Cleveland Wilhoit, "Newshole Allocation Policies of American Daily Newspapers," *Journalism Quarterly* 53 (Fall 1976): 434-440.

24. Robert W. Clyde and James K. Buckalew, "Inter-Media Standardization: A Q-Analysis of News Editors," *Journalism Quarterly* 46 (Summer 1969): 349-351.

25. Leon V. Sigal, *Reporters and Officials: The Organization and Politics of Newsmaking* (Lexington, Mass.: Heath, 1973), 119-130. Also see Leon V. Sigal, "Sources Make the News," in *Reading the News,* ed. Robert Karl Manoff and Michael Schudson (New York: Pantheon Books, 1987), 9-37.

26. The leading story is shared by all three major networks 43 percent of the time. Joe S. Foote and Michael E. Steele, "Degree of Conformity in Lead Stories in Early Evening Network TV Newscasts," *Journalism Quarterly* 63 (Spring 1986): 19-23.

27. The phrase is from Stanley K. Bigman, "Rivals in Conformity: A Study of Two Competing Dailies," *Journalism Quarterly* 25 (Autumn 1949): 127-131.

28. Daniel Riffe, Brenda Ellis, Momo K. Rogers, Roger L. Van Ommeren, and Kieran A. Woodman, "Gatekeeping and the Network News Mix," *Journalism Quarterly* 63 (Summer 1986): 315-321. For a discussion of variations in individual stories, see Luttbeg, "News Consensus," 484-488.

29. Sigal, *Reporters and Officials,* 66.

30. Joseph R. Dominick, "Geographic Bias in National TV News," *Journal of Communication* 27 (Fall 1977): 94-99.

31. Robert Rutherford Smith, "Mythic Elements in Television News," *Journal of Communication* 29 (Winter 1979): 75-82.

32. Ben Bagdikian, *The Information Machines* (New York: Harper and Row, 1971), 99-100.

33. Dunwoody and Shields, "Statehouse Reporting," 488-496.

34. David M. White, "The Gatekeeper," *Journalism Quarterly* 27 (Fall 1950): 383-390, replicated by D. Charles Whitney and Lee B. Becker, " 'Keeping the Gates' for Gatekeepers: The Effects of Wire News," *Journalism Quarterly* 59 (Spring 1982): 60-65. See also Guido H. Stempel III, "Gatekeeping: The Mix of Topics and the Selection of Stories," *Journalism Quarterly* 62 (Winter 1985): 791-796.

35. Judy VanSlyke Turk, "Information Subsidies and Media Content: A Study of Public Relations Influence on the News," *Journalism Monographs* 100 (December 1986): 1-29.

36. Drew and Wilhoit, "Newshole Allocation Policies," 434-440. Also see Leo Bogart, "How U.S. Newspaper Content Is Changing," *Journal of Communication* 35 (Spring 1985): 82-91.

37. Harriet Engel Gross and Sharyne Merritt, "Effect of Social/Organizational Context on Gatekeeping in Lifestyle Pages," *Journalism Quarterly* 58 (Autumn 1981): 420-427.

38. The first two headings have been adapted from Herbert Gans's study of news magazine and network television news. Herbert J. Gans, *Deciding*

What's News: A Study of CBS Evening News, NBC Nightly News, Newsweek & Time (New York: Pantheon Books, 1979), 8-31. See also Gaye Tuchman, *Making News: A Study in the Construction of Reality* (New York: Free Press, 1978).

39. Karen S. Johnson, "The Portrayal of Lame-Duck Presidents by the National Print Media," *Presidential Studies Quarterly* 16 (Winter 1986): 50-65.

40. Sandra William Ernst, "Baseball or Brickbats: A Content Analysis of Community Development," *Journalism Quarterly* 49 (Spring 1972): 86-90.

41. Gerald Stone, Barbara Hartung, and Dwight Jensen, "Local TV News and the Good-Bad Dyad," *Journalism Quarterly* 64 (Spring 1987): 37-44.

42. George Gerbner, Larry Gross, Michael Morgan, and Nancy Signorielli, "Charting the Mainstream: Television's Contributions to Political Orientations," *Journal of Communication* 32 (Spring 1982): 106-107. Small-town newspapers are more apt to highlight the positive, telling what is good rather than what is bad, because conflict is less tolerable in social systems where most of the leaders constantly rub elbows.

43. For evidence that media watchdog functions increase as differentiation and pluralism increase in a social system, see Clarice N. Olien, George A. Donohue, and Phillip J. Tichenor, "The Community Editor's Power and the Reporting of Conflict," *Journalism Quarterly* 45 (Summer 1968): 243-252. See also Bruce Cole, "Trends in Science and Conflict Coverage in Four Metropolitan Newspapers," *Journalism Quarterly* 52 (Fall 1973): 465-474.

44. The term is Michael J. Robinson's. See Robinson, "American Political Legitimacy in an Era of Electronic Journalism: Reflections on the Evening News," in *Television as a Social Force: New Approaches to TV Criticism,* ed. Richard Adler (New York: Praeger, 1975), 97-139. Stone and Grusin, "Bad News Bearer," 521, report that only 25 percent of nightly television news is "good news."

45. Stephen E. Rada, "Manipulating the Media: A Case Study of a Chicano Strike in Texas," *Journalism Quarterly* 54 (Spring 1977): 109-113. Also see Gadi Wolfsfeld, "Symbiosis of Press and Protest: An Exchange Analysis," *Journalism Quarterly* 61 (Autumn 1984): 550-555.

46. Klaus Bruhn Jensen, "News as Ideology: Economics Statistics and Political Ritual in Television Network News," *Journal of Communication* 37 (Winter 1987): 8-27; Thomas Skill, James D. Robinson, and Samuel P. Wallace, "Portrayal of Families on Prime-Time TV: Structure, Type and Frequency," *Journalism Quarterly* 61 (Summer/Autumn 1987): 360-368.

47. For a strong attack on status quo support, see Herbert J. Schiller, *The Mind Managers* (Boston: Beacon Press, 1973). See also Claus Mueller, *The Politics of Communication* (London: Oxford University Press, 1973).

48. Social forces are "more important than reporters' personalities in shaping the news" according to Warren Breed in "Social Controls in the Newsroom," *Social Forces* 33 (1955): 326-335. Reporters think otherwise. See Ruth C. Flegel and Steven H. Chaffee, "Influence of Editors, Readers, and Personal Opinions on Reporters," *Journalism Quarterly* 48 (Winter 1971): 645-651.

49. Sigal, *Reporters and Officials,* 119-130. On the use of government sources for economic news, see Stephen D. Reese, John A. Daly, and Andrew P. Hardy, "Economic News on Network Television," *Journalism Quarterly* 64 (Spring 1987): 137-144.

50. A comparison of war movies made with and without Pentagon aid showed that aided movies depicted the military in a more favorable light. Russell E.

Shain, "Effects of Pentagon Influence on War Movies, 1948-70," *Public Opinion Quarterly* 38 (Fall 1972): 641-647.

51. George Comstock and Robin Cobbey, "Watching the Watchdogs: Trends and Problems in Monitoring Network News," in *Television Network News: Issues in Content Research,* ed. William Adams and Fay Schreibman (Washington, D.C.: George Washington University, 1978), 47-63. For a fuller exploration of this issue, see David L. Altheide, *Creating Reality: How T.V. News Distorts Events* (Beverly Hills, Calif.: Sage, 1976); Gaye Tuchman, *Making News* (New York: Free Press, 1978); and Mark Fishman, *Manufacturing the News* (Austin: University of Texas Press, 1980).

52. But sensational news often contains a great deal of information. See C. Richard Hofstetter and David M. Dozier, "Useful News, Sensational News: Quality, Sensationalism, and Local TV News," *Journalism Quarterly* 63 (Winter 1986): 815-820.

53. Comstock and Cobbey, "Watching the Watchdogs," 53-55. Also see Neil J. Kressel, "Biased Judgments of Media Bias: A Case Study of the Arab-Israeli Dispute," *Political Psychology* 8 (June 1987): 211-226; and Lichter, Rothman, and Lichter, *The Media Elite,* 203-301.

54. Robert A. Peterson, George Kozmetsky, and Isabella C. M. Cunningham, "Perceptions of Media Bias Towards Business," *Journalism Quarterly* 59 (Fall 1982): 461-464.

55. Ron Aldridge, "New TV Rating System Stresses Quality Viewing," *Chicago Tribune,* April 25, 1983. Also see William Schneider and I. A. Lewis, "Views on the News," *Public Opinion* 8 (August/September 1985): 8-11, 58-59. The authors report the results of a *Los Angeles Times* nationwide survey in 1985 in which the public gave their newspapers a 96 percent positive rating when "very good" and "fairly good" ratings are combined. Local television received a 95 percent positive rating, and network television news ratings were 91 percent positive.

Readings

Altheide, David L. *Creating Reality: How TV News Distorts Events.* Beverly Hills, Calif.: Sage, 1976.

Brendon, Piers. *The Life and Death of the Press Barons.* New York: Atheneum, 1983.

Gitlin, Todd, ed. *Watching Television.* New York: Pantheon Books, 1987.

Goldstein, Tom. *The News at Any Cost: How Journalists Compromise Their Ethics to Shape the News.* New York: Simon and Schuster, 1985.

Manoff, Robert Karl, and Michael Schudson, eds. *Reading the News.* New York: Pantheon Books, 1987.

Matusow, Barbara. *The Evening Stars: The Rise of the Network News Anchors.* Boston: Houghton Mifflin, 1983.

Roshco, Bernard. *Newsmaking.* Chicago: University of Chicago Press, 1975.

van Dijk, Teun A. *News as Discourse.* Hillsdale, N.J.: Lawrence Erlbaum, 1988.

CHAPTER 4

Press Freedom and the Law

If prisoners confess to a visiting reporter that they have raped fellow prisoners, should the reporter be forced to reveal the assailants' identities? If a prominent army general becomes the subject of a documentary that allegedly libels him, must the media reveal how they compiled the story? Should journalists be allowed to destroy a citizens' privacy by disclosing his personal life simply because he has become involved in a well-publicized event?

The answers vary depending on whether a journalist or an average citizen outside the media ranks is polled. Most journalists agree that the press must be kept as free as possible to publish what it wishes and to shield the identity of the sources who provide sensitive information. The courts, especially at the highest levels, generally agree. But the public increasingly feels otherwise. In 1988 the Libel Defense Resource Center reported that the media lose nine out of ten libel cases heard by juries of ordinary citizens. Moreover, the monetary penalties assessed against the media at low judicial levels have increased sharply in recent years. Despite these indications of public dissatisfaction, the media victory score remains high, close to 90 percent, when libel cases dismissed before trial and those reversed on appeal are considered.[1]

The conflict between juries representing average citizens on the one side and media personnel and high-level judges on the other reflects perplexing dilemmas faced by democratic societies. How can freedom of the press to report all news be reconciled with protection of society from the dangers of unrestrained publicity? How can the right to compel needed testimony be squared with the media's need to protect news sources?

111

We will begin to answer those questions by probing the problems that arise when a free press claims the exclusive right to decide what to publish and what to omit, a right that often clashes with demands by citizen groups for newspaper space and air time to publicize social and political causes. Another problem the press has is gaining unrestrained access to information needed for a story when the government claims the right to conceal this information. Finally, we will examine barriers to publication that have been imposed by legislators and courts to safeguard private and public interests.

The First Amendment is the constitutional basis for most of the laws and court decisions about the right of access to the press and freedom to gather news and publish it. The amendment guarantees that "Congress shall make no law ... abridging the freedom of speech or of the press." This makes the fourth estate the only private business in America that is expressly protected by the Constitution. The dimensions of this protection, however, have fluctuated since the First Amendment was ratified in 1791. Moreover, similar protections in state constitutions have often been construed in ways that differ from interpretations at the national level.[2]

The Founding Fathers granted this special protection to the press because they believed that the right to collect and disseminate information and opinions is the bedrock of a free society.[3] If restraints are needed to protect society from harmful information, they must come through the deterrent effects of fear of punishment after publication, not through "prior restraint." Publication can be prevented only if it "will surely result in direct, immediate, and irreparable damage to our nation or its people." [4] The belief in the political importance of a free press has stood the test of time and remains a cornerstone of American democracy. Therefore, anything that affects the interpretation or the scope of this basic right is a matter of major political significance.

Access to the Media

The notion of government "by the people" seems to imply that the people have a right to make their voices heard. Ralph Nader's consumer protection movement or the tax revolt led by California activist Howard Jarvis could never have gathered widespread support throughout the country without mass media publicity. What would have happened if the media had refused to tell these stories? Did Nader and Jarvis have a right to mass media publicity for their views and for their organizing activities?

The answer is "no." In the absence of such a right, it is very difficult for most people, other than journalists or major public figures, to gain access to the media. In his book *Freedom of the Press for Whom?*

The Right of Access to the Mass Media, Jerome Barron, a lawyer interested in civil liberties, accused the media of fighting for broad rights of free expression for themselves while denying these same rights to the public.[5] Media personnel decide what stories to publicize and whose views to present. This leaves many who want to proclaim their views without a suitable public forum.

Barron argued that the First Amendment right to publish freely should be open to all individuals and groups, not only to news professionals. If individuals have a special cause or feel that some of the situations depicted by the mass media are not presented accurately, or that certain information is omitted, they should have an opportunity to use the mass media to state their views. Without this right, they may be doomed to political ineffectiveness.

Print Media

What rights of access to the mass media do individuals in private and public life have? To answer this question accurately, a distinction must be made between print and electronic media. American courts have usually held that the freedom of the print media to determine what they will or will not print, and whose views they will present, is nearly absolute. As long as the media stay clear of deliberate libel and slander and do not publish top-secret information, they may make publishing decisions unhampered by legal restraints. Even restraints on publishing false or misleading information are lacking.

The freedom of the press to publish or suppress information is delineated in the case of *Miami Herald Publishing Company v. Tornillo* (1974).[6] At issue was the constitutionality of a Florida statute that gave candidates for public office who had been personally attacked by a newspaper a right of reply. A candidate attacked on the editorial page had the right to reply on the editorial page in a format similar to that used by the accuser. If the attack appeared in the news pages, the candidate had the right to equal space, type, and position there. The law had been passed to deal with the problem of personal attacks published very late in a campaign, giving candidates little time for a rebuttal. The consequence might be loss of the election.

The case arose in 1972 when Patrick Tornillo, Jr., leader of the Dade County Teachers Union, was running for the Florida State Legislature. Just before the primary the *Miami Herald* published two editorials objecting to Tornillo's election because he had led a recent teacher's strike. Tornillo demanded that the paper print his replies to the editorials. The paper refused. After Tornillo lost the primary decisively, he brought suit against the paper.

The case went through the Florida court system, with lower court rulings overturned at higher stages. Finally, in 1974 it reached the U.S.

Supreme Court, which ruled unanimously that newspapers can print or refuse to print anything they like. Editors have an unlimited right to decide what goes in or what stays out of the paper. No one, including a candidate whose reputation has been damaged, has the right to demand space in a newspaper. Therefore, the Florida statute granting a right to reply was unconstitutional. The decision reaffirmed what had been the thrust of the law all along. Private citizens may request that a story or response to a personal attack be printed and that request may be granted, but they have no right to demand publication.[7]

Electronic Media

The rules are different for the electronic media, based on the view that limited spectrum space makes them semimonopolies. Unlike the print media business, which is open to anyone, entry into the electronic media business requires a license from the government. License holders are subject to government regulations, including rules ensuring that the license holders do not prevent public access to the airways in situations where access may be especially crucial.

The public's access rights fall under three categories: the *equal time provision,* the *fairness doctrine,* and the *right of rebuttal.* These access rights are based on Section 315 of the Communications Act of 1934 and its amendments and interpretations. The equal time provision requires that broadcasters who permit a candidate for political office to campaign on their stations must give equal opportunities to all other candidates for the same office. Under the fairness doctrine, broadcasters who air controversial issues of public importance must provide reasonable opportunities for the presentation of conflicting viewpoints. The right of rebuttal requires that an attack on the honesty, character, or integrity of an identified person or group entitles the targets of the attack to a reply. The broadcaster must notify the targets about the offending broadcast and must supply a transcript or summary. Thereafter, a reasonable opportunity to respond must be provided. All of the regulations that mandate public access are subject to one very important implicit condition: the rights arise only after the station has broadcast the information in question.

The Right to Equal Time. If a station gives or sells time to one candidate for a specific office, it must make the same opportunity available to all candidates for that office. Even if there are fifteen candidates for the same office, they all have a right to equal time, including those with few backers. By the same token, whenever the station denies time to all candidates for the same office, none of them has a right to demand access under the campaign coverage provisions of Section 315. The rules exclude coverage provided through regular news programs and selected talk shows that have been specifically exempted.

Stations constrained by the all-or-none equal time rule often opt for "none," particularly for state and local offices. This keeps many viable candidates off the air who might otherwise have gained exposure. But it saves stations from cluttering their programs with numerous campaign broadcasts that would be of little interest to their listeners and costly to the station in lost advertising revenues.

To make it possible to stage lengthy debates among mainline candidates for major offices without running afoul of the equal time provisions, Congress suspended these provisions in 1960. This permitted Kennedy and Nixon to debate. A different tactic was used in 1976 and 1980. To facilitate the Carter-Ford and Carter-Reagan debates, the Federal Communications Commission (FCC) permitted them to be staged as public meetings, which can be covered by the news media like regular news that is not subject to the equal time rule.

Billing the 1976 and 1980 presidential debates as public meetings arranged by the League of Women Voters and covered by the press like any newsworthy event was obviously a subterfuge to avoid the intent of the law. Several minor party candidates, eager to be included in the debates, sued in 1976 on the ground that this circumvention of equal time provisions was an illegal ruse. But the courts ruled against them. Finally, in November 1983 the FCC reversed its previous position by declaring that radio and television broadcasters were free to stage political debates at all political levels among candidates of their own choosing. The sole remaining restriction on debates is that broadcasters must not "favor or disfavor" any particular candidate. Candidates who feel that they have been unfairly shut out may appeal to the commission.[8]

The curbs on political dialogue other than debates have led to widespread dissatisfaction with the equal time rule. Many observers believe that the rule has done more political harm than good. It has blocked the public from receiving many important messages by current and prospective public officials. For instance, when President Gerald R. Ford set forth his farm policy in a speech to the Future Farmers of America in 1976, the networks shied away from full-length coverage because it might involve them in an equal time allotment for the Democratic candidate. Normally, they would have broadcast a presidential speech outlining major policy proposals. Critics are also unhappy about public sanction of subterfuges to evade the rule and about piecemeal legalized exceptions.

The Right to Fair Treatment. The fairness doctrine has a broader reach than the equal time provision because it is not limited to candidates for political office. Under the fairness doctrine reasonable time must be given for the expression of opposing views if a highly controversial public issue is discussed. What constitutes such an issue is a matter to be ultimately decided by the courts. In an average year fewer than 10 percent of the fifteen thousand charges of unfairness are sustained.

Like the equal time provision, the fairness doctrine has impoverished public debate by suppressing controversy. The media frequently shy away from programs dealing with controversial public issues to avoid demands to air opposing views in place of regular revenue-producing programs.

When controversial programs have been aired, it has been difficult to decide who has the right to reply. For instance, when President Richard Nixon justified America's incursion into Cambodia during the Vietnam War, three groups immediately demanded time to broadcast counterarguments: a group of Democratic senators, the Democratic National Committee, and a group of business executives organized to oppose the war. These three groups differed in their assessment of the errors committed by the president, and none was willing to yield to any of the others.

The media finally gave air time to the Democratic National Committee to speak for Nixon's opposition. Members of the Republican National Committee then claimed that the Democratic National Committee had used its time for political propaganda unrelated to the Cambodian situation. Therefore they asked for time to counter the views expressed by the Democrats. The whole affair became almost ridiculous. The courts settled the problem of choosing among opponents by ruling that no group has the right to expound its particular brand of opposition. Rather, it is up to the media to decide which opposing group will be heard.

This decision gives the media great control over the types of opposition views that will be aired. If media personnel favor certain views, they can select representatives of those views. Furthermore, the most prominent groups who wish to be heard are the most likely to be selected. For instance, if a group of senators and prestigious businesspeople is competing with members of a student organization to speak for the opposition, it is unlikely that the students will be selected as spokespersons. Groups that hold unconventional views or whose politics are on the extreme right or left are also unlikely choices. This sharply reduces their chances for challenging the power structure. It is one of many ways in which media practices perpetuate the established social order.

The media can entirely avoid the problem of air time for opposing views by including opposing views on controversial issues in their regular news programs. For instance, when Democratic party officials demanded air time in 1982 to rebut Republican television commercials that supported President Reagan's economic policies, the networks declined. The FCC upheld their position, ruling that opposition to Reaganomics had been fully aired in regular newscasts. Generally, the FCC and the courts have sustained the media's contentions if they are supported by reasonably good evidence. The courts have also ruled against an automatic right to oppose statements made during presidential news conferences, as long as the media air contrary views in news analyses immediately after the conferences.

The media thus retain control over the array of viewpoints that receive a hearing. Pressures and litigation, however, have made the media more receptive to featuring opposing views voluntarily. It has become traditional to allow spokespersons for the opposition to offer rebuttals after presidential, gubernatorial, and mayoral messages covering major policy issues. The temper of the times has thus curbed editorial freedom, even though legal rights remain unchanged.

Is there a right of reply to contentious statements made in business commercials? The oil industry, conservationists, and the drug industry, among other groups, have used commercials to raise questions about controversial public policies. Commercial firms and public interest groups have asked for time to respond. The question about response rights arises because First Amendment protections do not automatically extend to commercial messages. In fact, such messages have been subject to considerable restraints on the freedom of expression through truth-in-advertising laws administered by the Federal Trade Commission. If the media must make time available to respond to commercial messages, must it be free of charge? The answer is unclear.

A landmark case in 1969 seemed to indicate that there was a right to reply to commercial messages. It concerned television advertisements for cigarettes before such commercials were banned from television. John W. Banzhaf III, a young Manhattan lawyer and antismoking activist, accused the cigarette companies of promoting the glamour of cigarette smoking without advertising its dangers. He demanded the right to present views opposed to smoking, a life and death public health issue. The networks countered that opposition to smoking had been adequately presented by commercials and publications from various health organizations concerned with cancer and heart and lung disease. The Supreme Court sided with Banzhaf. It held that smoking involved such an extraordinarily important health issue that, contrary to usual rules, broadcasters must balance cigarette commercials with antismoking spots.[9]

This decision did not supply a yardstick to determine which issues are exceptional enough to warrant time for countercommercials. The case has turned out to be the exception rather than the rule. In all subsequent cases claims for countercommercial time have been refused. The law remains very unclear about the right to reply to commercial messages because the courts have spoken with forked tongues. The practice of media enterprises in allowing replies has also been quite mixed.

The Right of Rebuttal. Individuals who are assailed on radio or television in a way that damages their reputation have the right of rebuttal. The landmark case *Red Lion Broadcasting Co. v. Federal Communications Commission* (1969) established a rather broad scope for the right of reply.[10] The case arose because a book by Fred J. Cook, a very liberal newsman, about Barry Goldwater, a conservative senator, was attacked by the Rev. Billy James Hargis on a program conducted and paid for by the ultraconservative Christian Crusade. Fred Cook asked for broadcast time, free of charge, to reply. The station was willing to sell him reply time, but it refused to grant it free of charge, disclaiming responsibility for the content of programs for which various groups had bought television time. If the stations were forced to grant free rebuttal time for statements on such broadcasts, they could not afford to sell time to private broadcasters who might air controversial right- or left-wing views.

In the *Red Lion* case, to the delight of proponents of ready public access to the airwaves, the courts sided with the plaintiff. Cook was granted the right of rebuttal, at station expense, on the grounds that maligned individuals deserve a right to reply and that the public has a right to hear opposing views. The decision proved to be a hollow victory for supporters of free access, however, because it led to sharp curtailment of air time for controversial broadcasts.

The *Red Lion* case is one of many examples of political manipulation of the regulatory process. Cook's protest had been paid for and orchestrated by the Democratic National Committee as part of an effort to generate an avalanche of demands for rebuttals to conservative radio and television programs. The hope was that stations would then cancel these programs to avoid the costs of free rebuttal time.[11] This did, indeed, happen. By 1975 the Christian Crusade had been dropped by 300 of its 350 stations. Since 1969 the courts have retreated somewhat from their broad support for the right of rebuttal at station expense because of its chilling effects on controversial broadcasts. The flood of rebuttal requests also mired the FCC in a morass of claims and counterclaims that it could not process with its limited resources.

Reform Proposals. To halt the deleterious effects on programming and the flood of FCC proceedings, strong demands have been voiced by members of Congress and many broadcasters and communication scholars to do away with all the access provisions linked to Section 315 equal time, fairness, and right of rebuttal provisions. The pleaders contend that there is no longer any reason to consider electronic media as semimonopolies, in contrast to presumably competitive print media. In fact, print media in the age of one-newspaper towns face less competition than do electronic media with their competing networks and competition among multiple radio and television outlets. Besides, the distinction between print and electronic media is becoming increasingly blurred since newspapers can now transmit news and editorials through electronic channels for reception on television screens. Therefore, the electronic media should be just as free as the print media to make publishing decisions. The quality and fairness of programming decisions, and their success in presenting a wide array of viewpoints on controversial issues, should be judged from a long-range perspective at license renewal time rather than case by case. Renewal of a station's license should hinge on adequate performance over the entire five-year period. Such reforms, proponents claim, would encourage stations to air controversies while still providing a balance of views over a period of time.[12]

Opponents of reform point to the airing of many controversial programs despite Section 315. They warn that removal of access protections will leave the public at the not-so-tender mercies of media gatekeepers. As Jerome Barron has passionately lamented, "The myth says that if the press is kept 'free,' liberty of discussion is assured. But, in how few hands is left the exercise of 'freedom'!"[13] The vast influence of the electronic media on public perceptions requires safeguards stronger than ordinary market forces, others argue. If audience rights are paramount, as the *Red Lion* case affirms, shouldn't the audience be protected from media unfairness and misjudgment?[14]

To ensure survival of the fairness doctrine, Congress passed a bill making it law in the spring of 1987. President Reagan promptly vetoed the bill, and attempts to override the veto have failed. Subsequently, the FCC ruled unanimously that the fairness doctrine is unconstitutional.[15] Although the doctrine's goal had been fairness, it had "in fact resulted in 'blandness' or 'nothingness.'"[16] Major media organizations were delighted with the ruling and prepared to battle for its support by the courts, should that become necessary. Meanwhile, the fairness provisions are in limbo.

Problems of the Status Quo

Apart from the right to reply to a personal attack, to request time to express opposing views when controversial matters of public interest are aired, and the right of rival candidates to equal broadcast time, there are no access rights for individuals. Short of getting into the media business, there is no way to bring messages to public attention through the mass media if the media are unwilling. A federal court in Birmingham, Alabama, ruled in 1981 that public television enjoys complete editorial freedom as well. A group of citizens had sued the Alabama Education Television Network because it cancelled the film "Death of a Princess" in response to protests by Saudi Arabia's royal family and threats of economic boycott. The citizens had charged unfair denial of their right of access to information and claimed that the cancellation constituted political censorship. The court disagreed.[17]

Large news organizations increasingly guarantee exclusive broadcast rights to major events to a single media enterprise. This practice is another restraint on information dissemination. All news outlets, aside from the contract holder, are precluded from covering the event.[18] Exclusive contracts have been negotiated even for public spectacles such as the rededication of the Statue of Liberty during its centennial. The television networks have also been very restrictive in airing public information programs by professionals outside their own organization. Similarly, professional organizations have frequently restrained the flow of news to the general public. For instance, when scientists discovered that aspirin could prevent heart disease, they felt constrained to withhold the news for many months until the *New England Journal of Medicine,* a highly regarded professional publication owned by the Massachusetts Medical Society, had first published their reports. The power of the journal to act as the gatekeeper for major medical news springs from the fact that scientists prize the prestige derived from publication of their work in the journal. If they violate journal rules by releasing data to the lay public prior to publication in a medical journal, their story may be rejected for publication.[19]

People in public office who want access to the mass media to explain their views face problems quite similar to those of private individuals. Although the media are likely to be more sympathetic to their requests, on many occasions coverage is denied. For instance, Gov. Dan Walker of Illinois (1972-1976) repeatedly asked the media in his state to broadcast his speeches dealing with important public policies, such as appropriations for educational programs. The broadcast media refused his requests, saying that they had amply covered his policies in regular news broadcasts. They did not want to give him air time because it might force them to allot time for opposing views. When the governor challenged their right to deny air time in court, the judge supported the broadcasters. Not even a governor, the court ruled, has the right to access to the airwaves to explain his policies to the public.

Prior to the Nixon presidency (1969-1974), presidential requests for air time were routinely granted. This is no longer the case. Several speeches by Presidents Nixon, Ford, and Reagan were not broadcast at all because the media considered them partisan political statements or claimed that they contained nothing new. Others were carried by only a few stations, forcing the president to compete against regular entertainment broadcasts. This reduced the president's audience sharply. On still other occasions broadcasts of presidential speeches have been deferred until late evening, denying the president access to prime-time audiences. During the Carter and Reagan presidencies, such problems were often prevented by tailoring presidential requests for media time to the needs of the media. In particular, schedule conflicts with major sports events have been avoided.

The question of access rights to the airwaves also has been raised in connection with population groups whose concerns are different from those of the general public. Several public interest groups have objected to the lack of programs for young children and have asked for more programs, even though they would be of little interest to the majority of listeners and viewers. The FCC has concurred that children constitute an important special audience whose needs for distinctive programming must be met. Stations have been reluctant to add children's programs because revenues from them are comparatively low, particularly after the FCC, as a result of lobby pressures, reduced the amount of advertising permitted on children's programs. Curtailment of advertising was intended to spare immature viewers from the temptations offered by advertising.

Other audiences whose right of access to special programs has been recognized sporadically include blacks, Hispanics, and lovers of classical music. Occasional rulings have forced the electronic media to set aside time for broadcasts geared to such groups, whose needs might be ignored if the forces of the economic marketplace were allowed full rein. The FCC has further protected the interests of these groups by giving preference in license applications to stations whose output is likely to serve neglected clienteles. But in light of the growing number of television and radio outlets, making access easier for everyone, government protection of special interest groups is declining. In 1981 the Supreme Court freed the FCC from any obligation to weigh the effects of alternative program formats on various population groups when making licensing decisions. The Court's ruling arose from a series of cases in which radio stations had changed their format, for instance, from all news to all music.[20]

Other Approaches to Media Access

Attempts to gain access to the mass media through independently produced programs, individual requests for air time, and FCC rulings that support the interest of minority audiences have been only moderately successful. Other routes to access are even less satisfactory. Letters to the editor are an example. Due to lack of space, most papers publish few letters. The *New York Times,* for instance, receives more than sixty thousand letters a year and publishes 4 to 5 percent of them, limiting length strictly. Even with these stringent controls, space devoted to letters equals space for editorials in the *Times*. Editors select the letters to be published, using a variety of criteria that discriminate against those from average people. Letters that are unusual or are sent by someone well known are most likely to be printed.

Another avenue to access is the use of paid advertisements. Labor unions, business enterprises, lobby groups, and even foreign governments have placed advertisements in newspapers, such as the *New York Times* and *Wall Street Journal,* and on the air to present their side of disputes and public policy issues. This route is usually open to large companies, such as W. Grace and the Mobil Corporation, that can afford the steep purchase price, which may run into thousands of dollars for full-page advertisements and national broadcast exposure. However, print and electronic media have occasionally refused to print advertisements or sell air time when messages seemed to them too controversial—on topics like the energy crisis and deficit spending, for example.

Access to air time was also denied in 1975 to the Republican National Committee, which wanted to buy three half-hour slots on national television to explain the party's philosophy and goals to the public. The courts upheld the networks' right to refuse to sell time as long as this policy was applied evenhandedly for all similar organizations. The courts have also upheld the right of newspapers to refuse to sell advertising space as long as refusal is not used to discriminate against particular groups. However, the newspaper decisions have not been as clear-cut as the television decisions. In some instances courts have ordered papers to accept controversial advertising as long as advertising space for miscellaneous announcements was for sale.

Most people who would like to publicize their views cannot afford the high cost of advertising. This leads to periodic attempts to gain attention by creating a sensational event and inviting the media to witness it. A young draft resister used the tactic in 1969 when he invited the media to watch while he publicly burned his draft card. The ensuing free publicity reached well over 2 million people. It also led to the conviction of the draftee for draft law violations.[21] A worse fate befell a man who invited the media to a self-immolation to protest unemployment in 1983. Camera crews filmed the action while the protester suffered life-threatening burns. The story received nationwide coverage, but the emphasis was on the callousness of the film crew that did not stop the burning. The unemployment issue was well-nigh ignored.[22]

The rise of lobby groups eager to ensure broad access rights to people with minority viewpoints, and the FCC's sympathy with their pleas, have made broadcasters more sensitive to pressures for access by political activists. But even if radio or television station management is willing to grant access to such people, especially when they have engaged in newsworthy activities, there still is the problem of insufficient time to air every claimant's views. Despite the multiplication of television and radio channels in the wake of technological advancements, there will never be enough channels or even newspaper pages to publicize all important views to large audiences. Nor do concerned citizens have the time or capacity to listen to all significant views and put them into proper perspectives. In fact, the capacity to broadcast and publicize already far exceeds the audience's capacity to listen and assimilate. Studies of cable system users have shown that regardless of the number of channels available and the important stories that they may feature the average viewer rarely taps more than six.

Access to Information

Special Access for the Media?

The right to publish without restraint means little if information cannot be obtained. This raises the question of whether the media do and should have a special right of access to places where they wish to gather information. Supreme Court decisions have denied the existence of special rights. In *Zemel v. Rusk* (1965), for instance, a citizen sued to claim his right to a passport to visit Cuba and learn about conditions there. The Court upheld the State Department's ban on Cuban travel and ruled that neither ordinary citizens nor media personnel have a right to gather information. In the Court's words, "The right to speak and publish does not carry with it the unrestrained right to gather information." [23] A similar ruling was handed down in *Branzburg v. Hayes* (1972), a case involving a newsman's right to refuse testimony before a grand jury because he wanted to protect his sources. "It has generally been held," noted the Court, "that the First Amendment does not guarantee the press a constitutional right of special access to information not available to the public generally." [24] The press had argued that its status as the fourth branch of government, surveying the political scene for the public, entitled it to special rights of access.

The decisions denying such rights exclude journalists from access to many politically crucial events and thus deprive the public of important, albeit sensitive, information. Closed White House and Camp David meetings provide many examples. Other events that are often barred to the media are pretrial hearings and grand jury proceedings that determine the sufficiency of evidence of wrongdoing to justify indictments. Because grand jury proceedings frequently involve high political stakes, news about them has repeatedly been leaked to newspeople by participants. The press also has no right to attend conferences of the Supreme Court where the justices reveal why they decided to hear certain cases and refused to hear others. Media people may be barred from attending sessions of legislative bodies closed to the general public. Such sessions ordinarily deal with secret information that may require protection or with matters that might prove embarrassing to legislators.

Newspeople have no right to be admitted to sites of crimes and disasters when the general public is excluded. Nor do they have the right to visit prisons and interview and film inmates, even for the purpose of investigating prison conditions and rumors of brutality. In many cases where access has been denied, the Supreme Court has stressed that reporters could get the information they needed without special access privileges.[25] This may indicate that the Court is willing to grant access in situations where information about prison conditions is totally lacking.

Many of the Supreme Court's decisions in the early 1970s regarding access to information were highly controversial, as shown by 5 to 4 divisions in *Branzburg v. Hayes* (1972), *Pell v. Procunier* (1974), and *Saxbe v. Washington Post Co.* (1974).[26] This clash of views among the justices has made media access rights a very fluid and exciting area of legal development. A great deal of pressure has also been exerted on Congress to pass legislation that would clear up some of the uncertainties. Advocates of broadened access rights have been especially vocal.

By custom, although not by law, newspeople often receive preferred treatment in gaining entry to public events. Press passes ensure media access to the best observation points for inaugurations of chief executives, space shuttle landings, and political conventions. In many instances the media are admitted (for example, to the scene of accidents and crimes), while the general public is kept out. Access, however, is purely at the discretion of the public authorities in charge.

In wartime military officials often bar news personnel from combat zones. They keep them out by denying transportation to these areas or, as happened in Grenada in October 1983, by keeping invasion plans secret. Initial news accounts of American forces' invasion of this tiny Caribbean island were vague and often contradictory because the administration had banned the press. The closest reporters could get was the island of Barbados, some 150 miles away. Two days after the invasion, fifteen reporters were allowed to visit Grenada for a few hours under strict military supervision. On subsequent days two larger groups followed. Press restrictions remained in force for a full week.

Such tactics can effectively shut newspeople out of reporting crucial political events. Government spokespersons argued that the ban was necessary to ensure secrecy for the initial assault and to protect the safety of the journalists. Journalists disagreed on both scores and protested vigorously. The Grenada news blackout clearly exemplifies denial of access to news without any legal recourse. Subsequently, the Department of Defense issued new regulations to ensure limited media access in similar future situations.

Access to Government Documents

General Rules. Government documents are another extremely important source of political information to which access is frequently obstructed. The Freedom of Information Act, signed by President Lyndon B. Johnson on July 4, 1966 and amended in 1974 to make the act more enforceable, ostensibly opened many government files to the news media and the general public.[27] Burdensome application requirements, however, have limited its usefulness for news personnel. Nonetheless, the act led to important revelations such as the My Lai massacre in Vietnam, CIA involvement in political affairs in Chile and Cuba, and the failure of government to protect the public from unsafe nuclear reactors, contaminated drinking water, and ineffective drugs. Most reporters, however, are content to cover readily available current news rather than use the Freedom of Information Act to dig into government files to unearth past misdeeds.

The act has been used by organized crime and narcotics traffickers to spot threats to their activities and by business firms to spy on competitors. To cope with these and other abuses, the act was amended in 1986. Fees charged to businesses for information were raised to cover the full costs of inquiries. Fees were lowered for media enterprises to encourage their search for information. Although most of the changes garnered widespread approval, some First Amendment champions criticized provisions that broadened the right of government agencies to refuse requests for information.[28]

Many types of public documents remain unavailable to reporters. When journalism professor Elsie Hebert examined federal and state access policies, she was able to get data from only thirty-eight states and the federal government.[29] Ironically, the remaining twelve states declined to provide data about their freedom of information policies. As Hebert's study disclosed, some states are more liberal than the national government under the Freedom of Information Act in giving out information; others lag far behind. Most state laws provide for access to "public records," but the states define public records differently. The narrow common law definition has been broadened piecemeal, state by state. Laws obviously constitute a public record, but are citizens entitled to inspect the minutes of the meetings that preceded passage of a law, or tapes of the proceedings, or exhibits that a legislative committee considered before passing the law? In many states the term *public record* does not encompass any information about the genesis of laws and regulations.

Applicants for information often must demonstrate a special need for a particular set of data. A journalist or private citizen cannot go into a record center and say, "I would like to examine all your records on public health matters." Exactly what is wanted must be specified, which is difficult to do without knowing what is available. The kinds of interest that must be demonstrated and the degree of precision of information requests are determined by administrators.

A widely used rule of thumb about access to information is that disclosure must be in the public interest and must not do excessive harm. Access should be denied if the harm caused by opening records is greater than the possible benefit. Accordingly, if a reporter requested the records of welfare clients for a story on welfare cheating, this request would probably be denied because it is embarrassing to many people to have others know that they need public assistance. Because there are no precise guidelines for determining what is in the public interest and what degree of harm is excessive, the judgments of public officials who control documents are supreme. Many state legislatures are unwilling to leave access policies to the discretion of administrative officials. Therefore, they list the kinds of records that may or may not be disclosed. But that approach is unsatisfactory because legislators cannot possibly foresee all types of records that may be kept. Release of records may then be stopped simply because they are not specifically mentioned in the legislation.

Certain types of documents are routinely barred from disclosure. While the reasons are usually sound, closed access may not be in the public's best interest. For example, examination questions and answers for various tests given by government agencies are usually placed beyond public scrutiny. If questions and answers to civil service examinations were published, the value of these examinations might be totally destroyed. On the other hand, if the fairness and appropriateness of examination questions for public jobs are in doubt, public scrutiny of questions and answers might be beneficial. Favoritism in grading exams of the protégés of the powerful is a widely practiced tactic that also is difficult to expose without access to graded exams. A graphic example is the scandal in Chicago about the grades of Mayor Richard Daley's sons on a real estate broker exam. The grades came to public attention, as do many closed records, through a series of "leaks" by disgruntled public employees.

Other data frequently kept from media personnel are records that could give advantage to business competitors, such as bids for work to be performed for the government. In most states the law requires competitive bidding and mandates that contracts, with some exceptions, go to the lowest bidder. Because corruption is common in awarding government contracts, reporters often are very interested in what has been bid or what promises have been made in return for contract awards. Without access to the records, investigative reporting of suspected fraud or corruption is impossible. On the other hand, secrecy is warranted because publicizing the details of a bid would unfairly allow another firm to underbid by a few dollars and thus get the contract.

Clearly, some restraints on access are essential to protect individuals, especially now when access to computerized government information can make the average citizen's life an open book for anyone adept at using social security numbers to compile individual dossiers. Yet restraints may make betrayals of the public trust easier for potential offenders. The cloak of secrecy may conceal vast areas of corruption. Finding the right balance between protection of individuals and protection of the interests of the public through media access is an extremely difficult and controversial task.

Historical and National Security Documents. Access to the records that major public officials keep of their administration is limited. These records are usually unavailable to the media and the general public until thirty years after the death of the public official. The thirty-year limit was selected to spare possible embarrassment to people whose private and public lives were entangled with that of the official. Exceptions to the thirty-year rule arise when official papers are classified as public rather than private. Because the distinction between personal and public papers is not clear, exceptions frequently are contested in court. Former president Richard Nixon sued unsuccessfully to recover control of many of his records that had been released to the media.

The closure of the private records of public officials is part of the privacy protection afforded to all individuals, but it serves a public purpose as well. For uninhibited discussion in policy making, assurance of confidentiality is essential. Without it, people will posture for an audience rather than freely address themselves to the substance of the issues that are under consideration. The danger of inhibiting free discussion also explains why deliberations prior to legislative or judicial decisions are generally closed to public scrutiny.

Documents concerning matters of national security usually cannot be published. Examples are CIA intelligence data and information about prospective negotiations or sensitive past negotiations. News about specific new weapons adopted by the United States, or stories indicating that security devices are not operating properly, may also be restricted. In some cases, however, such information is available in open files and can be pieced together into a coherent story. Government efforts to stop the publication of this kind of story have been unsuccessful in recent years, except when prohibitions about publication were a matter of law. In 1982, for instance, it became a crime to publish the names of covert intelligence agents, even when they were taken from public documents.

In the absence of laws, the story may be different. Consider this 1979 case. The federal government was able to obtain an injunction to prohibit a Wisconsin magazine, *The Progressive,* from publishing descriptions, culled from open documents, of how a hydrogen bomb can be made. The injunction amounted to prior restraint. It delayed publication for six months but was lifted when other publications disclosed most of the same information the magazine article had contained. Since the government's chances of ultimately sustaining the injunction in the Supreme Court were slim, it decided to drop its efforts to stop the story.

Of course, most instances of security censorship never reach the lawsuit stage, leaving an enormous number of documents outside the public domain. Federal officials estimated in 1982 that up to 1 million documents are labeled as *classified* annually. Another 16 million are placed beyond easy access because they contain information taken from previously classified documents. Added to these staggering statistics at the federal level are massive numbers of documents withheld by state and local officials.[30]

The main problem with security censorship lies in the determination of what information is truly sensitive and must be protected and what information should remain available to media personnel and the public. The media and, to a lesser degree, Congress have been trying to expand the range of information that is made available for publication. The president and executive agencies, charged with protecting national security, have bent over backward to protect information that might compromise security.

The most graphic illustration of this perennial battle is the *Pentagon Papers* case. Daniel Ellsberg, a former aide to the National Security Council, a high-level executive agency that plans security policy, testified in court that he had become disillusioned about U.S. military activities in Vietnam. He claimed that foreign policy information contained in a study commissioned by the Defense Department about America's gradual entrapment in the Vietnam War had been improperly classified as top secret. Its release, he thought, would turn people against the war. He copied the information surreptitiously and gave it to prominent newspapers for publication. Because the war was still in progress, the executive branch considered this a criminal breach of security and sued Ellsberg and the media that printed the information. In *New York Times Co. v. United States* (1971), the Supreme Court absolved the media, ruling that the government had been overly cautious in classifying the information as top secret.[31] In the Court's view publication did not harm the country. The case brought against Ellsberg for leaking the information was also dismissed because evidence had been collected through illegal means. While the case cleared Ellsberg and the media of the specific charges brought against them, it left the government's contention unchallenged that officials may be prosecuted for jeopardizing national security by disclosing classified information to the press. Accordingly, Samuel Loring Morison, a naval intelligence analyst, was convicted in 1985 on espionage charges for providing a British military magazine with intelligence satellite photographs.[32]

The Supreme Court decision in the *Pentagon Papers* case and subsequent lower court rulings did not end the public controversy. Analysts still disagree about whether the disclosures from the *Pentagon Papers* damaged the foreign interests of the United States. Those who concur with the Court point out that much of the information released had already been available. Dissenters counter that the information had never been compiled in a single document and published in prominent sources such as the *New York Times* and *Washington Post*. They also refer to the dismay expressed by many European leaders about spotlighting events that they had deemed confidential.

Prior to the Nixon years, if a government agency decided that certain information needed to be kept from the media, the courts usually went along with the decision. This has obviously changed. Many people still believe that the decisions to disclose or withhold security-related information from the media and the public are political and should be made by the elected legislative and executive branches rather than by the nonelected courts. They contend that the agencies that routinely deal with military and foreign policy security information are infinitely better qualified to assess matters of public security than are judges whose training is narrowly legal. Wise decisions about disclosure of national security information are particularly difficult because both the clamor of the media to obtain access and the government's contention that the information requires protection are often self-serving. What is dubbed "the public interest" may be simply the reporters' interest in furthering their careers, or the publishers' interest in making money, or the government's interest in shielding itself from embarrassment.

At times, security issues are resolved through informal cooperation between the government and the media or through self-censorship. For instance, during the Iranian hostage crisis, six American hostages were sheltered in the Canadian embassy in Teheran for several weeks. Prominent news organizations, such as NBC, CBS, *Time, Newsweek,* and the *New York Times,* were privy to this information. Following requests from the White House and State Department, they decided to withhold the news to protect the hostages, even though it meant foregoing an excellent story. The story surfaced early in 1980, after the six hostages had been smuggled out of Iran.[33] Similarly, media have refrained from providing the public with details in a number of kidnapping incidents when news stories could have jeopardized delicate negotiations between kidnappers and the would-be rescuers of the victims.

Executive Privilege. The doctrine of executive privilege is deeply intertwined with the question of the limits of secrecy. Chief executives have the right to conceal information that they consider sensitive. This privilege extends to all of their personal communications to their staffs about public matters. Prior to the Nixon years the courts usually upheld executive privilege, but decisions since then suggest that the scope of the privilege is waning.

Silence by various government departments and agencies also sharply restricts political news available to the media. Undisclosed information frequently concerns failures, incidents of malfeasance, malfunctions, or government waste. Agencies guard this type of news zealously because disclosure might harm the agency or its key personnel. Chief executives at all levels of government often issue directives restraining top officials from talking freely to journalists. In March 1983 President Reagan even directed that lie-detector tests be given to check compliance with disclosure rules. In the face of opposition, the directive was later rescinded. Although not usually enforceable, directives that muzzle public officials tend to reduce the flow of information to the press and the public.

Except for the ever-present opportunity to get information through leaks, reporters find it difficult to penetrate the walls of silence erected by publicity-shy agencies. It is far easier to rely on press handouts or publicity releases supplied by the agency or on secondary reports from agency personnel. Handout information usually reflects the sources' sense of what is news rather than the reporters'.[34]

Private Industry Documents

While the problem of government secrecy as a restraint on information collection is formidable, it is small compared with the problem of access to news stories covering the private sector of society. Many enterprises, whose operations affect the lives of millions of Americans as much or more than many government agencies, shroud their operations in secrecy. If General Motors or International Telephone and Telegraph or General Mills wants to exclude reporters from access to information about their business practices, they can do so with impunity. So can drug companies, repair shops, or housing contractors.

The Freedom of Information Act does not cover unpublished records of private businesses, except for the reports made to the government about sales or inventory figures or customer lists. As noted earlier, many of these reports are withheld from the public on the ground that business cannot thrive if its operational data are made available to its competitors.[35] Moreover, the chances that withheld information will be disclosed through leaks are infinitely less in business than in government because suspects in the private sector can be summarily dismissed.

"Sorry, boys. I was told to keep my big mouth shut."

Drawing by Levin; © 1987 The New Yorker Magazine, Inc.

Individual Rights vs. the Public's Right to Know

Thus far we have mainly considered barriers to the free flow of information imposed by the mass media to protect editorial freedom or by government or industry to shield potentially sensitive information. Next we will discuss barriers to circulation of information imposed by individuals or on behalf of individuals for the purpose of protecting the right to privacy, the right to an unprejudiced trial, the right to gather information freely, and the right to a good reputation.

Privacy Protection

How much may the media publish about the private affairs of people in public and private life without infringing on the constitutionally protected right of privacy? How much is excluded from public scrutiny because of privacy rights? The answers depend on the status of the people involved. Private individuals enjoy broad protections from publicity; people who have become public figures because their lives are of interest to the public or because they are public officials do not.

In general, state and federal courts have been fairly lenient in permitting the media to cover details about the personal affairs of people whose lives have become matters of public interest. The right to publish has been upheld more often than the right to privacy. This trend is epitomized by a 1975 Georgia case about a young woman who had been raped and murdered. To protect its privacy, the family wanted to keep her name out of stories discussing the crime. The news media did not honor the family's request and published gruesome details of the crime, naming the victim. The family sued for invasion of privacy, claiming that there was absolutely no need to disclose the name and that Georgia law prohibited the release of the names of rape victims. The U.S. Supreme Court disagreed and overturned the Georgia law. It held that crime was a matter of public record, making the facts surrounding it of public interest and publishable, despite protests by victims and their families.[36]

Circumstances may turn private individuals into public figures. This happened to Oliver Sipple, a young man in a crowd of people watching President Gerald R. Ford. Sipple prevented an assassination attempt on the president by grabbing the would-be assassin's gun. Newspeople who interviewed him checked his background and discovered that he was part of San Francisco's homosexual community. Although this had nothing to do with his impromptu action in protecting the president, it was publicized. The disclosure caused Sipple great personal difficulties. He brought suit for invasion of privacy, but the courts denied his claim, saying that he had become an "involuntary public figure" by seizing the gun and had thus forfeited his right to privacy.

Individuals may also lose their right to privacy when they grant interviews to reporters. Once the interview is given, reporters are free to round the story out with observations that were not part of the interview. They are also free to publish those facts that were told to them in confidence. If reporters, without malice, misrepresent some of the facts, this, too, is tolerated. The rationale is that the public is entitled to a full story, if it gets any story at all, and that reporting should not be unduly inhibited by fears of privacy invasion suits.

Many privacy invasion cases involve unauthorized photographs of people in public life. Jacqueline Kennedy Onassis, the widow of President Kennedy, went to court to sue one particularly obnoxious photographer for taking photographs of her private life. The court ruled that even though she was no longer the first lady, she remained a public figure. Therefore, pictures could be taken and printed without her consent. The court, however, ordered the photographer to stop harassing her.[37]

To strengthen privacy protection, the courts in recent years have permitted subjects of unsolicited investigative reports to use trespass laws to stop the media. An example is the trespassing judgment won by the fashionable restaurant, *Le Mistral,* against CBS in 1976 after reporters had entered the premises and filmed a story showing violations of New York's health code.[38] The courts also have been increasingly willing to protect people against willful infliction of emotional pain by news media. However, the Supreme Court ruled unanimously in 1988, in a case brought by the Rev. Jerry Falwell against *Hustler* magazine publisher Larry Flynt, that the work of satirists and cartoonists enjoyed full First Amendment protection.[39] Falwell's plea for privacy protection and for compensation for emotional injury was denied.

Fair Trial and the Gag Rule

The broad scope of disclosure permitted about most people in public life could be contrasted with the limited scope of disclosure that the courts permit in their own bailiwick in criminal cases. The judiciary has zealously guarded the right of accused persons to be protected against publicity that might influence judge and jury and harm their case. This has been true even though scientific evidence demonstrating that media publicity actually influences the parties to a trial is scant and somewhat contradictory.[40]

The stern posture of the courts in censoring pretrial publicity is weakening, however. In 1983 two Supreme Court justices refused to block a nationwide television broadcast about a sensational murder case scheduled for trial three weeks later. The trial involved seven white New Orleans policemen accused of the revenge slaying of four black men suspected of participation in the murder of a white police officer. The trial had been moved from New Orleans to Dallas because of prejudicial publicity in New Orleans. Similarly, a federal court refused in 1983 to prevent television stations from showing tapes of a cocaine transaction incriminating John DeLorean, a well-known automobile maker and jet-set celebrity. DeLorean's attorneys had argued that the pretrial publicity would make it impossible to impanel an impartial jury. In another case the courts ruled that incriminating tapes used in a corruption trial of several members of Congress could be publicly shown, even though some of the defendants had not been tried as yet, and the convicted defendants were appealing the case.[41] When prominent national political figures have asked to have their trials moved out of Washington because of prejudicial pretrial publicity, their requests have been almost invariably refused.[42]

The question of the permissible scope of media coverage of court cases was brought to wide public attention by two murder cases, *Shepherd v. Florida* (1951) and *Sheppard v. Maxwell* (1966).[43] In these cases the Supreme Court held that the defendants, convicted of murder, had not had a fair trial because of widespread media publicity. As Justices

Robert H. Jackson and Felix Frankfurter put it in *Shepherd v. Florida,*
"The trial was but a legal gesture to register a verdict already dictated
by the press and the public opinion [it] generated." The convictions
therefore were overturned.

Judges have the right to prohibit the mass media from covering
some or all of a court case before and during a trial, even when the
public is allowed to attend courtroom sessions. As discussed in Chapter
7, judges may make rules restraining filmed coverage or may bar it
completely. No evidence need be brought that the information covered
by the "gag" order would impede a fair trial. Gag orders may extend
even to judges' rulings that tell the media to refrain from covering a
case. Thus the fact of judicial suppression of information may itself be
hidden.

Gag orders interfere with the media's ability to report on the
fairness of judicial proceedings. They also run counter to the general
reluctance of American courts to condone "prior censorship." Nonetheless, the courts have upheld gag laws as a necessary protection for
accused persons.

Numerous reporters have gone to jail and paid fines rather than
obey gag rules because they felt that the courts were overly protective of
the rights of criminal suspects and insufficiently concerned with the
public's right to know. A 1976 decision, *Nebraska Press Association v.
Stuart,* upholds to a certain degree the reporters' views.[44] In that case
the Supreme Court reversed a gag order that had been in effect for
several months concerning coverage of a murder trial. The Court declared that careless reporting that interferes with the rights of defendants should be forestalled by judicial maneuvers other than gag laws.
For instance, trials can be moved to different jurisdictions if there has
been excessive publicity locally. Suits also can be brought against media
enterprises or individual reporters who have acted irresponsibly by
publicizing testimony from closed sessions of the courts, taking unauthorized pictures, or bribing court personnel to leak trial testimony, for
example.

The policy on gag laws is still unclear, however. Some lower courts
have failed to comply with Supreme Court directives or have evaded the
spirit of decisions. For example, instead of gagging the press, judges
have placed gags on all the principals in a case, including the plaintiffs
and defendants, their lawyers, and the jury, to prohibit them from
talking about the case, particularly to members of the press. In an
increasing number of cases, judges have barred access to information by
closing courtrooms to all observers during pretrial proceedings as well as
trials. This has not, however, stopped legal personnel, including prosecutors, from leaking information to the press when that seems advantageous.

The Supreme Court during the 1980s began to strike down a number of these restrictions, or limit their use by specifying the circumstances under which media access may be denied. In *Richmond Newspapers v. Virginia* (1980), the Court ruled that the public and the press had an almost absolute right to attend criminal trials.[45] In the same vein the justices declared in 1984 that neither newspeople nor the public may be barred from observing jury selection, except in unusual circumstances.[46] The Supreme Court appears to be moving closer to the notion that the public's access to judicial proceedings is part of the First Amendment rights guaranteed by the Constitution.

Shield Laws

Digging into the affairs of public officials and other prominent citizens or exposing the activities of criminals or dissidents often requires winning the confidence of informants with promises to conceal their identity. Newspeople are hampered in their prepublication research if a court or legislative body has the right to know the identity of their sources, to examine unpublished bits of information, and to issue subpoenas for them. If reporters disclose such information, they break their word. Their sources are likely to dry up, whether they are public officials who have leaked confidential information or underworld informers.

On the other hand, failure to disclose information may allow criminals to go unpunished and innocent victims to be denied justice. This is why media organizations at times agree to comply with subpoenas fully or partially. For instance, the networks in 1985 agreed to surrender portions of unused film scenes from the hijacking of a TWA airliner that they deemed relevant for the prosecution of the hijackers.[47]

Shield laws that protect reporters against inquiries have become particularly urgent whenever law enforcement agencies find it difficult to penetrate dissident and deviant groups. At such times these agencies are tempted to use subpoenas to compel testimony from journalists, making them unwitting agents of the government. Shield laws are also needed to protect the physical safety of sources who disclose the activities of organized criminals or terrorists.

The Supreme Court has ruled that newspeople, like ordinary citizens, generally do not have the right to protect their sources in the face of a subpoena. They have no special right to be warned about a court-approved search of their premises to uncover evidence that might reveal their sources and the information provided by them.[48] Nor may they shield records or editorial deliberations from judicial scrutiny if these records are needed to prove deliberate libel. However, if the needed information is available from unshielded sources, the judges have often excused journalists from disclosure.[49]

Recognizing the ill effects of these common law-based compulsory disclosure rules on investigative reporting of crime and corruption, more than half of the states have passed shield laws to protect reporters from forced testimony. Shield laws give journalists most of the rights enjoyed by lawyers, doctors, and clergy to shield their sources' identity and information. Shield laws also may bar searches of news offices to discover leads to crimes. The Privacy Protection Act of 1980 prohibits government authorities at all levels from conducting surprise searches of newsrooms, except in a few, clearly specified situations.[50]

Shield laws usually do not ensure absolute protection. For example, when the right of reporters to withhold the names of their sources clashes with the right of other individuals to conduct a lawsuit involving serious matters (such as gathering evidence for a murder or conspiracy trial or a libel suit), state shield laws and common law protections must yield. In 1978 *New York Times* reporter Myron Farber was fined and jailed for thirty-eight days for disobeying a court order to provide information to a murder defendant. Farber's story about a series of deaths in a New Jersey hospital had led to the trial of the physician charged with murdering the patients. In 1983 the Maryland Supreme Court ruled that Loretta Tofani, a *Washington Post* reporter, must testify about prisoners in a suburban jail who had told her about committing rape and being rape victims. The reporter's articles had won a Pulitzer Prize.[51] Likewise, CBS News was required to give Gen. William Westmoreland the text of its in-house investigation of a 1982 television documentary that had allegedly libeled the general. The documentary on the Vietnam War had charged Westmoreland with falsifying enemy troop figures. In his libel suit Westmoreland contended that producers of the documentary had deliberately omitted information that exonerated him. The U.S. District Court in New York City rejected the network's contention that its in-house report was protected by First Amendment guarantees; the network had referred in court to findings contained in the report.[52]

Some journalists advocate a federal shield law to protect all newspeople throughout the country. Others, fearing that such a law would provide conditional shielding only, prefer to do without shield laws of any kind; they contend that the First Amendment constitutes an absolute shield. These differences of opinion have taken steam out of the pressure for a federal shield law.[53] Members of the judiciary also deny that shield laws are needed, but for different reasons. In the words of Justice Byron R. White, "From the beginning of our country, the press has operated without constitutional protection for press informants and the press has flourished." Hence absence of shield laws has "not been a serious obstacle to either the development or retention of confidential news sources by the press." [54]

The power of congressional committees to compel testimony is equal to the power of the courts in this regard. A prominent 1976 case involved CBS reporter Daniel Schorr, who had received secret information about the proceedings of a congressional committee investigating CIA activities. He refused to tell the committee the name of the source who had leaked the information. Although the committee had the power to cite Schorr for contempt of Congress and punish him accordingly, it chose not to do so. Insiders saw this decision as evidence of the general trend in the post-Watergate era to permit shielding when it helps reporters investigate government misconduct.[55]

Libel Laws

For years libel suits, even when they were lost in court, had a dampening effect on investigative reporting. Then in 1964 that changed substantially for cases involving public officials. An action for libel was brought by the police chief of Montgomery, Alabama. An advertisement in the *New York Times* had charged him with mishandling civil rights demonstrations. The Supreme Court absolved the newspaper, ruling in *New York Times v. Sullivan* that a public official who claims libel must be able to show that the libelous information was published "with knowledge that it was false or with reckless disregard of whether it was false or not."[56]

The "Sullivan rule" has made it very difficult for public officials to bring suit for libelous statements made about them. Malicious intent and extraordinary carelessness are hard to prove, especially since the courts give the media the benefit of the doubt. By the same token, the Sullivan rule has made it much easier for media to publish adverse information about public officials without extensive checking of the accuracy of the information prior to its publication.

Since its 1974 decision in *Gertz v. Robert Welch,* the Supreme Court has applied more restrictive interpretations of the meaning of "public figure."[57] In that case the Court held that a prominent lawyer, whose name had been widely reported in the news, was not a public figure and could therefore sue for libel. A person who had not deliberately sought publicity, the Court ruled, would be deemed a public figure only in exceptional circumstances. What these circumstances are remains unclear.[58] However, even a private figure, suing a news organization for libel, must prove that damaging statements are false if they involve "matters of public concern."[59] Otherwise, the burden of proof that the statements are true rests on the media.

The battle between freedom of the press and the right of individuals to be protected from harmful publicity is full of confusing developments.[60] The courts have pulled back from the position that made individual rights, except the right to a fair trial, largely subordinate.

They have done so by distinguishing the rights of private individuals from those of public figures and by construing the category of "public figures" more narrowly. This leaves private individuals with substantial rights to bar the media from publishing potentially libelous or embarrassing facts, so long as those facts are not a matter of public record. Whether libel suits may be brought to challenge expressions of opinions remains controversial.[61]

By and large, laws and court decisions protecting private individuals have not greatly benefited people in public life. The principle that full publicity for the activities of public officials and institutions is essential has been reaffirmed repeatedly, most recently in the *Hustler v. Falwell* case, which strongly reaffirmed the Sullivan rule.[62] The Supreme Court has even discouraged libel suits by public figures by requiring that such suits be dismissed by the federal courts before trial if the evidence fails to suggest libel with "convincing clarity."[63] The best protection for public figures from unscrupulous exposure by the media are the informal and formal codes of ethics (discussed in Chapter 2) by which most journalists abide most of the time. The increasing number of suits by public figures against media people have also become a damper on careless reporting because these suits are costly in time and money, even when the media are exonerated. By 1983 the investigative television show "60 Minutes" had successfully defended itself in 150 libel actions, but the costs were staggering. Financially weaker programs could not have paid them; neither could they have risked multi-million-dollar judgments against them, should they lose a libel suit.

Other Restrictions on Publication

As discussed in Chapter 1, all governments prohibit the publication of certain information on the grounds that the public interest would be harmed. The United States is no exception. The areas where censorship is most prevalent are national security involving external dangers, national security involving internal dangers, and obscenity. In each category there is general agreement that certain types of information should not be publicized. There is very little agreement, however, about where the line ought to be drawn between permitted and prohibited types of material. We have already discussed the controversy surrounding the release of the *Pentagon Papers* as well as the government's efforts to prohibit publication of a magazine article detailing, on the basis of available but dispersed information, how a hydrogen bomb might be manufactured. Additional examples involving external security will be presented in Chapter 10.

Internal security news primarily entails investigations of allegedly subversive groups and reports on civil disturbances. Several relevant cases are discussed in Chapter 9. Such news also involves media portrayal of asocial behavior that might lead to imitation. Various attempts to limit the portrayal of crime and violence, either in general or on programs to which children have access, are examples. They are discussed in Chapter 5.

Closely related to restraints on the depiction of crime and violence are restraints on publication of indecent and obscene materials and broadcasts that include offensive language or portray sexual matters or human excretion. It is feared that such broadcasts may corrupt members of the audience, particularly children, and lead to imitation of undesirable behavior. Although reports of the Presidential Commission on Obscenity and Pornography have cast doubt on the claim that such broadcasts are socially dangerous, many foes of obscenity and "dirty" words remain unconvinced.

In addition, proponents of obscenity restraints argue that publication of indecent and obscene materials, particularly in visual form, offends community standards and should therefore be prohibited by law. This argument rests on the notion that the public, as represented generally by self-selected spokespersons and organized protest groups, should have the right to prohibit the dissemination of material that offends the sense of propriety of many citizens. Despite the popularity of pornography, as shown by the millions of citizens who read pornographic magazines, go to pornographic movies and stage shows, and rent pornographic videos, laws in many places bar free access to such information. Nationally, the FCC requires that indecent programming be featured only between midnight and 6:00 a.m., when children are unlikely to be watching TV. Obscene programming is barred at all times. Indecent material has been defined by the FCC as "material that depicts or describes, in terms patently offensive by contemporary community standards for the broadcast medium, sexual or excretory activities or organs." Obscenity has been defined by the Supreme Court as "something that, taken as a whole, appeals to the prurient interest; that depicts or describes in a patently offensive way sexual conduct, and that lacks serious artistic, political and scientific value." [64] The Supreme Court has repeatedly upheld these types of restrictions.

Another example of protective censorship is the ban since 1971 on cigarette advertising on radio and television. It is designed to protect susceptible individuals from being lured into smoking by seductive advertisements. Pressures for additional areas of protective censorship have been considerable and range from pleas to stop liquor, sugared cereal, and casino gambling advertisements to requests to bar information dealing with abortion or drug addition. Legislatures and courts have rejected most of them except when advertising on children's programs was involved. But the future is unclear. Some of these matters have become election issues. If candidates have committed themselves to censoring abortion or drug information, for example, they may be compelled to follow through on their promises by working for appropriate laws after election.

So-called "hate" broadcasters also remain a gray area in broadcast law. Contrary to the expressed public policy of the nation, many small stations or individual programs routinely attack racial, ethnic, and religious groups. Like broadcasts with obscene language, these attacks violate the sense of propriety of many citizens. Nevertheless, the FCC has been reluctant to withhold licenses from the offending parties because genuine freedom of expression includes "freedom for the thought we hate," as Supreme Court Justice Oliver Wendell Holmes said long ago.

The case of KTTL-FM, a small country-music station in Dodge City, Kansas, illustrates the dilemma. The station has attacked blacks, Asians, Roman Catholics, Jews, public officials, the courts, and the Internal Revenue Service. It has suggested hanging public officials, "cleansing the earth" of "black beasts," and preparing militarily for an impending racial Armageddon. But despite protests to the FCC from Kansas lawmakers and members of the public, KTTL-FM's license is unlikely to be revoked so long as no actual violence can be linked to its broadcasts.[65]

Summary

In a democratic society citizens have the right and civic duty to inform themselves and to express their views publicly. The press, as the eyes and ears of the public, shares these rights and must be protected against restraints that could interfere with its ability to gather information and disseminate it freely. In this chapter we have seen how these important basic principles have been modified to meet the realities of political life in the United States. Despite legislation such as the Freedom of Information Act of 1966, a great deal of information about government activities remains shrouded from the public's eyes. Either it has been classified as secret for security reasons, or it is not released to the public because it could embarrass individuals or lead to undesirable business practices. The public and press also are excluded from many executive sessions of legislatures, grand jury sessions, pretrial proceedings in the courts, and other official meetings if the participants so desire.

Nearly all of these exclusions have been challenged in the courts because they constitute restrictions on the right of access to information. The courts have ruled that most of them are compatible with constitutional guarantees of free speech and press. They also have ruled, for the most part, that news professionals enjoy neither greater rights of access to information than does the general public, nor, in the absence of shield laws, greater freedom to protect their access to information by refusal to disclose their sources.

The right to publish information is also limited. Here the public is most seriously restricted because newspeople claim the exclusive right to determine what to publicize and what to omit. The power of print media to refuse a forum to most citizens is nearly absolute, aside from social pressures mandating that stories of widely recognized public concern be published. Under current rules and regulations the electronic media must grant equal access to the air to political candidates for the same office. The fairness rule mandates air time for people who hold opposing views on controversial issues that have been aired. Although put to rest for the time being, the rule remains a lively ghost that may well rise again. The right of rebuttal is likely to share the fate of the fairness rule—either death is in the cards, or a reincarnation in the form of congressional legislation.

Even when access to a media forum is ensured, the right to publish is not absolute. News has been suppressed because of public policy considerations, such as the need to safeguard external and internal security and the need to protect the moral standards of the community. The scope of permissible censorship has been the subject of countless inconclusive debates and conflicting decisions by the courts.

The right to publish also conflicts on many occasions with the rights of individuals to enjoy their privacy, to be protected from disclosure of damaging information, true or false, and to be safeguarded from publicity that might interfere with a fair trial. The courts have been the main forum for weighing these conflicting claims, and the scales have tipped erratically from case to case. Two trends stand out from the haze of legal battles: the right to a fair trial generally wins out over the freedom to publish, and private individuals enjoy far greater protection from publicity than do people in public life. Shifting definitions of what turns a private person into a public person have blurred this distinction, however.

When one looks at the massive restraints on the rights of access to information, the rights of access to publication channels, and the right to publish information freely, one may feel deep concern about freedom of information. Is there cause for worry? Taking a bright view, one can point out, as Justice Byron White did in the 1972 *Branzburg* case, that "the press has flourished. The existing constitutional rules have not been a serious obstacle" stopping the press from investigating wrongdoing.[66] The press as watchdog may be chilled by legal restraints, but it is not frozen into inaction. From the perspective of champions of First Amendment rights, that may be small comfort. Many current political and judicial trends point toward greater restraints and greater public tolerance for restraints, especially when national security is involved. Constant vigilance is the price that will have to be paid to preserve the heritage of freedom of thought and expression.

Notes

1. Robert L. Hughes, "Rationalizing Libel Law in Wake of *Gertz:* The Problem and a Proposal," *Journalism Quarterly* 60 (Autumn 1985): 540-547.
2. Robert F. Copple, "The Dynamics of Expression Under the State Constitution," *Journalism Quarterly* 64 (Spring 1987): 106-113.
3. For an analysis of how well these rights have been used, see Doris A. Graber, "Press Freedom and the General Welfare," *Political Science Quarterly* 101 (Summer 1986): 257-275.
4. Justice Potter Stewart in *New York Times v. U.S.,* 403 U.S. 713 (1971).
5. Jerome Barron, *Freedom of the Press for Whom? The Right of Access to the Mass Media* (Bloomington, Ind.: Indiana University Press, 1973).
6. 418 U.S. 241 (1974).
7. For a full discussion of the case, see Fred W. Friendly, *The Good Guys, the Bad Guys and the First Amendment: Free Speech vs. Fairness in Broadcasting* (New York: Random House, 1977), 192-198.
8. Phil Gailey, "F.C.C. Lets Broadcasters Hold Political Debates," *New York Times,* November 9, 1983.
9. *Banzhaf v. Federal Communications Commission,* 405 F. 2d 1082 (D.C. Cir. 1968); cert. denied, 396 U.S. 842 (1969).
10. 395 U.S. 367 (1969).
11. Friendly, *The Good Guys,* 32-42.
12. Ibid., 199-236.
13. Barron, *Freedom of the Press,* 5.
14. For a discussion of these issues, see Jerome S. Silber, "Broadcast Regulation and the First Amendment," *Journalism Monographs,* no. 70 (Lexington, Ky.: Association for Education in Journalism, November 1980). Court cases testing the First Amendment rights of cable television broadcasters are analyzed in Peter Kerr, "Cable TV Pressing Free-Speech Issue," *New York Times,* April 5, 1984.
15. See the March 28, June 27, and August 8, 1987, issues of the *Congressional Quarterly Weekly Report.*
16. "Excerpts from F.C.C. Statement," *New York Times,* August 5, 1987.
17. *Barnstone v. University of Houston,* 514 F. Supp. 670 (D. Tex. 1980). First Amendment problems encountered when governments own media are discussed by William Hanks and Lemuel Schofield, "Limitations on the State as Editor in State-Owned Broadcast Stations," *Journalism Quarterly* 63 (Winter 1986): 797-801. The right of public broadcasters to editorialize was upheld in *League of Women Voters v. FCC,* 104 S. Ct. 3106 (1984).
18. Paula J. Lobo, "First Amendment Implications of Exclusive Broadcast Contracts," *Journalism Quarterly* 60 (Spring 1983): 41-47.
19. Lawrence K. Altman, "Medical Guardians: Does New England Journal Exercise Undue Power on Information Flow?" *New York Times,* January 28, 1988.
20. *FCC v. WNCN Listeners Guild,* 450 U.S. 582 (1981).

21. *U.S. v. Kiger*, 421 F.2d 1396 (2d Cir. 1970); cert. denied, 398 U.S. 904 (1970).
22. W. Lance Bennett, Lynne A. Gressett, and William Haltom, "Repairing the News: A Case Study of the News Paradigm," *Journal of Communication* 35 (Spring 1985): 50-68.
23. *Zemel v. Rusk*, 381 U.S. 1 (1965). See also Louis A. Day, "Broadcaster Liability for Access Denial," *Journalism Quarterly* 60 (Summer 1983): 246-261.
24. *Branzburg v. Hayes*, 408 U.S. 665 (1972) at 684.
25. See, for instance, 417 U.S. 817 (1974); *Saxbe v. Washington Post Co.*, 417 U.S. 843 (1974); and *Houchins v. KQED, Inc.*, 438 U.S. 1 (1978).
26. These and related cases are discussed more fully in John J. Watkins, "Newsgathering and the First Amendment," *Journalism Quarterly* 53 (Autumn 1976): 406-416. Citations in notes 24 and 25.
27. The act was an amendment to the 1946 Administrative Procedure Act—5 U.S.C.A. 1002 (1946)—which provided that official records should be open to people who could demonstrate a "need to know" except for "information held confidential for good cause found" (sec. 22). The 1966 amendment stated that disclosure should be the general rule, rather than the exception, with the burden on government to justify the withholding of a document, if challenged in court (5 U.S.C.A. Sec. 552 and Supp. 1, Feb. 1975).
28. Linda Greenhouse, "Agencies Get New Power to Withhold Investigative Reports," *New York Times*, October 29, 1986.
29. Elsie Hebert, "How Accessible Are the Records in Government Records Centers?" *Journalism Quarterly* 52 (Spring 1975): 23-29.
30. Robert Pear, "Information Curb Assailed by Panel," *New York Times*, August 9, 1982.
31. 403 U.S. 713 (1971).
32. Stuart Taylor, Jr., "Federal Judge Rules Espionage Laws Apply to Disclosures to Press," *New York Times*, March 15, 1985.
33. Deirdre Carmody, "Some News Groups Knew of 6 in Hiding," *New York Times*, January 31, 1980.
34. Judy Van Slyke Turk, "Information Subsidies and Media Content: A Study of Public Relations Influence on the News," *Journalism Monographs* 100 (December 1986): 1-29. For comparative views of government secrecy, see Itzhak Galnoor, ed., *Government Secrecy in Democracies* (New York: Harper and Row, 1977).
35. Richard B. Kielbowicz, "The Freedom of Information Act and Government's Corporate Information Files," *Journalism Quarterly* 55 (Autumn 1978): 481-486.
36. *Cox Broadcasting Corp. vs. Cohn*, 420 U.S. 469 (1975).
37. *Gallella v. Onassis*, 487 F. 2d 986 (1973).
38. *Le Mistral Inc. v. Columbia Broadcasting System*, 402 N.Y.S. 2d 815 (1978).
39. *Hustler v. Falwell*, No. 86-1278, 1988. See also Robert E. Drechsel, "Mass Media Liability for Intentionally Inflicted Emotional Distress," *Journalism Quarterly* 62 (Spring 1985): 95-99.
40. Interestingly, the courts maintain the fiction that judges can command jurors to strike improper information presented in court from their memory. Presumably, judges are unable to do the same for media information that jury members might have received outside the courtroom. The issue is examined in Judith M. Buddenbaum et al., "Pretrial Publicity and Juries: A Review of Research," research report 11 (Bloomington, Ind.: School of Journalism, Indiana University, March 1981).

41. See, for example, *U.S. v. Alexandro,* 675 F. 2d 34 (1982); cert. denied, 103 S. Ct. 78 (1982); *U.S. v. Jannotti,* 673 F. 2d 578 (1982); cert. denied 457 U.S. 1106 (1982); *U.S. v. Myers,* 692 F. 2d 823 (1982); *U.S. v. Williams,* 705 F. 2d 603 (1983); and *U.S. v. Kelly,* 707 F. 2d 1460 (1983).

42. A recent example is Michael K. Deaver, a White House aide indicted for perjury. In his request for a change of venue, he presented the court with 471 hostile news clips from Washington, D.C., papers. Philip Shenon, "Like Others in the Past, Deaver Says Fair Trial Isn't Possible in Capital," *New York Times,* April 22, 1987.

43. 341 U.S. 50 (1951); and 384 U.S. 333 (1966).

44. 427 U.S. 539 (1976).

45. 448 U.S. 555 (1980). The implications for the right of access are discussed in Roy V. Leeper, "*Richmond Newspapers, Inc. v. Virginia* and the Emerging Right of Access," *Journalism Quarterly* 61 (Autumn 1984): 615-622. Subsequent cases are discussed in Ann L. Plamondon, "Recent Developments in Law of Access," *Journalism Quarterly* 63 (Spring 86): 61-68.

46. Glen Elsasser, "High Court Curbs Secret Jury Selection," *Chicago Tribune,* January 19, 1984. The controversy arose because the Riverside County, California, Superior Court closed jury selection in a rape and murder case. The Press-Enterprise Company of Riverside sued to gain access to the court proceeding and to the relevant transcripts.

47. Alex S. Jones, "CBS Compromises on Subpoena for Videotapes of Hostage Crisis," *New York Times,* July 27, 1985.

48. *Zurcher v. The Stanford Daily,* 436 U.S. 547 (1978).

49. *Anthony Herbert v. Barry Lando and the Columbia Broadcasting System Inc.,* 441 U.S. 153 (1979).

50. The impact of the law is discussed in Tony Atwater, "Newsroom Searches: Is 'Probable Cause' Still in Effect Despite New Law?" *Journalism Quarterly* 60 (Spring 1983): 4-9.

51. *Tofani v. State of Maryland,* 297 Md. 165 (1983).

52. "Westmoreland/CBS Controversy," *Historic Documents of 1983* (Washington, D.C.: Congressional Quarterly, 1984), 401-412.

53. Jonathan Friendly, "Prosecutors Increase Efforts to Make Press Name Sources," *New York Times,* November 26, 1983.

54. *Branzburg v. Hayes,* id. at 699.

55. However, Schorr lost his job with CBS as a result of the incident. By suspending Schorr, the network discouraged this kind of coverage, even though Schorr's right to shield his sources was not challenged.

56. 376 U.S. 254 (1964) at 279-280.

57. 418 U.S. 323 (1974).

58. *Time Inc. v. Firestone,* 424 U.S. 448 (1976); *Hutchinson v. Proxmire,* 443 U.S. 111 (1979); and *Wolston v. Reader's Digest,* 443 U.S. 157 (1979). Also see Hughes, "Rationalizing Libel Law."

59. *Philadelphia Newspapers Inc. v. Hepps,* 106 S. Ct. 1558 (1986).

60. On fact/opinion distinctions, see Harry W. Stonecipher and Don Sneed, "Libel and the Opinion Writer: The Fact-Opinion Distinction," *Journalism Quarterly* 64 (Summer-Autumn 1987): 491-498. The problem of proving damages is discussed in David A. Anderson, "Presumed Harm: An Item for the Unfinished Agenda of *Times v. Sullivan,*" *Journalism Quarterly* 62 (Spring 1985): 24-30.

61. Hughes, "Rationalizing Libel Law, 541-542.

62. *Hustler v. Falwell,* No. 86-1278, 1988.

63. *Anderson v. Liberty Lobby,* 106 S. Ct. 2505 (1986). Also see *Bose Corporation v. Consumers Union of United States,* 104 S. Ct. 1949 (1984).
64. *Miller v. California,* 413 U.S. 5 (1973) at 15. Quoted in Irvin Molutsky, "F.C.C. Rules on Indecent Programming," *New York Times,* November 25, 1987.
65. Reginals Stuart, "F.C.C. Bars Penalty on Racism on Air," *New York Times,* April 29, 1985.
66. *Branzburg v. Hayes,* id. at 699.

Readings

Carter, T. Barton, Marc A. Franklin, and Jay B. Wright. *The First Amendment and the Fifth Estate: Regulation of Electronic Mass Media.* Mineola, N.Y.: The Foundation Press, 1986.

Chamberlin, Bill F., and Charlene J. Brown, eds. *The First Amendment Reconsidered.* New York: Longman, 1982.

Devol, Kenneth S., ed. *Mass Media and the Supreme Court: The Legacy of the Warren Years.* New York: Hastings House, 1982.

Drechsel, Robert E. *News Making in the Trial Courts.* New York: Longman, 1983.

Hemmer, Joseph J., Jr. *The Supreme Court and the First Amendment.* New York: Praeger, 1986.

O'Brien, David M. *The Public's Right to Know: The Supreme Court and the First Amendment.* New York: Praeger, 1981.

Pember, Don R. *Mass Media Law.* Dubuque, Iowa: William C. Brown, 1981.

Tunstall, Jeremy. *Communications Deregulation: The Unleashing of America's Communications Industry.* Oxford, England: Basil Blackwell, 1986.

CHAPTER 5

Media Impact on Attitudes
and Behavior

In the spring of 1987, television news featured a story about four teenagers in Bergenfield, New Jersey, who had committed suicide by inhaling carbon monoxide fumes from an automobile engine turned on in a closed garage. The pictures of the roped-off garage, funeral ceremonies, and bereaved relatives were gripping. Within a day two young women in Alsip, Illinois, committed suicide in the same manner. Once more the media recounted the circumstances in considerable detail. Within a few days five more teenagers in the Chicago area took their own lives. A suburban police chief in one of the grieving communities accused reporters of enticing the victims to suicide.

A few months later an elderly couple was severely burned when their daughter set their bedroom on fire after watching a similar incident in the television movie "The Burning Bed." Every year television conveys thousands of potentially destructive social messages: the thrills of alcohol and drug consumption and of illicit sexual encounters, unmarred by concerns about pregnancy, disease, and death; violence as a routine solution to conflicts between nations and individuals; distorted views of the societal roles played by women, minorities, the elderly, and the handicapped in today's America. Concern about the impact of media images often pervades the highest circles of government. In 1983 after ABC television broadcast the movie "The Day After," depicting how Kansas City, Kansas, might fare in a nuclear attack, President Ronald Reagan dispatched cabinet members to allay the public's worries about the threat of nuclear war. The administration feared—and antinuclear forces hoped—that the movie would drive millions of citizens into the budding movement against nuclear weapons.

These examples dramatize the many puzzling questions so often asked about the impact of mass media on children and adults. Does violence in television fiction and news programs cause violence in real life? Did reporters entice those suicide victims in Illinois? How much do people learn from the media, and what do they learn? Are people's attitudes and values about society and politics influenced by what they read and see?

In this chapter we will examine these questions, beginning with the assimilation of attitudes that occurs as an unintended byproduct of media exposure. By and large, newspeople do not try to teach political attitudes and values, nor do people try to learn them. Rather, exposure to individual, dramatic events or the incremental impact of the total flow of information over prolonged periods of time leads to "incidental" learning about the political world. We also will consider the ways in which people choose the media to which they will pay attention and the sorts of things they will learn. Finally, we will address the question posed at the start: To what degree does exposure to the mass media influence behavior in politically significant ways?

Differential Effects of Print and Broadcast News

Most Americans are exposed to combinations of all the media either directly or indirectly through contacts with people who have been exposed. We may know that American astronauts have walked on the moon. We may view this as a scientific miracle that raised the sagging prestige of the United States abroad and at home. And we may feel pride about the venture and yet some unease about its high price tag. But which of these thoughts and feelings come from television, or newspapers, or conversations, or from a combination of media? It is well-nigh impossible to disentangle such strands of information.[1]

Each medium, however, does make unique contributions to learning. For example, television, because of its visuals, is especially powerful in transmitting realism and emotional appeal. It does less well conveying the substance of events. In one fairly typical study researchers asked viewers to relate the main points of specific stories; they failed on 72 percent of them. Miscomprehension rates for individual stories ranged from 16 percent to 93 percent.[2]

Print media excel in conveying abstract ideas. Since most tests of learning from the media focus on abstract knowledge, print media are generally credited with conveying more knowledge than audio-visual media do. In fact, media scholar Neil Postman warns that massive use of television will turn America into a nation of dilettantes who avoid serious thinking and crave only entertainment. He contends that television trivializes the problems of the world. It gives people the illusion of being knowledgeable when, in fact, they are distracted from probing issues in depth.[3]

The claim that the nature of the medium accounts for differences in knowledge gain is not as clear-cut as it may seem, however. Demographic differences among media users make it difficult to judge the significance of the finding that heavy newspaper users tend to be better informed than persons who do not read the paper. Heavy users generally enjoy higher socioeconomic status and better formal education. Their status in life, therefore, provides above-average incentives for learning. Attitudes toward the media matter as well. Print media are viewed by most people as sources of information, while electronic media are viewed as sources of entertainment. However, when asked to choose either television or print news as an information source, most people opt for television for nearly all kinds of news. Television news is also deemed more credible than print news because "seeing is believing."[4] These attitudinal differences, rather than the nature of each medium, may explain the differences in effects.

Television's greatest political impact, compared with that of other media, is derived from its ability to reach millions of people simultaneously with the same images. Major broadcasts enter nearly every home in the nation instantaneously and simultaneously. Televised events become shared experiences: "The reality that lives is the reality etched in the memories of the millions who watched rather than the few who were actually there."[5] America's print media have never attained such a reach and the power that flows from it. Moreover, 23 million American adults are functionally illiterate and therefore are almost entirely beyond the reach of print media.[6] What the poorly educated now learn about politics from television may be fragmentary and hazy, but it represents a quantum leap over their previous exposure and learning.

In short, the research on the differential effects of various types of media reveals that different types present stimuli that vary substantially in nature and content. It would be surprising, therefore, if their impact were identical, even when they deal with the same subjects. Because current research does not provide adequate answers about the precise effects of these stimulus variations and about the processes by which individuals mesh a variety of media stimuli, we will focus on the end product—the combined impact of all print and electronic media stimuli.

The Role of Media in Political Socialization

Before considering the role that mass media information plays in shaping our attitudes toward society, the political importance of these attitudes must be assessed. Political socialization—the learning and internalizing of customs, rules, structures, and environmental factors governing political life—is important because it affects the quality of interactions between citizens and their government. Political systems do not operate smoothly without the support of most of their citizens, who must be willing to abide by the laws and to support government through paying taxes or performing other duties such as military service.

Support is most readily obtained if citizens are convinced of the legitimacy and capability of their government and if they feel strong emotional ties to it. If political socialization fails to instill such attitudes, policies and laws that depend on public support, such as energy conservation or traffic regulations, may become unenforceable. Refusal to pay taxes may force the government to sharply curtail its activities. If citizens hold government in contempt or regard it as illegitimate, the result may be political apathy, civil disobedience, revolution, or civil war.

In societies where the government relies on popular participation through elections and through continuous scrutiny of the government's activities, political socialization must equip citizens with sufficient knowledge to participate effectively. If it fails to do this, elections, at best, become a sham; people go through the motions of making a choice without understanding what this choice means. At worst, elections become a mockery in which clever politicians manipulate an ignorant electorate. Likewise, surveillance of government activities is impossible if people lack a grasp of the nature of government and public policies.

Childhood Socialization

Since political socialization starts in childhood, it is first conveyed by the small child's environment. From their families children usually learn basic attitudes toward authority, property, decision making, and veneration for political symbols. When children enter the more formal school setting, teaching about political values becomes quite systematic. At school, children also learn new factual information about their political and social world.

The people who teach children rely heavily on mass media for much of the information and values that they transmit. Hence children receive a great deal of media-based information indirectly from the very beginning of their intellectual development. Children's direct contacts with the media are equally abundant. In the United States millions of babies watch television. In the winter youngsters between two and eleven years of age spend an average of thirty-one hours a week in front of the television set—more time than in school. Between the ages of twelve and seventeen, this drops to twenty-four hours.[7] Eighty percent of the programs children see are intended for adults and therefore differ substantially from the child's limited personal experiences. Children watch military combat, funerals, rocket launchings, courtships, seductions, and childbirth. If they can understand the message, its impact is likely to be great since, lacking experience, they are apt to take it at face value.

This strong impact of the mass media on children's political socialization has been convincingly demonstrated by research. When asked for the sources of information on which they base their attitudes about subjects such as economic or race problems, or war and patriotism, high school students mention the mass media far more often than they mention their families, friends, teachers, or personal experiences.[8] Comparisons of youngsters who use the media heavily with those who are light users confirm that school-aged children gain substantial information from the media and that this influences their attitudes toward society. Heavy mass media users, particularly those who read newspapers, know most about current political events and show most interest in them.[9] They also show greater understanding and support for basic American values, such as the importance of free speech and the right to equal and fair treatment.[10] Media use and level of political knowledge have a greater impact on a child's political behavior than the child's grade in school, the method of instruction, or the parents' media-use patterns.[11]

The finding that mass media strongly influence socialization runs counter to earlier socialization studies that showed parents and teachers as the chief socializers. Several reasons account for the change. The first is the increasing pervasiveness of television, which makes it easy for even the youngest children to be affected by mass media images. This pervasiveness dates back only to the early 1960s, even though network television broadcasts in the United States took place as early as 1940.

The second reason involves deficiencies in measurement. Much of the early research discounted all media influence unless it came through direct contact outside the classroom between the child and the media. That excluded indirect media influence, that is, being exposed to parents and teachers who convey media information to the child. These exclusions sharply reduced findings of media effects.

Finally, research designs have become more sophisticated. In the early studies children were asked to make their own general appraisal of learning sources. A typical question might be: "From whom do you learn the most, your parents, your school, or newspapers and television?" The questions used in recent studies have been more specific. Gary Coldevin, a Canadian researcher, asked high school students in Canada and the United States what they knew about particular subjects, such as immigration policy, government in general, or education policy. Then he asked them to state arguments for and against certain policy positions. Only after the students had written down their ideas were they asked for the chief sources for their facts and, separately, the chief sources affecting how they evaluated these issues. In nearly every case the mass media were the chief sources of information and evaluations for U.S. as well as Canadian students. However, the media were slightly less important, and parents and schools slightly more important, as sources of evaluations than as information sources.[12]

What children learn from the mass media and how they evaluate it depends heavily on their stage of mental development. According to child psychologist Jean Piaget, children between two and seven years of age are keenly aware of the objects they see and hear.[13] But they do not independently perceive the connections among various phenomena or draw general conclusions from specific instances. Many of the lessons presumably taught by media stories therefore elude young children. Complex reasoning skills are fully developed only at the teen-age level. Children's interests in certain types of stories also change sharply with age, as do their attention and information-retention spans.[14] Given these variations, research on the impact of the mass media on children should focus on narrow age spans. Such research has been comparatively rare.

Researchers do know that children are likely to be highly supportive of the political system during their early years, when they learn basic facts about prominent politicians.[15] The president and the police officer are next to father and God. By their teen-age years youngsters have often become quite disillusioned about authority figures. This skepticism diminishes as education is completed and the young adult enters the work force. What role the media play in this transformation is unclear. It is also unclear to what extent children and adolescents imitate behavior depicted by media stories, how long they remember stories, and how long the effects of exposure last.

Adult Socialization

The pattern of heavy media exposure continues from childhood to adulthood. The average American adult spends nearly three hours a day watching television, two hours listening to radio, twenty minutes reading a newspaper, and ten minutes reading a magazine. Time spent with the mass media has jumped by 40 percent since the advent of television, mostly at the expense of other leisure activities. However, this redistribution of time has stabilized now, and there have even been occasional declines in television viewing.[16] On the average day 80 percent of all Americans are reached by television and newspapers. On a typical evening the television audience is close to 100 million people, nearly half the entire population.

This massive exposure contributes to the lifelong process of political socialization and learning. The mass media form

> the mainstream of the common symbolic environment that cultivates the most widely shared conceptions of reality. We live in terms of the stories we tell, stories about what things exist, stories about how things work, and stories about what to do. . . . Increasingly, media-cultivated facts and values become standards by which we judge.[17]

Once basic attitudes toward the political system have been formed, they usually stabilize, and later learning largely supplements and refines earlier notions. Established attitudes filter subsequent experiences. Major personal or societal upheavals may lead to more or less complete resocialization and revised political ideas. Short of drastic changes, the need to cope with information about new events and shifting cultural orientations also forces the average person into continuous learning and gradual readjustments. But the basic value structure generally remains intact, even when attitudes are modified.[18]

Much of what the average person learns about political norms, rules, values, and events, and about the way people cope with these political happenings, comes of necessity from the mass media. Those with the widest exposure to political news in the mass media generally are most aware of political issues and have more opinions about them. Personal experiences are severely limited compared with the range of experiences that come to us directly or indirectly through the media.

Although not explicitly political, most media content is full of implicit messages about the social order and political activities. An accident report, for example, may suggest that police and fire forces respond too slowly and that emergency facilities in the local hospital are inadequate. In fact, such seemingly nonpolitical stories are the most widely used sources for political information. Surveys show that only one-half to two-thirds of the adult public regularly consumes explicit political news. Half of the population does not watch television news at all.[19] Only a very small proportion of the television news audience pays serious attention to news broadcasts.

People's opinions, feelings, and evaluations about the political system may spring from their own processing of facts supplied by the media; from attitudes, opinions, and feelings explicitly expressed by the media in news or entertainment programming; or from a combination of the two.[20] It is important to distinguish between learning of facts and learning of opinions. The media play a very large role in conveying information and a much smaller role in conveying attitudes and opinions.[21] Many people who use the media for information, and as a point of departure for formulating their own appraisals, reject or ignore attitudes and evaluations that are supplied explicitly or implicitly by media stories. In fact, survey data show that, on an average, two-thirds of the people do not know their newspaper's position on specific economic, social, and foreign policy issues.[22]

A widely publicized incident on September 1, 1983, demonstrates the distinction between fact and opinion learning. A Soviet jet fighter's heat-seeking missile downed a South Korean passenger plane after it strayed over Soviet territory on a flight from New York to Seoul. Two hundred sixty-nine people died. These were the undisputed facts. The U.S. Congress denounced the shooting, calling it a "cold-blooded barbarous attack" and "one of the most infamous and reprehensible acts in history." From the Soviets' perspective it was nothing of the kind. Soviet officials claimed that the plane, which they said resembled an American electronic reconnaissance plane, had been on a spy mission and had ignored warnings by intercepting military aircraft. They alleged that the United States was exploiting the tragedy as a propaganda spectacle to whip up anti-Soviet sentiments throughout the world. Apprised of the air disaster by media stories, U.S. citizens could side with the opinion of Congress or of the Soviet government, or they could form their own distinctive opinions.

Most people are prone to accept newspeople's views in those areas where they have not had personal experience or guidance from social contacts. When audiences have direct or vicarious experiences to guide them, and particularly when they have already formed opinions grounded firmly in their personal values, they are far less likely to be swayed by the media. In practice, this means that the least informed and least interested are most likely to reflect the viewpoints expressed in the media, particularly television. Parroting of viewpoints espoused by political commentators explains why people uninterested in politics often hold quite sophisticated opinions if they have been extensively exposed to news stories.[23]

Although people can and do form opinions independently on many issues, particularly those concerning local problems, complete independence is impossible.[24] Rarely do they have enough information and understanding to form their own views about all national and international issues that confront them in bewildering succession. This puts people at the mercy of the media, not only for information, but also for interpretation. Even when people think that they are forming their own opinions about familiar issues, they often depend on the media more than they realize. Research by George Gerbner and his associates provides evidence that "those who spend more time watching television are more likely to express views, beliefs, and assumptions that are congruent with television's portrayal of life and society." [25] If the media fail to supply adequate information, people's opinions may rest on unsound foundations. Gerbner, for instance, claims that extensive television exposure leads to "mainstreaming." It turns people into bland middle-roaders with a basically uniform outlook on political life.

The 1984 presidential debates between President Ronald Reagan and Sen. Walter Mondale, D-Minn., exemplify the effectiveness of the media in guiding opinions, even on comparatively simple matters. A telephone survey conducted immediately after the first debate showed that a slight majority of the viewers thought that the president had won the debate. The media, however, strongly attacked the president's performance, and consequently viewers' appraisals changed. Two days after the debates Mondale's winner ratings had surpassed the president's by forty-nine points.[26]

Many graphic examples of the persuasive power of the media come from advertising research, which has documented how messages can affect consumers' perceptions of unfamiliar products and activities and thus change their behavior. Broadcasting may even lead to religious conversions. Radio and television evangelists attract more than 25 million Americans each week, and thousands phone program hosts to announce their conversion or financial support.[27]

Media's persuasiveness does not mean that exposure is tantamount to learning and mind changing. Far from it! Most media stories are promptly forgotten. Stories that become part of an individual's fund of knowledge tend to reinforce existing beliefs and feelings. Acquisition of new knowledge or changes in attitude are the exception rather than the rule. Still, they occur often enough to be highly significant.

Differences in Media Use and Socialization

Just as population groups differ in their cultural environment, economic interests, and psychological make-up, media preferences differ as well. We will outline some of these differences and assess the effects that they are apt to have on political socialization. The picture is extremely complex. For example, if we look at racial differences, we cannot simply talk about characteristic media exposure and impact patterns for nonwhites and whites; sex, age, education, income, region, and city size must also be specified. Additional variations come from commonly ignored factors such as lifestyle and social setting, family size, personality characteristics, and social and job pressures. Of course, the mere fact that individuals belong to a certain demographic category or social group does not mean that they necessarily share the media exposure characteristics of that category or group. For many individuals, group ties may be weak, with little impact on behavior. Group influence may also be weakened for people who are subject to conflicting group pressures. For instance, college students whose peer groups revel in left-wing literature may also be exposed by their families to conservative media fare. Predicting their media exposure and impact patterns from these different group affiliations would be hazardous.

Demographic Factors

Blacks and whites in America diverge in political knowledge and attitudes. Although firm proof is lacking, different media exposure patterns may be a partial explanation.[28] Most importantly, blacks pay considerably less attention to newspapers than do whites. Fifty-nine percent read a daily newspaper, compared with 72 percent for whites. While whites show no sex differences in newspaper reading, blacks do. Black women, despite high rates of employment outside the home, trail black men by six percentage points in readership. In general, employed women show higher readership rates than do women working at home. Unemployed blacks are half as likely as unemployed whites to read a daily newspaper. Since newspapers are the medium that supplies the most ample amounts of standard political news, more black than white citizens lack this information. In turn, this makes blacks less likely to share the political images and judgments of their white fellow citizens.

Blacks rely less on the mass media for political information than do whites. For example, only 22 percent of blacks polled in a low-income Los Angeles neighborhood said that they relied on print media for most of their political information, and only 23 percent said that they relied on radio or television. Many named instead interpersonal sources such as their families or public agencies. By comparison, 40 percent of the whites mentioned print media as major sources of political news, and 43 percent mentioned radio and television. Hispanics found print and electronic media even less useful for keeping themselves politically informed than did blacks. Only 12 percent of the Hispanics said that they got most of their political information from newspapers, and only 5 percent called radio or television their most important sources. Such alienation from major sources of political information may hamper the political effectiveness of Hispanics and blacks in dealing with the majority culture.[29]

Nonwhites prefer to get their news from different papers and stations than whites, especially when media oriented to their racial group are available. Minority groups who primarily use ethnically oriented media are apt to live in different communication and socialization environments than do people in the majority culture. Substantial differences among racial groups in attitudes toward government agencies, and in trust in government and feelings of political efficacy, lend credence to the belief that diverse media images, combined with different life experiences, produce distinctive socialization patterns.

Blacks and whites extract different information even when they use the same media. Blacks are more apt than whites to believe that factual as well as fictional stories presented by the media are true to life. Therefore, the images that many blacks form about lifestyles or societal patterns are more likely to mirror the distortions found in media presentations.[30] A study of the diffusion of information about six assassinations showed that each racial group dwelled heavily on news that dealt with its own race. While all blacks and whites had heard about the deaths of Martin Luther King, Jr., and John and Robert Kennedy, many more blacks (10 to 24 percent more) knew about the assassinations of black leaders Medgar Evers and Malcom X. Similarly, many more whites than blacks knew about the death of white Nazi leader George Lincoln Rockwell.[31]

There are many possible explanations for demographic variations in media use and socialization patterns. Despite the successes of the civil rights movement, most blacks in the 1970s and 1980s belonged to different social groups than did whites, and they led lives quite unlike those of the white middle class to whose tastes most media cater. The social status of many older blacks kept them alienated from the northern urban culture in which they found themselves, often after a childhood spent in the rural South. Understandably, they were less interested in news that focused heavily on city life and politics. More blacks than whites fell into youthful age brackets where readership is generally lower. Fewer blacks than whites drive to work; hence fewer listen to radio news. For the many blacks whose schooling has been poor, deficient reading skills make newspaper reading unattractive. Television is an appealing alternative. Accordingly, blacks on an average watch about 15 percent more television than do whites.[32]

Some researchers have questioned whether the apparent differences between blacks and whites are based on race-linked cultural differences or spring instead from the fact that the black population is more frequently poor and educationally deprived. Bradley Greenberg and Brenda Dervin contend that within the subculture of poverty, blacks and whites use the media in similar ways.[33] They attribute differences in media habits and socialization to economic and educational differences. Other scholars argue that race and its cultural consequences are indeed important factors in media exposure and impact. Leo Bogart, for example, found racial differences in media-use patterns regardless of socioeconomic status.[34] The unresolved issues thus revolve around the causes of subcultural differences rather than their existence. If differences spring from race-linked cultural differences, they may be resistant to change. If they are linked to socioeconomic status, they may change readily with rising incomes, better education, and improved occupational status.

Sex, age, income, education, and region and city size, in addition to race, help explain differences in newspaper reading, radio listening, and television viewing. For instance, men and women differ sharply in daytime television viewing; age has a bearing on newspaper reading; southerners listen to much less radio than do northerners. Program preferences vary as well. Women over fifty are the heaviest viewers of television news, followed by men over fifty. Twelve- to seventeen-year-olds are the lightest news watchers. Men far exceed women in following sports coverage, while women spend more time on television drama.

Differences in media-use patterns are particularly pronounced between income levels. High-income families, who usually are better educated than poor families, use print media more and television less than the rest of the population. Variations in education produce similar patterns. For instance, 79 percent of college graduates interviewed in one 1979 study said that they read a newspaper "yesterday," compared with 73 percent of high school graduates and 57 percent of people lacking a high school diploma. The story is reversed for television viewing. College graduates were watching 19.8 hours of television per week, compared with 23.3 hours for high school graduates and 25.9 hours for those without a high school diploma.

more educated = more print, less TV

Upper income people also use a greater variety of media. Among the upper economic groups 57 percent are multimedia users compared with 27 percent in the lower economic groups. Thus the well-to-do potentially have much more information and a greater variety of information available to them. This helps them to maintain and increase their influence and power in American society.

In part, the poor pay less attention to print media because these media carry less information of interest to them. In fact, lack of interest in politics and disillusionment with government are the chief reasons given for failure to read newspapers. The urban poor need consumer information on prices, goods, and services more than coverage of new business regulations or city politics. Yet the print media rarely supply adequate consumer information. While print media are largely unattractive to the poor, television and radio programs appeal to them because these programs are easy to grasp and carry a great deal of light entertainment. They allow the poor to escape from the grim reality that surrounds their lives.

Unifying Forces

The notion of vastly different communications environments for various population groups should not be carried too far, however. The bulk of media entertainment and information is similar throughout the country and is shared by all types of media audiences. The same network television and cable programs are broadcast on the East Coast and the West Coast, in big cities and small towns. Differences among individual networks are slight. Hence television comes close to being a single, nationwide source of news and commentary. Radio is more diverse, but even many radio news programs are little more than national wire service reports. Insofar as newspaper stories are based on wire service information, they, too, are fairly uniform everywhere.

In Chapter 3 we saw that news media cover basically the same categories of stories in the same proportions. Specific stories vary, of course. Newspapers on the West Coast are more likely to devote their foreign affairs coverage to Asian affairs than are newspapers on the East Coast, which concentrate on Europe and the Middle East. Tabloids, such as the *New York Daily News,* put more stress on sensational crime and sex stories than does the staid *New York Times.* Nevertheless, news sources everywhere provide a large common core of information and interpretation that imbues their audiences with a shared structure of basic values and information.

Choosing Media Stories

Uses and Gratifications Theories

General patterns of media use do not reveal *why* people pay attention to specific stories, but a number of theories have been formulated to help explain how and why such individual choices are made. Currently, one of the most widely accepted of these theories is the "uses and gratifications" approach. Put most simply, proponents of this approach contend that individuals ignore personally irrelevant and unattractively presented messages and pay attention to the kinds of things that they need and that they find gratifying, provided the expense in time and effort seems reasonable.[35]

Uses and gratifications may be behavioral, emotional, or intellectual. For instance, people pay attention to stories that help them in making political decisions, such as voting or participating in protest demonstrations. They also use the media to gain a sense of security and social adequacy. Media stories help people to know what is happening in their political environment and to take part in discussions with friends and coworkers. They feel gratified if the media reinforce what they already know and believe. Finally, the media are used to while away time, reduce loneliness, participate vicariously in exciting ventures, and escape the frustrations of everyday life.[36] Of course, there is no guarantee that the gratifications that are sought are routinely attained. In fact, media may produce anxieties and fears as well as hatred and alienation. When radio and television were shut down by a long strike in Israel in 1987, the public reacted with relief rather than dismay. David Hartman, the Israeli philosopher, gave this explanation: "When television and radio become the prisms through which you look at reality, you come away saying, 'What an ugly place this is.' But when you take away those prisms and people's perceptions of reality are derived exclusively from their own daily experiences, which are for the most part prosaic, they inevitably become more relaxed and stable." [37]

Table 5-1, based on interviews with 6,564 adults in ten small cities throughout the United States, indicates the twenty-five newspaper content areas that are read most widely. People were asked to rate thirty to thirty-five common newspaper topics on a scale of 1 to 5. A score of 1 denoted that they always ignored the topic; a score of 5 denoted that they always read it whenever it appeared. Presumably, the topics earning the highest scores supply the broadest array of gratifications.

Special subcultural needs may lead to significant variations in attention patterns. For instance, a Jewish person may be particularly attentive to news from the Middle East and other places that concern Israel. A person of Polish ancestry may look for news about food shortages and political developments in Poland. Women who favor increased job opportunities for women are apt to notice stories about women's expanding presence in the business world.

What people actually select depends very much on their lifestyle and the context in which they are exposed to information. What is useful and gratifying in one setting may be less so in another. When people change their lifestyles, such as moving from daytime to nighttime work or trading a desk for a travel job, media patterns may change drastically to bring about closer accord with the people encountered in the new environment. [38]

Lifestyle also determines the time available for media use and hence the quantity of news that can be selected. In early adulthood when people begin their careers or raise children, the demands of home and job may leave little time for attention to the media. The cost of newspaper and magazine subscriptions may be prohibitive on a tight budget. Conversely, older people, whose home and job duties have become lighter and whose financial obligations are decreasing, frequently have much more time for reading or watching television. Lifestyle also determines what media are readily available. People may expose themselves to media that are of little intrinsic interest to them when this is convenient or socially appropriate. Table 5-2 shows the kinds of reasons people give when asked why they paid attention or failed to pay attention to particular news stories.

Selective Exposure Theories

Although people pick up what is personally useful and gratifying, they ignore many other bits of information, regardless of their political and social significance. Most of these omissions are random. People simply fail to notice certain information or have no time or inclination to pursue it, even when it comes to their attention. But systematic

Table 5-1   Rankings of Top Twenty-five Content Categories and Average Ratings Across Ten Markets

Rank	Rating
1. Natural disasters and tragedies	3.93
2. Stories and columns on the national economy (prices, unemployment, inflation)	3.87
3. News of the local economy	3.82
4. Column on local people and events	3.72
5. Stories about national politics and the president	3.72
6. Service information (TV listings, weather, movie listings, etc.)	3.71
7. News of international leaders and events	3.70
8. Stories on energy, conservation, and the environment	3.67
9. Stories on things to see and do in the area	3.66
10. Good Samaritan stories (people helping people)	3.60
11. Humorous stories and features	3.56
12. Accident and crime news	3.52
13. Health and medical advice	3.42
14. How fast the community is growing	3.33
15. Editorials and letters to the editor	3.32
16. Schools and education	3.31
17. City council and local politicians	3.30
18. News about the governor and state legislature	3.27
19. Consumer stories and advice	3.27
20. Stories about human psychology (the way we think and act)	3.22
21. Nature and outdoor stories	3.19
22. How-to advice on such things as crafts, auto and home repairs	3.19
23. News of record (births, deaths, weddings, etc.)	3.10
24. Space and exploration	3.10
25. Science and technology	3.08

Source: Judee K. Burgoon, Michael Burgoon, and Miriam Wilkinson, "Dimensions of Content Readership in 10 Newspaper Markets," *Journalism Quarterly* 60 (Spring 1983): 79. Reprinted by permission of the Association for Education in Journalism and Mass Communication, publishers of *Journalism Quarterly.*

Note: Ratings are based on a 1 to 5 scale. A rating of 1 means never read; a rating of 5 means always read.

omissions occur as well. Various cognitive balance theories try to explain these omissions. According to these theories, people avoid information that disturbs their peace of mind, offends their political and social tastes, or conflicts with information, attitudes, and feelings they already hold. Social scientists explain selective exposure by pointing out that people are uncomfortable when they are exposed to ideas that differ from their own or that question the validity of their ideas. To avoid discomfort, people select information that is congruent with their existing beliefs.

Selectivity then leads to diversification of socializing influences and

Table 5-2   Reasons for Attention or Inattention to News Stories

Reasons for attention	Percent	Reasons for inattention	Percent
Personal relevance	26	Missed	47
Emotional appeal	20	No interest	28
Societal importance	19	Too remote	10
Interesting story	15	Too busy	6
Job relevance	12	Doubt media	3
Chance reasons	1	Too complex	3
Miscellaneous	7	Redundant/boring	2
		Doubt story	1

Source: Doris A. Graber, *Processing the News: How People Tame the Information Tide,*
2d ed. (New York: Longman Inc., 1988), 102. Copyright © 1988 by Longman Inc. Reprinted
by permission of Longman Inc.

Note: $N = 453$ for reasons for attention, 1,493 for reasons of inattention.

lays the groundwork for differential attitudes toward politics. It also
reduces the already slim chances that an individual's beliefs, attitudes,
and feelings will be altered once they have become established. Selective
exposure therefore helps to explain the considerable stability that exists
in cognitions and orientations such as party allegiance or isolationism or
interventionism in foreign affairs.

Over the years scholars have repeatedly examined the various selective exposure phenomena and have modified their earlier theories in
accordance with new findings. They now believe that selective exposure
occurs to a lesser extent than was thought initially. Many people find it
too bothersome to select news stories carefully, particularly when using
electronic media. For instance, when television news carries stories that
are objectionable to a viewer, there is no easy way to screen out the
undesired stories and still watch the rest of the broadcast.

Many people are actually curious about discrepant information or
pride themselves on being open-minded and receptive to all points of
view. For instance, Democrats may want to hear what Republicans are
saying to find out how the opposition is stating its case. They may also
want to determine what counterarguments need to be formulated. Many
people even enjoy news that contradicts their own ideas. At worst,
exposure to discrepant information is not as universally painful as
previously thought. It can be ignored, overlooked, or distorted. The
source can be discredited and the message disbelieved.[39]

Much of the evidence for markedly selective exposure has come
from settings in which available media supported the preferences of the

audience. No choice was necessary; selection was de facto rather than deliberate. For example, unionized workers with friends and associates who are also in unions may encounter a lot of pro-union information at home and at work. They may not have to make a special effort to seek out pro-union information or reject anti-union opinions. In fact, anti-union information may be unavailable. Genuine rather than de facto selective exposure does occur, of course, but it operates more like a preference than a total exclusion rule. It appears to be most prevalent for those relatively few people who recognize dissonance and find it painful.

Agenda-Setting Theories

If selections of news items were entirely determined by personal needs and pleasures, news selection patterns would show infinite variations. This is not the case. Similarities in the political environment of average Americans and social pressures produce common patterns in the selection of news. As previously mentioned, gatekeeping practices largely account for the similarity in news supply, which is a powerful unifying force. Media also tell people in fairly uniform fashion which individual issues and activities are most significant and deserve to be ranked highly on the public's agenda of concerns.[40] Importance is indicated through cues such as banner headlines or front-page placement in newspapers, or first-story placement on television. Frequent and ample coverage also implies significance.

Many people readily adopt the media's agenda of importance, often without being aware of it, rather than selecting or rejecting news on the basis of what is personally gratifying or displeasing. We look at the front page of the newspaper and expect to find the most important stories there. We may watch the opening minutes of a telecast eagerly and then allow our attention to slacken. Consequently, agenda setting by the media leads to uniformities in exposure as well as in significance ratings of news items. When the media make events seem important, politicians are likely to comment about them and to take action. This enhances the perceived importance of these events and ensures even more public attention.

Numerous studies confirm the agenda-setting influence of the media.[41] In one intensive study of information processing, several thousand responses by small panels of voters showed that the panelists largely agreed on the current issues that were salient to their personal lives. The lists of issues mentioned by the panelists as most important to them personally, most talked about, and most salient to their community corresponded to cues in the news sources that they used in their communities.[42] However, agenda setting varied in potency. The audience followed media guidance but not slavishly.[43] Past and current

experiences, conversations with others, and independent reasoning provided alternatives to media guidance.

Comparisons of media agendas with public opinion polls and
reports about political and social conditions show that media guidance
is most important for new issues that have not been widely discussed
and for issues beyond the realm of personal experience.[44] Prominent
media coverage does ensure that an issue will be noticed, but it does
not guarantee that the audience will assign it the same relative rank
of importance that media play has indicated. Likewise, information that
is useful or gratifying to the audience will be noted, even if it is on
the back pages, receives minuscule headlines, or is briefly reported at
the tail end of a newscast.[45] The need for raw material for conversation
with friends and associates is a particularly strong force in selecting
stories.

Learning Processes

Media-Audience Interactions

The forces that make for diversity and for uniformity in the selection of news have been discussed. But what happens after the news has
been selected? The early models that depicted a straight stimulus-
response relationship have been disproven. There is no "hypodermic
effect": information presented by the media is not injected unaltered
into the minds of the audience. Rather, media and audience interact;
the images conveyed by the media stimulate perceptions in audience
members that reflect each individual's perceptual state at the time the
message was received.

Recent research indicates that from childhood on people develop
ideas about how the world operates and feelings about various aspects of
these operations. Cognitive psychologists call these mental configurations by various names, including *schemata* and *scripts*.[46] Items of news
are selected, interpreted, and integrated in accordance with a number
of culturally influenced rules of reasoning. For instance, in Marxist-
oriented societies, most political events are attributed to economic
forces. Hence Marxist observers interpreted racial rioting in the United
States in the late 1960s as proletarian uprisings, whereas most Americans viewed them as protests against racial injustice and its consequences.

In the United States much subcultural diversity exists despite the
basic uniformity created by the shared dominant culture. Most political
schemata developed by average Americans come from the mass media
rather than from direct experiences. This is a strong homogenizing
influence. Coherence also springs from the human effort to organize
perceptions into internally consistent images that are meaningful to the

perceiver.[47] As journalist Walter Lippmann explained more than sixty years ago:

> For the most part we do not first see, and then define, we define first and then see. In the great blooming, buzzing confusion of the outer world, we pick out what our culture has already defined for us, and we tend to perceive that which we have picked out in the form stereotyped for us by our culture.[48]

Because individuals pick up information that is related to things they already know and for which they have developed appropriate schemata, numerous "knowledge-gap" studies show that political elites and other well-informed people tend to absorb a great deal more mass media information than do the poorly informed.[49] It is not functionally advantageous for the poorly informed to acquire knowledge that carries little meaning for them. This explains why information-poor population groups, although they are heavy consumers of the mass media, generally extract far less political information than do more politically sophisticated audiences. Thus during the course of a lifetime the knowledge gap between the privileged and underprivileged widens. Those with the least political knowledge are likely to remain politically impotent. Moreover, the knowledge gap between the privileged and underprivileged makes mutual understanding more difficult. Improved public education, which might shrink the gap, remains a distant goal.

Transient Influences

Many transitory factors impinge on news processing. A person's frame of mind may be accepting or rejecting. Attention may be focused totally on the news story or partly diverted. Up to half of the television audience eats dinner, washes dishes, reads, or talks on the phone while watching television. Examination time at school, illness in the family, or the year-end rush at work may preempt the time normally devoted to media.

The other people present when news is received or discussed are also significant. For instance, if one watches or talks about a presidential inauguration with friends who are making fun of the way the president talks and acts, the occasion loses solemnity and becomes banal. If one watches or talks about the event with a group who admire the president, one comes away feeling inspired. Researchers cannot predict the effect of media messages without knowing the group context in which exposure or conversation took place.[50]

How a person interacts with information also depends on the format of that information. If news reports present conflicting facts or opinions, if they are overly long or overly short, if they are repetitious, dull, or offensive, their effect is apt to be diminished. Moreover, the total communications matrix affects the influence of its parts; the impact of print news may be blunted by prior presentations on television and radio that have removed the edge of novelty.[51]

Source credibility and appeal are other significant factors in news processing. Once President Richard Nixon had lost his credibility and respect in the wake of Watergate disclosures, any statement he made was suspect for many Americans. His manner and bearing were more closely watched for clues to his general state of mind. Partisanship, too, may play an important role in source appraisal. It may cast a rosy glow over fellow partisans and a pall over the opposition.

Perceptual and Image Factors

When people receive new information they combine it with existing beliefs. But does the new reshape the old or the old reshape the new in the final images? Research has shown that images of political candidates are largely perceiver-determined for those aspects for which the audience already has developed complex schemata. For instance, people assume that Democratic presidential candidates will pursue policies typically associated with Democrats. They read or view the news in that vein, picking up bits of information that fit and rejecting, ignoring, or reinterpreting those that do not fit. The same is likely to hold true for information about big business or big labor, the Arab world, or the Soviet Union. Average Americans are likely to interpret big business and big labor news negatively. Similarly, if reports about the Arab world and about the Soviet Union permit a choice between favorable and unfavorable interpretations, the unfavorable image is apt to prevail.

Information about aspects of events or people that are not widely known or stereotyped leads to stimulus-determined images. How the media frame these political issues and depict people largely determines what the audience perceives. Candidates' personalities, assessments of their capabilities, and appraisals of the people with whom they surround themselves, for example, usually are stimulus-determined, except when a candidate is already well known.[52] Likewise, when the media describe present-day China, when they cast doubt on the safety of nuclear energy production, or when they praise the merits of a new wage-insurance plan, they create images that are likely to dominate people's schemata.

The general rule that media are most influential in areas where the audience knows least does not apply to specialized publications. Professional journals, for instance, often have a strong impact on their readers' images or professional matters. This happens because of the high credibility of the sources, which makes the professionals who read these publications subordinate their own views to those of the published experts.

Learning Effects: Knowledge and Attitudes

Measurement Problems

What kinds of politically relevant knowledge, attitudes, feelings, and actions spring from people's contacts with the media? Because of the limitations of measuring instruments, the answer is difficult. In Chapter 1 we pointed out the impossibility of isolating media influence when it is one of many factors in a complex environment.[53] For instance, the rising levels of cynicism about the U.S. government that occurred following the disclosure of the Watergate scandal in the Nixon administration cannot be directly and solely attributed to the disclosure stories. It is possible that cynicism was produced primarily by the experience of paying higher prices in the grocery store, facing motor fuel shortages at the gas station, or living through a public transit strike. Until researchers can trace an individual's mental processes and isolate the components that interact and combine to form mental images, the impact of media on knowledge and attitudes cannot be fully assessed. Nor can researchers understand completely just what is learned from media.

Research up to now has focused on very small facets of learning (for example, specific facts about political candidates or about a few public policies). Even within such narrow areas, testing has been severely limited, zeroing in on learning the substance of explicit messages rather than on assessing total knowledge gains. For instance, election coverage of a presidential candidate teaches more than facts about the candidate. It may also inform the audience about the role played by White House correspondents in campaign coverage and about living conditions in other cities. Because researchers usually ask only about learning campaign information, such ancillary learning, however important it may be, is overlooked. Much learning may even be subconscious. People may be unaware that they have learned something new and may not mention it when asked what they have learned. At times new information may be temporarily forgotten, only to reenter consciousness a short while later.

Although many assumptions about learning that seem intuitively correct remain untested, media practices continue to be judged as if these assumptions were true. The assumption that people deduce important social lessons from specific stories presented by the media is one example. Media researcher Joshua Meyrowitz argues, for instance, that television has radically changed social roles by stripping them of mystery and holding them up to continuous public scrutiny. Isolated housewives have learned about the attractive roles open only to males in American society, and the successes and failures of the women's movement have affected the behavior of these housewives. Television allows children to experience the adult world long before they are physically and emotionally prepared to cope with these experiences. In the age of television, political heroes have become ordinary mortals, and authority figures are no longer respected because the mystery of social distance has been stripped away.[54]

We believe that adults as well as children often model their behavior after the behavior of characters they encounter in the media. We assume that unfavorable stereotypes will hurt the self-esteem of the groups so characterized, and so we urge newspeople to present these groups in a better light. Accordingly, the television image of blacks has improved dramatically since the 1960s, although the image of Hispanics remains predominantly negative.[55] News reports and dramatic shows presumably teach people how lawyers or police officers or hospitals conduct their business. Presumably, impressionable people who watch these shows and like what they see will be motivated to aspire to these professions; conversely, distortions in the portrayal of these roles will mislead inexperienced people who regard them as accurate.

Although we assume these effects, and there is every reason to believe that many are quite common, most of them remain unmeasured. An important exception has been the Cultural Indicators project conducted since the mid-1960s at the University of Pennsylvania's Annenberg School of Communications. Using "cultivation analysis" the investigators studied trends in the dramatic content of network television and the conceptions of social reality produced in viewers. Their findings confirm that heavy viewers of television drama (more than four hours daily) see the world as television paints it and react to that world rather than to reality more than do light viewers of the same demographic background and similar circumstances. For instance, heavy viewers, exposed to large doses of crime in television drama, believe that the dangers of becoming a crime victim are far greater than they actually are.[56] They fear crime more and are more distrustful and suspicious than are persons who view television less often. They also are generally more pessimistic and tend to gravitate toward the middle-of-the-road of "mainstream" politics depicted on television.

Like most research on mass media effects, these findings have been challenged on the grounds that factors other than mass media exposure account for the results. The characteristics of viewers rather than their exposure to television may be responsible for their images of the world and their addiction to television. The technical aspects of the Cultural Indicators project have also been challenged. Such scientific controversies indicate that research on mass media effects needs a lot more refinement before the findings can be considered definitive.

A neglected research sphere concerns forgetfulness. Much that is learned from the media is evanescent. When Iran is engulfed by revolution or Philadelphia rocked by a patronage scandal, the salient names and facts are on many lips, but after the crisis has passed, this knowledge evaporates rapidly. How rapidly seems to depend on a number of factors, most importantly, the ability to store and retrieve information. After three months of neglect, most ordinary stories have been forgotten, even by people with good memories. If stories are periodically revived with follow-ups or with closely related stories, memory becomes deepened and prolonged. In fact, a few crucial incidents are so deeply etched into human memory that they become permanent. The Great Depression, World War II, and the assassination of President John F. Kennedy are examples.[57]

Factual Learning

Given these limitations on initial learning and on remembering, what can be said about the extent of political learning from the mass media? The data that follow come from the research project in which the information supply and political learning of four small panels of adults living in Evanston, Illinois; Indianapolis, Indiana; and Lebanon, New Hampshire, were monitored intensively throughout an entire year.[58] When asked about topics covered by their news sources, the panelists in the Three Sites Project could identify many, but the mix of topics varied from person to person. Seven broad topic areas were recognized by nearly every panel member as receiving "a lot of coverage" during the interview year. The list was dominated by economic and foreign policy issues. Sixteen other topics were recalled by a somewhat smaller majority of the panel members—all in all an impressive array of politically important topics to be remembered by an average mass media audience.

However, people do not seem to gain much specific knowledge from the media. They recognize information if it is mentioned to them, but fail to recall it without such assistance.[59] For instance, the panelists in the Three Sites Project were asked open-ended questions at the height of the 1976 presidential campaign about the positions of presidential candidates Gerald R. Ford and Jimmy Carter on the issues of inflation and unemployment—issues of personal importance to the panelists and discussed by them with friends and associates. Yet as Table 5-3 indicates, specific knowledge was abysmally small. Half of the answers were "don't know's." Specific information about each policy was contained in less than 10 percent of the answers on unemployment and less than 5 percent of the answers on inflation. Women, especially those forty years of age and under, recalled much less information than did the men. Age, education, and even prior knowledge and exposure to several news sources did not produce major differences in learning scores.

Similarly, when John Robinson and Dennis Davis tested comprehension of the main points of thirteen television news stories within hours of viewing, the results were quite uniform. As Table 5-4 shows,

Table 5-3   Recall of Specific Information on Unemployment and Inflation (in percentages)

	UNEMPLOYMENT							
	Ford				Carter			
	Women		*Men*		*Women*		*Men*	
Responses	O	Y	Y	O	O	Y	Y	O
Statistics	0	0	0	2	4	0	2	11
Policy data	12	8	9	12	3	4	3	5
General information	41	38	44	43	43	41	48	35
Don't know	47	55	47	43	50	55	46	48

	INFLATION							
	Ford				Carter			
	Women		*Men*		*Women*		*Men*	
Responses	O	Y	Y	O	O	Y	Y	O
Statistics	1	0	1	0	0	0	1	0
Policy data	1	2	2	0	3	2	6	6
General information	38	34	39	42	34	29	29	27
Don't know	59	63	59	58	63	69	64	67

Source: Doris Graber, "Agenda-Setting: Are There Women's Perspectives?" in *Women and the News*, ed. Laurily Keir Epstein (New York: Hastings House, 1978), 22. Copyright © 1978 by Laurily Keir Epstein. Reprinted by permission.

Note: N = 1,716 replies. O stands for older women and men (over age forty). Y stands for younger women and men (age forty and under). *Statistics* means that the respondent was able to cite precise figures for unemployment and inflation rates and/or rate changes. *Policy data* means that the respondent was able to refer to specific proposals made by Ford or Carter to cope with the inflation or unemployment problem. *General information* means that the respondent knew whether general trends were changing or stable, and knew whether action was planned, without being able to give specifics.

comprehension scores hovered around 40 percent with only minor differences among various age groups. Use of additional media boosted comprehension only slightly. Education and prior information levels produced the largest variations in scores with the best informed scoring 13.8 percentage points higher than the poorly informed; grade school and college graduates' scores were separated by a 12.2 percent gap.

The paucity of factual learning by average individuals has disturbed many people because it is an axiom of democracy that good citizens must be well informed. Political scientists Scott Keeter and Cliff Zukin titled their intensive study of voter knowledge gains during

Table 5-4 Television News Comprehension Scores

Viewer characteristics	Group size	Score
Age		
18-29 years	97	42.3%
30-44 years	110	41.4
45-59 years	98	43.7
60 and older	82	38.8
Education		
Grade school	42	34.4
High school graduate	119	40.8
Some college	119	42.4
College graduate	107	45.6
Information base (name recognition test)		
Low	145	34.7
Medium	150	44.6
High	82	48.5
Additional news media use		
Newspaper		
Nonreader	185	40.7
Reader	202	42.3
Radio		
Nonlistener	274	41.8
Listener	113	41.3
News magazine		
Nonreader	249	40.5
Reader	128	43.7

Source: Adapted from John P. Robinson and Dennis K. Davis, "Comprehension of Single Evening's News," in *The Main Source: Learning from Television News*, ed. John P. Robinson and Mark R. Levy (Beverly Hills, Calif.: Sage, 1986), 122-126.

Note: Score is the percentage of a perfect score for the entire broadcast. A perfect score of 8 points for the thirteen stories amounts to 104 points. It required comprehending the central point of each story plus three or more important details. There were 387 viewers selected through national probability sampling.

the 1976 and 1980 presidential elections *Uninformed Choice.* They argued that citizens are too uninformed to make intelligent political choices.[60] Earlier studies had registered even less knowledge than Keeter's and Zukin's research. These judgments may be unduly harsh. In many studies knowledge is gauged largely by a citizen's ability to recall the names of prominent officeholders and to recite facts from the U.S. Constitution. Such factual information tests seem inappropriate for judging political knowledge and competence. What really matters is that citizens understand major political issues, not that they can recall the names of politicians or the length of the term of a Supreme Court justice.

Are people aware of major political issues and their significance? Are they able to place them in the general context of current politics? When these genuinely important questions are asked, the picture of the public's political competence brightens considerably. People may not remember the content of political speeches very well, but, as mentioned already, they are aware of a wide range of current issues. Moreover, when interviewers probe for understanding, rather than for knowledge of specific facts, they often discover considerable political insight. For instance, people who cannot define either *affirmative action* or *price deregulation* may have fairly sophisticated notions about these matters. Panelists in the Three Sites Project and others who had very little formal education knew about government price controls on some goods and services and fully understood the burdens faced by people hampered in finding a job because of their race or sex.[61]

Learning General Orientations

Some media stories leave the audience with politically significant feelings that persist long after facts have faded from memory. Although many details of the 1986 explosion of the *Challenger* space shuttle have been forgotten, Americans still retain vivid feelings of horror, sympathy, grief, and disappointment. Often news that etches a few facts into people's memories may leave them with generalized feelings of trust or distrust. For instance, prominently featured stories of serious corruption in government may lower the public's esteem for the integrity of government. A 1974 national survey showed that people who had read newspapers severely critical of various actions taken by the government expressed significantly less trust in government than did respondents exposed to favorable views. People who had not gone beyond grade school seemed to be particularly susceptible to erosion of trust in the wake of mass media criticism.[62] A number of laboratory and field experiments demonstrate similar linkages, positive as well as negative. Favorable publicity enhances esteem for government; unfavorable publicity diminishes it. Cynical people, in turn, tend to participate less than others in civic activities such as voting and lobbying.[63]

As political scientist Murray Edelman has noted, media stories may produce an overpowering sense of a world out of control, or they may reassure the audience that all is going well. Feelings of both insecurity and security may make people quiescent because they become fearful of interfering with crucial government actions or else complacent about the need for public vigilance. Fear that dissension weakens the government may decrease tolerance for dissidents. Edelman also warns that political quiescence leads to acceptance of faulty public policies, poor laws, and poor administrative practices—significant political effects.[64]

On a more personal level, millions of people use the media to keep in touch with their environment. This helps to counter feelings of loneliness and alienation because information becomes a bond among individuals who share it.[65] Media may also arouse desires that can change the course of life of individuals and societies. The models of life depicted by the media create wants and expectations as well as dissatisfactions and frustrations. These feelings may become powerful stimulants for social change for the society at large or for selected individuals within it. Whether media-induced changes are considered positive, negative, or a mixture of both depends, of course, on one's sociopolitical preferences.

Deterrents to Learning

Lack of motivation for political knowledge and distrust for the media, as well as deficiencies in the information supply deter the average individual from learning through media exposure. Most people do not need detailed knowledge of current affairs for either their jobs or their social relationships. Rather than discussing politics, which they see as a touchy topic, they prefer to talk about sports, or the weather, or the local gossip. In fact, as the level of abstract, issue-oriented content of political news rises, the size of the attentive audience shrivels.[66] People scan the news for major crises without trying to remember specific facts. However, when they sense that events will greatly affect their lives, or when they need information to make voting choices, political interest and learning perk up quickly and often dramatically.[67]

Occasionally, serious programs on radio and television become highly popular. Most of them involve themes of corruption, violence, or other wrongdoing, which may account for their popularity. Examples are "60 Minutes," which probes a variety of social ills; "The Winds of War," a made-for-TV movie that recapitulated World War II; and documentaries dealing with rape, child-snatching, and prison violence. Broadcasts of congressional hearings on Watergate and the Iran-contra affair or of the Panama Canal debates in the Senate fall into this category. These are exceptions, however.

Like a straw fire, widespread public interest in most political crises flares up and then dies quickly. For instance, attention was relatively brief in 1987 to the Iran-contra scandal even though it involved highly dramatic events like hostages, secret weapons deals, and circumvention of congressional mandates. After a few weeks audiences began to complain that stories about the affair usurped too much media time. Attention spans are erratic and brief, even though most Americans believe that, as good citizens, they ought to be well informed about political news, and they feel guilty, or at least apologetic, if they are not.[68]

Learning is further inhibited by the alienation of many population groups from the media. Some white ethnics and police and union members, for instance, consider most mass media to be opposed to them. They believe that the media lie and distort when they cast police as trigger-happy oppressors of the disadvantaged, or unions as corrupt and a barrier to economic progress.[69]

Public opinion polls in the 1980s showed considerable erosion over time of public confidence in the trustworthiness of the media. On a scale ranging from "a great deal of confidence in people running the media," to "only some," to "hardly any," a 1987 National Opinion Research Center poll recorded only 19 percent high confidence. Low confidence stood at 25 percent. By comparison, the Supreme Court earned a 38 percent high confidence rating, major companies stood at 31 percent, and organized labor at 11 percent.[70]

How media information is presented also affects learning. The public is bombarded daily with more news than it can handle. Most of the news is touted as significant even though much is trivial. The constant crisis atmosphere numbs excitement and produces boredom. The presentation of stories in disconnected snippets further complicates the task of making sense out of them and integrating them with existing knowledge. This is especially true when stories are complex. People who feel that they cannot understand what is happening are discouraged from spending time reading or listening. Featuring conflicting stories and interpretations, without giving guidance to the audience, also hinders learning.[71]

Television news deters the kind of factual and conceptual learning that social scientists measure and prize. Instead, it concentrates on conveying the essence of personalities and vistas of places and events.[72] Moreover, the average half-hour television news program covers the equivalent in words of only one newspaper page. If several newscasts are watched, about half the material is repetitive. Even within a single newscast a large proportion of every item is background information that puts the item into perspective for viewers seeing it for the first time. Moreover, as Tony Schwartz points out in *The Responsive Chord,* most television programs are not primarily designed "to get stimuli across, or even to package . . . stimuli so they can be understood and absorbed." Rather, television tries "to evoke stored information . . . in a patterned way" to make use of what the audience already knows.[73] These deterrents to learning are not outweighed by positive factors such as the interest generated by the picture and sound combination and the high confidence in familiar newscasters.

Viewing purposes are also important. Because most people watch television news to be entertained and because it is structured according to show business guidelines, audiences are not likely to try hard to learn much from it. "Happy-time" news formats and exciting film footage encourage the feeling that news should be viewed as lighthearted diversion. Of course, an entertaining format does not preclude learning; people do learn even from pure entertainment fare. Nevertheless, this kind of format reduces motivation to learn.[74]

The internal structure of television newscasts also impedes learning. Three-quarters of all news stories take up less than three minutes, yet they are crammed with information that cannot possibly be absorbed in that time (see Table 5-5). In addition to the abundance of pictures that is noted in the table, each news story contains verbal information. The average ratio is three factual statements for every two pictorial scenes. For the fifteen to eighteen stories that make up a typical newscast, viewers are asked to absorb an average of eighteen factual statements and eleven picture scenes per story. Furthermore, in most news programs disparate items are tightly packaged with few pauses to allow viewers to absorb information. Pauses are essential for learning. When they are absent, it is not surprising that half the audience after the lapse of a few hours cannot recall a single item from a television newscast. Many people watch television while cooking dinner or playing games, and these distracting activities do not help either.[75]

Some social scientists even contend that television has destroyed learning incentives because it takes the place of personal interactions and real life experiences. People who participate in life passively, watching the world through a television set, do not need to acquire information for talking with others and do not learn through action.[76]

Despite all of the deterrents to learning that have been discussed thus far, compared with other people in the world, Americans still rank quite high in political information levels. Education heightens the need for and salience of information. As the American population becomes better educated, this record should improve even further. Americans who routinely engage in political conversation already show greatly superior learning scores; however, many Americans rarely discuss poli-

Table 5-5   Network Television News Characteristics

Story length (seconds)	Percentage	Picture exposure (seconds)	Percentage	Number of pictures	Percentage
Less than 60	29	1-10	47	1-4	38
60-179	47	11-20	29	5-10	13
180-299	16	21-30	12	11-20	26
300+	8	31+	13	21-54	23

Source: Author's research based on a sample of 149 news stories from early evening newscasts on ABC, CBS, and NBC.

tics.[77] Americans are also well socialized into the American system. They may be disappointed and cynical about particular leaders or policies, but relatively few question the legitimacy of the government, object to its basic philosophies, or reject its claims to their support. If one believes in the merits of the system, this finding is, indeed, cause for satisfaction with current political socialization.

Learning Effects: Behavior

Because the media shape people's knowledge, attitudes, and feelings, they obviously can influence behavior. To assess the extent of behavioral effects, two areas that have long been of great political concern will be examined: imitation of crime and violence, particularly among adolescents, and stimulation of economic and political development in underdeveloped regions. In Chapter 6 we will discuss the effects of media coverage on voting behavior and in Chapter 9 the impact of the media on behavior in various societal crises.

Crime and Violent Behavior in Children

Many social scientists believe that violence and crime portrayed in the media, particularly on television, lead to learning and imitation. Children and young adults are deemed to be particularly impressionable. Because crime and violence are serious problems in American society, the possible link between television exposure and deviant behavior has been thoroughly investigated. The Surgeon General's office has produced a bookshelf of information.[78] Congressional committees have spent countless hours listening to conflicting testimony by social scientists about the impact of television violence. Meanwhile, violent content, particularly in fiction programs, has escalated. In 1986 nine out of ten entertainment programs broadcast during prime time contained violence at an average rate of eight violent incidents per hour. Weekend children's programs topped this rate with twenty-seven acts of violence packed into each hour.[79]

What have studies of the impact of television violence revealed? Despite the strong inclination of many of the researchers to find that crime fiction causes asocial behavior, the evidence provides only modest support. Some children do copy violent behavior, especially when they have watched aggression that was left unpunished or was rewarded and when countervailing influences from parents and teachers were lacking.[80] But, aside from immediately copying television examples when tempted to do so, children do not ordinarily become violent after exposure to violence in the mass media. Most children lack the predisposition and usually the opportunity for violence, and their environment discourages asocial behavior. In fact, exposure to crime makes

1985 CHICAGO TRIBUNE

Reprinted by permission: Tribune Media Services.

some children more sympathetic toward the suffering of crime and violence victims.[81] A crude cause and effect model is therefore invalid.

The percentage of imitation-prone pre-adolescents and adolescents in the population is not known at this time. However, the wide dispersion of television throughout American homes makes it almost certain that the majority of children susceptible to violence will be exposed. Even in the absence of television, many other triggers could arouse these young people to violence. Whatever the source of arousal, even if the actual number of highly susceptible pre-adolescents and adolescents is tiny and statistically insignificant, the social consequences can be profound.

Other confounding factors in assessing the impact of television on children are age-linked comprehension differences. Younger children may not be able to comprehend many of the events presented by the media in the same way that adolescents do. Several studies of preschool-age and early grade-school-age children suggest that much of what adults consider to be violent does not seem so to children. Cartoon violence is an example. When an enemy drops Donald Duck on his head, or pummels Mickey Mouse, or flattens Fred Flintstone with a boulder, most children view it as funny make-believe.[82] For them, it is not a behavior model for action in the real world. Many of the programs that adults consider to be dangerous actually may be harmless.

Children not only see things differently from adults, but they also are less adept at drawing inferences. The complex social reasoning that adults often ascribe to even young children does not develop until youngsters reach their teens. For instance, after seeing a series of shows with the implied message that the big bully who hits everybody always wins, children presumably conclude that similar behavior on their part will yield similar results. In actuality, they may not draw such a conclusion. Although young children often imitate what they have seen, they are rarely able to generalize or respond to implied messages. Without a better understanding of how the average child at various stages of development interacts with stories presented by the media, we cannot completely assess media effects on subsequent behavior. Nor can we plan program content with any assurance that it will encourage children of all ages and in diverse social settings to engage in approved behaviors and to abstain from undesirable activities.

Behavior Change in Adults

What about imitation of socially undesirable behavior by adults? The same broad principles apply. Imitation depends on the setting at the time of media exposure and on the personality and attitudes viewers bring to the situation. Widespread societal norms seem to be particularly important. For instance, the 1970 report of the Presidential Commission on Obscenity and Pornography noted that exposure to aberrant sexual behavior led to comparatively little imitation. In fact, there was some evidence that greater availability of obscene and pornographic materials reduced sex crimes and misdemeanors because vicarious experiences were substituted for actual ones.[83] By comparison, there was a great deal more evidence that exposure to criminal behavior encourages imitation. The difference may be more apparent than real, however, since crime is more likely to be reported, while sexual perversions remain hidden.

In sum, the precise link between exposure to media images and corresponding behavior remains uncertain. Legislative tampering with media offerings therefore appears premature. It will take a great deal more research and experimentation to determine how media fare can be presented to produce desirable results and avoid undesirable ones. Even assuming that this goal could be reached, it is questionable whether a democratic society should attempt to manipulate the minds of its citizens to protect them from temptations to violate social norms. It may be best to leave control of the content of entertainment programs to widely based informal social pressures. Whether social pressures should be allowed to interfere with reporting real-world violence poses even more difficult dilemmas. The possibly adverse effects on behavior must be balanced against the need to keep informed about the real world.

Socioeconomic Modernization

The assumed potential of the media to guide people's behavior has led to great efforts to use media as tools for social and political development. The results have been mixed—some successes and many failures.

Psychic Mobility. The hope of using the media to bring about industrialization, improved social services, and greater political participation in underdeveloped areas of the industrialized nations, such as parts of the American South or in Third World nations, ran very high at mid-century. The psychological key to human and material development was then assumed to be a personality characteristic that political scientist Daniel Lerner labeled *empathic capacity.* The media were thought to be the stimuli; when media present new objects and ideas, they presumably stimulate people to empathize and imagine themselves to be involved with these objects and ideas. For instance, when the media show how slum dwellers have converted old tires into sandals, or how flood victims have purified their polluted water supply, audience members begin to wonder, "How could I make this work for me?"

Before mass media became widely available to average people, this "psychic mobility" was generated when people came into direct contact with strangers with different lifestyles and experiences. Because contacts usually were limited to relatively few people, changes spread very slowly to wider groups. The broad diffusion of mass media, however, made it possible for the first time in human history to reach millions of people with comparative ease and to expose them to developmental stimuli, either directly or through contact with others reached by the media. Transistor radios and satellite television have opened even remote and inaccessible regions to modern communication and brought news of current lifestyles to isolated communities.

Social scientists who credit the media with a major role in modernization have made three assumptions. First, the mass media can create interest and empathy for unfamiliar experiences. Second, the mass media provide graphic examples of new practices, which are then readily understood and copied. (For instance, films and videotapes can show people how to build a cinder block house, how to purify water, or how to plant potatoes more efficiently.) Third, development, once started, creates an incentive for people to increase their knowledge and skills. Where formal education is not readily accessible, the media provide information and enhance the capacity to learn. Proof of these assumptions is seen in the progress in urbanization, industrialization, per capita income, and literacy that has followed media development in many regions.[84]

Psychological Barriers to Modernization. While many poor and technologically underdeveloped regions have shown measurable progress, with the media apparently serving as catalysts, modernization has been far slower and more sporadic than expected. A number of psychological and physical obstacles have kept the dreams of the development theorists from coming true. Most damaging has been outright hostility by individuals or communities to change and unwillingness to alter long-established patterns. Mass media may actually become a negative reference point so that people condemn the modern lifestyle depicted by the media.

For instance, when several federal government agencies attempted in the 1960s to improve poverty conditions in Knox County, Kentucky, where per capita income was one-fourth of the U.S. average, they found great resistance in tightly knit, homogeneous communities. Mass media programs designed to change health, child-rearing, and employment practices fell on deaf ears. In more heterogeneous communities in the country, success was moderate.[85]

People who are not overtly hostile to change, still may be totally uninterested in changing. This has been called the "housewife syndrome" because it happens most frequently with women who are isolated in their homes. Or it may spring from insecurity about ability to cope with changes and reluctance to further complicate a difficult life. Women and men exhibiting this mental state cannot be reached by the mass media without the intervention of a trusted person, such as a priest, physician, or family member. Mass media influence then becomes a "two-step flow" reaching its targets through selected opinion leaders.

Putting modern skills into words and concepts that people with little formal education can understand has also turned out to be exceedingly hard. For instance, teaching new ways to keep baby food pure, or to apply for aid from a government agency, or to construct cinder block houses involve concepts that may require schooling to grasp. The disparity in social backgrounds between journalists and their audiences further confounds the problem of communication. It creates *heterophily* (a gap between social backgrounds) that complicates communication rather than *homophily* (similarity in backgrounds) that eases it.

Changes that require adopting new social values or abandoning old habits are the most difficult of all and the least likely to occur. For example, people whose religious and social values favor large families are unlikely to be persuaded by the media to settle for small ones. Ingrained habits, such as driving without seatbelts, rarely change voluntarily. In the 1970s the Insurance Institute for Highway Safety broadcast advertisements in a number of cities about the importance of wearing seat belts. Even though these public service commercials were shown on prime-time television more than one hundred times each month, roughly 70 percent of the people who had seen and agreed with them did not use car seat belts. In the absence of penalties for noncompliance, the National Highway Traffic Safety Administration, which had spent nearly $10 million annually on its seat belt campaign, was able in 1975 to raise usage by only 4 percentage points, from 11 to 15 percent.[86]

Adoption of Changes. How can the mass media bring about socially desirable changes? We will outline five steps involved in change and indicate how the mass media fit into the picture.

The first step is an awareness of the possibility for change. Here the media are especially helpful. Radio can inform people about new energy-saving devices or new child-rearing methods. Television and movies can show new technologies and new styles of political participation.

The second step is understanding how to accomplish the suggested changes. For example, people may be aware that public assistance is available, but they may not know how to apply for it. Mass media usually fail to supply detailed information. On the average, only one-third of all stories that might inspire action of various types, such as environmental protection or energy conservation, contain implementing information.[87] Unless this gap is filled, the chain leading to the adoption of innovations is broken.

The third step is evaluation. People assess the merits of the innovation, given their circumstances, and decide whether they want to adopt it. Innovations often fail to take root because prospective users consider them bad, inappropriate, too risky, or too difficult. Media messages alone may not be persuasive enough. It may be crucial to have a trusted person urge or demonstrate adoption of the innovation.

The fourth step is trial. The effect of the media in getting people to try innovations is limited. Factors beyond media control are more important, such as social and financial costs of the change as well as the audience's willingness to change. Generally, young men are most receptive to innovations; older people are most skeptical and cautious.

Finally, trials may be followed by adoption. The media contribute most to this phase by encouraging people to stick with the changes that they have made part of their life and work styles. For example, adoption of birth control is useless unless it is continuous. The same holds true for many health and sanitation measures or improved work habits. To ensure continuity, mass media must cover a topic regularly, stressing long-range goals and reporting progress.

Predicting which media campaigns designed to change behavior will succeed and which will fail has proved to be difficult. The federal government spends millions of dollars each year on public service advertisements and consumer education programs, but it has reaped little from these efforts. Numerous carefully planned projects to motivate poor people and elderly shut-ins to listen to vitally needed information about nutrition, medical care, and social security benefits have failed. On the other hand, campaigns to get people to study pesticide labels more carefully, to learn about employment for the mentally retarded, or to win support for environmental protection programs have succeeded. The reasons why have thus far eluded researchers in most cases.[88]

Douglas S. Solomon, who studied health campaigns conducted by private and public institutions, believes that four factors account for success or failure. To succeed, campaigns must set well-specified, realistic goals that are tailored to the needs of various target groups. They must carefully select appropriate media and media formats and present them at key times and intervals. Messages must be properly designed for greatest persuasiveness. There also must be continuous evaluation and appropriate readjustments.[89]

In some instances the media's efforts to mobilize people have produced unanticipated attitudes and changes in behavior. For instance, when television was introduced in several Canadian Eskimo communities in the 1970s, programs were designed to show the viewers how to modernize their living conditions and to acquaint them with Canadian affairs generally. Rather than aspiring to modernize their lifestyles, Eskimo adults in the television communities turned their eyes to the past. They wanted to return to traditional Eskimo ways. This attitude was not apparent in localities without television. Whether it sprang from nostalgia for the past or aversion to the lifestyle changes foreshadowed by television is unclear. Interestingly, the adults who yearned for traditional ways aspired to a modern lifestyle for their children following the introduction of television.[90]

Above all, the success of the mass media in bringing about change hinges on the receptivity for change. Ongoing efforts to use the media to modernize underdeveloped areas or bring socially helpful information to the poor, the elderly, or the handicapped must concentrate on identifying the specific circumstances most likely to bring success. Responding to requests initiated locally, rather than designing information campaigns from the outside, and integrating local traditions into modern approaches seem to hold the most promise.[91]

Summary

The mass media play a major role in *political socialization,* the learning and accepting of norms and rules, structures, and environmental factors that govern political life. Contrary to earlier findings that indicated limited impact, the media are very influential and consequently a tremendously powerful political force.

However, the impact of the media on political socialization and other aspects of political learning is not uniform for all members of the media audience. The media affect individuals of different lifestyles and circumstances in different ways. Psychological, demographic, and situational factors influence perceptions and the ensuing political consequences. So does the manner of news presentation and the perspectives from which news is presented.[92]

Although many factors contribute to diversity in socialization and learning, there are also powerful unifying forces. Most Americans are exposed to similar information and develop roughly similar outlooks on what it means and ought to mean to be an American both politically and socially.

Various theories explain why and how individuals select particular information to remember. Learning of specific facts presented by the media is sparse. Nonetheless, people become aware of many political problems and appreciate their basic significance, even without remembering details about them. Equally important, exposure to the media produces apathy, cynicism, fear, trust, acquiescence, and support— moods that condition participation in the political process, which may range from total abstinence to efforts to overthrow the government by force.

The media may also produce or retard behavior that affects the quality of public life. In this chapter we assessed the role of the media in fostering socially undesirable behaviors, such as crime and violence, and in the political and social development of poor and industrially backward population groups. Media influence is greatest in informing people and creating initial attitudes; it is least effective in changing attitudes and ingrained behaviors.

Given the many largely uncontrollable variables that determine media influence, concerted efforts to manipulate media content to foster societal goals are risky at best. They could set dangerous precedents for inhibiting the free flow of controversial ideas or for using the media as channels for government propaganda.

Notes

1. Impact differences between print and electronic media are discussed in Peter Clarke and Eric Fredin, "Newspapers, Television and Political Reasoning," *Public Opinion Quarterly* 42 (Summer 1978): 143-160; Lee B. Becker, Idowu Sobowale, and William E. Casey, "Newspaper and Television Dependencies: Their Effects on Evaluations of Public Officials," *Journal of Broadcasting* 23 (Fall 1979): 465-475; Robert D. McClure and Thomas E. Patterson, "Print vs. Network News," *Journal of Communication* 26 (Spring 1976): 23-28; and Marion Just and Ann Crigler, "Public Learning

from the News Media" (Paper presented at the annual meeting of the American Political Science Association, Chicago, Ill., 1987).

2. Jacob Jacoby and Wayne D. Hoyer, "Viewer Miscomprehension of Televised Communications: Selected Findings," *Journal of Marketing* 46 (Fall 1982): 12-26.

3. Neil Postman, *Amusing Ourselves to Death: Public Discourse in the Age of Show Business* (New York: Viking Penguin, 1985). For a good discussion of the differences between the effects of print and television news, see Joshua Meyrowitz, *No Sense of Place: The Impact of Electronic Media on Social Behavior* (New York: Oxford University Press, 1985), 94-106.

4. Ronald Mulder, "Media Credibility: A Use-Gratifications Approach," *Journalism Quarterly* 57 (Fall 1980): 474-477; and Cecilie Gaziano and Kristin McGrath, "Measuring the Concept of Credibility," *Journalism Quarterly* 63 (Autumn 1986): 451-462. Alan M. Rubin, "Ritualized and Instrumental Television Viewing," *Journal of Communication* 34 (Summer 1984): 67-77, distinguishes between goal-directed and ritualized media use, with the former producing more learning than the latter.

5. Gladys Engel Lang and Kurt Lang, *Politics and Television Re-Viewed* (Beverly Hills, Calif.: Sage, 1984).

6. Stephen D. Reese and M. Mark Miller, "Political Attitude Holding and Structure: The Effects of Newspaper and Television News," *Communication Research* 8 (April 1981): 167-188. Also see Steven H. Chaffee and Joan Schleuder, "Measurement and Effects of Attention to Media News," *Human Communication Research* 13 (1986): 76-107.

7. George Comstock, "Social and Cultural Impact of Mass Media," in *What's News: The Media in American Society,* ed. Elie Abel (San Francisco: Institute for Contemporary Studies, 1981), 246. Also see Bruce Watkins, "Television Viewing as a Dominant Activity of Childhood: A Developmental Theory of Television Effects," *Critical Studies in Mass Communication* 2 (1985): 323-337. Average high school graduates have spent 15,000 hours watching television and 11,000 hours in the classroom. They have seen 350,000 commercials.

8. Gary Coldevin, "Internationalism and Mass Communications," *Journalism Quarterly* 49 (Summer 1972): 365-368. Also see M. Margaret Conway, Mikel L. Wyckoff, Eleanor Feldbaum, and David Ahern, "The News Media in Children's Political Socialization," *Public Opinion Quarterly* 45 (Summer 1981): 164-178; and Gina M. Garramone and Charles K. Atkin, "Mass Communication and Political Socialization: Specifying the Effects," *Public Opinion Quarterly* 50 (Spring 1986): 76-86.

9. M. Margaret Conway, A. Jay Stevens, and Robert G. Smith, "The Relations Between Media Use and Children's Civic Awareness," *Journalism Quarterly* 52 (Autumn 1975): 531-538; and Steven H. Chaffee, H. L. Scott Ward, and Leonard P. Tipton, "Mass Communication and Political Socialization," *Journalism Quarterly* 48 (Winter 1970): 647-659.

10. Leo Bogart, *Press and Public: Who Reads What, When, Where, and Why in American Newspapers* (Hillsdale, N.J.: Lawrence Erlbaum, 1981), 1. See also Suzanne Pingree, "Children's Cognitive Processes in Constructing Social Reality," *Journalism Quarterly* 60 (Fall 1983): 415-422; and Charles K. Atkin, Bradley S. Greenberg, and Steven McDermott, "Television and Race Role Socialization," *Journalism Quarterly* 60 (Fall 1983): 407-414.

11. Conway et al., "The News Media," 176.

12. For a good review of the political socialization literature, see Sidney Kraus

and Dennis Davis, *The Effects of Mass Communication on Political Behavior* (University Park: Pennsylvania State University Press, 1976), 8-47. See also Charles K. Atkin, "Communication and Political Socialization," in *Handbook of Political Communication,* ed. Dan D. Nimmo and Keith R. Sanders (Beverly Hills, Calif.: Sage, 1981), 299-328.

13. Jean Piaget, *The Language and Thought of the Child,* 3d ed. (New York: Harcourt Brace, 1962).

14. George Comstock, Steven Chaffee, Natan Katzman, Maxwell McCombs, and Donald Roberts, *Television and Human Behavior* (New York: Columbia University Press, 1978), 261-287. See also W. Andrew Collins, "Cognitive Processing in Television Viewing," in *Television and Behavior: Ten Years of Scientific Progress and Implications for the Eighties,* vol. 2, ed. David Pearl, Lorraine Bouthilet, and Joyce Lazar (Rockville, Md.: National Institute of Mental Health, 1982).

15. This research is summarized in Comstock et al., *Television and Human Behavior,* 172-287.

16. Alexander Szalai et al., eds., *The Use of Time* (The Hague, Netherlands: Mouton, 1972); and John P. Robinson, *How Americans Use Time: A Social-Psychological Analysis of Everyday Behavior* (New York: Praeger, 1977). On declines in viewing, see John P. Robinson, "Television and Leisure Time: A New Scenario," *Journal of Communication* 31 (Winter 1981): 120-130.

17. George Gerbner, Larry Gross, Marilyn Jackson Beeck, Suzanne Jeffries Fox, and Nancy Signorielli, "Cultural Indicators: Violence Profile No. 9," *Journal of Communication* 28 (Summer 1978): 178, 193. See also George Gerbner, Larry Gross, Michael Morgan, and Nancy Signorielli, "Political Correlates of Television Viewing," *Public Opinion Quarterly* 48 (Summer 1984): 283-300. The media's role in changing social attitudes is discussed in Hans Mathias Kepplinger and Michael Hachenberg, "Media and Conscientious Objection in the Federal Republic of Germany," in *Political Communication Research,* ed. David L. Paletz (Norwood, N.J.: Ablex, 1987), 108-128.

18. George Comstock, "The Impact of Television on American Institutions," *Journal of Communication* 18 (Spring 1978): 12-28.

19. Paula M. Poindexter, "Non-News Viewers," *Journal of Communication* 30 (Autumn 1980): 58-65.

20. Entertainment programming can supply general information, such as problem-solving techniques, or specific information, such as the social roles of women and minorities. For examples see Gary W. Selnow, "Solving Problems on Prime-Time Television," *Journal of Communication* 36 (Spring 1986): 63-72; Bradley S. Greenberg, *Life on Television* (Norwood, N.J.: Ablex, 1980); and W. James Potter and William Ware, "Traits of Perpetrators and Receivers of Antisocial and Prosocial Acts on TV," *Journalism Quarterly* 64 (Summer/Autumn 1987): 382-391.

21. Doris A. Graber, *Processing the News: How People Tame the Information Tide,* 2d ed. (New York: Longman, 1988), 90-93.

22. William Schneider and A. I. Lewis, "Views on the News," *Public Opinion* 8 (August/September 1985): 5-11, 58-59.

23. Reese and Miller, "Political Attitude Holding," 182.

24. L. Erwin Atwood, Ardyth B. Sohn, and Harold Sohn, "Daily Newspaper Contributions to Community Discussion," *Journalism Quarterly* 55 (Autumn 1978): 570-576; and Harold G. Zucker, "The Variable Nature of News

Media Influence," in *Communication Yearbook 2,* ed. Brent D. Ruben (New Brunswick, N.J.: Transaction Books, 1978), 225-240.

25. Gerbner et al., "Political Correlates," 286.
26. Michael J. Robinson, "News Media Myths and Realities: What the Network News Did and Didn't Do in the 1984 General Campaign," in *Elections in America,* ed. Kay Lehman Schlozman (Boston: Allen and Unwin, 1987), 149. For additional evidence of changes in political opinions produced by commentary, see Frederick T. Steeper, "Public Response to Gerald Ford's Statements on Eastern Europe in the Second Debate," in *The Presidential Debates: Media, Electoral and Policy Perspectives,* ed. George F. Bishop, Robert G. Meadow, and Marilyn Jackson-Beeck (New York: Praeger, 1978), 81-101.
27. Kenneth D. Wald, *Religion and Politics* (New York: St. Martin's Press, 1987), 209.
28. Comstock et al., *Television and Human Behavior,* 307-309. Also see Robert T. Bower, *The Changing Television Audience in America* (New York: Columbia University Press, 1985). Unfortunately, the book relies on 1980 data. For evidence that similarity in exposure leads to similar socialization, see Alexis S. Tan, "Media Use and Political Orientations of Ethnic Groups," *Journalism Quarterly* 60 (Spring 1983): 126-132.
29. Frederick Williams, Herbert S. Dordick, and Frederick Horstmann, "Where Citizens Go for Information," *Journal of Communication* 27 (Winter 1977): 95-99.
30. Comstock et al., *Television and Human Behavior,* 295-306.
31. Sheldon G. Levy, "How Population Subgroups Differed in Knowledge of Six Assassinations," *Journalism Quarterly* 46 (Winter 1969): 685-698.
32. Bogart, *Press and Public,* 76-79.
33. Bradley Greenberg and Brenda Dervin, "Mass Communication Among the Urban Poor," *Public Opinion Quarterly* 34 (Summer 1970): 224-235. Also see Bradley S. Greenberg, Michael Burgoon, Judee Burgoon and Felipe Korzenny, *Mexican Americans and the Mass Media* (Norwood, N.J.: Ablex, 1983). For partly contradictory evidence, see Tan, "Media Use."
34. The statistics in the next three paragraphs are from Bogart, *Press and Public,* 56, 66, 77. See also Leo Bogart, "Negro and White Media Exposure: New Evidence," *Journalism Quarterly* 49 (Spring 1972): 15-21; and George Comstock and Robin E. Cobbey, "Television and the Children of Ethnic Minorities," *Journal of Communication* 29 (Winter 1979): 104-115.
35. Karl Erik Rosengren, Lawrence A. Wenner, and Philip Palmgreen, eds., *Media Gratifications Research: Current Perspectives* (Beverly Hills, Calif.: Sage, 1985). Also see Gina M. Garramone, "Motivation and Political Information Processing: Extending the Gratifications Approach," in *Mass Media and Political Thought,* ed. Sidney Kraus and Richard Perloff (Beverly Hills, Calif.: Sage, 1985), 201-222.
36. Michael Morgan, "Heavy Television Viewing and Perceived Quality of Life," *Journalism Quarterly* 61 (Autumn 1984): 499-504; Philip Palmgreen, Lawrence A. Wenner, and J. D. Rayburn II, "Relations Between Gratifications Sought and Obtained: A Study of Television News," *Communication Research* 7 (April 1980): 161-192; Robert W. Kubey, "Television Use in Everyday Life: Coping with Unstructured Time," *Journal of Communication* 36 (Summer 1986): 108-123.
37. Thomas L. Friedman, "No TV? Israel Is Savoring the Silence," *New York Times,* November 6, 1987.

38. Graber, *Processing the News*, 133-136. See also Stuart H. Schwartz, "A General Psychographic Analysis of Newspaper Use and Life Style," *Journalism Quarterly* 57 (Autumn 1980): 392-401.

39. Lewis Donohew and Philip Palmgreen, "A Reappraisal of Dissonance and the Selective Exposure Hypothesis," *Journalism Quarterly* 48 (Autumn 1971): 412-420. See also Michael A. Milburn, "A Longitudinal Test of the Selective Exposure Hypothesis," *Public Opinion Quarterly* 43 (Winter 1979): 507-517; and Steven H. Chaffee and Yuko Miyo, "Selective Exposure and the Reinforcement Hypothesis: An Intergenerational Panel Study of the 1980 Presidential Campaign," *Communication Research* 10 (January 1983): 3-36.

40. Percy H. Tannenbaum, "The Indexing Process in Communication," *Public Opinion Quarterly* 19 (Fall 1955): 292-302. Also see Roy L. Behr and Shanto Iyengar, "Television News, Real-World Cues, and Changes in the Public Agenda," *Public Opinion Quarterly* 49 (Spring 1985): 38-57.

41. Donald L. Shaw and Maxwell E. McCombs, *The Emergence of American Political Issues: The Agenda-Setting Function of the Press* (St. Paul: West Publishing Co., 1977). See also Maxwell E. McCombs, "The Agenda-Setting Approach," in *Handbook*, 121-140; Shanto Iyengar and Donald R. Kinder, *News That Matters: TV and American Opinion* (Chicago: University of Chicago Press, 1987); and Benjamin I. Page, Robert Y. Shapiro, and Glenn R. Dempsey, "What Moves Public Opinion?" *American Political Science Review* 81 (March 1987): 23-43.

42. Doris A. Graber, "Agenda-Setting: Are There Women's Perspectives?" in *Women and the News*, ed. Laurily Keir Epstein (New York: Hastings House, 1978), 15-37.

43. For a relevant case study, see Tony Atwater, Michael B. Salwen, and Ronald B. Anderson, "Media Agenda-Setting with Environmental Issues," *Journalism Quarterly* 62 (Summer 1985): 393-397.

44. Zucker, "News Media Influence," 227. See also James H. Watt, Jr., and Sjef van den Berg, "How Time Dependency Influences Media Effects in a Community Controversy," *Journalism Quarterly* 58 (Spring 1981): 43-50; Behr and Iyengar, "Television News"; and Michael B. MacKuen and Steven L. Coombs, *More than News: Media Power in Public Affairs* (Beverly Hills, Calif.: Sage, 1981).

45. The importance of personal and contextual factors in news selection and evaluation is discussed in Lutz Erbring, Edie Goldenberg, and Arthur Miller, "Front-Page News and Real World Cues: Another Look at Agenda-Setting by the Media," *American Journal of Political Science* 24 (February 1980): 16-49; and David B. Hill, "Viewer Characteristics and Agenda Setting by Television News," *Public Opinion Quarterly* 49 (Fall 1985): 340-350. For a discussion of problems in measuring the relative impact of various factors, see Howard Schuman, Jacob Ludwig, and Jon A. Krosnick, "The Perceived Threat of Nuclear War, Salience, and Open Questions," *Public Opinion Quarterly* 50 (Winter 1986): 519-536.

46. Graber, *Processing the News*, 27-31, and, for details on learning processes, chaps. 7-9.

47. David Krech and Richard S. Crutchfield, "Perceiving the World," in *The Process and Effects of Mass Communications*, rev. ed., Wilbur Schramm and Donald F. Roberts (Urbana: University of Illinois Press, 1971), 235-264.

48. Walter Lippmann, *Public Opinion* (New York: Harcourt Brace, 1922), 31.

49. Phillip J. Tichenor, George A. Donohue, and Clarice N. Olien, "Mass Media

Flow and Differential Growth in Knowledge, *Public Opinion Quarterly* 34 (Summer 1970): 159-170; and Cecilie Gaziano, "The Knowledge Gap: An Analytical Review of Media Effects," *Communication Research* 10 (October 1983): 447-486. For evidence of shared reactions to television programs, irrespective of educational level, see W. Russell Neuman, "Television and American Culture: The Mass Medium and the Pluralist Audience," *Public Opinion Quarterly* 46 (Winter 1982): 471-487.

50. Eliot Freidson, "Communication Research and the Concept of the Mass," in *The Process and Effects of Mass Communication,* 197-208. See also Steven H. Chaffee, "Television and Social Relations, Introductory Comments," in *Television and Behavior,* 260-263.

51. Larry L. Burriss, "How Anchors, Reporters and Newsmakers Affect Recall and Evaluation of Stories," *Journalism Quarterly* 64 (Summer/Autumn 1987): 514-519.

52. Roberta S. Sigel, "Effects of Partisanship on the Perception of Political Candidates," *Public Opinion Quarterly* 28 (Summer 1964): 488-496. See also Shanto Iyengar, "Television News and Citizens' Explanations of National Affairs," *American Political Science Review* 81 (September 1987): 815-831.

53. For example, when a sample of citizens was asked why their worries about nuclear war had increased, the following mixture of reasons was cited: increased media coverage (52%); Reagan administration policies (19%); new weapons/new technology/proliferation (19%); unrest in the Third World (13%); East/West tensions (11%); Soviet belligerence (4%); children/grandchildren's lives (4%); other reasons (2%); don't know/no answer/can't explain (5%). Michael A. Milburn, Paul Y. Watanabe, and Bernard M. Kramer, "The Nature and Sources of Attitudes Toward a Nuclear Freeze," *Political Psychology* 7 (December 1986): 672.

54. Joshua Meyrowitz, *No Sense of Place: The Impact of Electronic Media on Social Behavior* (New York: Oxford University Press, 1985).

55. S. Robert Lichter, Linda S. Lichter, Stanley Rothman, and Daniel Amundson, "Prime-Time Prejudice: TV's Images of Blacks and Hispanics," *Public Opinion* 10 (July/August 1987): 13-16. More cynical observers claim that improvement of the images of blacks reflects the desire to boost audience ratings by tapping the large audience of black viewers.

56. The chances of becoming a crime victim are small in real life, but 30 to 64 percent in TV life. See Gerbner et al., "Cultural Indicators," 106-107; Paul Hirsch, "The 'Scary World' of the Nonviewer and Other Anomalies: A Reanalysis of Gerbner et al.'s Findings on Cultivation Analysis," parts 1 and 2, *Communication Research* 7 and 8 (Winter 1980 and Spring 1981): 403-457 and 3-37; and Michael Hughes, "The Fruits of Cultivation Analysis: A Re-examination of the Effects of Television Watching on Fear of Victimization, Alienation, and the Approval of Violence," *Public Opinion Quarterly* 44 (Summer 1980): 287-303. Exposure to news about actual crime predicts salience of crime better than does personal exposure to crime. Edna F. Einsiedel, Kandice L. Salomone, and Frederick P. Schneider, "Crime: Effects of Media Exposure and Personal Experience on Issue Salience," *Journalism Quarterly* 61 (Spring 1984): 131-136. See also Hugh M. Culbertson and Guido H. Stempel III, " 'Media Malaise': Explaining Personal Optimism and Societal Pessimism About Health Care," *Journal of Communication* 35 (Spring 1985): 180-190.

57. John Stauffer, Richard Frost, and William Rybolt, "The Attention Factor in

Recalling Network Television News," *Journal of Communication* (Winter 1983): 29-37.

58. Graber, "Agenda-Setting," 23.

59. Teun A. Van Dijk, *News as Discourse* (Hillsdale, N.J.: Lawrence Erlbaum, 1988), 139-174; and John P. Robinson and Mark R. Levy, *The Main Source: Learning from Television News* (Beverly Hills, Calif.: Sage, 1986, 57-175.

60. Scott Keeter and Cliff Zukin, *Uninformed Choice: The Failure of the New Presidential Nominating System* (New York: Praeger, 1983).

61. V. O. Key, with the assistance of Milton C. Cummings, Jr., *The Responsible Electorate* (Cambridge, Mass.: Harvard University Press, 1965), 7, reached the same conclusion.

62. Arthur H. Miller, Edie N. Goldenberg, and Lutz Erbring, "Type-Set Politics: Impact of Newspapers on Public Confidence," *American Political Science Review* 73 (March 1979): 67-84.

63. Michael J. Robinson, "Public Affairs Television and the Growth of Political Malaise: The Case of 'The Selling of the Pentagon,'" *American Political Science Review* 70 (June 1976): 409-432. See also Garrett J. O'Keefe, "Political Malaise and Reliance on Media," *Journalism Quarterly* 57 (Spring 1980): 122-128.

64. Murray Edelman, *Politics as Symbolic Action* (New York: Academic Press, 1976).

65. Comstock et al., *Television and Human Behavior*, 289-309.

66. W. Russell Neuman, *The Paradox of Mass Politics: Knowledge and Opinion in the American Electorate* (Cambridge, Mass.: Harvard University Press, 1986), 137.

67. The desire to be politically informed varies widely. For details, see ibid. News selection criteria are discussed in Graber, *Processing the News*, chap. 4.

68. Doris A. Graber and Young Yun Kim, "Why John Q. Voter Did Not Learn Much from the 1976 Presidential Debates," in *Communication Yearbook 2*, 414-419.

69. Glasgow University Media Group, *Bad News* (London: Routledge and Kegan Paul, 1976).

70. *Public Opinion* 10 (September/October 1987): 25. Age differences in media appraisals are discussed in Michael J. Robinson, "An Absence of Malice: Young People and the Press," *Public Opinion* 9 (November/December 1986): 43-47.

71. James W. Tankard, Jr., and Stuart W. Showalter, "Press Coverage of the 1972 Report on Television and Social Behavior," *Journalism Quarterly* 54 (Summer 1977): 293-298; Philip Palmgreen, "Mass Media Use and Political Knowledge," *Journalism Monographs*, no. 61 (May 1979): 20-33; and Edwin Diamond, *The Tin Kazoo: Television, Politics, and the News* (Cambridge, Mass.: MIT Press, 1975), 50-56.

72. Daniel C. Hallin, "We Keep America on Top of the World," in *Watching Television*, ed. Todd Gitlin (New York: Pantheon Books, 1986), 9-41.

73. Tony Schwartz, *The Responsive Chord* (Garden City, N.Y.: Anchor Press, Doubleday, 1974), 25. For an excellent analysis of learning from television, see Robinson and Levy, *The Main Source*, chaps. 3-7.

74. C. Richard Hofstetter and Terry Buss, "Motivation for Viewing Two Types of TV Programs," *Journalism Quarterly* 58 (Spring 1981): 99-103; and Mihaly Csikszentmihalyi and Robert Kubey, "Television and the Rest of Life: A Systematic Comparison of Subjective Experience," *Public Opinion Quarterly* 45 (Fall 1981): 317-328.

75. Richard M. Perloff, Ellen A. Wartella, and Lee B. Becker, "Increasing Learning from TV News," *Journalism Quarterly* 59 (Spring 1982): 83-86.
76. Jarol B. Manheim, "Can Democracy Survive Television?" *Journal of Communication* 26 (Spring 1976): 84-90.
77. Robinson and Levy, *The Main Source,* 97.
78. None of these studies focuses on the effects of exposure to nonfictional violence in the media since the First Amendment would be a strong bar to censorship of news. Surgeon General's Scientific Advisory Committee on Television and Social Behavior, *Television and Growing Up: The Impact of Televised Violence* (Washington, D.C.: U.S. Government Printing Office, 1971). For a critical review of the 1981 follow-up report, see Thomas D. Cook, Deborah A. Kendzierski, and Stephen V. Thomas, "The Implicit Assumptions of Television Research: An Analysis of the 1982 NIMH Report on 'Television and Behavior,' " *Public Opinion Quarterly* 47 (Spring 1983): 161-201. See also Richard A. Dienstbier, "Sex and Violence: Can Research Have It Both Ways?" *Journal of Communication* 27 (Summer 1977): 176-188.
79. "Violent Family Hour," *Society* 24 (January/February 1987): 2.
80. George A. Comstock, *The Evidence on Television Violence* (Santa Monica, Calif.: Rand Corporation, P-5730, 1976); Jerome L. Singer, Dorothy G. Singer, and Wanda S. Rapaczynski, "Family Patterns and Television Viewing as Predictors of Children's Beliefs and Aggression," *Journal of Communication* 34 (Summer 1984): 73-89. The politics of research on the effects of television violence are discussed by Willard D. Rowland, Jr., *The Politics of TV Violence: Policy Uses of Communication Research* (Beverly Hills, Calif.: Sage, 1983).
81. James M. Carlson, *Prime Time Law Enforcement: Crime Show Viewing and Attitudes Toward the Criminal Justice System* (New York: Praeger, 1985).
82. Robert P. Snow, "How Children Interpret TV Violence in Play Context," *Journalism Quarterly* 51 (Spring 1974): 13-21.
83. Presidential Commission on Obscenity and Pornography, *Report of the Commission on Obscenity and Pornography* (New York: Bantam Books, 1970). See also the *Attorney General's Commission on Pornography: Final Report,* published in 1986; and Dienstbier, "Sex and Violence," 177-180.
84. David O. Edeani, "Critical Predictors of Orientation to Change in a Developed Society," *Journalism Quarterly* 58 (Spring 1981): 56-64. The carefully measured impact of the introduction of television into a Canadian community is presented in Tannis MacBeth Williams, ed., *The Impact of Television: A Natural Experiment in Three Communities* (Orlando, Fla.: Academic Press, 1985).
85. Lewis Donohew, "Communication and Readiness for Change in Appalachia," *Journalism Quarterly* 44 (Winter 1967): 679-687; and Lowndes F. Stephens, "Media Exposure and Modernization Among the Appalachian Poor," *Journalism Quarterly* 49 (Summer 1972): 247-257.
86. Leon S. Robertson, "The Great Seat Belt Campaign Flop," *Journal of Communication* 26 (Autumn 1976): 41-45.
87. James B. Lemert, Barry N. Mitzman, Michael A. Seither, Roxana H. Cook, and Regina Hackett, "Journalists and Mobilizing Information," *Journalism Quarterly* 54 (Winter 1977): 721-726.
88. Ronald J. Rice and William Paisley, eds. *Public Communication Campaigns* (Beverly Hills, Calif.: Sage, 1981).

89. Douglas S. Solomon, "Health Campaigns on Television," in *Television and Behavior,* 316-319.
90. Sheldon O'Connell, "Television and the Canadian Eskimo: The Human Perspective," *Journal of Communication* 27 (Autumn 1977): 140-144; and Gary O. Coldevin, "Anik I and Isolation: Television in the Lives of Canadian Eskimos," *Journal of Communication* 27 (Autumn 1977): 145-153.
91. Everett M. Rogers, "The Rise and Fall of the Dominant Paradigm," *Journal of Communication* 28 (Winter 1978): 64-69; and Wilbur Schramm and Daniel Lerner, eds., *Communication and Change: The Last Ten Years— and the Next* (Honolulu: University Press of Hawaii, 1976).
92. Stuart J. Sigman and Donald L. Fry, "Differential Ideology and Language Use: Readers' Reconstructions and Descriptions of News Events," *Critical Studies in Mass Communication* 2 (December 1985): 307-322.

Readings

Ball-Rokeach, Sandra, Milton Rokeach, and Joel W. Grube. *The Great American Values Test: Influencing Behavior and Belief Through Television.* New York: The Free Press, 1984.

Bryant, Jennings, and Dolf Zillmann, eds. *Perspectives on Media Effects.* Hillsdale, N.J.: Lawrence Erlbaum, 1986.

Graber, Doris A. *Processing the News: How People Tame the Information Tide.* 2d ed. New York: Longman, 1988.

Jensen, Klaus Bruhn. *Making Sense of the News.* Aarhus, Denmark: Aarhus University Press, 1986.

Meyrowitz, Joshua. *No Sense of Place: The Impact of Electronic Media on Social Behavior.* New York: Oxford University Press, 1985.

Robinson, John P., and Mark R. Levy. *The Main Source: Learning from Television News.* Beverly Hills, Calif.: Sage, 1986.

Stover, William James. *Information Technology in the Third World: Can It Lead to Humane National Development?* Boulder, Colo.: Westview Press, 1984.

van Dijk, Teun A. *News Analysis: Case Studies of International and National News in the Press.* Hillsdale, N.J.: Lawrence Erlbaum, 1988.

_____. *News as Discourse.* Hillsdale, N.J.: Lawrence Erlbaum, 1988.

CHAPTER 6

Elections in
the Television Age

Who will rule the people? In times past the contenders often were put through the ordeal of hand-to-hand combat. In the modern age the ordeal of television frequently decides this question, sometimes in strange and unexpected ways. So it happened in November 1987 when Harold Washington, Chicago's first black mayor, died unexpectedly after a heart attack. He had left no designated political heir. The scramble for the empty seat of power began almost immediately, at first largely behind closed doors while the public witnessed the burial rites. Even there, political contenders for the post, struggling to become symbolically linked to the fallen leader, postured before the television cameras.

During the night of the funeral, rumors abounded that a deal had been struck between the city's white power brokers and Eugene Sawyer, the longest serving black alderman on the City Council. Sawyer was opposed by Alderman Timothy Evans, the late mayor's floor leader on the Council. Evan's supporters staged a huge memorial rally for Mayor Washington, which became, in effect, a political rally for their candidate. After the service the noisy demonstration moved to City Hall, shouting support for Evans and disdain for Sawyer. The size of the crowd was intended to demonstrate the strength of the opposition to Sawyer and the strength of support for Evans.

Sawyer's forces watched this display with concern. Candidate Sawyer wavered, fearing a disabling split in the hitherto united black electorate. Despite strong prodding by his supporters, he refused to test his candidacy through a City Council vote. Any alderman who could muster majority support on the Council would win the office. Close to midnight Sawyer watched a television interview in which Evans accused

Sawyer of lying about the strength of Sawyer's backers on the City Council. An angry Sawyer then decided that he would let a Council vote prove his strength. And so in the early morning hours Sawyer was elected mayor of Chicago by a vote of 29 to 19. Besides himself, only five of the city's black aldermen voted for him. As media critic Steve Daly put it, the election of Eugene Sawyer was a story "made-for TV, and made-by TV." [1]

But was it really? Eugene Sawyer was an experienced politician with a long record in Chicago politics. As chairman of the Rules Committee and president pro tempore of the City Council, he was one of the most visible aldermen in the group of fifty from which a candidate had to be chosen. Support from the Rev. Jessie Jackson had hurt Evans' candidacy among anti-Jackson aldermen on the Council. The mass demonstrations designed to show the television audience that Sawyer lacked the support of the black community were scheduled after Sawyer already was the apparent front-runner within the City Council. Despite heavy coverage of the rallies and of Sawyer's opponents, Sawyer won in the end.

As in so many election contests, factors other than media coverage may have determined the outcome. Media coverage, however, could have been the deciding factor. Although the link between media and elections has been studied more thoroughly than other media-politics linkages, the verdict remains unclear. Definitive answers are lacking for most cause-effect questions such as those posed by the Sawyer-Evans showdown in Chicago.

The State of Research

Understanding the role of the mass media in elections is hampered by imbalances in research. Presidential elections have been extensively studied, and congressional elections have drawn the attention of more and more scholars. Far less is known about the media's role in gubernatorial elections and practically nothing about their impact on local, judicial, or school board elections. The limited evidence available suggests that the role of the media varies substantially, depending upon the particular office being contested, and the news appeal of a campaign. In congressional elections, for example, exciting campaigns are covered, while routine ones are ignored. Television coverage tends to be sparse because the boundaries of media markets and congressional districts match poorly. With relatively few voters in a television market interested in a particular congressional race, market-wide coverage reaches too many uninterested viewers and hence wastes scarce time.[2]

Even at the presidential level little research has been done to point up differences in the role of the media as candidates and issues change from one election to the next.[3] High costs have discouraged researchers from studying media influences throughout the entire campaign from the preprimary period to the general election. The crucial early stages in the campaign when candidate selection takes place were largely ignored prior to Ronald Reagan's election in 1980.

The influence of factors such as incumbency, three-way competition, or major national crises was not thoroughly investigated either. It stands to reason that the impact of the media will vary depending on the changing political scene, the type of coverage chosen by newspeople, and the fluctuating interests of voters. Comparable studies of media impact on elections in Canada, Great Britain, France, Germany, and elsewhere have been plagued by similar problems.[4]

Another serious obstacle to understanding is the dearth of media content analyses. Election news content and its setting within the context of general news have been examined only rarely because content analysis is very costly. But without knowing the exact content of news, it becomes impossible to test what impact, if any, it had on viewers' perceptions. Another problem is failure to ascertain media exposure accurately. Investigators frequently assume that people have been exposed to media without checking precisely which stories have come to the attention of various individuals and what these individuals learned from these stories.

A shortage of good data also prevents researchers from isolating the effects of political advertising on political campaigns.[5] Candidates and their supporters spend a large share of their campaign budgets on political advertising displayed on bumper stickers and billboards, printed in newspapers, disseminated through video tapes, or broadcast with clockwork regularity on radio and television. The precise impact of these advertisements on target audiences is uncertain because it is difficult to untangle effects of commercials from the effects of other types of campaign publicity.

In their investigation of the impact of television commercials during the 1972 presidential campaign, Thomas Patterson and Robert McClure found that major campaign issues were covered more extensively in television commercials than in network newscasts. For instance, between September 18 and November 6, 1972, more than sixty-five minutes of advertising time were used to tell about Nixon's policies regarding Vietnam, China, Russia, and America's allies. The average television network spent only fifteen minutes on these stories.[6] Most viewers—particularly those who did not read newspapers and were poorly informed—remembered more from the commercials, which each took only five minutes or less of air time, than from the television news. Simplicity of content, expert eye-ear appeal, and repetition of the message combined to produce this result.

Although people learned facts about campaign issues from commercials, they apparently failed to influence viewers' evaluations of the candidates. Commercials are perceiver-determined. People see in them pretty much what they want to see—attractive images for their favorite candidates and unattractive ones for the opponent. If attempts to glamorize political actors and hide their weaknesses succeed, the effect lasts for only a short time. Commercials of opposing candidates and people's cynicism about campaign propaganda see to that. By and large, commercials have not altered ultimate voting choices in recent presidential campaigns, although they seem to have had some impact during early primaries. The claims that television commercials can manufacture fairyland candidates and make them believable to credulous audiences apparently are vastly exaggerated whenever voters have alternative means to know the candidates.[7]

Whether commercials can inject crucial issues into a campaign remains debated. In the heat of campaigns, wins and losses are often attributed by the candidates to particular commercials or to the ability of the candidates to buy ample television time. Scholarly corroborations are lacking for most of these claims. Nevertheless, the battle of the airwaves has been steadily increasing in recent campaigns, especially during primary contests. It has also begun to branch out from over-the-air television to cable outlets. Advertising rates are cheaper on cable television—an attractive medium because messages can be more readily tailored to the needs of the smaller cable audiences.

Television commercials often provide the only chance to gain information about the many candidates who are ignored by the media.[8] At the lower levels of political office, voters lack alternative sources of information, and therefore the impact of commercials can be decisive. Indeed, wisely spent advertising funds can buy elections.[9] Michael Robinson concluded that commercials for congressional candidates "can work relative wonders," especially when they are not challenged by the other side. "A well-crafted, heavily financed, and uncontested ad campaign does influence congressional elections—1980 is substantial proof."[10]

The Consequences of Media Politics

The advent of television and its ready availability in every home, the spread and improvement of public opinion polling, and the use of computers in election data analysis have vastly enhanced the role of the mass media in elections. In this era of "media politics," what major changes have been wrought by the new technologies? Four consequences will be considered: a decline in party influence, an increase in the power of media personnel to influence the selection of candidates, the need for candidates to "televise well," and the importance of made-for-media campaigns.

Decline in Party Influence

Foremost among the changes is the declining influence of political parties, particularly in presidential elections. During the 1940s, when social scientists first investigated the impact of the mass media on the outcome of presidential elections, party allegiance was the most important determinant of the vote. It was followed by voters' feelings of allegiance to a social group, assessment of the candidate's personality, and consideration of issues, in that order.

Since the full flowering of the electronic age more than two decades later, the order has been reversed. The candidate as a personality has become the prime consideration at the presidential level. Second are issues associated with the candidate, followed by party affiliation and group membership.[11] When voters base their decisions on a candidate's personality or stand on issues, the media become more important because they are the chief sources of information about these matters.

Correspondingly, political parties take on less importance. When voters can see and hear candidates in their own living rooms, they can make choices that differ from those made by the party. Split ticket voting, that is, voting for candidates of different parties, has become common. Candidates can also defy and thereby weaken party control because radio and television give them direct access to voters. More candidates can enter the race and campaign on their own strengths, raising their own money and building their own organizations. New candidates with the aid of the media can gain a wide following rapidly. This new independence of voters and candidates makes primary and general election races more crowded and less predictable. Party regulars who have groomed themselves for years to attain positions of power may find themselves bypassed.

Party affiliation remains very important at the state and local levels where the average voter knows little about most candidates, and media information is scant, particularly on television. This is not true, however, when candidates run without overt or covert party designation and endorsement, or when candidates of the same party compete against each other in primary elections. When party choice criteria are lacking and personal experience or advice from opinion leaders is unavailable, voters turn to whatever guidance the media may offer. Some will follow expressed or implied media endorsements; others will take them as cues to vote the opposite way. In either case what the media say about the candidates influences the voting decision.

Media as King Makers

More than ever before media personnel can influence the selection of candidates and issues.[12] Candidates, like actors, depend for their success as much on the roles into which they are cast as on their acting ability. In the television age media people usually do the casting for presidential hopefuls, whose performance is then judged according to the assigned role. Strenuous efforts by campaign directors and public relations experts to dominate this aspect of the campaign have been only moderately fruitful.

Casting occurs early in the primaries when newspeople, on the basis of as yet slender evidence, must predict winners and losers in order to narrow the field of eligibles. Concentrating on the front-runners in public opinion polls makes newspeople's tasks more manageable, but it often forces trailing candidates out of the race prematurely. As *New York Times* political writer R. W. Apple candidly admits, "Such early calculations are highly speculative. . . . But early calculations have a life of their own because they are the backdrop against which politicians and the media tend to measure the performance of the various candidates in their early confrontations." [13]

Perhaps the best example of this occurred in the 1976 Democratic primaries. Almost a dozen candidates were running, but the media covered Jimmy Carter, the little known former governor of Georgia, far more heavily and favorably than the other contenders. Months before the primaries, Carter's campaign staff worked assiduously to gain for their candidate extensive newspaper coverage. Massive television coverage followed after the New Hampshire primary in February in which Carter received 30 percent of the Democratic vote. NBC's Tom Pettit called Carter "the man to beat." *Time* magazine labeled his campaign as the only one "with real possibilities of breaking far ahead of the pack." It featured him on its front cover, as did *Newsweek*. Along with the front-cover picture in *Time* went a 2,630-line feature story, compared with 300 lines devoted to all other Democrats in the race.

Sen. Henry Jackson of Washington and Rep. Morris Udall of Arizona did well in the early Democratic primaries, but between them received less than one-third of the television coverage that Carter received. Subsequent primary defeats, such as Carter's poor showing in Massachusetts in early March, were characterized as exceptions that merely slowed his momentum, rather than as disastrous defeats. Gallup poll ratings in early February that credited Carter with only 5 percent of the national vote were given little publicity. [14]

Carter's handling of the media was astute. He managed to convince newspeople that his election successes were far greater than could be reasonably expected. Such expectations, which are media creations, are based on poll results, projections from past campaigns, and more or less educated guesses. They are the uncertain yardsticks by which newspeople measure winners and losers. Candidates who exceed expectations win; candidates who fall short lose. [15] Carter won his prized "winner" status after less than 5 percent of the primary delegates had been selected. The emphasis that the media place on early victories creates psychological momentum that enhances a candidate's chances for winning successive primaries and getting the nomination. Media legitimation is particularly important for political unknowns such as Democratic hopeful Gary Hart in 1984. His second-place finish in the Iowa caucuses convinced newspeople that he, not John Glenn, was the runner-up to Walter Mondale. In the week after Iowa and before the New Hampshire primary, Hart received more coverage than did Mondale. Media attention propelled him to victory in New Hampshire.[16]

The winner or loser image may become a self-fulfilling prophecy because supporters and money, as well as media coverage, flow to the front-runner, especially when lesser contenders have dropped out of the race after poor showings in early contests. In Hart's case the money and support needed for a full-scale campaign in 1984 became available after his victories in Iowa and several New England states had attracted press attention. Even then the boost was insufficient to match the resources of front-runner Mondale whom news stories continued to designate as the likely winner of the presidential primary sweepstakes, albeit with lowered odds.

Media coverage and public opinion polls tend to move in tandem, especially in the early months of a campaign. Candidates who receive ample media coverage usually do well in the polls. Good poll ratings bring more media coverage. Once the caucus and primary season has started in the spring of the election year, the outcomes of these contests become more important predictors of media attention. The winners and candidates whose scores seem surprising receive heavy media coverage; the media neglect the losers. One other pattern prevails. The substance of stories tends to be favorable for trailing candidates in the race and unfavorable for front-runners. For instance, after Hart's smashing triumph over Mondale in New Hampshire, the typical "attack the front-runner" strategy began. A media blitz questioning Hart's competence and credibility culminated on the eve of Super Tuesday when five primaries and four caucuses took place.[17]

The media's role as king maker or killer of the dreams of would-be kings is often played over a long span of time. Image making for presidential elections now begins on a massive scale more than a year before the first primary. The "pre-pre-campaign," on a more limited scale, begins shortly after the finish of the previous election. By the end of 1981, for instance, thirty Democrats and fourteen Republicans had already been mentioned as potential presidential candidates for 1984.[18] Senators who receive favorable publicity over many years may gradually come to be thought of as likely presidential nominees.

Captains of the media industry have often been able to use their personal influence and the power of the media under their control to support nominations for their favorites and to harm opponents. For instance, publisher Henry Luce enticed popular war-hero Dwight Eisenhower to run for the presidency in 1952. Luce put his publications, such as *Time* and *Life,* at Eisenhower's service. Kyle Palmer and the Chandler family, through their control of the *Los Angeles Times,* were instrumental in getting Richard Nixon a seat in the House of Representatives in 1946 and a U.S. Senate seat in 1950. Col. Robert McCormick used the powerful *Chicago Tribune* to defeat policies of the Roosevelt and Truman administrations and to put Republican politicians into office in Illinois.[19]

The power of the media also can be wielded to destroy candidacies. This happened to two Democratic candidates for the presidency in 1988, Senator Joe Biden of Delaware and Gary Hart. Biden was forced out of the campaign by widely publicized charges that his speeches contained plagiarized quotes from other political leaders. Hart withdrew temporarily after charges of philandering. News of trysts with model Donna Rice on the yacht *Monkey Business* and in his Washington home made headlines across the country. In December 1987 Hart reentered the presidential contest. He ended his campaign shortly after Super Tuesday when it became clear that his political reputation was beyond repair. Recurrent media references to the Chappaquiddick incident, a damaging personal affair in Senator Edward Kennedy's past, also have dampened efforts by his supporters to draft him as a presidential contender.

Media images can also become vastly important during the general election campaign. For instance, the Kennedy-Nixon television debates of 1960, the Reagan-Carter debates of 1980, and the Reagan-Mondale debates of 1984 helped to remove public impressions that John F. Kennedy and Ronald Reagan were unsuited for the presidency. Kennedy was apparently able to demonstrate that he was capable of coping with the presidency despite his youth and inexperience and Reagan in 1980 conveyed the impression that he was neither trigger-happy nor physically or mentally decrepit. Four years later, however, his inauspicious start in the opening debate made some viewers wonder whether advancing age had made him unfit for a second term. Demonstration of physical and mental vigor during subsequent debates helped reverse the unfavorable image that could have cost Reagan the election. No other medium could have equaled the reach and impact of television.[20] In fact, the risks of televised debates so awed presidential candidates after the 1960 encounter that a repeat performance did not occur for sixteen years. Since then they have become plentiful, with a veritable flood of debates during the 1988 race. Their impact has fluctuated, ranging from inconsequential to decisive.

Presidents Lyndon Johnson and Jimmy Carter saw their chances

The Re-entry.

for a second term diminish sharply in the wake of adverse media coverage.[21] In Carter's case the media chose to commemorate the anniversary of a major foreign policy failure—the American hostages' prolonged captivity in Iran—just prior to the 1980 presidential election. In Johnson's case the media chose to publicize only certain statements from the full record of Johnson's public statements justifying his Vietnam policies. Evidence suggests that media message selection gutted the case the president needed to make himself a strong second-term candidate in 1968.[22] Johnson decided not to seek another term.

Media-operated public opinion polls are yet another weapon in the arsenal for king-making. The CBS-*New York Times* poll, the NBC-Associated Press poll, and the ABC-*Washington Post* poll all conduct popularity ratings and issue polls throughout presidential elections and publicize them widely. During the final election week in 1984, the *New York Times* devoted one-third of its election coverage to poll reports.[23] These widely publicized poll results become bench marks for voters, telling them who the winners and losers are and what issues should be deemed crucial to the campaign. Depending on the nature and format of the questions asked by the pollsters and the political context in which the story becomes embedded, the responses spell fortune or misfortune for the candidates.

Polls may determine which candidates enter the fray and which keep out. Reagan was encouraged to enter the 1976 presidential race because President Gerald Ford's poll ratings were low prior to the Republican presidential nominating convention of that year.[24] With these low poll ratings as backdrop, Ford's subsequent rise in the polls was widely interpreted as a show of real political strength. Similarly, President Carter's poor poll ratings early in the 1980 campaign encouraged Kennedy's candidacy and gave Carter an image of political weakness that he was unable to shed even when his ratings improved. A Harris poll reported by ABC News in June 1980 boosted financial and volunteer support for Republican John Anderson when it showed that 31 percent of the respondents would vote for him "if the polls showed" that he had a real chance of winning the election. Ironically, poll predictions hastened Anderson's political downfall when he dropped below expected support in the crucial primary in his home state of Illinois.

Television-Age Recruits

A third important consequence of the new politics is the change it has wrought in the types of candidates likely to be politically successful. Because television can bring the image of candidates for high national and state office directly into the homes of millions of voters, political recruiters have become extremely conscious of a candidate's ability to look impressive and to perform well before the cameras. People who are not telegenic have been eliminated from the pool of available recruits. Abraham Lincoln's rugged face probably would not have passed muster in the television age. President Harry S. Truman's "Give 'em Hell, Harry," homespun style would have backfired if presented to nationwide groups rather than small gatherings. Franklin D. Roosevelt's wheelchair appearances would have spelled damaging weakness. Roosevelt, in fact, was keenly aware of the harmful effects that a picture of himself in a wheelchair might have and never allowed photographs to be taken while he was being lifted to the speaker's rostrum.

Actors and celebrities from other walks of life who are adept at performing before the public now have a much better chance than ever before to be recruited for political office. Reagan, a former actor; John Glenn, an ex-astronaut; and Jesse Jackson, a charismatic preacher, are examples of typical television-age recruits whose chances for public office would have been much smaller in an earlier era. As columnist Marquis Child has put it, candidates no longer "run" for office; they "pose" for office.[25]

In fact, good pictures can counterbalance the effects of unfavorable verbal comments. During the 1984 presidential campaign favorable pictures coincided with favorable poll results even when verbal commentary was predominantly negative. For example, CBS reporter Leslie Stahl verbally attacked the president for falsely posturing as a man of peace and compassion, but the pictures accompanying her script told a different story:

> The president basking in a sea of flag-waving supporters, beaming beneath red-white-and-blue balloons floating skyward, sharing concerns with farmers in a field, picnicking with Mid-Americans, pumping iron, wearing a bathing suit and tossing a football . . . , getting the Olympic torch from a runner, greeting wheelchair athletes at the handicapped Olympics, greeting senior citizens at their housing project, honoring veterans who landed on Normandy, honoring youths just back from Grenada, countering a heckler, joshing with the press corps, impressing suburban school children, wooing black inner city kids. . . [26]

A Reagan assistant promptly thanked Stahl for showing four-and-a-half minutes of great pictures of the president, noting that "that's all the American people see." [27] Aware of the power of visuals, he was not in the least concerned about the scathing remarks.

Candidates who perform poorly on television now spend considerable time and money being coached by professionals. These television advisers have become year-round regular members of presidential and gubernatorial staffs. Names of media experts such as David Sawyer, Gerald Rafshoon, Tony Schwartz, David Garth, Philip Dusenberry, or Joseph Napolitan have become almost as well known as the political bosses of yesteryear. These experts create commercials for the candidates and generate and handle general news coverage of the campaign.

In 1984 media expenses represented 30 to 50 percent of the budget spent by all candidates and parties in elections at all levels. Total campaign spending was estimated at $1.8 billion.[28] Radio and television expenses for the Republicans and Democrats for the postnomination campaign totaled $22.9 million and $18.2 million, respectively, nearly half of all campaign costs. Additional money was spent on media during the prenomination campaign, which cost even more than the final campaign.[29] However, the transmission of audio-visual election messages via satellites may lower costs, starting with the 1988 campaign.[30]

Given the high cost of television commercials and of gaining news exposure, a candidate's ability to raise money remains an important consideration, even when federal funding is available. Wealthy candidates who can draw on personal resources have an advantage. Activities and statements likely to alienate donors are shunned. While there is evidence that the best-financed candidates do not always win, folklore says they do. Hence falling behind in the race for money to finance media exposure is a sharp brake on political aspirations. The political consequences in recruitment and postelection commitments that spring from such financial considerations are enormous.

Campaigning for the Media

A fourth major aspect of the new politics is the fact that mass media coverage has become the campaign's pivotal point. Campaigns are expressly arranged for the best media exposure before the largest suitable audience. To attract media coverage candidates concentrate on press conferences, talk show appearances, or trips to interesting locations. Even when candidates meet voters personally through rallies, parades, or shopping center visits, they generally time and orchestrate these events to attract favorable media coverage.

Incumbents have a distinct advantage over challengers. Although they may attract about the same number of campaign stories, incumbents receive additional attention through coverage of their official duties.[31] Incumbents may also be able to dictate time and place for media encounters. When a president schedules a meeting for reporters in the White House Rose Garden, ample coverage is ensured. There even is a quasi-incumbency status for promising challengers. Once they have attained wide recognition as front-runners, newspeople compete for their attention. Their power to grant or withhold it can be translated into influence over quality and quantity of coverage.

Candidates plan their schedules to dovetail with media coverage habits. They spend disproportionate amounts of time campaigning in Iowa and New Hampshire where media coverage is heavy. During the 1984 campaign, Walter Mondale spent thirty days in New Hampshire, John Glenn spent thirty-two. Gary Hart topped this with fifty-two days, Ernest Hollings with sixty, and Reubin Askew with more than seventy.[32] Ample media coverage does not guarantee benefits at the polls. In 1988 Pete Du Pont spent ninety-one days and $560,000 in Iowa, but he received only 7 percent of the Republican vote.

A survey of 1984 ABC, CBS, NBC, and *New York Times* coverage showed that Iowa and New Hampshire, which have less than 3 percent of the U.S. population, received almost one-third of the total media coverage during the 1984 primaries. New York, California, Pennsylvania, New Jersey, and Illinois, which combined have 31 percent of the U.S. population, received another third, leaving primaries in the other forty-three states, where two-thirds of all Americans live, with slightly over one-third of the coverage.[33]

To keep a favorable image of their candidates in front of the public, campaign managers arrange newsworthy events to familiarize potential voters with their candidates' best aspects. Because most television producers do not like "talking heads"—shots of the faces of speakers—candidates may engage in meaningless activities merely to provide

attractive, action-oriented pictures. Most of these pictures are deliberately packed with symbols to convey stock messages quickly and easily.
For instance, showing candidates with old people, or black workers, or
college students proclaims affinity for these groups. Leslie Stahl thus
describes how Carter courted the voters in 1980:

> What did President Carter do today in Philadelphia? He posed, with as
> many different types of symbols as he could possibly find.
>
> There was a picture at the day care center. And one during the game of
> bocce ball with the senior citizens. Click, another picture with a group of
> teenagers. And then he performed the ultimate media event—a walk
> through the Italian market.
>
> The point of all this, obviously, to get on the local news broadcasts and
> in the morning newspapers. It appeared that the President's intention was
> not to say anything controversial. . . . Simply the intention was to be seen.[34]

Many campaign events are now staged as prime-time, live coverage
television spectacles. Aside from occasional presidential debates, the
conventions used to be the biggest single media event of presidential
campaigns. Both major parties still select the convention cities with an
eye to effective television coverage. Convention managers try to keep a
tight rein on speakers and demonstrations. They want to make sure that
desirable images are conveyed and that important speeches are made
when the television audience is likely to be at a peak. For their part,
media people who cover conventions try to structure the flow of words
and pictures to cover unfolding events and still tell a coherent dramatic
story. The difficulty of sustaining interest in nominating conventions
when the identity of the nominee has already been firmly established
has sharply reduced live coverage. The gap has been filled in part by
gavel-to-gavel coverage by the Washington-based Cable Satellite Public
Affairs Network (C-SPAN).

Structuring and staging campaign activities such as conventions to
make them newsworthy by the standards of modern American media
has enhanced showmanship at the expense of substance. As California
governor Jerry Brown's campaign manager put it in 1976:

> "Newsworthy" means featuring disagreement, conflict, and contrast. It
> means painting campaign participants as heroes and villains. It means
> making one's point briefly, at the start of a speech, and using popular,
> emotionally stirring symbols. It means tailoring one's speech to the needs of
> the moment and capturing the audience's fancy.[35]

Conspicuous by its absence from this definition is any mention that
newsworthy means saying something important or enlightening to the
audience.

Because conflict is deemed attractive and memorable, journalists
often goad campaigners into confrontations by asking questions that
point up existing conflicts or that may lead to new battles. During the

1980 presidential campaign, the media encouraged challengers to attack President Carter's energy policies and his handling of cabinet appointments. When journalists select the battlegrounds for the presidential contest, they shape the political agenda not only during the campaign but afterwards as well. Campaign statements may be subsequently construed as commitments to act.

Campaign stories are judged by general news criteria. Therefore minor candidates and newcomers whose chances for success are questionable do not get much coverage. Their efforts to attract the media are apt to fail since they simply are not "big news" to the mass audience. Lack of coverage, in turn, makes it extremely difficult for them to become well known and increase their chances of winning elections. This is another example of unintentional media bias that redounds to the benefit of established politicians.

Media Content

What kinds of newspaper and television coverage have recent elections received? How have the media evaluated presidential candidates' qualifications and issue positions? Did the media sufficiently cover the issues that would be likely to require attention from the new president? Were adequate criteria supplied to enable voters to decide which of several policy options would best suit their priorities? Were voters informed about each viable candidate's positions on the issues? Did they receive enough information about each candidate's personality, experience, and ability to evaluate the candidate's likely performance as president? We will now address these questions and assess the adequacy of the information supply for making voting choices in the manner that democratic theorists consider rational and desirable.

Any evaluation of how the media perform their task must also take their concerns into consideration. It is extremely difficult for the media to mesh the public's preference for simple, dramatic stories with the need to present sufficient information for issue-based election choices. Information that may be crucial for voting decisions may not appeal to much of the audience and will therefore be ignored. Hence newspeople feel compelled to feature exciting, humanly touching aspects of the election, even when they are trivial, without totally neglecting essential, unglamorous information useful for issue-based decision-making.

Patterns of Coverage

The following information on mass media output comes from an extensive content analysis of newspapers and national and local television newscasts of the 1968, 1972, 1976, and 1980 presidential campaigns.[36] To simplify the presentation, most tables focus on newspaper data, thereby tapping the richest election data source. Three out of four voters use newspapers, often along with television, during a presidential campaign.

Prominence of Election Stories. In a presidential election year election stories receive about the same amount of news attention as do foreign affairs news and crime coverage. In 1968, 1972, 1976, and 1980 they constituted roughly 13 percent of all newspaper political news and 15 percent of television political news. They were not featured unusually prominently in terms of headline size, front-page or first-story placement, and inclusion of pictures, although they were slightly longer than average. Election stories, although more prominent when primaries, conventions, and significant debates are held, do not dominate the news. Normally, it is quite possible to read the daily paper without noticing election news and to come away from a telecast with the impression that election stories are just a minor part of the day's political developments. Election news competes for audience attention with many other types of stories; this accounts, in part, for its limited impact.

Uniformity of Coverage Patterns. Patterns of presidential election coverage are remarkably uniform, regardless of a newspaper's partisan orientation. Media personnel at highly regarded papers everywhere select the same kind of stories and emphasize the same types of facts, despite the wealth of diverse materials available to them. The major difference generally is that small newspapers carry fewer election stories and that news stories vary in their evaluation of candidates, issues, and campaign events.[37] Television news patterns are also uniform.

Content analysis studies during congressional, state, and local campaigns show similar patterns. The political portraits that various media paint of each candidate match well in basic outlines and in most details.[38] For example, all major television stations and the three major local newspapers covered the 1983 mayoral campaign in Chicago in nearly identical fashion. One might expect that the need to compete against each other and the controversial nature of the race would have produced more diverse treatment.

Table 6-1 illustrates the similarity in patterns of coverage of the primary and general elections by the *Chicago Tribune* and *Chicago Sun-Times,* two major competing dailies in Chicago that are owned and operated by distinct enterprises, and the *Defender,* a paper owned and operated by black business leaders that caters to Chicago's large black community.

Election news patterns are quite stable in successive elections and uniform for all media covering a particular election. Thus Americans

Table 6-1 Distribution of Coverage Areas in the 1983 Chicago
Mayoral Primary and General Elections
(in percentage of story themes)

Coverage area	Primary election			General election		
	Tribune	Sun-Times	Defender	Tribune	Sun-Times	Defender
Campaign	43	46	53	42	41	44
Policy	28	24	19	20	21	23
Ethics	13	11	7	8	8	8
Qualities	11	14	19	19	19	14
Party	5	5	3	12	13	11

Source: Doris A. Graber, "Media Magic: Fashioning Characters for the 1983 Mayoral
Race," in *The Making of the Mayor: Chicago 1983*, ed. Melvin G. Holli and Paul Green
(Grand Rapids, Mich.: Eerdmans, 1984), 84. Reprinted by permission.

Note: For primary election, $N = 639$ for the *Tribune*, 748 for the *Sun-Times*, and 303 for
the *Defender*; for general election, $N = 1,133$ for the *Tribune*, 1,288 for the *Sun-Times*,
and 635 for the *Defender*.

receive similar information on which to base their political decisions.
Similarity of coverage of election campaigns has benefits as well as
drawbacks. The large degree of homogeneity introduced into the elec-
toral process is an advantage in a heterogeneous country, such as the
United States, where it can be difficult to develop political consensus.
But it also means uniform neglect of many topics and criteria for
judging candidates. Shared knowledge is marred by shared ignorance.
Uniformity throttles needed diversity.

A uniform information base obviously has not produced totally
uniform political views throughout the country. Differences in political
evaluations, even among audiences that share the same news, must be
attributed to news commentators' varying interpretations of the same
facts and to the different outlooks that audiences bring to the news. As
pointed out in the previous chapter, the impact of news frequently is
perceiver- rather than stimulus-determined.

Of the factors that encourage uniform coverage, the professional
socialization that is common to journalists appears to be the most
important. As noted in Chapter 3, newspeople share a sense of what is
newsworthy and how it should be presented. Pack journalism also
characterizes election reporting, as Timothy Crouse pointed out so
vividly in *The Boys on the Bus*, a tale of reporters accompanying
candidates on their odysseys.[39] Uniform coverage apparently cannot be
attributed to common use of wire service stories, quotes from the same

speeches, or shared columnists. In the presidential elections that were examined extensively, only one-fourth of all campaign stories were based on similar wire service stories or relied on quotes to make their main points. Papers that use very few wire service stories for campaign coverage still showed the same news patterns. The campaign stories that were based on the writings of columnists (15 percent) involved a wide array of writers.

Uniform coverage patterns might be produced if the media followed what has been called the *campaign model* of reporting.[40] In this model—the utopia of campaign managers—the rhythm of the campaign as produced by the candidates and their staffs determines what is covered. Reporters dutifully take their cues from the candidates. Comparisons of the campaign activities with media coverage show that this model does not prevail. Press coverage conforms instead to an *incentive model.* Whenever exciting stories provide an incentive for coverage, they are published in a rhythm dictated by the needs of the media and the tastes of their audiences. The needs and tastes of the candidates may be ignored. Media coverage routinely lags behind the acceleration of campaign activity just prior to nominations and primary and general elections because newspeople are waiting to cover the outcome.

The incentive model explains the handling of news substance. Producing exciting stories means concentrating on conflicts, real or concocted, keeping score about who is ahead or behind in the race, and digging out tidbits about the personal and professional lives and foibles of the actors in the political drama. Complex election stories, stuffed with statistics and strange names, may be shunned. The incentive model is also apparent in election coverage by specialized media. For instance, papers geared to ethnic audiences focus on the aspects of the campaign that are of primary concern to those audiences and ignore the rest. Business and labor publications put extraordinary emphasis on the campaign's relation to the economy, featuring stories ignored by general audience publications.

Political and Structural Bias. Does election coverage give a fair and equal chance for all viewpoints to be expressed so that media audiences can make informed decisions? Are the perennial charges of bias leveled by disappointed candidates evidence that newspeople always show favoritism? Or are they merely reactions to coverage that did not advance their cause? Generally, media people try to produce balanced coverage for all major candidates for the same office. This holds true for print journalists who have no legal obligation to keep coverage balanced as well as broadcasters who are obliged to give equal coverage for special election programs but who are free to indulge in unequal exposure in regular news programs. However, there are no universally accepted standards of fairness and balance. Newspeople traditionally aim for rough parity in the number of stories about each candidate and rough parity in the balance of overtly favorable and unfavorable stories. Fairness does not mean discussing the candidates from the same perspectives, quoting their friends and enemies in equal proportions, or giving their stories similar time, space, or placement. It does not mean proportionate coverage of major political orientations. For example, during the 1984 Democratic National Convention, 85 percent of the interviews were conducted with liberal Democrats, although they constituted only 56 percent of the Democrats in Congress.[41]

Table 6-2 demonstrates the unfair imbalance that ensues when the media give the lion's share of coverage to those candidates who have the best chance for election. Republican contender Bernard Epton received practically no coverage during the 1983 Chicago mayoral primary elections. Most stories discussed Democratic contenders Jane Byrne, the incumbent, Cook County prosecutor Richard M. Daley (the son of the longtime mayor), and U.S. representative Harold Washington. Even during the general election, when Epton's chances for victory had risen dramatically because he was running against a black challenger in a racially polarized city, Epton lagged way behind his opponent. There also was imbalance in another coverage aspect—the choice of friendly and hostile sources. Typically, incumbents receive harsher treatment than challengers because their records in office always provide targets for criticism. In the 1983 mayoral election, for example, the Jane Byrne story, with one minor exception, reflected predominantly the views of her enemies.

Completely fair and balanced reporting may be impossible because candidates' newsworthiness and willingness to talk to reporters vary. Incumbent president Reagan, dubbed "the Great Communicator," was far more newsworthy throughout 1984, thanks to his official position, than Walter Mondale, his challenger. In the Chicago mayoral campaign Harold Washington was a charismatic candidate, while his Republican challenger was lackluster. There was keen interest in exploring the changes that a black mayor might bring about for the city. No wonder the media found Washington far more newsworthy than his opponent.

One may even question whether it is fair to attempt to balance coverage when the situation surrounding candidates is not comparable. Reducing an incumbent's coverage to that accorded to a challenger seems unfair and inappropriate since the public needs to know what officeholders are doing. It would be equally inappropriate to automatically expand a challenger's coverage to an incumbent's proportions. Imbalanced coverage in these instances results from *structural bias,* which is caused by the circumstances of news production. This differs from *political bias,* which involves slanting the news for partisan rea-

Table 6-2   Source Orientation in the 1983 Chicago Mayoral Primary
and General Elections (in percentage of story themes)

Source orientation	Primary election			General election		
	Tribune	Sun-Times	Defender	Tribune	Sun-Times	Defender
Jane Byrne						
Pro	17	27	12	9	9	2
Anti	29	26	17	11	14	7
Richard Daley						
Pro	23	24	10	1	1	—
Anti	8	2	6	—	—	1
Harold Washington						
Pro	20	21	52	34	38	72
Anti	2	1	3	19	11	2
Bernard Epton						
Pro	1	1	—	18	20	5
Anti	—	—	1	8	8	10

Source: Graber, "Media Magic," in *The Making of the Mayor*, ed. Holli and Green, 62.
Reprinted by permission.

Note: For primary elections, $N = 639$ for the *Tribune*, 748 for the *Sun-Times*, and 303 for
the *Defender;* for general elections, $N = 714$ for the *Tribune*, 828 for the *Sun-Times*, and
508 for the *Defender.*

sons. Structural bias, although devoid of partisan motives, may profoundly affect people's perceptions about campaigns.[42]

Political bias, by contrast, is highly unusual. Outright editorial
comment in election news stories is practically nil. Veiled criticism is
somewhat more common and can be detected in 1 to 4 percent of the
stories, if one considers all types of media and all types of elections. At
times it may be difficult to judge to what extent structural bias is fueled
by political bias. In the Chicago election, for instance, newspeople could
argue that the heavy emphasis on negative stories about incumbent
Byrne was structural: there were many mayoral failures to cover. One
could also claim that newspeople reveled in digging up negative news
about her, while seeing and hearing comparatively little evil about her
challengers. Editorials, of course, are intrinsically biased since their
primary purpose is to express opinions.

As part of the editorial function, many news media endorse candidates. Republican candidates have received the bulk of endorsements
for the presidency in this century; nonetheless, ten Democrats have
succeeded in the twenty-two presidential elections during this period.
Endorsements for less exalted offices have been more influential, particularly in elections in which voters had little information to make their

own decisions.⁴³ Influential papers, such as the *Los Angeles Times,* the *Washington Post,* or William Loeb's *Manchester Union Leader,* can be extraordinarily successful in promoting the election of candidates they have endorsed and in defeating unacceptable contenders. At the presidential level news coverage tends to be essentially evenhanded, regardless of the candidate endorsed. Below the presidential level the media tend to give more coverage to their endorsed candidates than to those they have not endorsed.

The effort to keep coverage balanced does not extend to third-party candidates. Anyone who runs for the presidency who is not a Republican or Democrat is out of the mainstream of newsworthiness and slighted or even ignored by the news profession. Especially newsworthy third-party candidates, such as George Wallace of the American Independent party, Robert La Follette of the Progressive party, and John Anderson of the National Unity Campaign, were notable exceptions. Newsworthiness considerations also account for the sparse coverage of vice-presidential candidates despite the importance of the office. Vice presidents frequently become president, but that possibility always seems remote until it happens. Ninety-five percent of the coverage in a typical presidential election goes to the presidential contenders and only 5 percent to their running mates.

Substance of Coverage: Candidates

Judging from the highly consistent patterns of the 1968-1980 period, it is clear that the media discuss the qualifications of presidential candidates more amply than campaign events and issues. On an average, personal and professional qualifications of the candidates are referred to in 60 percent of the comments and issues in 40 percent (actually, a somewhat higher percentage since some of the discussion of professional qualities relates to ability to cope with issues).⁴⁴

The qualifications highlighted by the media fall into two broad groups: those that are generally important in judging a person's character and those specifically related to the tasks of the office. Included in the first group are personality traits (such as integrity, reliability, and compassion), style characteristics (such as forthrightness or folksiness), and image characteristics (such as the ability to appear productive and level-headed). Professional qualifications at the presidential level include the capacity to conduct foreign and domestic affairs, the ability to mobilize public support, and a flair for administration. The candidate's political philosophy is also a professional criterion.

Within these two broad categories some forty qualities were mentioned repeatedly, in quite similar proportions, in all the news sources that we examined for four presidential elections. However, only ten qualities were stressed heavily, and more than half of these involved primarily personal capacities. Over the years presidential candidates have been most frequently assessed in terms of their trustworthiness, strength of character, leadership capabilities, and compassion. As one wit has phrased it, the crucial question is, "Would you buy a used car from him?" For the media and the public as well, the question of trustworthiness has been paramount because American political executives, especially presidents, wield tremendous unchecked power. After trustworthy, the seven most frequently mentioned qualities were principled, compassionate, inspirational, forthright, strong, administratively competent, and capable in foreign affairs. Style and image characteristics, although important, pale before the prominence given to personality traits.

When it comes to professional capacities—the very qualities that deserve the fullest discussion and analysis—media coverage in recent presidential elections has been comparatively scanty and often vague even when an incumbent was running. Only a handful of professional qualifications have been mentioned with any frequency. These include general appraisals of the capacity to handle foreign affairs, which has been deemed crucial throughout the twentieth century, and the capacity to handle domestic affairs. The latter has primarily involved the capacity to sustain an acceptable quality of life for all citizens by maintaining the economy on an even keel and by controlling crime and internal disorder.

Although the same specific qualities reappear from election to election, treatment of individual candidates is dissimilar. For instance, in the 1983 Chicago mayoral campaign the proportions of stories allotted to individual candidates in major areas of concern varied widely. The *Chicago Tribune* devoted 42 percent of its discussion about candidate ethics to incumbent Byrne, compared with 21 and 9 percent, respectively, for her chief rivals, Washington and Daley. Each of the other papers had its unique allotments of space: each treated the candidates unequally. Such disparate coverage makes it very difficult for the electorate to compare and evaluate the candidates on important dimensions. Effective comparisons are also hindered by contradictions in remarks reported about the candidates. Bound by current codes of objective reporting and neutrality in electoral contests, the media rarely give guidance to the audience for judging conflicting claims.

Verbal news commentary about political candidates is generally quite negative, especially for incumbents. Choices therefore involve selecting the lesser evil. Table 6-3 shows the negative treatment 1984 presidential candidates received on the evening network news between Labor Day and the election. In 1988 the chief Democratic contenders were derisively labeled "the seven dwarfs." The lead paragraph in a *Time* magazine story at the end of the 1980 race between Reagan and

Table 6-3   Candidate Evaluations in Post-Labor Day Network
Television News, 1984

Candidate	Score	Candidate	Score
Ronald Reagan	−33	Walter Mondale	−10
George Bush	−55	Geraldine Ferraro	−28

Source: Data from Maura Clancey and Michael Robinson, "The Media in Campaign '84:
General Election Coverage, Part I," *Public Opinion* 7 (December/January 1985): 53.

Note: Scores constitute the balance between all explicitly positive and negative references
to the candidate. Neutral comments have been omitted. $N = 625$ news stories from ABC,
CBS, and NBC early nightly news.

Carter sums up the typical downbeat mood of recent presidential elections: "For more than a year, two flawed candidates have been flounder-
ing toward the final showdown, each unable to give any but his most
unquestioning supporters much reason to vote for him except dislike of
his opponent." [45]

Newspeople's comments are a comparatively minor reason for the
negative cast of the news. The main reason lies in story selection and
choice of sources to quote. As the 1983 Chicago mayoral campaign
demonstrated so well, newspeople quote amply from hostile sources,
dwelling on stories that make candidates look bad. Good news and good
press are often considered "Pollyanna pap"; bad news and bad press
and confrontations are deemed exciting drama.

On the whole, newspaper and television coverage are quite similar,
except that the features are starker on television. If newspapers stress
personality qualities heavily, television stresses them more. If newspapers concentrate on few qualities, television concentrates on even fewer.
The usual one- or two-minute story gives little chance for in-depth
reporting and analysis. It does permit creation of simple, graphic images
that illustrate selected themes about the candidate and the campaign.
Viewers can readily absorb and use such interpretive portrayals as a
basis for making decisions.

To conserve their limited time, television newscasters create stereotypes of the various candidates early in the campaign and then build
their stories around these stereotypes by merely adding new details to
the established image. During the 1980 presidential campaign, Reagan
was typecast as an amiable dunce stumbling into the presidency almost
by mistake.[46] Reporters dwelled on his frequent misstatements of facts
and mangling of names and statistics. They focused extensively on his
much ridiculed comments that the trees in large forests and the volcanic
eruption of Mt. St. Helens caused more pollution than cars and indus-

tries did. Carter, typecast in the 1976 race as the decent small-time loner who had ventured into a hostile Washington, by 1980 had become the J. R. Ewing candidate. He was constantly portrayed as mean, petty, and manipulative. Anderson was pictured as a twentieth-century Don Quixote, battling all sorts of evils in hopeless struggles. His running mate, Pat Lucey, was cast in the role of Sancho Panza, an admiring but ineffectual sidekick to his master.

The impact of television typecasting is vast because television reaches nearly every voter in national and state-wide campaigns. For instance, once Carter had been tagged as "fuzzy" in the 1976 campaign there was, according to his press secretary Jody Powell, "no way on God's earth we could shake the fuzziness question . . . no matter what Carter did or said. He could have spent the whole campaign doing nothing but reading substantive speeches . . . and still have had the image in the national press." [17] The general feeling in such cases seems to be that leopards do not change their spots.

Substance of Coverage: Issues and Events

Issue and events coverage usually lags behind coverage of personal characteristics in print and broadcast news. This imbalance bothers social scientists; they contend that the electorate ought to judge the candidates on their issue positions. It also runs counter to the common impression that the print media emphasize issues while television shows off personalities. Actually, electronic and print media display surprisingly similar patterns, although television lags behind print media in the range and depth of issue coverage.

The overriding consideration in choosing issues, as in other political coverage, is newsworthiness rather than intrinsic importance. This is why the changing record of happenings on the campaign trail, however trivial, receives extended coverage. Even when ample time is available to explore serious issues in depth, as happens when presidential nominating conventions are covered in full, the emphasis is on brief, rapidly paced, freshly breaking events. In fact, the amount of coverage for particular issues often seems to be in inverse proportion to their significance. For instance, during the 1976 campaign the media extensively covered Ford's questionable statement that "there is no Soviet domination of Eastern Europe" and Carter's comments about lust and sex in his life made during an interview with *Playboy* magazine.

Three major features stand out in coverage of issues and events during the 1968, 1972, 1976, and 1980 presidential campaigns. First and most significantly, the media devoted the bulk of their stories to campaign hoopla and the horse-race aspects of the contests. They slighted political, social, and economic problems facing the country and said little about the merits of the solutions proposed, unless these issues could be made exciting and visually dramatic. Second, information about issues was patchy because the candidates and their surrogates addressed only issues that would help their campaigns and that would not alienate any portion of the huge and disparate electorate from which all were seeking support. Third, newspeople, in turn, focused selectively on controversial issues that lent themselves to appealing stories. They rarely attempted systematic coverage of all-important issues. The issue positions of vice-presidential candidates remained virtually unexplored.

Table 6-4 shows the proportions of stories allotted to various types of issues and events during the final months of these four, quite typical campaigns.[48] Stories about campaign incidents dominated, except in 1968 when election-related Vietnam War stories captured the most coverage. In 1972, 1976, and 1980, emphasis on foreign affairs dropped sharply. Next to campaign events, the issues that normally receive the heaviest coverage concern general domestic politics. These stories, which are available from regular beats, are usually tied to familiar names and widely salient domestic events. Therefore they require little background information, and pictorial coverage is easily arranged. All of these considerations make it very tempting to report domestic politics stories.

Social problems, like poverty or the plight of the elderly, usually lack novelty and are complex to describe. They frequently involve highly controversial and emotionally charged policies about which candidates and media keep silent for fear of alienating large segments of the public. Social issues therefore receive scanty coverage in election stories, except when they erupt into violence, as happened in 1968 when racial tensions turned into racial riots.

Coverage of economic issues, like unemployment, inflation, and taxes, is also limited because these issues are hard to explain and dramatize and rarely produce exciting pictures. Although these are issues of personal concern to the average voter, most people are unwilling to wrestle with a difficult subject that newspeople have not yet learned to simplify and dramatize.[49] Rather than write complex campaign stories that most of the audience probably would ignore, newspeople prefer to feature the horse-race glamour of campaign developments.

Candidates frequently complain about the media's reluctance to cover issues. As Carter put it in an interview in 1976:

> The traveling press have zero interest in any issue unless it's a matter of making a mistake. What they are looking for is a 47-second argument between me and another candidate or something like that. There's nobody in the back of this plane who would ask an issue question unless he thought he could trick me into some crazy statement.[50]

Table 6-4 Newspaper Issue Coverage in the Last Month of the 1968, 1972, 1976, and 1980 Presidential Campaigns (in percentages)

Issue	1968	1972	1976	1980
Campaign events	14	42	51	52
Domestic politics	21	24	19	29
Foreign affairs	30	18	14	5
Economic policy	13	10	11	7
Social problems	22	7	5	6

Source: Doris A. Graber, "Hoopla and Horse-Race in 1980 Campaign Coverage: A Closer Look," in *Mass Media and Elections: International Research Perspectives,* ed. Winfried Schulz and Klaus Schönbach (München: Verlag Olschläger, 1983), 286. Reprinted by permission.

Note: The 1980 data come from the *New York Times.* Data for earlier elections come from twenty newspapers. Because news distribution patterns are quite similar among all papers, the data for a single paper are representative. $N = 3,538$ for 1968, 11,187 for 1972, 11,027 for 1976, and 147 for 1980.

Nevertheless, candidates continue to emphasize issues. As Table 6-5 indicates, the dearth of issue information should not be blamed on them. The table is based on a content analysis of the candidates' campaign rhetoric.[51] Issues made up more than 50 percent of the content of campaign oratory of presidential candidates Reagan, Carter, Anderson, and of one vice-presidential candidate, Mondale. During the primaries, five of eleven major-party candidates devoted better than half of their rhetoric to issues. Reagan and Edward Kennedy topped 70 percent.

Overall, some twenty-five issues have surfaced constantly in the press and some twenty on television in recent presidential campaigns. Typically, only half of these received extensive and intensive attention. Media issue coverage thus is considerably narrower than party platforms, which cover well over fifty issues. The media omit many important policy questions likely to arise during the forthcoming presidential term. While candidates like to talk about broad policy issues, such as war and peace or the health of the economy, newspeople prefer to concentrate on narrower, specific policy positions on which the candidates disagree sharply.[52] Comparisons of candidates' speeches with television newscasts show that two-thirds of the issues mentioned by candidates are broad, designed to attract wide support from an anxious electorate. By contrast, only one-quarter of the issues featured on television are broad. The rest deal with controversial matters like abortion, or busing, or military aid for a specific country.[53]

Table 6-5   Issue Mention by Presidential and Vice-Presidential
Candidates During the 1980 General Election
(in percentages)

Topic	Ronald Reagan	George Bush	Jimmy Carter	Walter Mondale	John Anderson	Patrick Lucey
Issues	71	44	59	65	61	37
Campaign events	5	27	14	16	15	53
Other	24	29	27	19	24	10

Source: Darrell M. West, "Rhetoric and Agenda-Setting in the 1980 Presidential Campaign" (Paper presented at the annual meeting of the Midwest Political Science Association, Milwaukee, Wisconsin, April 1982), 8. West's data are discussed more fully in *Mass Media and Elections,* ed. Schulz and Schönbach, 290. Reprinted by permission.

Note: N = 549 for Ronald Reagan, 216 for George Bush, 574 for Jimmy Carter, 175 for Walter Mondale, 392 for John Anderson, and 19 for Patrick Lucey.

As is the case for coverage of presidential qualifications, issues discussed in connection with individual candidates vary. Voters thus receive little aid from the media in appraising and comparing the candidates on the issues. This makes it tempting to rest voting decisions on general personality characteristics, which are more amply presented and far easier to evaluate. Television images of the candidates can be judged by many of the same techniques that people use routinely to appraise the characteristics of persons whom they meet. Readers who find newspaper coverage confusing and depressing therefore turn to television for a simpler and more encouraging image of the unfolding electoral scene.

Television news usually displays more uniform patterns of issue coverage for all the candidates and involves a more limited range of issues than does print news. The drama of campaigning receives even heavier emphasis than in the print media. Television stories are briefer, touch on fewer aspects of each issue, and contribute to the stereotypic images developed for particular candidates. Stripping information to its bare bones and covering what is left as a theatrical event apparently appeals to the public. Television news and commercials have become the primary sources of presidential election information for the majority of people, ranking well ahead of newspapers.

Substance of Coverage: "Medialities"

Media coverage should be assessed not only in terms of the numbers of stories devoted to various topics, but also in terms of its political significance. Story substance should be examined as well as the political context in which a story appeared and the play it received throughout the country from various news channels. There are times when the public and politicians are particularly vulnerable to campaign stories so that a few stories carry extraordinary weight. Rapid diffusions of these stories throughout the major media enhances their impact. Michael Robinson calls such featured events *medialities*—"events, developments, or situations to which the media have given importance by emphasizing, expanding, or featuring them in such a way that their real significance has been modified, distorted, or obscured." [54]

During the 1988 presidential campaign, medialities included:

- The Iran-contra hearings that suggested that the Reagan administration was inept and contemptuous of the law. It tarnished the luster of several Republican contenders, especially Vice President George Bush.

- The stock market crash of October 19, 1987, which also called the capability of the administration into question. American voters are especially sensitive to pocketbook issues.

- The character tarnishing of several candidates, involving charges of premarital sex (Pat Robertson and Jackson), philandering (Hart), plagiarism (Biden and, to a lesser degree, Jackson), and unfair campaign practices (Michael Dukakis, Bush, and others).

Such key stories can have a far more profound impact on the campaign than thousands of routine stories and should be appraised accordingly.

Adequacy of Coverage

How adequate is current election coverage? Do the media help voters enough to make decisions according to commonly accepted democratic criteria? As the 1983 Chicago mayoral election and presidential campaigns since 1968 demonstrate, appraisal of candidates and issues is not made easy for voters. In presidential contests information is ample about the personal qualifications of the major, mainstream candidates and about the day-to-day campaign events. It is sketchy and often confusing about most professional qualifications, on substantive issues, and on the policy options involved in these issues. Most primary contenders, candidates of minor parties, and the vice-presidential candidates are largely ignored. This is not surprising because the field of candidates is usually much larger than most Americans realize. In 1984, for example, 229 persons were formal candidates for the presidency. The prevalence of negative information makes it seem that all of the candidates are mediocre or even poor choices. This negative cast appears to be a major factor in many voters' decision to stay home on election day. In the 1983 mayoral election, issue coverage was more complete and less confusing primarily because many issues at that level are less complex and closer to the voters' personal experiences.

Coverage trends in congressional elections are similar to those in presidential contests; challengers receive only a fraction of the coverage bestowed on incumbents. A study of newspaper coverage of forty-one incumbents and forty-one challengers in 1978 congressional races showed that challengers' share of total coverage was 28 percent in discussions of personal and political characteristics and 34 percent in issue discussions. In name mentions, challengers' share was 42 percent, and in positive commentary it was 30 percent.[55] As Table 6-6 shows, challengers' coverage is also inferior in quality. The table indicates the major content themes in fourteen tight congressional races in which an incumbent was running.

In presidential contests the deficiencies of media coverage are most noticeable during the primary period when a large slate of same-party candidates is running in each primary. The media solve the dilemma of covering a multitude of candidacies by giving uniformly skimpy treatment to all candidates except for those designated as front-runners. For instance, in 1980, 71 percent of all mentions of presidential contenders referred to the campaigns of Carter, Reagan, and Kennedy. If Anderson is added, that figure mounts to 81 percent. The remaining 19 percent of the coverage was shared by six second-tier contenders—George Bush, Howard Baker, Jerry Brown, John Connally, Philip Crane, and Robert Dole.

The balance between discussion of qualifications and of issues and campaign events during the primaries is the reverse of what it is in the general election. In 1976, for example, 61 percent of all primary commentary referred to issues and events and only 39 percent to presidential qualities, despite the need to acquaint voters with a host of unfamiliar personalities. Moreover, horse-race and hoopla news predominated in issue coverage at the expense of substantive matters. As Thomas Patterson has noted, "Issue material is but a rivulet in the news flow during the primaries, and what is there is almost completely diluted by information about the race."[56]

Although the quality of coverage during the primaries may be thin, the quantity is substantial. A check of the *New York Times* in 1980 showed that 34 percent of all campaign stories appeared from January to March. The Iowa caucuses and the New Hampshire primary were especially well covered, making political events in these states disproportionately influential, considering their size and political unrepresentativeness. Another 30 percent of all stories covered the April-May-June period. The reduction in coverage is more significant than it seems because twenty-five primaries, many of them in large states, occurred in this period. They thus received substantially less coverage than did the twelve earlier primaries.

The July-August time span following the primary season includes

Table 6-6 Median Number of Local Newspaper Paragraphs
Mentioning Selected Themes in Fourteen Tight
Congressional Races, September 27-November 7, 1978

Themes	Incumbent News	Challenger News
Campaign organization	22	27
Personal characteristics	10	13
Political attributes	49	4
Issues/ideology/group ties	29	12

Source: Peter Clarke and Susan H. Evans, *Covering Campaigns: Journalism in Congressional Elections* (Stanford, Calif.: Stanford University Press, 1983), 61. Reprinted by permission.

the nominating conventions. This is an important period because approximately 25 percent of the voters usually make up their minds in the wake of the conventions. In 1980, 31 percent of the campaign coverage fell within those two months. Most surprising was the dearth of coverage of the final campaign, following the Labor Day holiday in September. Although two presidential debates were held during the last two months of the campaign in 1980, this period garnered only 5 percent of the campaign coverage. What might have been a last-minute media blitz to rehearse the public for the political climax fizzled into a tired media anticlimax. Issue content did rise by 14 percentage points during the final campaign weeks, and election stories received slightly greater prominence in display as the campaign neared its end. This increased the likelihood that information on the candidates' positions on the issues would come to the voters' attention as the day of decision approached.

It would be unfair to blame low voter turnout in presidential primary elections entirely on inadequate election news. Many factors are involved, ranging from the quality of the candidates to voter registration rules and weather conditions. But interviews with voters show that poor coverage does play a significant part. Voters find election stories interesting, but they do not feel that these adequately prepare them to make choices. Media images depict campaigns as tournaments where voters sit on the sidelines and watch the bouts and wait to see who is eliminated and who remains. Winning and losing are presented as all-important, rather than what winning and losing mean in terms of the political direction of the country in general or the observer's personal situation in particular. Taking its cues from the media, the audience accepts election news as just another story rather than as an important tale that will directly affect its own welfare in real life.

Media Effects

Learning About Candidates and Issues

What do people learn from campaign coverage? It varies, of course, depending on their interest in the campaign, prior political knowledge, desire for certain information, and political sophistication. But several general trends emerge from national surveys, such as those conducted biannually by the Survey Research Center at the University of Michigan, and from intensive interviews of smaller panels of voters, such as those conducted by the author of this book.

The foremost impression from interviews with voters is that they learn very little specific information in a presidential campaign. National surveys show that only 16 percent of the electorate reach genuinely high scores; 59 percent score below the mean in election knowledge.[57] These figures are based on the numbers of responses people are able to give when asked open-ended questions about parties and candidates. During the 1980 presidential primaries, an average of only 17 percent of the respondents in the National Election Survey increased their knowledge between February and June. An average of 10 percent actually lost ground over the course of the primaries.[58]

The interest that most citizens take in a campaign thus does not mean that they learn a great deal about it beyond who is winning and losing, how the candidates look, and how they go about fighting political battles. Interest in the campaign competes with interest in other events and issues. For instance, a panel of voters who kept diaries on the important news stories that came to their attention throughout the 1976 election year devoted only 11 percent of their entries to election stories. When asked to name "major current events or issues," 38 percent of the panelists never named the primary election in the four interviews conducted during the primary season.[59] Similarly, during the early months of the 1988 campaign, 69 percent of the respondents to a national Gallup poll said that they had paid very close attention to news accounts about Jessica McClure, a Texas toddler who was trapped in an abandoned well for several days. Forty percent of the respondents said that they had followed the news of the 1987 stock market plunge closely, and 37 percent had done the same for accounts about the U.S. Navy's escort of Kuwaiti tankers through the Persian Gulf. The presidential campaign ranked lowest among the prominent news events about which the respondents were questioned. Only 15 percent claimed to have paid close attention to the Democratic race, and only 13 percent alleged close interest in the Republican contest.[60]

A comparison of election information supplied by the newspapers with information mentioned by survey respondents reveals roughly similar patterns, as Table 6-7 shows. A nationwide sample of people was

Table 6-7 Presidential Qualities Mentioned by the Public and by Newspapers, 1976 (in percentages)

Qualities	Likes		Dislikes		Newspapers
	Carter	*Ford*	*Carter*	*Ford*	
Personal comments					
Personality traits	49	38	39	18	36
Presidential image	15	37	21	24	25
Style	5	4	16	10	16
Total	69	79	76	52	77
Professional capacities					
Capacities	21	17	16	43	7
Relations with public	1	—	—	—	3
Philosophy	9	4	8	5	12
Total	31	21	24	48	22

Source: Survey data from 1976 Election Survey, Center for Political Studies, Survey Research Center, University of Michigan; newspaper data from author's research.

Note: The percentages are based on responses to the question, "Now I'd like to ask you about the good and bad points of the two major candidates for president. Is there anything in particular about (name of candidate) that might make you want to vote for him? Is there anything about (name of candidate) that might make you want to vote against him? What is that? Anything else?" $N = 2,182$ for Carter likes, 2,337 for Ford likes, 2,125 for Carter dislikes, and 1,747 for Ford dislikes. $N = 17,423$ mentions of qualities by newspapers.

asked to mention good and bad points about 1976 presidential nominees Ford and Carter that might affect their voting choices. The similarity between media content and the public's views was greatest for heavy users of newspapers.

Media and public images, however, differ in emphases and richness of detail. The public mentions fewer issues and qualities and describes them less precisely. For instance, when asked about the reasons for voting for a candidate, a respondent may say, "I like him," but may be unable to name any specific reasons. A query about the issues that figured in the voter's appraisal of the candidates is likely to elicit a broad reference to foreign or domestic policy in general rather than to specific issues. Facts and figures are rarely recalled, and a good deal of misinformation surfaces when specifics are mentioned. Complex policy positions are remembered far less often than are positions involving simple yes or no choices.

Overall, three out of four answers people give when asked what they have learned about candidates and issues or why they would vote or refrain from voting for a certain candidate concern personality traits.[61] People are interested in the human qualities of their elected leaders, particularly their trustworthiness, principled character, strength, and compassion. The media provide ample data on these traits. In many instances people apparently make their choice first, commonly on the basis of quick judgments about personality or vague feelings of party allegiance, and then later acquire information to justify that choice.

Much of the information the media make available is ignored. In a typical election, such as the 1976 presidential race, fully 43 percent of the people in a nationwide poll could comment on only one candidate's strengths and weaknesses. Less than 20 percent could state three or more likes or dislikes about either candidate. Appraisals commonly were limited to one or two statements. The issues people mentioned as important in the campaign represented a much abbreviated and imprecise version of media issue coverage. As Table 6-8 indicates, people stress economic and social issues much more than do the media. This is not surprising; these issues are personal. People do not need media coverage to know that inflation, unemployment, poverty, crime, race relations, and environmental pollution are serious problems requiring attention from presidents. Nor is it surprising that people put much less emphasis on campaign hoopla, covered so plentifully by the media. Although they find these fleeting events entertaining, people make little effort to remember them long.

Knowledge Base for Voting

Many social scientists worry about the public's limited preparation for voting and fault the media for doing a poor job, particularly in covering issues. But the worry and blame are largely misplaced. Although election news definitely stresses personality traits over issues, it does supply a fair amount of issue coverage. Voters who want to base their decisions on the candidates' stands on specific issues can usually find that information. When voters are poorly informed about issues, it is chiefly because they do not consider elections important enough to take the time to learn about them.

The average voter concentrates heavily on personal qualities of the candidates—a choice that can be defended as sound and rational given the realities of politics. Forming opinions about complex issues like arms limitation or monetary policies is time consuming and difficult, particularly when experts' policy recommendations conflict. Moreover, voters do not know what issues will actually arise during a president's term and what obstacles the incumbent will face in implementing campaign promises. Therefore they ignore most issues, paying attention to only a few that are of major interest generally or personally.

The kind of thing that most people can judge, often quite expertly, is a candidate's competence and integrity. People have learned through personal experience how to pick a doctor, minister, or mechanic without

Table 6-8 Comparison of Percentage of Mention of Issues and Events by Newspapers, Television, and Survey Responses, 1976

Issues and events	Newspapers	Television	Survey responses
Campaign events	51	63	0
Domestic politics	19	14	5
Foreign affairs	14	10	5
Economic policy	11	9	75
Social problems	5	4	14

Source: Survey data come from the 1976 Election Survey, Center for Political Studies, Survey Research Center, University of Michigan; media data from author's research.

Note: Survey responses specify the most important national problem. $N = 11,027$ for newspapers, 1,355 for television, and 2,263 for survey responses.

understanding medicine, religion, or machines. They know how to judge others in terms of trustworthiness and general ability. The information that media provide most plentifully is geared toward such evaluations of personal character.

Although the media furnish most people with more information than they are willing or able to use, the media fall short of supplying the needs of political elites. Opinion leaders, and the mass public that often relies on their guidance, would benefit from greater clarity of presentation in the daily press, more point-by-point comparisons of candidates and policies, and more ample evaluations of the political significance of differences in candidates and their programs.

Although most people gain little specific knowledge, they may retain conclusions drawn from long-forgotten facts. Voting choices often match approval of a candidate's policy positions, even when voters cannot recall the candidate's stands or the specifics of the policy.[62] Facts may condense into politically significant feelings and attitudes, which then may be remembered long after the facts have been forgotten. For instance, a general impression, developed during a series of elections, that one's party is fielding candidates of poor caliber may ultimately destroy party allegiance.

Voting Behavior

Does campaigning via the media change votes? The answer to this perennial question so dear to the hearts of campaign managers, public relations experts, and social scientists hinges on the interaction between audiences and messages. Crucial variables include the voter's receptivity to a message urging change, the potency of the message, the appropriateness of its form, and the setting in which it occurs. A vote change is most likely when voters pay fairly close attention to the media and are ambivalent in their attitudes toward the candidates. Messages are most potent if they concern a major and unpredicted event, such as a successful or disastrous foreign policy venture or corruption in high places, and if individuals find themselves in social settings where a change of attitudes will not constitute deviant behavior. This combination of circumstances is fairly uncommon, which explains why changes of voting intentions are comparatively rare. Fears that televised campaigns can easily sway voters and amount to "electronic ballot box stuffing" are therefore unrealistic.

However, even small numbers of media-induced vote changes may be important. Many elections at all levels are decided by tiny percentages of votes, often less than 1 percent. The media may also have a crucial impact on election outcomes whenever they are able to stimulate or depress voter turnout. This is a more likely consequence of media publicity than changes in voting choices. It has led to concern about the changes in turn-out that may be produced by broadcasts that predict election results before voting has ended. In the 1980 presidential election, for instance, NBC projected Reagan as the winner at 8:15 p.m. Eastern Standard Time, several hours before the polls closed on the West Coast. This could have reduced the late turnout on the West Coast, affecting presidential, congressional, and state contests. Despite several investigations of the problem, the precise impact of early forecasts on elections remains disputed. Current evidence indicates that the effects, if they do occur, have rarely been substantial.[63]

Attempts to stop immediate dissemination of projections of winners and losers have run afoul of First Amendment free speech guarantees. This may explain why the laws passed in more than half of the states to restrain exit polling are seldom enforced.[64] A bill now before the Congress mandates simultaneous poll closing times of 9:00 p.m. Eastern Standard Time in all states except Alaska and Hawaii in presidential elections. Concomitantly, the major television networks have pledged to refrain from projecting the outcome of a presidential election until the polls have closed. The concern about the impact of exit polls and early forecasts seems overdrawn. Voters are bombarded throughout the election year with information likely to determine their vote and turnout. Why should there be squeamishness on the very last day of the campaign?

The most important influence of the media on the voter does not lie in changing votes, once predispositions have been formed, but in shaping and reinforcing predispositions and influencing the initial selection of candidates. When newspeople sketched out the Jimmy Carter image and held him up as a potential winner during the 1976 primaries, ignoring most of his rivals, they made "Jimmy-Who?" into a viable candidate. Millions of voters would never have cast their ballot for the obscure Georgia politician had not the media thrust him into the limelight as a likely winner.

By focusing the voters' attention on selected individuals, their characteristics, and issue stands, the media also determine to a large extent the crucial issues by which the competence of the candidates will be gauged. Very early in the campaign, often long before formal campaigning starts, media interpretations of the significance of issues can shape the political and emotional context of the election.[65]

President Carter's chances for reelection in 1980 hinged on the images that the media resurrected from his four years in office. In the same way Watergate revelations created public moods that doomed many Republicans in the 1974 elections, Newspeople shape election outcomes by molding the images of political reality that lead to voting decisions rather than by suggesting voting choices to an electorate that prefers to make up its own mind. As Leon Sigal has noted, they "play less of an independent part in creating issues, sketching imagery, and coloring perceptions of the candidates than in getting attention for their candidacies. Newsmen do not write the score or play an instrument; they amplify the sounds of the music makers." [66] Although voters pay most concentrated attention to media coverage just before elections, the crucial attitudes that determine voting choices may already be so firm that the final vote is a foregone conclusion.

Summary

The role played by the media, especially television, in recent campaigns is powerful and growing all the time. Three results of the new media politics are striking: the shrinking contributions of political parties and other political actors, the domination of the campaign strategies and schedules by media demands, and the emergence of the media as king makers in political recruiting and promotion of candidates, particularly at the presidential level.

In this chapter we also scrutinized newspapers and television election coverage throughout the campaign. General coverage patterns and the problem of political and structural bias, the substance and slant of coverage, and the manner of presentation were considered as well. The media emphasize personal rather than professional qualities of the candidates and campaign events rather than substantive issues. Stories are chosen for their newsworthiness, not their educational value.

Lastly, we examined the effects of media output on the people who are exposed to it. Although the public complains about the skimpiness and shallowness of election coverage, it absorbs only a small portion of it. This does not necessarily lead to lack of political understanding or irrational voting. The bits of information that people absorb permit sound choices based on appraisal of a chosen candidate's character. Minute changes brought about by the media in final voting decisions or voter turnout may alter the outcome of a close election and the course of political life.

Claims that the media influence elections very little rest on election studies in the 1940s and 1950s that have become obsolete. This early research preceded the age of television dominance and was concerned primarily with changes in the final voting decision. More recent research has cast the net much wider to include media effects on all phases of the election campaign, from the recruitment and nomination stages to the strategies that produce the final outcome. In addition to media impact on the final voting choice, social scientists look at political learning during campaigns and the information base that supports the voting decision. Television, in particular, has changed the election game rules, especially at the presidential level. Candidates and media are inextricably intertwined. Those who aspire to elective office must play the new politics, which is media politics.

Notes

1. Steve Daley, "TV Captures City Council, Warts and All," *Chicago Tribune,* December 3, 1987; and James Strong and Robert Davis, "Allies Couldn't Get Sawyer to Run, but his Main Opponents Finally Did," *Chicago Tribune,* December 3, 1987.
2. For a good review of the presidential election process, see Herbert Asher, *Presidential Elections and American Politics: Voters, Candidates and Campaigns Since 1952,* 3d ed. (Homewood, Ill.: Dorsey Press, 1984); Stephen J. Wayne, *The Road to the White House: The Politics of Presidential Elections,* 3d ed. (New York: St. Martin's Press, 1988); and Nelson W. Polsby and Aaron Wildavsky, *Presidential Elections,* 7th ed. (New York: Scribner's, 1988). For reports on congressional campaigns, see John Carey, "How Media Shape Campaigns," *Journal of Communication* 26 (Spring 1976): 50-57; Peter Clarke and Susan H. Evans, *Covering Campaigns: Journals in Congressional Elections* (Stanford, Calif.: Stanford University Press, 1983); Edie N. Goldenberg and Michael W. Traugott, *Campaigning for Congress* (Washington, D.C.: CQ Press, 1984); and Jan Pons Vermeer, *Campaigns in the News: Mass Media and Congressional Elections* (New York: Greenwood Press, 1987). For state contests involving ballot issues, see Betty Zisk, *Money, Media, and the Grass Roots: State Ballot Issues and the Electoral Process* (Beverly Hills, Calif.: Sage, 1987). On gubernatorial contests see John W. Windhauser, "Reporting of Campaign Issues in Ohio Municipal Election Races," *Journalism Quarterly* 54 (Summer 1977): 332-340; Leonard Tipton, Roger D. Haney, and John R. Baseheart, "Media Agenda-Setting in City and State Election Campaigns," *Journalism Quar-*

terly 52 (Spring 1975): 15-22; and Jan Pons Vermeer, *"For Immediate Release":: Candidate Press Releases in American Political Campaigns* (Westport, Conn.: Greenwood Press, 1982).

3. For comparisons of election coverage in various years, see John H. Kessel, *Presidential Campaign Politics: Coalition Strategies and Citizen Response*, 3d ed. (Homewood, Ill.: Dorsey Press, 1988); Richard L. Rubin, *Press, Party and Presidency* (New York: Norton, 1981); and Gary King and Lyn Ragsdale, *The Elusive Executive: Discovering Statistical Patterns in the Presidency* (Washington, D.C.: CQ Press, 1988). Comparisons with election campaigns in foreign countries are presented in Edie N. Goldenberg and Michael W. Traugott, eds., "Mass Media in Legislative Campaigns," *Legislative Studies Quarterly* 12 (August 1987): 313-456.

4. For examples, see Winfried Schulz and Klaus Schönbach, eds., *Mass Media and Elections: International Research Perspectives* (München: Olschläger, 1983).

5. Kathleen Hall Jamieson, *Packaging the President: A History and Criticism of Presidential Campaign Advertising* (New York: Oxford University Press, 1984); Dorothy Davidson Nesbit, *Videostyle in U.S. Senate Campaigns* (Knoxville, Tenn.: University of Tennessee Press, 1988); Richard Joslyn, *Mass Media and Elections* (Reading, Mass.: Addison-Wesley, 1984), chap. 7; and Wayne, *The Road to the White House*, 209-218.

6. Thomas Patterson and Robert McClure, *The Unseeing Eye* (New York: Putnam's, 1976), 102-108. See also C. Richard Hofstetter and Cliff Zukin, "TV Network News and Advertising in the Nixon and McGovern Campaigns," *Journalism Quarterly* 56 (Spring 1979): 106-115; and Richard Joslyn, "The Content of Political Spot Ads," *Journalism Quarterly* 57 (Spring 1980): 92-98.

7. Michael J. Robinson, "The Media in 1980: Was the Message the Message?" in *The American Elections of 1980*, ed. Austin Ranney (Washington, D.C.: American Enterprise Institute, 1981), 179-180. For contrary views, see Joe McGinniss, *The Selling of the President, 1968* (New York: Trident Press, 1969), 31.

8. Joslyn, *Mass Media*, chap. 7; and Michael J. Robinson, "Three Faces of Congressional Media," in *The New Congress*, ed. Thomas E. Mann and Norman J. Ornstein (Washington, D.C.: American Enterprise Institute, 1981).

9. James D. Nowlan and Mary Jo Moutray, "Broadcasting Advertising and Party Endorsements in a Statewide Primary," *Journal of Broadcasting* 28 (Summer 1984): 361-363.

10. Robinson, "The Media in 1980," 186.

11. Walter DeVries and V. Lance Tarrance, *The Ticket Splitters* (Grand Rapids, Mich.: Eerdmans, 1972). Kessel, *Presidential Campaign Politics*, 251-253, defines *issues* very broadly. This leads him to the conclusion that issues are most important in voting.

12. For a well-reasoned argument questioning television influence, see Michael J. Robinson, "News Media Myths and Realities: What the Networks Did and Didn't Do in the 1984 General Campaign," in *Elections in America*, ed. Kay Lehman Schlozman (Boston: Allen and Unwin, 1987), 143-170. An equally well-reasoned argument supporting television influence is presented in Dean Alger, "Television, Perceptions of Reality and the Presidential Election of '84," *PS* 20 (Winter 1987): 49-57.

13. F. Christopher Arterton, "Campaign Organizations Confront the Media—

Political Environment," in *Race for the Presidency: The Media and the Nominating Process*, ed. James David Barber (Englewood Cliffs, N.J.: Prentice Hall, 1978), 21.

14. Ibid., 22. See also Michael J. Robinson, "TV's Newest Program: 'The Presidential Nominations Game,' " *Public Opinion* 1 (May/June 1978): 41-46.

15. Larry M. Bartels, "Expectations and Preferences in Presidential Nominating Campaigns," *American Political Science Review* 79 (September 1985): 804-815. The importance of the winner image is discussed in Henry E. Brady and Richard Johnston, "What's the Primary Message: Horse Race or Issue Journalism?" in *Media and Momentum: The New Hampshire Primary and Nomination Politics*, ed. Gary R. Orren and Nelson W. Polsby (Chatham, N.J.: Chatham House, 1987), 127-186.

16. William G. Mayer, "The New Hampshire Primary: A Historical Overview," in *Media and Momentum*, 23.

17. William C. Adams, "Media Coverage of Campaign '84: A Preliminary Report," *Public Opinion* 7 (April/May 1984): 9-13.

18. Richard Stout, "The Pre-Pre-Campaign-Campaign," *Public Opinion* 5 (December-January 1983): 17-20, 60.

19. Rubin, *Press, Party and Presidency*, 129, 138.

20. The potency of visual information is discussed in Doris A. Graber, "Kind Pictures and Harsh Words: How Television Presents the Candidates," in *Elections in America*, 115-141; Shawn W. Rosenberg with Patrick McCafferty, "The Image and the Vote: Manipulating Voters' Preferences," *Public Opinion Quarterly* 51 (Spring 1987): 31-47; Shawn Rosenberg, Lisa Bohan, Patrick McCafferty, and Kevin Harris, "The Image and the Vote: The Effect of Candidate Presentation on Voter Preference," *American Journal of Political Science* 30 (February 1986): 108-127.

21. Michael J. Robinson, "A Statesman Is A Dead Politician: Candidate Images on Network News," in *What's News: The Media in American Society*, ed. Elie Abel (San Francisco: Institute for Contemporary Studies, 1981).

22. Walter Bunge, Robert Hudson, and Chung Woo Suh, "Johnson's Information Strategy for Vietnam: An Evaluation," *Journalism Quarterly* 45 (Autumn 1968): 419-425.

23. Thomas E. Patterson and Richard Davis, "The Media Campaign: Struggle for the Agenda," in *The Elections of 1984*, ed. Michael Nelson (Washington, D.C.: CQ Press, 1985), 124.

24. Anthony Broh, "Presidential Preference Polls and Network News," in *Television Coverage of the 1980 Presidential Campaign*, ed. William C. Adams (Norwood, N.J.: Ablex, 1983), 21.

25. Quoted in Edwin Diamond, *Sign-Off: The Last Days of Television* (Boston: MIT Press, 1982), 175.

26. Martin Schram, *The Great American Video Game: Presidential Politics in the Television Age* (New York: William Morrow, 1987), 25.

27. Ibid., 26.

28. Herbert E. Alexander and Brian A. Haggerty, *Financing the 1984 Election* (Lexington, Mass.: Heath, 1987), 81-83. Also *U.S. News & World Report*, October 8, 1984, 74.

29. Wayne, *The Road to the White House*, 31.

30. Andrew Rosenthal, "Via Satellite, Candidates Make Their Own News," *New York Times*, July 21, 1987.

31. James Glen Stovall, "Incumbency and News Coverage of the 1980 Presiden-

tial Campaign," *Western Political Quarterly* 37 (December 1984): 628. The effects of incumbency are similar at the congressional level.

32. Emmett H. Buell, Jr., " 'Locals' and 'Cosmopolitans': National, Regional, and State Newspaper Coverage of the New Hampshire Primary," in *Media and Momentum*, 66.

33. William C. Adams, "As New Hampshire Goes . . . ," in *Media and Momentum*, 45.

34. Michael J. Robinson and Margaret Sheehan, "Traditional Ink vs. Modern Video Versions of Campaign '80," in *Television Coverage*, 18.

35. J. D. Lorenz, "An Insider's View of Jerry Brown," *Chicago Tribune*, February 12, 1978.

36. The 1980 analysis was limited to the *New York Times* because earlier analyses had shown great similarity in coverage patterns among news sources throughout the country. In 1968, 1972, and 1976 the newspaper sample consisted of twenty newspapers from communities of different size and political orientation from all parts of the country. The sample is broadly representative of the American press, although slightly skewed toward papers that media critics consider above average in performance. The papers were the *New York Times, Philadelphia Inquirer, Boston Globe, Bangor Daily News, Chicago Tribune, Cleveland Plain Dealer, Detroit Free Press, Topeka Daily Capital, Houston Chronicle, Miami Herald, Raleigh News and Observer, Atlanta Constitution, Los Angeles Times, Seattle Daily Times, Denver Post, Salt Lake City Tribune, Chicago Daily Defender, National Observer, Wall Street Journal*, and *Washington Post*. Papers were selected with the assistance of editors to be representative of the American press. Criteria for sample selection included representation of all sections of the United States, diversity of community size, representation of high and low population density regions, diversity of endorsement and audience political affiliation, reflection of various types of newspaper competition ranging from near-monopoly status to highly competitive markets, and inclusion of papers designed for special interest audiences. The television sample came from the early evening national news presented by ABC, CBS, and NBC, as well as local Chicago area CBS and NBC newscasts. Television data for 1980 came from CBS and are based on Michael J. Robinson and Margaret A. Sheehan, *Over the Wire and on TV: CBS and UPI in Campaign '80* (New York: Sage, 1983). Tapes and abstracts for coding broadcasts for 1968, 1972, and 1976 were made available by the Vanderbilt Television News Archive, described in Fay C. Schreibman, "Television News Archives: A Guide to Major Collections," in *Television Network News: Issues in Content Research*, ed. William Adams and Fay C. Schreibman (Washington, D.C.: George Washington University, 1978), 89-110.

37. Buell found that two small New Hampshire papers differed in coverage from the *New York Times, Washington Post*, and *Boston Globe*. They gave minor candidates more equal coverage, had more features devoted to a single candidate, and covered issues more amply. See Buell, " 'Locals' and 'Cosmopolitans,' " 76-97.

38. See Carey, "How Media Shape Campaigns"; Windhauser, "Reporting of Campaign Issues"; and Clarke and Evans, *Covering Campaigns*. For an exception in a senatorial campaign, see Jon F. Hale, "The Scribes of Texas: Newspaper Coverage of the 1984 U.S. Senate Campaign," in *Campaigns in the News*, 91-107.

39. Timothy Crouse, *The Boys on the Bus* (New York: Ballantine, 1976).
40. C. Richard Hofstetter, *Bias in the News: Network Television Coverage of the 1972 Election Campaign* (Columbus: Ohio State University Press, 1976), 39-41.
41. William C. Adams, "Convention Coverage," *Public Opinion* 7 (December/January 1985): 45.
42. Wenmouth Williams, Jr., and William D. Semlak, "Structural Effects of TV Coverage on Political Agendas," *Journal of Communication* 28 (Autumn 1978): 114-119; and Hofstetter, *Bias in the News*, 32-36. For an interesting discussion of the special concerns involved in covering black candidates, see Jannette Lake Dates and Oscar H. Gandy, Jr., "How Ideological Constraints Affected Coverage of the Jesse Jackson Campaign," *Journalism Quarterly* 62 (Autumn 1985): 595-600.
43. G. Cleveland Wilhoit and Taik Sup Auh, "Newspaper Endorsements and Coverage of Public Opinion Polls in 1970," *Journalism Quarterly* 51 (Winter 1974): 654-658; and Byron St. Dizier, "The Effect of Newspaper Endorsements and Party Identification on Voting Choice," *Journalism Quarterly* 62 (Autumn 1985): 589-594.
44. The proportions are even more favorable for issues when in each story every single issue is coded rather than only three. Doris A. Graber, "Hoopla and Horse-Race in 1980 Campaign Coverage: A Closer Look," in *Mass Media and Elections*, 283-300.
45. Anthony King, "How Not to Select Presidential Candidates: A View from Europe," in *The American Elections,* 305.
46. Typecasts have been extracted from Robinson, "A Statesman Is a Dead Politician," 178-182.
47. F. Christopher Arterton, "The Media Politics of Presidential Campaigns," in *Race for the Presidency,* 36.
48. The data are based on coding up to three issues per story. An experiment involving coding of all 1980 issues mentioned in every story showed campaign events at 37 percent, domestic policy at 19 percent, foreign affairs at 12 percent, economic policy at 20 percent, and social problems at 13 percent. This indicates that many stories stressing hoopla and horse-race aspects do have subordinate coverage of substantive issues. The usual, more limited coding procedures do not capture this. However, it is questionable whether most readers will notice these less obvious story elements.
49. Seymour Martin Lipset and William Schneider, *The Confidence Gap: Business, Labor, and Government in the Public Mind* (New York: The Free Press, 1983), chap. 5.
50. Robert C. Sahr, "Energy as a Non-Issue in 1980 Coverage," in *Television Coverage,* 135.
51. Darrell M. West, "Rhetoric and Agenda-Setting in the 1980 Presidential Campaign," quoted in Graber, "Hoopla and Horse-Race," 289-290.
52. Benjamin I. Page, *Choices and Echoes in Presidential Elections: Rational Man and Electoral Democracy* (Chicago: University of Chicago Press, 1978), chap. 6.
53. Thomas E. Patterson, "Television and Election Strategy," in *The Communications Revolution in Politics,* ed. Gerald Benjamin (New York: The Academy of Political Science, 1982), 28.
54. Robinson, "The Media in 1980," 191.
55. Goldenberg and Traugott, *Campaigning for Congress,* 127-128. Also see Clarke and Evans, *Covering Campaigns,* 57-72.

56. Thomas Patterson, *The Mass Media Election: How Americans Choose Their President* (New York: Praeger, 1980), 168.

57. Kessel, *Presidential Campaign Politics,* 250.

58. Scott Keeter and Cliff Zukin, *Uninformed Choice: The Failure of the New Presidential Nominating System* (New York: Praeger, 1983), 80. The figures are based on Reagan, Kennedy, Bush, Brown, Connally, Baker, and Dole data. Learning data for 1984 are presented in Brady and Johnston, "What's the Primary Message?" 164-168.

59. Doris A. Graber, *Processing the News: How People Tame the Information Tide* (New York: Longman, 1988), 140.

60. "The Girl in the Well Outpolls the Men in the Race," *New York Times,* November 19, 1987.

61. Some scholars report that for making voting decisions issues are more important than the candidates' personality traits. For examples, see Kessel, *Presidential Campaign Politics,* 267-293. The disagreements are explained in part by different definitions of what constitutes either an issue or a personality comment and by different practices in the choice of items to be coded. Kessel reports that there has been a rise in issue emphasis since 1976. For 1984 his data show that 28.1 percent of the comments made by voters concerned candidates, 8.9 percent referred to parties, and 62.9 percent related to issues. By contrast, pollster Richard Wirthlin reports that 29 percent of Reagan's voters cited issues, as did 44 percent of Mondale's voters. The Reagan/Mondale vote ratio was 59:41. Peter Hart and Richard Wirthlin Interview, "Moving Right Along? Campaign '84's Lessons for 1988," *Public Opinion* 7 (December/January 1985): 10.

62. Richard W. Boyd, "Popular Control of Public Policy: A Normal Vote Analysis of the 1968 Election," *American Political Science Review* 66 (June 1972): 429-449; Philip E. Converse, "The Concept of Normal Vote," in *Elections and the Political Order,* ed. Angus Campbell, Philip E. Converse, Warren E. Miller, and Donald Stokes (New York: Wiley, 1966), chap. 2; and Graber, *Processing the News,* 85-89.

63. Paul Wilson, "Election Night 1980 and the Controversy over Early Projections," in *Television Coverage,* 152-153; and Percy H. Tannenbaum and Leslie J. Kostrich, *Turned-On TV/Turned-Off Voters: Policy Options for Election Projections* (Beverly Hills, Calif.: Sage, 1983).

64. For a discussion of how state laws have fared in the courts, see Stephen Bates, "Lawful Exits: The Court Considers Election Day Polls," *Public Opinion* 8 (Summer 1986): 53-54.

65. Arthur T. Hadley, *The Invisible Primary* (Englewood Cliffs, N.J.: Prentice-Hall, 1976).

66. Leon V. Sigal, "Newsmen and Campaigners: Organization Men Make the News," *Political Science Quarterly* 93 (Fall 1978): 465-470.

Readings

Arterton, F. Christopher. *Media Politics: The News Strategies of Presidential Campaigns.* Lexington, Mass.: Heath, 1984.

Clarke, Peter, and Susan H. Evans. *Covering Campaigns: Journalism in Congressional Elections.* Stanford, Calif.: Stanford University Press, 1983.

Joslyn, Richard. *Mass Media and Elections*. Reading, Mass.: Addison-Wesley, 1984.

Kaid, Lynda Lee, Dan Nimmo, and Keith R. Sanders, eds. *New Perspectives on Political Advertising*. Carbondale: Southern Illinois University Press, 1986.

Nesbit, Dorothy Davidson. *Videostyle in U.S. Senate Campaigns*. Knoxville, Tenn.: University of Tennessee Press, 1988.

Orren, Gary R., and Nelson W. Polsby. *Media and Momentum: The New Hampshire Primary and Nomination Politics*. Chatham, N.J.: Chatham House, 1987.

Robinson, Michael J., and Austin Ranney, eds. *The Mass Media in Campaign '84*. Washington, D.C.: American Enterprise Institute, 1984.

Robinson, Michael J., and Margaret A. Sheehan. *Over the Wire and on TV: CBS and UPI in Campaign '80*. New York: Russell Sage Foundation, 1983.

Schram, Martin. *The Great American Video Game: Presidential Politics in the Television Age*. New York: William Morrow, 1987.

CHAPTER 7

The Struggle for Control:
News from the White House,
Congress, and the Courts

Walter Cronkite once remarked, "Politics and media are insepara-
ble. It is only the politicians and the media that are incompatible." [1]
There is a love-hate relationship between government officials and the
media. To perform their functions adequately, each needs the other.
But they have conflicting goals and missions and operate under different institutional constraints.

The Adversary Relationship

To retain public support and maintain its power, the government
wants to influence what information is passed on to the public and to
other officials. It wants to be able to define situations and project
images in its own way to further its social and political objectives. As
critics of government, newspeople take special pains to expose wrongdoing by public officials. They often view the world from a different
perspective than do politicians and describe the situation accordingly.
They feel bound by the economics of the news business to present
exciting stories that will attract large audiences. This often means
prying into conflict, controversy, corruption, or ordinary wheeling and
dealing—matters that government officials would like to shield. Government wants its portrait taken from the most flattering angle, at least
from a perspective that resembles average conditions. The media, however, prefer candid shots that show government in awkward poses and
compromising situations.

In this chapter we will examine more closely the interrelationship of
government and the media, considering in turn the executive, legisla-

tive, and judicial branches. Casual as well as systematic observations readily establish that the media devote a great deal of attention to the affairs of the national government, particularly the presidency. As Table 7-1 shows, during the twelve-month span from July 1986 to June 1987, the early evening broadcasts of ABC, CBS, and NBC ran an average of 172 network television stories per month about some aspect of the presidency. They featured an average of 450 national political news stories in general, so presidential coverage represents a sizable 38 percent.

The numbers for Congress and the Supreme Court were much lower, with a monthly average of twenty-four Congress stories. However, many of the stories about domestic and foreign affairs cover congressional activities, even when Congress is not explicitly mentioned. When such indirect coverage is added to the Congress score, the gap between Congress and the president narrows considerably. The Supreme Court averaged sixteen stories per month, with a lot of monthly peaks and valleys. Congressional and presidential monthly patterns were much steadier.

The president received roughly seven and one-half hours of television news coverage each month from the networks, compared with slightly over one hour for Congress and one-half hour for the Supreme Court. Differences among the three networks in number of stories and time allotments were minimal. Newspaper coverage patterns resembled television.[2]

Similarity in patterns does not mean that the media project identical images of public officials. A local newspaper, an elite newspaper, and network television all covered a proposal by President Reagan to cut taxes and the president's 1984 trip to Europe. Researchers found, however, three different sets of images in the stories.[3] The *Durham Morning Herald,* a local paper with limited resources for independent news analysis, presented uncritical factual accounts drawn largely from the wire services. These stories featured the themes, ideas, and perspectives provided by the White House and cast the president and the events into a favorable light. Although the elite *New York Times* reported the White House version of events, it subjected them to critical analysis. The views of prominent foes of the president and his policies were given ample space. This created a much less rosy impression of the state of affairs. CBS evening news presented a more mixed picture. Verbal images were predominantly negative, whereas visual images, based on presidentially controlled photo opportunities, were highly favorable. Audiences for these three news sources thus were informed about the same events, but the tint of the interpretive lenses varied from rosy, to a darkish blend of black and white, to a pattern of sharply contrasting light and dark shades.

Table 7-1 Evening Network News Coverage of the Three Branches of
Government, July 1986-June 1987

Month	President		Congress		Supreme Court	
	N	*Time*	N	*Time*	N	*Time*
1986						
July	158	5:53	26	0:47	29	0:56
August	183	5:44	13	0:28	21	0:39
September	159	6:46	17	0:28	12	0:23
October	204	9:29	15	0:31	12	0:24
November	167	9:28	27	2:18	13	0:14
December	166	9:58	21	1:40	4	0:10
1987						
January	181	7:16	24	0:59	12	0:16
February	190	8:31	30	1:24	9	0:14
March	178	6:37	30	1:07	17	0:35
April	129	5:22	29	0:57	16	0:29
May	166	8:14	30	1:42	11	0:22
June	184	7:16	22	0:46	41	1:17
Total	2,065	90:34	284	13:07	197	5:59
Average	172	7:33	24	1:05	16	0:30

Source: Computed by author from the Vanderbilt Television News Archives Indexes.

Note: Numbers of stories are based on the story divisions made by the Vanderbilt
Television News Archive Indexes. The time is listed in hours and minutes. Figures for the
three networks have been combined.

The Media and the Executive Branch

Four Major Functions

The media perform four basic functions for presidents and other
government executives such as governors and mayors.[4] First, they inform them about current events, including developments in other parts
of the government. This information sets the political scene for policies.
When the media highlight problems, executive action often follows. Not
infrequently, media furnish daily news faster than can bureaucratic
channels. President John F. Kennedy, for instance, would read the *New
York Times* before beginning his official day because stories about
foreign affairs often reached him twenty-four hours earlier through the
Times than through State Department bulletins that had to be coded
and then decoded.

Second, the media keep executive branch officials throughout the
government attuned to the major concerns of the American people.
They do this directly by reporting on public opinion and indirectly by

featuring the stories likely to shape public opinion. Public officials assume that newspeople keep in touch with popular concerns to be able to write stories that are meaningful to their readers and viewers. Readers and viewers, in turn, take their cues about what is important and worthy of discussion from the media.

Third, the media enable executives to convey their messages to the general public as well as to political elites within and outside of government. These channels of communication, to which presidents have access almost at will, provide unparalleled opportunities to explain administration policies, publicly attack opponents' positions, and force them to take stands they may want to avoid. Political elites need these channels as much as the public does because there is no effective communication system that directly links government officials who are dispersed throughout the country.[5]

Fourth, the media allow chief executives to remain in full public view on the political stage, keeping their human qualities and professional skills on almost constant display. Newspapers, television, and radio supply a steady stream of commentary about a president's daily routines. Coverage of personal life may be minute. For instance, when President Dwight D. Eisenhower had a heart attack in Denver in 1955, his news secretary James Hagerty held five news briefings a day, seven days a week, for three weeks. The media dutifully reported intimate details of the president's condition, including the color of his morning toast and the number of bowel movements recorded on his medical chart. Beyond providing human interest tidbits, this coverage was intended to reassure the public that it was fully informed about the president's disability and his fitness to continue his official functions. Human interest stories help to forge close personal ties between people and their leaders and may contribute to the relation of trust that turns people into willing followers.

Media Impact

The political significance of the relationship between the media and the executive branch is greater than the few functions just described. Media coverage is the very lifeblood of politics because it shapes the perceptions that form the reality on which political action is based. Media do more than depict the political environment; they *are* the political environment. Because direct contact with political actors and situations is limited, media images define situations for nearly all participants in the political process.

As we saw in previous chapters, the age of television politics that began in the 1950s has vastly enhanced media impact and hence media power. In the past a story might have caused ripples on the political seas when thousands of people in one corner of the country read it in the

paper or heard it on the radio. Today that same story can cause political tidal waves when millions nationwide see and hear it simultaneously on television. A politician now can visit with millions of potential followers in their living rooms, creating the kinds of emotional ties that hitherto came only from personal contact. An appearance on television may affect the political future of a member of Congress more than service on an important congressional committee.

By attracting new participant-observers to politics and creating new types of politicians, television has tipped the political scales of power among the three branches of government in favor of the presidency. The first and second laws of "video politics" explain why: "television alters the behavior of institutions in direct proportion to the amount of coverage provided or allowed," and "the more coverage an institution secures, the greater its public stature and the more significant its role."[6]

We have already described how strongly media in general, and television in particular, influence who becomes eligible for presidential office and how profoundly the media affect the conduct and outcome of elections. After elections the success of presidential policies, the length, vigor, and thrust of a president's political life, and the general level of support for the political system depend heavily on the images that the media convey. For instance, support for the Vietnam War ebbed after television news showed American marines leveling Vietnamese villages and reported massacres of Vietnamese civilians by American troops. Television news generated "greater receptivity to darker news about Vietnam. . . . It was the end of the myth that we were different, that we were better." [7] Television also bestowed respectability on vocal opponents of the war by publicizing antiwar activities. President Lyndon B. Johnson considered it hopeless to try to recapture public support for the war after Walter Cronkite announced in 1968 that the war could not be won. As David Halberstam put it: "It was the first time in American history a war had been declared over by an anchorman." [8] Although it is difficult to prove conclusively that Vietnam War coverage had the massive effects that Halberstam claims, circumstantial evidence supports his verdict.

The media frequently raise issues that presidents and other public officials would prefer to keep out of the limelight. Many observers believe that publicizing problems created by school busing has strengthened opposition to federally mandated racial integration of schools. The Watergate scandal of 1973, which led to the resignation of President Richard Nixon, is a prime example of how constant media prodding can put a damaging issue at the top of the public agenda despite presidential efforts to downplay it. The list of major and minor scandals that the media have highlighted to the government's dismay is seemingly endless—misdeeds of the Central Intelligence Agency, racial discrimination within the Agriculture Department, shady dealings by the National Security Council, tasteless jokes by members of the president's cabinet, and so on.

Media coverage can increase as well as undermine public support for a president's policies. This is particularly important in national emergencies when backing by Congress and the public is vital. For instance, in August 1964 only 42 percent of the American public supported President Johnson's Vietnam policies. Many questioned his ability to continue to raise men and money for the war. After the president broadcast an explanation, however, these doubts were apparently dispelled; approval ratings of his Vietnam policies rose to a comfortable 72 percent. Similarly, President Nixon's dispatch of troops to Cambodia in April 1970 won a 50 percent approval rating after he explained it on television. Prior to the broadcast, only 7 percent of the public had approved. Favorable ratings for President Jimmy Carter's foreign policy jumped by 34 percentage points from 22 to 56 percent after the news media announced that the 1978 Camp David meeting had produced a peace settlement between Egypt and Israel. But such steep gains may be short lived because memories fade quickly. Following the Camp David stories, the monthly ratings dropped steadily by about 4 percentage points, until six months later when the trend was reversed by a new announcement of Middle East successes.

By highlighting problems, requesting government action, or reporting demands for action, media stories may spur new policies or change existing policies. For instance, a 1982 CBS television documentary called "People Like Us" prompted the Reagan administration to take action. Fearing a backlash from this documentary on three destitute American families hurt by the administration's budget cuts, officials of the Department of Health and Human Services promptly investigated the three cases. Soon the wheels of government were spinning to make sure that truly needy people could "rest assured that the social safety net of programs they depend on are exempt from any cuts." [9] Sometimes the mere threat of publicity has been used by media personnel to force presidents and bureaucrats to act.

Sensational adverse publicity can kill as well as generate programs. For instance, the publicity following an accident at a nuclear plant in Three Mile Island, Pennsylvania, in 1979 predictably resulted in sharp curbs in the production of nuclear energy. Welfare programs, such as Head Start's prekindergarten training for poor children or financial aid for minority businesses, were sharply cut in the wake of news about inefficient management and corrupt handling of money.

Media publicity can also be crucial in determining whether a presidential appointee will be confirmed by the Senate. Griffin Bell, President Carter's nominee for attorney general, almost missed confirmation in 1977 because of adverse press reports about his racial views. During the Nixon administration, highly unfavorable media publicity was instrumental in killing the nominations to the Supreme Court of Clement F. Haynsworth, Jr., accused of conflicts of interest, and G. Harrold Carswell, accused of racial prejudice. Similarly, negative publicity about Robert H. Bork's legal views and Douglas Ginsburg's marijuana use cost these nominees of Ronald Reagan a seat on the Court.

Direct and Mediated Transmission

Audio-visual and print images about government are conveyed either directly or indirectly. Direct conveyance allows government officials to transmit their messages with a minimum of shaping by the media. President Harry S. Truman was the first to use the direct mode by broadcasting his entire State of the Union message in 1947 to a nationwide audience. In January 1961 President Kennedy further expanded direct coverage by allowing telecasts of news conferences to be broadcast live. Among public officials, presidents enjoy the greatest opportunities for uncontrolled access to the American people. As noted in Chapter 4, political leaders competing with the president for power and public support have tried for matching privileges with only moderate success.

Of course, even live television and radio broadcasts are not totally devoid of media influence because camera angles and other photographic techniques slant all presentations somewhat. For example, when President Reagan, in 1985, visited a military cemetary in Bitburg, Germany, CBS wanted to convey the essence of the controversy by filming the president against the backdrop of Nazi storm troopers' graves. The White House, disclaiming any intent to honor fallen Nazi soldiers, tried but failed to persuade the network to film the scene from a different angle.[10]

Instant commentary following presidential remarks has often blunted their impact. Likewise, print news stories describing a presidential news conference, even when they are followed by the full transcript, involve shaping by media personnel. Compared with the great leeway that newspeople usually have in choosing and interpreting information about the presidency, this type of control is minimal, however.

Indirect or mediated transmission—the shaping of news presentations by media personnel—lies at the heart of the tensions between media and government because it bestows more power upon the media than governments like to surrender. Mediated transmission permits journalists to pick and choose from among the facts given to them. They routinely chop lengthy official statements into one- or two-sentence quotes and then weave them into an account often supplemented with information gathered from hostile sources. Thus the story is presented in a framework chosen and controlled by the media. By judiciously selecting spokespeople for specific points of view, newspeople can evaluate public officials and policies at will. Frequently, these appraisals are negative, especially when the popularity of an administration is already falling. Newspeople are often accused of using mediated coverage deliberately, or at the least carelessly, to hurt public officials and their policies.

As Table 7-2 shows, the trend toward negative coverage is accelerating. During the seventeen-year period from January 1968 to January 1985, news about the president, his family, his staff, and his foreign and domestic policies was primarily positive in only five years.

Media Goals and Tactics

Media personnel refute the charge that they go out of their way to show incumbent administrations in a bad light. They contend that they are looking for lively, significant stories that will earn them the respect of their colleagues and the acclaim of their readers and viewers. They see themselves as guardians of the public interest who help to make government more honest and efficient, and they believe that they have a duty to report the government's problems and wrongdoings. The actors who produced the unfortunate situation, not the newspeople who reported it, should be blamed, they argue. Politicians who attack the

Table 7-2 Tone of CBS News Coverage of the President, January 1968-January 1985 (in percentages)

Administration	Positive	Neutral	Negative	Balance
Nixon				
First	28	51	20	+8
Second	10	50	39	−29
Ford	20	59	21	−1
Carter	17	55	28	−11
Reagan	13	57	30	−17
Average	18	54	28	−10

Source: Adapted from Fred Smoller, "The Six O'Clock Presidency: Patterns of Network News Coverage of the President," *Presidential Studies Quarterly* 16 (Winter 1986): 40. Reprinted by permission of the Center for the Study of the Presidency, publisher of *Presidential Studies Quarterly.*

Note: Balance equals positive score minus negative score. N = 5,500 stories. The Reagan score does not include the Iran-contra affair and the stock market crash, events that occurred later.

media for focusing on bad news are accused of resembling the ancient Greeks who often killed bearers of bad tidings. This is what newsman William J. Small had in mind when he entitled his book on government and the media *To Kill a Messenger.*[11]

As noted earlier, many of the stories journalists choose to cover reflect badly on government because they deal with socially undesirable or unusual behavior. Media personnel assigned to the presidential beat regularly feature harsh criticism of presidential programs, particularly if it is voiced by politically influential opponents. Minor sins are often blown up as if they were major transgressions. For example, Martin Plissner, the political editor of CBS News, dug out from the back pages of the *New York Daily News* President Carter's incriminating remarks that he saw nothing wrong with preserving the ethnic purity of neighborhoods. Then he asked one of his reporters to question the president about them at a press conference. Carter fell into the trap, and the story became front-page news.[12]

A Rocky Marriage

In general, chief executives complain about their coverage. All presidents profess to believe in a free press and to run an open government, but they rapidly develop a distaste for many of the reports about their administration. As President Kennedy told a news conference midway into his term in 1962, "[I am] reading more and enjoying it less." [13]

A classic attack on presidential press coverage occurred on November 13, 1969, in Des Moines, Iowa. Vice President Spiro Agnew lashed out at the media for their instant adverse commentary on a televised address by President Nixon. Agnew charged that a tiny, anonymous group of men based in New York and Washington, who represented nobody but their own privileged fraternity, took it upon themselves to impugn the truthfulness and capabilities of the elected head of the nation. He challenged the networks to give the American people "a full accounting of their stewardship," warning that "we would never trust such power over public opinion in the hands of a small and unelected elite." The media were outraged, but the many people who called stations to comment on the address sided with Agnew two to one.[14]

Presidents' displeasure with media coverage is readily understandable. Media coverage not only deprives them, to varying degrees, of control over the definition of political situations; it also forces them to talk in clichés and quotable oversimplifications and, in the process, to put themselves on record in ways that may narrow their options for future action. Media disclosures of secret activities, such as an impending military intervention or a planned price freeze, may actually force the president's hand. Bargaining advantages may be lost through premature publication of news; trivia, conflict, and public wrongdoing may receive undue emphasis.

In the rocky marriage between the press and the president, open battles are comparatively rare. Despite traded accusations that the government manipulates and lies and the press distorts and entraps, each side is fully aware that it depends on the other. The president and members of the executive branch control valuable information that the media need each day and must publish quickly while it is fresh. In fact, the president *is* the story in many instances. If presidents refuse to talk to reporters, as happened unusually often during the Nixon and Reagan years, or if they instruct their staffs and major departments and agencies to refuse interviews, the story cannot be covered firsthand. Alienating the prime news maker and source of government news is a major catastrophe for any news organization. Even when information from outside sources is available, "official" sources are preferred. Reporters' eagerness to get the news firsthand gives the president a tremendous advantage in influencing the substance and spin of news stories.

The media, for their part, can withhold publicity that the president needs or force publicity that he does not want. They can stress the positive or accent the negative. They can give instantaneous live coverage or delay broadcasts until a time of their choosing. In 1987, for example, two of the three major networks refused a request for live coverage of President Reagan's speeches in support of his embattled nomination of Judge Robert Bork to the Supreme Court. All three networks refused to air his plea for additional funding for antigovernment forces in Nicaragua.

The upshot of such an even match between the press and the government is a good deal of fraternizing and cronyism among these two "enemies," often to the dismay of those who would have the press be "pure." Each side works hard to cultivate the other's friendship. They often collaborate in examining political issues and problems. This coziness may reduce journalists' zeal to investigate government's misdeeds. Indeed, charges of collusion have been made when media time and again have suppressed news at the request of government departments or the White House.

Many of these instances have concerned questions of national security. In 1980 the press delayed publicizing plans for a U.S. invasion of Iran to rescue American hostages. In 1987 it suppressed technical data about eavesdropping devices designed to intercept information from Soviet marine cables. Reports about the forthcoming Bay of Pigs invasion of Cuba in 1961 were also toned down under government pressure. With the wisdom of hindsight, President Kennedy acknowledged later that the news blackout might have been a mistake. Publicity might have averted the ill-fated venture.[15]

The relationship between the media and the chief executive often displays three distinct phases.[16] Initially, there is a honeymoon period, a time of cooperation when the media convey the president's messages about organization of the new administration, appointment of new officials, and plans and proposals for new policies. At this early stage few policies and proposals have been implemented, so there is little opportunity for adverse criticism. Presidents and their advisers, eager to get their story across, make themselves readily available to the media and supply them with ample information.

Once the administration embarks on controversial programs and becomes vulnerable to criticism of its record, the honeymoon ends. This seems to be happening earlier and more abruptly now than in the past.[17] The administration, stung by adverse publicity, then tries to manipulate the media. This is quite difficult, especially since top officials have become immersed in their work by midterm and often delegate contact with the media to lower level officials, particularly those charged with press relations. The media, in turn, try to avoid manipulation by developing more unofficial sources that can supply them with the information that they do not get directly from the top.

If the rifts between media and the executive branch become particularly severe, there may be a third period in which both sides retreat from their mutually hostile behavior to a more moderate stance. Frequently, this phase coincides with a reelection campaign during which newspeople try harder to provide impartial coverage, and presidents are more eager to keep newspeople happy. For instance, relations between President Gerald R. Ford and the news media brightened considerably during his 1976 campaign to retain the presidency.

Administrations' ability to get along with the media differ considerably. The president's interpersonal skills as well as the nature of the political problems faced by the administration account for much of the variation. In recent history the Kennedy and Reagan administrations have been particularly good at press relations, while the Nixon administration was especially bad. In fact, Nixon's Watergate problems might never have developed into a major scandal if he had been able to charm the press in the Kennedy manner.

The relationship between the executive and media varies not only from one administration to the next but also from one part of the country to another. Frictions are greatest between the White House and the Washington press corps because they are most interdependent, and familiarity breeds a certain amount of contempt. The northeastern seaboard press has a reputation of being more critical than the press in the rest of the country. For this reason most presidents occasionally circumvent the eastern press by scheduling news conferences in other parts of the country and by making major policy announcements away from the East Coast. As Jeb Stuart Magruder, deputy director of Richard Nixon's reelection campaign, explained in his account of the Nixon years, "We were involved in media politics, and we were seeking not only to speak through the media in the usual fashion—press releases, news conferences—but to speak around the media, much of which we considered hostile, to take our message directly to the people." [18]

Similarly, presidents Carter and Reagan arranged to visit small communities throughout the country to bask in the adulation of local audiences and local media for the benefit of nationwide television viewers. Reagan even presented brief radio broadcasts every Saturday afternoon in the hope of attracting front-page coverage in Sunday papers. The Mutual Broadcast System, the national radio network that supplies programs to radio stations, ultimately refused to carry these talks, and the Democrats' rebuttal, on a regular basis. It claimed that many of the talks were a "rehash" of old news. Unedited versions of presidential pronouncements are broadcast by an electronic news service especially created in 1985 for that purpose. The system transmits live proceedings directly to subscribing local media enterprises throughout the nation. The White House also makes the president and top-level administrators available for satellite interviews by local anchors. The interviews are transmitted through the Local Program Network (LPN), which is financed by a nationwide group of local stations.[19]

Presidential Goals and Tactics

Besides circumventing the eastern press, presidents use an array of other tactics to control the substance and tenor of news. Three tactics are particularly common. First and most important, they try to win reporters' favor. This is not difficult because presidents are constantly surrounded by people who must have fresh news to earn their pay. Second, presidents try to shape the flow of news to make good publicity more likely and bad publicity less likely. Finally, they pace and arrange their work schedules to produce opportunities for favorable media coverage. Each of these tactics will be discussed in turn.

Winning Favor. To woo reporters, presidents offer good story material as well as occasional scoops that may bring distinction to individual reporters. They cultivate reporters' friendship by being accessible, treating them with respect, and arranging for their creature comforts. To keep reporters in line, presidents may threaten them directly or obliquely with withdrawal of privileges. These may include accommodations in the presidential plane, special interviews, or answers to their questions during news conferences. Presidents may attack individual reporters or their organizations for undesirable reporting, as President Kennedy did when he found Halberstam's reports about Vietnam in the *New York Times* objectionable. The *Times* did not follow Kennedy's suggestion to remove Halberstam from location in Vietnam, and he later won a Pulitzer Prize for his on-the-scene reporting. Kennedy also dispatched Gen. Maxwell Taylor, chairman of the Joint Chiefs of Staff, to complain personally to publisher Henry Luce about reporters who had made inaccurate statements concerning the Bay of Pigs disaster. But the protest was to no avail. No heads rolled in consequence.[20]

Shaping the News Flow. Presidents try to guide the flow of news by the thrust of their commentary and by controlling their subordinates' contacts with the press. In 1986, for example, after no agreements could be reached during a meeting of U.S. and Soviet leaders in Iceland, the American press put most of the blame for the failure on President Reagan. To shift the blame to General Secretary Mikhail Gorbachev, the president and his cabinet deluged the country with public appearances in which the administration's version of the story was given. Given the high status of the speakers, extensive media coverage was certain.

To control news flow, presidents may prohibit their staffs, on pain of dismissal, from publicly disagreeing with their policies. In addition, they may require administrative departments to clear interviews through the White House to avoid conflicting pronouncements on matters such as unemployment statistics or oil conservation policies. The Carter and Reagan administrations insisted that officials privy to sensitive information receive approval of their superiors prior to granting interviews to the press. Criticism by the eastern press has been averted by withholding advance copies of speeches or timing them late enough in the evening to preclude adequate coverage in the morning papers in the East.

Presidents also may space out releases so that there is a steady, manageable flow of news. If they want emphasis on a particular story, they may withhold competing news that breaks simultaneously. Sometimes a barrage of news is released or even created to distract attention from sensitive developments. For instance, at the end of the 1976 presidential campaign, Carter feared losses in California and New Jersey. To deemphasize them, and to focus media attention on his expected victory in Ohio, he altered his travel plans to campaign primarily in Ohio. He also called Chicago's mayor, Richard Daley, just before a mayoral press conference to emphasize that Ohio would be the key state to win—a message Daley immediately passed on to the press. Carter's staff later claimed credit for deflecting media attention from the California and New Jersey primaries and making Ohio the critical state. As Pat Caddell, Carter's pollster, put it: "We orchestrated that. We were in trouble in New Jersey but we knew we were going to win Ohio. Then Daley did it. Of course, we orchestrated that too!" [21]

Orchestrating Coverage. Ways of arranging activities to create favorable publicity are numerous. They include the scheduling of campaign events, the heightening of suspense through news blackouts prior to major pronouncements, and the manufacturing of picturesque pseudo-events. Timing speeches for broadcast during television hours and at times when there are no competing sports events or television spectacles is another example. Political successes may be coupled with political failures in hopes that publicity for the success will draw attention away from the failure. The Carter administration reportedly timed its announcement of the opening of formal relations with the People's Republic of China late in 1978 to buffer negative publicity if its attempts to clinch a peace settlement between Israel and Egypt failed. Similarly, the Reagan administration hoped that pictures of the American marines' successful military takeover of the tiny island of Grenada would counteract the images of the 1983 bombing of American marines in Lebanon.

News management may even go to the point of deceiving the press in order to present a smoke-screen message to the public. For instance, in 1961, the Kennedy administration told Miami reporters that five thousand U.S. troops had invaded Cuba's Bay of Pigs. This news was intended to encourage Cubans to rise up in support of a large invasion force. In actuality, only one thousand troops had been sent. When the troops ran into trouble, officials circulated stories that only a few hundred American troops had been involved and that their chief mission had been to land supplies for anti-Castro guerrillas in Cuba rather than to invade the country. When reporters discovered that they had been used to spread false stories, they were furious. The inevitable result was a credibility gap between the executive branch and the media and between the media and the public.

Institutional Settings

On the President's Side. A president can shape the news indirectly through appointments to the Federal Communications Commission (FCC) and other public agencies concerned with the media and through informal contacts with personnel in these agencies. Financial lifelines can be controlled through the Office of Management and Budget, which screens the budgetary requests of all federal agencies, including those related to communications. Control can also be wielded through the Justice Department. For instance, the Antitrust Division challenged the FCC's approval of a merger between the American Broadcasting Company and the International Telephone and Telegraph Company. In that case the Justice Department carried a series of appeals through the courts and ultimately to the Supreme Court.

Presidents involve themselves directly in media policy making through various White House organizations, study commissions, and task forces. In 1970 President Nixon created the Office of Telecommunications Policy—the first permanent agency within the White House to plan communications policy. The Carter administration replaced this office with a less powerful organization within the Commerce Department, the National Telecommunications and Information Administration. By downgrading the agency, Carter gave the impression that the White House had distanced itself from communications policy questions and would leave the FCC free from White House pressure. However, a small policy planning staff remained in the White House to advise the president. This divorce of planning from operations still characterizes federal communications policy and has impeded strong executive leadership.

Other White House media agencies include the Office of the Press Secretary and the Office of Media Liaison. By custom, the press secretary meets almost daily with the White House press corps to make announcements and take questions. These briefings supply reporters with the president's interpretation of events. The Office of Media Liaison sets up meetings twice a month between the president and groups of editors, publishers, and reporters from various parts of the country. The often hostile Washington press corps is excluded from these gatherings and does not get transcripts until those in attendance have had a chance to file their stories. As part of the White House organization, there is also a press release office and a research office that provides information on what the president has said in the past. In addition, executive departments and agencies have their own press secretaries.[22] To structure his activities so that they would receive the best possible media coverage, President Carter in 1978 appointed a special assistant for communication. Although widely viewed as the "Great Communicator," President Reagan felt the need to do the same. Altogether, 25 percent of White House senior staff during the Reagan years was involved in public relations work.[23]

On the Media's Side. The White House press corps consists of some seventy newspeople who cover the president regularly. Many have considerable experience and reputations to match. The *New York Times, Washington Post, Los Angeles Times, Chicago Tribune, Philadelphia Inquirer,* and other major newspapers have full-time reporters exclusively assigned to the president. So do a number of newspaper chains, such as the Scripps-Howard papers, the Hearst press, and the Newhouse papers. Alternatively, smaller papers may send their Washington bureau chiefs to the White House whenever there is news of special interest to their region.

Each of the major broadcast networks has three or four reporters at the White House on a regular basis; smaller networks have one. The Cable Satellite Public Affairs Network (C-SPAN), a twenty-four-hour cable news operation with a staff of more than fifty people, provides White House coverage as well as gavel-to-gavel coverage of the House of Representatives. C-SPAN sends its signal to more than 1,500 cable systems throughout the country. Although C-SPAN has the potential to reach more than 30 million people, so far the actual audience for government coverage has been quite small. The White House also is covered by several other all-news cable services, weekly news magazines, several periodicals, as well as photographers and their supporting staffs. Much of the photographic coverage of the president, however, is handled by White House staff photographers.[24]

Most of the country's dailies (more than 70 percent) do not have a regular Washington correspondent or part-time "stringer" to cover the White House. The same still holds true for most of the country's television and radio stations. Inexpensive satellite time, however, has lowered news transmission costs and boosted the numbers of stations that can afford direct coverage of the Washington scene. Satellites have enabled many small stations to view the activities of the national government through the prism of local interests. News organizations without Washington staffs rely heavily on wire service news. Both of the major wire services in the United States, Associated Press (AP) and United Press International (UPI), have three full-time reporters accredited to the White House who cover the beat continuously, including all presidential trips. Other news organizations alternate coverage of presidential trips, taking turns at assigning a reporter to the "pool" of reporters scheduled to accompany the president. Two foreign wire services, the British Reuters and the French Agence France-Presse, also have one regular reporter each assigned to the White House.

The White House press corps spends much of its time waiting for news from the president's staff. Reporters often find this frustrating and even humiliating. Their press passes give them unlimited access to the White House press room only. Other parts of the White House and executive offices are off limits except by special appointments, which are given out selectively. For public ceremonies in the East Room or Oval Office or Rose Garden, reporters usually are escorted as a group. Some have likened this to being herded like cattle. Many also object to the hero worship and protectiveness that they sense in the president's staff and the frequent occasions when presidents make personal or public moves without first alerting the press corps.

Forms of Contact. The release of news by chief executives or their aides takes a number of routinized forms. Most of these represent a concerted effort to control news output. The most common is the *news release,* a story prepared by government officials and handed to members of the press, usually without an opportunity for questions. It can be used verbatim, and officials hope that it will be. To make sure that the release appears at the most opportune time, it often has a date line that stipulates the earliest time when it may be published. If an administration wants to give the appearance of great activity or to distract reporters' attention from areas of undesired publicity, it may publish a flood of releases simultaneously. The Carter administration also initiated a program of taping thirty- to forty-second radio spots to be distributed to stations around the country on request. In this way stations receive the news in a ready-made version controlled by the White House.

In a *news briefing* reporters have an opportunity to ask the press secretary about the news releases. But because executive officials furnish the news for the briefing, they control the substance and tone of the discussion. Although most press secretaries, as well as members of the press, believe that daily news briefings are unnecessary and could be covered just as well by press releases, the briefings have become traditional.

While a *news conference* may appear to be a wide-open question period, it is usually controlled tightly by the official being questioned. News conferences are a form of political theater, staged, directed, and partially written by top executives to cast themselves in praiseworthy roles. Seemingly spontaneous answers usually have been carefully prepared by experts on the executive's staff and rehearsed during extensive briefings that precede news conferences.

Since the days of Theodore Roosevelt, the first president to summon reporters to the White House regularly, presidents have initiated news conferences. They often begin the event with a lengthy statement designed to set the conference's tone. The president may lead off with topics for which he wants headlines, or he may seek to divert media attention away from politically embarrassing issues. Presidents may generate questions by letting it be known ahead of time that certain types of queries will receive very interesting answers. They can often control the subject and tone of a news conference by recognizing friendly reporters for questions and avoiding follow-up questions. But no president has been able to squelch embarrassing questions entirely or to deny reporters the chance to use their questions as opportunities to express their own views about controversial issues.[25] Reporters revel in acting like prosecutors trying to extract a confession of major crimes from a hapless subject. Through posing leading questions, they try to force the president into making statements that he does not wish to make.

Some news conferences are off-the-record *backgrounders* called by high officials to give newspeople important background information that they are honor bound to keep entirely secret or to publish only without revealing its source. Various forms of vague attribution are usually permitted, such as "government sources say," "it has been reported by reliable sources," or even more specifically, "the White House discloses" or the "Defense Department indicates."

Government officials like backgrounders because they permit them to bring a variety of policy ideas before their colleagues and the public without openly identifying with them. In other words, they are a relatively safe way to "test the waters." Secretary of State Henry Kissinger used backgrounders to submit foreign policy options for public debate and to warn foreign countries that their behavior was unacceptable to the United States. To discourage the Soviet Union's support of India in a war with Pakistan, Kissinger told reporters in a backgrounder that Russia's policy might lead President Nixon to cancel a planned trip to Moscow. If the statement had been officially attributed to Kissinger, it would have constituted a threat that might have undermined détente with the Soviet Union.

Similarly, Secretary of Defense Caspar Weinberger summoned reporters to a secret briefing in 1982 to provide them with data on Soviet military capacity that would substantiate the administration's claim that the Soviet Union posed a grave military threat to the United States and Europe. The data—photographs produced by satellites and secret electronic systems—had been withheld because of fears that disclosure might alert the Soviet Union to U.S. surveillance tactics. Weinberger hoped that in the wake of a confidential viewing of these photographs, reporters would no longer publicly question the administration's claims of danger. Public support for Reagan's defense policies might then increase.

Unlike government officials, reporters are ambivalent about backgrounders. They like having access to news that might otherwise be unavailable, but they dislike being prevented from publishing all aspects of the story or from giving the source of the information so that the story can be placed in its proper perspective. At times reporters have evaded the prohibition on source disclosure by refusing to attend a background briefing and then reporting the story as told to them by reporters who attended. To prevent such leaks, government officials have occasionally solicited written pledges from reporters that they would not reveal information released during briefings. Usually reporters refuse to sign.

In addition to formal encounters, reporters and the president or White House staff meet informally in work or social settings. Frequently, the most probing stories about White House activities come from reporters not ordinarily assigned to cover the president. The regulars would be too vulnerable to retaliation by the White House if they wrote such penetrating reports.

Top government officials, and occasionally the president, may agree to be interviewed on programs such as "Nightline," "Good Morning America," the "Today" show, "Meet the Press," or "Face the Nation." Questioning on these shows can resemble a brutal inquisition. Executive officials participate anyhow because these programs provide excellent opportunities to present the administration's position to an interested nationwide audience. Besides, if questioning becomes excessively harsh, the audience often feels sorry for the targets and sides with them.

An even less formal release of news occurs through leaks, the surreptitious release of information by government sources who wish to remain anonymous. Officials may leak information that they are not authorized to release or that they do not wish to release formally. Sometimes low-level officials leak information to gain attention from top officials.

Leaks are mixed blessings. They can destroy the timing of negotiations, alienate the parties whose secrets have been betrayed, and cause great harm by disclosing politically sensitive matters. They also may bring important suppressed issues to needed public attention, serve as trial balloons, and permit government officials to release information anonymously. Although presidents frequently leak confidential stories, they passionately hate news leaks by others. Because the source is hidden, personal confrontation and punishment are impossible. All recent presidents have therefore used federal investigative agencies such as the Federal Bureau of Investigation and the Central Intelligence Agency to find the sources of news leaks.[26]

A typical leak occurred in 1987 when unidentified U.S. officials leaked information about U.S. intelligence successes in intercepting messages between the Libyan government and its Berlin embassy. The information, which was eagerly picked up by American media, was allegedly leaked to build public support for the Reagan administration's decision to bomb Libya as punishment for its role in international terrorism. Unfortunately, the disclosures alerted Libya that its codes had been broken and undoubtedly led to security countermeasures.[27]

The harm that leaks cause must be weighed against their benefits. In a system in which the executive maintains tight control over the formal channels of news, leaks provide a valuable counterbalance. President Reagan's controversial budget proposals in 1983 are a case in point. Administration insiders, eager to bring their concerns to the public and Congress, resorted to almost daily leaks of economic appraisals that contradicted the president's views. An irate Reagan proclaimed, "I've had it up to my keister with these leaks," but he modified his budget plans nonetheless.[28]

The Media and Congress

According to political folklore, the presidency basks in the limelight of publicity at all times while Congress waits in the shadows. The television age has permanently altered the balance of political power, making the president dominant and the legislature inferior, political observers claim. As Sen. J. William Fulbright of Arkansas told Congress in 1970, "Television has done as much to expand the powers of the President as would a constitutional amendment formally abolishing the co-equality of the three branches of government." [29]

Image vs. Reality

If one probes beyond these impressions to the underlying facts, the situation appears less clear. When coverage of areas of legislative concerns is added to coverage that mentions Congress explicitly, Congress and the presidency receive roughly the same amount of national news attention. In fact, content analysis of twenty-two newspapers and the evening news of the three television networks during a typical week in 1978 showed that Congress held the edge by 54 to 46 percent in newspaper coverage. The edge was reversed for television, with the president ahead, 59 to 41 percent.[30] But much television coverage was highly negative, reducing its usefulness as a booster for the president.[31]

In terms of substance, presidential coverage and congressional coverage differ noticeably. Table 7-3 presents a comparison of thirteen issues that emerged for the president and Congress when the three most heavily covered issues were tallied on a monthly basis. Six of the thirteen issues were shared, but differed in rankings based on the amount of time devoted to each issue. The only exception was the Iran-contra scandal, the leading item by far in both presidential and congressional coverage. The figures on the Iran-contra affair are a graphic example of media obsession with a highly dramatic topic at the expense of other important news. During a four-month span in late 1986 and early 1987, more than one-third of network television news time was devoted to the scandal. The main emphasis of these stories was on personalities, "whodunit" questions, and the issue of presidential leadership. The important policy issues raised by the affair were largely ignored.[32]

Overall, presidential coverage put more emphasis on foreign policy, while congressional coverage stressed economic affairs more. Since foreign policy issues usually are more glamorous and attract audiences more than do economic affairs, this difference spells an advantage for the president. However, it must be remembered that the bulk of coverage of Congress comes through stories about individual members published in their home states. Although local coverage does not generally attract national attention, it is politically crucial to each member.

Why does Congress fare worse than the presidency in media coverage? There are several reasons. Most importantly, the presidency makes a better media target because it is a single-headed institution readily personified, filmed, and recorded in the visible person of the chief executive. This gives the media and media audiences a familiar, easily dramatized focus of attention. Even stories originating from congressional sources frequently feature the president as the main actor. Stephen Hess reports that 71 percent of news stories about the president or Congress come from legislative sources, but Congress is the main actor in only 48 percent. Conversely, in the 29 percent of stories about the president or Congress that originate with the executive branch, 52 percent focus on the executive.[33]

The president is like a super star surrounded by a cast of supporting actors. As the personification of the nation, the president can usually command national television or radio time, often at prime time and simultaneously on all major networks. During a recent ten-year period, three out of eleven congressional requests for television coverage were granted, compared with forty-four out of forty-five for the president.[34]

In contrast to the presidency, Congress, like the sparsely covered bureaucracy, is a many-headed hydra with no single widely familiar

Table 7-3   Issue Focus of Evening Network News Coverage of the
President and Congress, July 1986-June 1987

PRESIDENT

Issue	Story rank 1	2	3	Time
Iran-contra affair	5	1	2	29:31
Arms control	3	2	4	13:23
Appointments	—	4	1	5:24
Persian Gulf	2	—	1	4:56
Soviet relations	1	1	—	4:22
South Africa	1	—	—	2:06
Lebanon	—	1	—	1:47
Central America	—	1	1	1:30
Venice economic conference	—	1	—	1:19
Congress	—	—	1	1:00
Reagan's health	—	1	—	0:56
State of Union address	—	—	1	0:35
Health issues	—	—	1	0:25

CONGRESS

Issue	Story rank 1	2	3	Time
Iran-contra affair	5	2	3	6:20
Persian Gulf	1	1	—	0:53
Central America	—	4	—	0:51
Budget	3	—	1	0:46
South Africa	1	2	—	0:26
Health issues	—	1	3	0:25
Foreign trade	—	1	1	0:16
Television news	1	—	—	0:12
Saudi Arabia	—	—	2	0:10
Taxes	1	—	—	0:08
Highway funding	—	—	1	0:06
Philippines	—	1	—	0:06
Congress	—	—	1	0:05

Source: Computed by the author from the Vanderbilt Television News Archives Indexes.

Note: The numbers are combined monthly scores for ABC, CBS, and NBC early evening
newscasts. They indicate how often each issue reached the top three ranks in frequency of
mention during the year. The time is listed in hours and minutes. Italicized issues were
covered in both presidential and congressional news.

personal focus.[35] Its activities are conducted simultaneously in more than one hundred locations on Capitol Hill. No individual member can command nationwide media coverage at will. Even well-known senators and representatives are viewed as spokespersons for their own or their party's views, or as potential presidential candidates, not as spokespersons for Congress as an institution. Their celebrity status often has little to do with their legislative activity in Congress. In fact, there has never been a single spokesperson for Congress in general, or even for the Senate or House, because senators and representatives are loathe to designate one of their number as *primus inter pares.* Consequently, most stories about Congress deal with individual members or legislative activity on specific issues rather than with the body as a whole.

Another reason why stories on Congress escape wide attention lies in the nature of its work. The legislative branch plans action, makes compromises among conflicting interests, forges shifting coalitions, and works out legal details. Stories about the executive branch that describe *what* is actually done are far more memorable than reports about *how* the laborious process of hammering out legislation works. Besides, the most interesting aspect of the legislative process, the shaping of broad guidelines for policy, is usually reported by the media as part of the work of the executive branch. Congress, to quote Chris Matthews, Speaker Thomas P. O'Neill's press secretary, is "the Hamburger Helper to the White House Story." [36]

Congressional coverage is frequently not as useful to the public as it could be because the media concentrate on readily available stories. In the early stages of the legislative process, when there is still time for citizens to influence a bill, congressional coverage has been least ample. Coverage usually focuses on final action that merely ratifies the work of committees and subcommittees. Citizens learn what the new policies are without being exposed to the pros and cons and the political interplay that led to the ultimate compromise.[37] Live television coverage of congressional sessions is changing this and is making Congress more vulnerable to constituent and interest group pressures.

Fearing that legislative floor sessions would present an unedifying, boring spectacle, Congress resisted live radio and television coverage of most sessions until the late 1970s. Prior to 1979 only selected committee hearings were televised, primarily those involving spicy topics such as labor racketeering, Communists in government, or high-level corruption. These televised sessions became highly dramatic morality plays, with casts of sinners brought to justice and congressional knights battling evil before the public. Senators such as Harry Truman and Estes Kefauver and beetle-browed Sam Ervin were catapulted into the national limelight by these hearings. Many of the targets of the investigations, on the other hand, were harmed by the damaging publicity, even when they were later officially exonerated of any misdeeds. Few ordinary congressional sessions could provide comparable drama. As the *Philadelphia Inquirer* noted after the hearings an organized crime conducted by Senator Kefauver's committee, there is simply "no show like watching people thrown to the lions." [38]

In 1979 the House of Representatives lifted the prohibition on televising its floor sessions. The action was prompted in part by the desire to counterbalance the political advantages reaped by the executive branch from heavy media attention. House sessions began to be telecast by a House-run closed circuit system. The rules for coverage are strict: only the member speaking may be filmed, *not* the listeners. This stipulation bars the public from seeing the typically near-empty House chamber and inattentive members. Commercial, cable, and public television systems have access to the House broadcasts but rarely cover them. The broadcasts have received their widest dissemination through live gavel-to-gavel coverage by C-SPAN.

In 1986 the Senate finally followed suit and permitted live coverage of its proceedings. It was prodded by the concern that the Senate was "fast becoming the invisible half of Congress," in the words of Sen. Robert Byrd, D-W.Va. Byrd thus phrased the political rationale: "We cannot hold our own with the White House and the House of Representatives when it comes to news coverage of the important issues of the day." [39] Sen. Robert Dole, R-Kans., called televised proceedings "an electronic bridge to the American people." [40] Judging from initial broadcasts, television enhanced debate participation; an unusually large number of senators crossed that bridge dressed more nattily than usual and sporting well-polished rhetoric.

Televised sessions have not changed the publicity balance between the president and Congress. For the reasons outlined, Congress has not become a first-rate "show." A few interesting and unexpected results of congressional coverage have been reported, however. Representatives themselves are apparently among the most avid watchers of House coverage because the television cameras permit them to monitor sessions that they previously missed. Now they can keep up on floor action and issues reported by committees other than their own.[41] Members of Congress are generally unable to edit their videotaped remarks before they are broadcast, unlike their statements in the *Congressional Record*. This has made the legislators more cautious in their televised utterances. They do not wish to create images that may haunt their careers. Rather they try to use their appearances to create favorable images for themselves and their pet political projects.

Brief, quotable statements made by members in time to appear on the evening news have multiplied. Some members have claimed that recent sharp increases in the time spent to pass legislation are largely due to television coverage.[42] The added publicity also may make incumbent representatives even more unbeatable at the polls than they are now. In addition, broadcasting may make it more difficult for congressional leaders to keep the voices of dissident members muffled. It may be harder to reach legislative compromises once representatives have publicly committed themselves to definite positions. However, there is no solid proof thus far that television coverage has harmed consensus-building in the chamber.

Writing Congress Stories

Newspeople assigned to the congressional beat use general criteria of newsworthiness and gatekeeping to decide who and what will be covered and who and what will be ignored. Exciting, novel, or controversial topics that can be made personally relevant to the public and simply presented have precedence over recurrent complex and mundane problems, such as congressional reorganization or the annual farm bill. Orderly, dispassionate debate usually is passed over in favor of purple rhetoric and wild accusations that can produce catchy headlines. Heated confrontations are more likely to occur in the more intimate committee hearings than in full sessions. In fact, the chance for making headlines may provoke disputes when they might not otherwise occur.[43] Accordingly, committee hearings attract most extensive coverage, particularly on television.

Since Congress is a regular beat, daily press briefings are conducted by the leaders of each chamber. Major media organizations such as the *Washington Post* and the *New York Times,* major newspaper chains such as Gannett, Hearst, and Knight, and the television networks and wire services have full-time reporters covering Congress. Some of these reporters are specialists in various policy areas. Some wire service reporters, for example, concentrate on news of interest to specific regions such as the West or South. There are also Washington "stringer" bureaus whose reporters serve assorted subscriber news services throughout the country. Specialized news services such as Congressional Quarterly cover the congressional beat in detail for professional audiences. In all, more than two thousand correspondents are accredited to the press galleries in the House and Senate. About four hundred of these cover Congress exclusively.[44]

Congressional press releases and written reports provide news sources without a regular reporter on Capitol Hill with much of their information about Congress. These documents are prepared and distributed because wire service reporters are unable to attend the many hearings occurring simultaneously. Press releases enable members of Congress to tell their stories in their own words. They give an advantage to members whose offices can turn out interesting public statements.[45]

In 1970 only 16 percent of House offices reported that they had a staffer with press responsibilities; by 1984 that figure had risen to 72 percent.[46]

Senators generally receive considerably more press coverage than do representatives, even though an equal number of reporters cover both houses. On network television, stories about senators outnumber those about representatives more than six to one, probably because senators have greater prominence, prestige, and publicity resources and their larger constituencies make them of interest to a wider audience. In general, high media visibility for senators as well as representatives hinges on serving in important leadership positions and being a congressional veteran. By contrast, sponsoring legislation or service on important committees matters little. Who one is obviously counts more than what one does. In practice, this means that more than 40 percent of the congressional membership receives no national television exposure at all. A mere twenty members of the Senate garner the lion's share of attention.[47] Unlike the president, neither senators nor representatives enjoy automatic coverage of whatever they say and do, even though they issue frequent press releases and call occasional news conferences. However, on certain topics, such as tax policy or investigation of executive activities, congressional spokespersons, rather than the president, are routinely sought out. Additionally, many members of Congress receive regular local coverage through their own news columns or radio or television programs. They usually find their relations with the local media far more congenial than relations with a national press corps that cares little about focusing on the problems of particular congressional districts. Local media depend on senators and representatives for local angles to national stories because local slants make these stories more attractive to the target audiences. Since their Washington-based senators and representatives are ideal sources, newspeople are loathe to criticize them.

Functions of Media

The functions performed by the national media for Congress and by Congress for the national media parallel press-presidency relations. There are major qualitative differences, however, in the relationship. Neither Congress nor the media needs the services of the other as much as the presidency needs the press. The national media can afford to alienate some legislators without losing direct access to congressional news. Similarly, except when major controversial laws are involved, legislators can ignore national publicity and rely instead on publicity in their districts. News about national events and national public opinion is also somewhat less important to most members of Congress than to the president. Senators and representatives are most interested in news that will affect their own constituency. The home media are particularly important to legislators as sources of news and as channels for transmitting messages back to the home district while they are at work in Washington.

National as well as local media provide senators and representatives with a forum to express their views on political issues and to attract public support for themselves and their causes. This publicity reassures constituents that their elected representatives are aware of problems and are trying to solve them. It may produce action to remedy publicized abuses such as faulty tires, unnecessary surgery, or pesticides in food. Publicity by itself may bring about reform without the need for legislation or judicial action.

For a few members of Congress, national media attention may be a springboard to legislative effectiveness and to higher office, including the presidency. Once members achieve visibility, their fame often grows by its own momentum. They become regulars on interview shows, and their opinions are solicited when national issues are debated. However, members rarely receive the intimate personal coverage that presidents get. For most members media attention may do little more than make them visible targets for lobby groups. This may lead to reelection support from these groups or research support for pet projects. Publicity also may fuel support for the opposition. It may provide ammunition for rival candidates during the next election campaign.[48]

For members of Congress who are not aspiring to higher office and who do not need nationwide attention to achieve their legislative goals, national publicity may be practically irrelevant. By contrast, favorable media coverage in their districts is essential to let their constituents know what they are doing and to pave the way for reelection. As indicated, local publicity is usually easy for members to obtain. Several members of Congress even own mass media outlets, which ensures them of ample favorable coverage. Lyndon Johnson is a prominent example; he held extensive broadcast properties in Texas during his years in Congress. Many members also communicate through newsletters and individual letters sent to selected constituents.

In addition to full- or part-time media consultants, senators and representatives have studios available on Capitol Hill where they can produce low-cost video tapes, films, and audio tapes to distribute to their constituents.[49] Seventy-five percent of the House members and 80 percent of the Senate members use these facilities to make broadcasts for home-town distribution. Relationships between Congress members and journalists also benefit from the liaison services performed by the nonpartisan press galleries maintained by each chamber. In operation for more than a century, these galleries handle matters affecting the credentials and working facilities of the press.

A Cautious Marriage

Just as the functions that media perform are similar for the executive and legislative branches, so is the love-hate relationship. But it, too, is less ardent for Congress, even though mutual recriminations are plentiful. Senators and representatives, competing with peers for media attention, bemoan lack of coverage of their pet projects and pronouncements. They complain that reporters treat them as if they were scoundrels conspiring to defraud the public. As Table 7-4 indicates, they have reason to lament the little positive coverage they receive. In fact, congressional coverage is considerably more negative than coverage of the presidency or the Supreme Court.[50] Members of Congress resent the cross-examinations that reporters love to conduct with a prosecutor's zeal and an air of infallibility. They charge and can prove that the media emphasize trivia, scandals, internal dissent, and official misconduct, but often ignore congressional consensus and passage of significant legislation. They blame the media for the declining prestige of Congress.

The media, in turn, complain with justification about legislators' efforts to manage the news through their professional publicity staffs. They point to members' lack of candor and to their exclusion of media personnel from many congressional meetings and executive sessions. Broadcasters also resent the strict controls placed on their coverage of congressional sessions. They are barred from taping their own stories and are limited in the views they can photograph.

But senators and representatives realize that they need the media for information and for the publicity that is crucial to passing or defeating legislation. They know that the media will discreetly ignore their personal foibles so long as no official wrongdoing is involved. Newspeople, in turn, realize that they need individual legislators for information about congressional activities and as a counterfoil and source of leaks to check the executive branch. Members are valuable for inside comments that can personalize otherwise dull stories. Congress often creates story topics for the media by investigating dramatic ongoing problems like auto or mine safety. A congressional inquiry may be the catalyst that turns an everyday event into a newsworthy item. The story then may ride the crest of publicity for quite some time, creating its own fresh and reportable events until it recedes into limbo once more. Newspeople do not want to dry up these sources; nor do they want to forgo the financial rewards generated by paid campaign commercials.

Congress and Communications Policy

The media, particularly radio and television, are aware of the power Congress has over regulatory legislation. In the past Congress made little use of its power to legislate communications policy, viewing it as a hornet's nest of political conflict best left alone. The major exception

Table 7-4 An Evaluation of Press Coverage of Congress (in percentage of stories)

Newspaper	Positive	Negative	Neutral	Editorial ratio[a]
Atlanta Constitution	9	34	56	1:2.1
Boston Globe	14	32	53	1:1.8
Chicago Sun-Times	5	26	68	1:3.8
Dallas Morning News	5	18	78	1:1.8
Denver Post	12	32	57	1:1.1
Los Angeles Times	4	20	75	1:10
Miami Herald	6	27	67	1:2.4
Minnesota Star	5	29	66	1:2
Philadelphia Inquirer	8	40	53	1:3
Washington Post	5	21	75	1:2.4

Source: Adapted from Charles M. Tidmarch and John J. Pitney, Jr., "Covering Congress: An Analysis of Reportage and Commentary in Ten Metropolitan Newspapers," *Polity* 17 (Spring 1985): 480. Reprinted by permission.

Note: N = 2,299 stories, including news, analysis, editorials, op-ed items, and cartoons. The data in the table are based on content analysis of all Congress-related stories that appeared during thirty days spanning July and August 1978.

[a] Ratio of positive to negative editorials with neutral editorials excluded.

was passage of the Communications Act of 1934 that granted broad authority to the Federal Communications Commission (FCC) and of supplementary laws dealing with technical innovations. Periodic attempts to supersede the act have usually floundered, but the power to legislate communications policy remains. If and when strong, unified pressures from industry or consumer groups develop, Congress's powers to legislate communications policy could become important. Meanwhile, there is a vacuum in both policy formulation and oversight of administration that neither the president nor the FCC has attempted to fill.[51] Communications industry representatives have occasionally jumped into the breach. They are in a strong position to push their ideas because they enjoy a near monopoly over the basic information needed to make policy.

The communications subcommittees of the Commerce, Science, and Transportation Committee in the Senate and of the Energy and Commerce Committee in the House control communications policy largely through the power of investigation. The FCC has been investigated more frequently than most other regulatory bodies. In fact since 1970 more than fifty different congressional committees and subcommittees have reviewed various FCC activities. But there have been few dramatic results beyond spending a significant share of the commission's limited resources on responding to these investigations. Investigations have included reviews of specific FCC actions, studies of FCC operations and structures, examinations of broad policy issues such as the impact of television's portrayal of the aged or of alcohol and drug abuse, and studies of corruption in television-sponsored game shows. The appropriations committees have wielded their power over the FCC's purse in a desultory way. They occasionally have denied funds for the commission or explicitly directed what particular programs should be funded.[52] However, monetary control may be stricter in the future because Congress switched the FCC in 1982 from the status of a permanently authorized agency to one requiring biennial renewal.

Although the Senate has seldom used confirmation hearings to impress its views on new FCC commissioners, this does not mean that the views of powerful senators have been ignored. Prospective commissioners are likely to study past confirmation hearings carefully and take their cues from them. Most presidential nominees have been confirmed. Appointments are usually made to reward the politically faithful.[53] While congressional control over the FCC has generally been light, there is always the possibility of stricter control. All the parties interested in communications policy, including the White House and the courts, pay deference to that possibility.

Congressional control over the media also includes matters such as postal rates and subsidies, legislation on permissible mergers and chain control of papers, and laws designed to keep failing newspapers alive. Copyright laws, which affect print and electronic media productions, are involved, too. So are policies and regulations about telecommunication satellites, broadcast spectrum allocations, and cable television. The vast, congressionally guided changes in the telephone industry are yet another area of major concern to media interests.

Laws regulating media procedures occasionally have a strong impact on media content and policies. For instance, FCC encouragement of diversification of radio programs was largely responsible for the development of a sizable number of FM rock music stations. These stations were able to provide alternatives to more conventional programs. Congressional scrutiny of documentaries may chill investigative reporting. Congress probed the circumstances surrounding a documentary on drug use at a major university because the events were allegedly staged, and it also looked into the accuracy of charges of illicit public relations activity by the Pentagon. Former Democratic senator John Pastore of Rhode Island, who was deeply concerned about television violence, helped create the Surgeon General's Advisory Committee on Television and Social Behavior, which has investigated violence in television shows in preparation for congressional action.[54] Congressional failure to act may also have far-reaching consequences for the mass media. For instance, failure to regulate cable television has left the FCC and the courts in control of this medium.

News Impact on Congress Members

On the whole, despite ample negative coverage, the media treat congressional leaders and Congress with a fair amount of deference and respect. Media critic Ben Bagdikian has even charged that the media are an effective propaganda arm for Congress that virtually guarantees the reelection of any incumbent who is willing to run. "Most of the media are willing conduits for the highly selective information the member of Congress decides to feed the electorate," he argues.[55] This claim is exaggerated; many factors unrelated to media coverage contribute to the high reelection rate of incumbents. Besides, the media often present incumbents in an unfavorable light, and they do not publish the bulk of their self-promoting press releases. A study of the Third Congressional District in Wisconsin showed that papers published only 7 percent of the available news release copy from their representative. Senatorial publicity fared even worse. Many papers did not publish any news releases; the most generous papers published no more than 30 percent of the news release copy they received.[56] Nonetheless, there is some truth to Bagdikian's charges of kid-glove treatment.

Michael Robinson's detailed analysis of the impact of media coverage on Congress revealed several major effects. The media have increased the reelection chances of incumbents, but only in the House of Representatives where local coverage, which is generally favorable, is most important. In the Senate the negative tenor of the national media and the greater attention to challengers seeking Senate seats have reduced the reelection chances of incumbents. Newsletters, direct mail, and campaign brochures and advertisements partially fill gaps left by mass media coverage. They also serve as counterweights to the adverse news coming from newspapers and television. Skill in dealing with the media has become a crucial talent not only for presidents but also for would-be members of Congress. They must know how to "show-boat" to get coverage from newspapers and television.[57]

Compared with the presidency, the institution of Congress has suffered a decline in image and power. This springs partly from stories that usually picture it as lobby-ridden, incompetent, and slow and partly from the fact that the White House has provided more exciting copy.[58] However, individual presidents have been more bloodied by adverse publicity than have individual members of the House. Thus the media have fostered a stronger presidency, but weaker presidents, and a weaker Congress, but more durable representatives.

The Media and the Courts

Of the three branches of government, the judiciary receives the least publicity for its officials. As Table 7-1 shows, this holds true even of the Supreme Court when compared with the president or Congress. At the federal level, aside from hearings during initial appointments to the federal bench, judges are rarely in the limelight. Judges infrequently grant interviews, almost never hold news conferences, and generally do not seek or welcome media attention, primarily because they fear their impartiality might be compromised. Remoteness enhances the impression that judges are a breed apart, doling out justice to lesser mortals. At the state and local levels, where many judges are elected rather than appointed to office, media coverage is somewhat more common, and the aura of judicial majesty recedes accordingly.

The courts as institutions also receive comparatively little coverage. There are exceptions, of course. The courts' difficulties in coping with the flood of legal actions, the problems of disparate sentencing policies, and the flaws in the correction system have all been the subject of sporadic media investigations. Speeches by Supreme Court justices to public bodies such as the American Bar Association have been telecast and reported nationwide. Chief Justice Warren E. Burger even allowed himself to be questioned routinely about his annual "State of the Judiciary" speech. The news conference before the speech remained off the record, however, and the chief justice could not be quoted directly.

Although justices and court systems are not very newsworthy because they generally do not become embroiled in open battles about policies, their products—judicial decisions—do make the news. This is particularly true of U.S. Supreme Court decisions, which frequently have major consequences for the political system. For example, *Brown v. Board of Education* (1954) was widely publicized because it declared unconstitutional the separate schooling of children of different races, and *Baker v. Carr* (1962) received ample media attention because it led to massive changes in electoral districting in the United States.[59] In more recent decisions the Court has made important news with its major rulings on abortion, obscenity, capital punishment, and affirmative action.

Impact of Coverage

Publicity about Supreme Court decisions informs public officials at all government levels, as well as the general public, about the substance of selected decisions. A small corps of reporters is responsible for choosing the decisions to be covered. At the Supreme Court, full- and part-time reporters combined number about fifty people. Of these only the correspondents for the major wire services and four major newspapers are full time.

Supreme Court coverage is difficult; the reporters must digest voluminous and often contradictory opinions supporting or dissenting from a given decision. This must be done quickly and without help from the justices who authored the opinions. Advice from outside commentators, including legal experts, is usually unavailable initially since they are not allowed to preview the opinions. Leaks of advance information are very rare. The Supreme Court does have a press office, which provides some reference materials and bare-bones records of the Court's activities. In addition, brief analyses of important pending cases are available to the media through publications sponsored by the legal profession.

Because of the shortage of skilled reporters, much court reporting, even at the Supreme Court level, is imprecise and sometimes even wrong. Justice Felix Frankfurter once complained that editors who would never consider covering a baseball game through a reporter unfamiliar with the sport regularly assigned reporters unfamiliar with the law to cover the Supreme Court. This situation has improved considerably in recent years, but it is far from cured.

Engle v. Vitale, a 1962 decision on school prayer, and *Baker v. Carr* illustrate faulty reporting.[60] An analysis of stories about these two decisions in sixty-three metropolitan daily papers showed that headlines were misleading, and coverage was sketchy and uninformative.[61] Ill-informed statements by well-known people opposing the Court's decisions made up the major part of the stories. Several stories contained serious errors. For instance, the wrong clause of the Constitution was cited as the basis for the decision outlawing classroom prayer in public schools. Arguments made in lower courts were erroneously attributed to Supreme Court justices. Moreover, the media covered the prayer decision most heavily because it was relatively easy to grasp and presented an emotionally stirring story. They slighted the duller reapportionment decision, which was of far greater political significance because it forced states to reapportion legislative districts on a massive scale.

Many important decisions are completely ignored. During one typical Supreme court term even the *New York Times* failed to mention one-quarter of all written opinions. In the stories about the remaining 112 opinions, 49 lacked essential information. The *Detroit News,* a more average paper, failed to mention 70 percent of the written opinions.[62]

The thrust of judicial complaints about sketchy, inaccurate reporting is the same as for coverage of the presidency and Congress. However, reporting of court activities seems to be more superficial and flawed than its presidential and congressional counterparts.[63] The reasons are not difficult to understand. The volume of decisions is huge, frequently clustering near the end of the annual term. The subject matter is often highly technical, hard for reporters to understand and make understandable. With notable exceptions, stories about judicial decisions lack the potential to become exciting, front-page news. They are hard to boil down into catchy phrases and clichés. The Supreme Court beat tends to be understaffed. All of these factors make it very difficult for assigned reporters to prepare interesting, well-researched accounts.

The information supplied to the public, though inadequate for providing important insights into the law and the judicial process, usually sustains respect for the judiciary and compliance with its rulings. Most people are poorly informed about the Supreme Court, but they still hold it in high esteem.[64] Occasionally Court publicity has the opposite effect, however. For instance, widespread adverse publicity about Supreme Court decisions outlawing prayer in the public schools has encouraged individuals and entire school systems to ignore that ban. It also has led to an abortive movement to pass a constitutional amendment to permit prayers in the public schools. Justice Tom Clark, one of the participants in the 1962 prayer decision, complained that misunderstanding of *Engel v. Vitale* made this ruling unpopular. He blamed inadequate reporting for the misunderstanding and lack of compliance. Public reactions to Supreme Court decisions, in turn, may affect future decisions of the Court. Justices themselves are influenced in their work by what they read and hear from the media. Media reports of crime waves, or price gouging by business, or public opposition to aid for parochial schools are likely to influence Court decisions and set boundaries to judicial policy making.[65] Recent research indicates that the amount of publicity given to a crime influences prosecutors at lower judicial levels. When there is little publicity, prosecutors are less likely to press for a trial of the case and more likely to agree to a plea-bargain settlement.[66]

Publication of decisions by the Supreme Court and lower courts is by no means the only significant news about the judiciary. General news about crime and the work of the justice system is also important in creating images of the quality of public justice. Here a plentiful media diet is available. In a typical year news about crime and the justice system constituted 25 percent of all newspaper stories in Chicago, 20 percent of all local television stories, and 13 percent of all national television stories. Even when the large number of stories reporting individual crimes were subtracted from the totals, the figures remained impressive, particularly when compared with stories about other social problems. The combined total of stories about health issues and minorities, for example, received less than one-third of the coverage given to crime and the justice system. Like stories about government activities, crime and justice system stories tend to focus on sensational events, often at the expense of significant trends and problems in the legal system that might benefit from greater public attention.[67]

Judicial Censorship

Although crime and justice system news is amply covered by the media, there are important omissions. The Supreme Court bars reporters from all of its deliberations prior to the announcement of decisions. On the few occasions when information about a forthcoming decision has been leaked ahead of time, justices have reacted with great anger and have curtailed the contacts between newspeople and Court personnel. Television cameras are barred from the Supreme Court and other federal courts, and proceedings may not be broadcast directly.

For years many state courts prohibited radio and television reporters from covering trials and other proceedings. This restriction was grounded in fears that electronic equipment might produce a carnival atmosphere that would intimidate participants and harm the fairness of the proceedings. Sensational coverage of the Lindbergh kidnapping trial in 1935 spawned such bans. Now, however, they appear to be on the wane. By 1988 most states permitted electronic coverage of judicial proceedings in their courts, but some of the permissions were on a trial basis.[68]

Restraints on live audio and video coverage are not the only limitations on judicial publicity. In the interest of ensuring fair trials, courts also limit the information that may be printed about court proceedings. These types of restrictions were discussed in Chapter 4.

Communications Law

Judges' views on communications law are also of interest to newspeople. The FCC's vague legislative mandate has given rise to numerous court battles, as has the interpretation of the First Amendment's free press provisions. Since federal courts are frequently asked to interpret compliance with constitutional and statutory restraints, media lobbies have attempted to influence the appointment of federal judges and have often been parties in cases that involve communications law. They have tried to steer these cases to sympathetic judges during appeals from FCC rules and licensing decisions.

In an average year fifteen to twenty appeals involving various aspects of communications policy are brought from the FCC to the courts, most often to the Court of Appeals for the District of Columbia. The law permits any person who is "aggrieved" or whose interests are "adversely affected" by the orders of the FCC to seek a court review, and these provisions have been liberally interpreted. Such easy access has enhanced concern about the potentially large role of the courts in communications policy making.

The federal Court of Appeals has upheld the majority of FCC rulings, although this may be changing. In the late 1970s the court frequently substituted its own policy analysis and preferences for those of the commission.[69] The limited number of cases that have reached the Supreme Court, usually because violation of First Amendment rights was alleged, have generally upheld the FCC's rulings. While influence over the FCC itself thus seems more important for policy impact than the role played by the courts, it is difficult to gauge how much impact the prospects of judicial review have on FCC activities. Agencies frequently modify their behavior to avoid reversals by the judiciary.

The vagueness of the power granted to the FCC provides immense leeway to the courts as well as to the commission. As Daniel Polsby and Kim Degnan have observed, "If 'the public interest' leaves the FCC in a trackless normative wilderness in which it is free to make up the rules of the game, the court's discretion to pass on those rules for reasonable or substantial correspondence with record evidence is not less broad." [70] Interpretation of the scope of the FCC's mandate therefore inevitably involves the courts in shaping communications policy.

Summary

In this chapter we have examined the relationship between the media and the three branches of the national government. Coverage is ample, but the goals of the media differ from those of government officials. Officials want stories that report them and their work accurately and favorably. They also want to dominate the news-sifting process so that published news mirrors their sense of what is important and unimportant. Newspeople, on the other hand, want stories that are newsworthy, judged by the usual criteria. They believe that their publics are more interested in exciting events and human interest tales than in academic discussions of public policies, their historical antecedents, and their projected impact expressed in statistics. Newspeople also feel a special mission, like Shakespeare's Mark Antony, "to bury Caesar, not to praise him." And, like Brutus, they claim that their criticism is not disloyalty. They do not love the government less; they only love the nation more.

Each side in this tug of war uses wiles and ruses as well as clout to have its own way. The outcome is a see-saw contest in which both sides score victories and suffer defeats, but each is most attuned to its own failures rather than to its victories. The public interest is served in equally uneven fashion. If we equate it with a maximum of intelligible information about important issues and events, media presentations fall short. But coverage is good in that it is continuous, often well-informed, with sufficient attention to audience appeal to make dry information palatable. Investigative reporting has brought to light many shortcomings and scandals that otherwise might have remained hidden. The fear of exposure by the media has undoubtedly kept government officials from straying into many questionable ventures, although this effect is hard to document. On the negative side, fear of media coverage and publicity has probably inhibited desirable actions.

Because the contacts between officials of the national government and the media are so constant, a formal institutional structure has been established to handle these interactions. The fairly elaborate setup at the presidential level and the simpler arrangements for Congress and the Supreme Court have been described. We also have indicated some of the problems that newspeople face in covering a flood tide of complex news expeditiously, accurately, and with a modicum of critical detachment and analysis.

Problems in communications policy making remain. All three branches of government shape communications policy, but there is little coordination among them. Even within the executive and legislative branches, where most policy should be made, control is dispersed among so many different committees and agencies that drift rather than direction has resulted. Few major policy decisions have been made except in times of crisis, and even then the weaknesses of government structures have made it easy for industry spokespersons to dominate decision making.

The government's weakness in this area may be a blessing in disguise and in the spirit of the First Amendment. Because the Constitution commands that Congress shall make no law abridging the freedom of the press, it may be well to keep all communications policy making to the barest minimum. As Chief Justice John Marshall warned at the start of the nation's history, the power to regulate is the power to destroy.[71] Policy making and regulation overlap. A uniform, well-articulated communications policy, however beneficial it may seem to many people in public and private life, still puts the government imprint indelibly on the flow of information.

Notes

1. James F. Fixx, ed., *The Mass Media and Politics* (New York: Arno Press, 1971), ix.
2. Doris A. Graber, *Crime News and the Public* (New York: Praeger, 1980), 24-25.
3. David L. Paletz and K. Kendall Guthrie, "The Three Faces of Ronald Reagan," *Journal of Communication* 37 (Autumn 1987): 7-23
4. For information on the impact of the media on the presidency in general, see Robert E. Denton, Jr., and Dan F. Hahn, *Presidential Communication: Description and Analysis* (New York: Praeger, 1986); and John Tebbel and Sarah Miles Watts, *The Press and the Presidency* (New York: Oxford University Press, 1985). Books about the relations of individual presidents with the press include Kenneth W. Thompson, ed., *Ten Presidents and the Press* (Lanham, Md.: University Press of America, 1983); William C. Spragens, *From Spokesman to Press Secretary: White House Media Oper-*

ations (Lanham, Md.: University Press of America, 1980); and James Deakin, *Straight Stuff: The Reporters, the White House and the Truth* (New York: William Morrow, 1984). State government coverage is discussed in Delmer Dunn, *Public Officials and the Press* (Reading, Mass.: Addison Wesley, 1969); Frederick Fico, "Search for Statehouse Spokesman: Coverage of the Governor and Lawmakers," *Journalism Quarterly* 62 (Spring 1985): 74-80; and Lewis W. Wolfson, *The Untapped Power of the Press: Explaining Government to the Press* (New York: Praeger, 1985), 137-151. For coverage of local politics, see Chapter 9 of Wolfson's book.

5. As John Kenneth Galbraith has noted, "Nearly all of our political comment originates in Washington. Washington politicians, after talking things over with each other, relay misinformation to Washington journalists who, after further intramural discussion, print it where it is thoughtfully read by the same politicians. It is the only completely successful system for the recycling of garbage that has yet been devised." Quoted in William L. Rivers, *The Other Government: Power and the Washington Media* (New York: University Books, 1982), 19.

6. Michael J. Robinson, "A Twentieth-Century Medium in a Nineteenth-Century Legislature: The Effects of Television on the American Congress," in *Congress in Change: Evolution and Reform,* ed. Norman J. Ornstein (New York: Praeger, 1975), 241, 256.

7. David Halberstam, *The Powers That Be* (New York: Knopf, 1979), 49.

8. Ibid., 514. Also see Daniel C. Hallin, *The "Uncensored War": The Media and Vietnam* (New York: Oxford University Press, 1986).

9. Tony Schwartz, "Protest on CBS Show: 'Fairness' Dispute Renews," *New York Times,* April 23, 1982.

10. Martin Linsky, *Impact: How the Press Affects Federal Policymaking* (New York: Norton, 1986), 37-38.

11. William J. Small, *To Kill a Messenger* (New York: Hastings House, 1970).

12. Jules Witcover, *Marathon: The Pursuit of the Presidency, 1972-1976* (New York: Viking, 1977), 302.

13. *Kennedy and the Press: The News Conferences* (New York: Crowell, 1965), 239.

14. The quotes are from the *Collected Speeches of Spiro Agnew* (New York: Audubon Books, 1971), 89. See also William E. Porter, *Assault on the Media: The Nixon Years* (Ann Arbor: University of Michigan Press, 1976), 47.

15. Small, *To Kill a Messenger,* 29, 102; and Stephen Engelberg, "Slamming the Press in Daylight," *New York Times,* October 14, 1987. See also Daniel D. Kennedy, "The Bay of Pigs and the *New York Times:* Another View of What Happened," *Journalism Quarterly* 63 (Autumn 1986): 524-529.

16. Michael Baruch Grossman and Martha Joynt Kumar, "The White House and the News Media: The Phases of Their Relationship," *Political Science Quarterly* 94 (Spring 1979): 37-53.

17. Fred Smoller, "The Six O'Clock Presidency: Patterns of Network News Coverage of the President," *Presidential Studies Quarterly* 16 (Winter 1986): 42.

18. Jeb Stuart Magruder, *An American Life: One Man's Road to Watergate* (New York: Atheneum, 1974), 101.

19. George de Lama, "White House Aims Sky High for Added TV Exposure," *Chicago Tribune,* February 16, 1986.

20. William J. Small, *Political Power and the Press* (New York: Norton, 1972), 162.

21. F. Christopher Arterton, *Media Politics: The News Strategies of Presidential Campaigns* (Lexington, Mass.: Heath, 1984), 181.
22. Stephen Hess, *The Government/Press Connection: Press Officers and Their Offices* (Washington, D.C.: Brookings, 1984).
23. Linsky, *Impact*, 4.
24. John Herbers, *No Thank You, Mr. President* (New York, Norton, 1976).
25. For a thorough analysis of press conferences, see Jarol B. Manheim, "The Honeymoon's Over: The News Conference and the Development of Presidential Style," *Journal of Politics* 41 (February 1979): 55-74; and Frank Cormier, James Deakin, and Helen Thomas, *The White House Press on the Presidency: News Management and Co-Option* (Lanham, Md.: University Press of America, 1983).
26. Small, *Political Power and the Press*, 163.
27. Douglas Frantz and James O'Shea, "CIA Shifts Aim to Network for News Leaks," *Chicago Tribune*, May 21, 1986.
28. Steven R. Weisman, "Reagan, Annoyed by News Leaks, Tells Staff To Limit Press Relations," *New York Times*, January 11, 1983. For a list of measures taken by the Reagan administration to stop leaks, see Ronald Berkman and Laura W. Kitch, *Politics in the Media Age* (New York: McGraw-Hill, 1986), 195-197.
29. Robert O. Blanchard, ed., *Congress and the News Media* (New York: Hastings House, 1974), 105.
30. Stephen Hess, *The Washington Reporters* (Washington, D.C.: Brookings, 1981), 98. The figures are based on 921 newspaper and 87 television stories. Also see Lynda Lee Kaid and Joe Foote, "How Network Television Coverage of the President and Congress Compare," *Journalism Quarterly* 62 (Spring 1985): 59-65.
31. Michael Robinson, Maura Clancey, and Lisa Grand, "With Friends Like These . . . ," *Public Opinion* 6 (June/July 1983): 3.
32. "The Tower Report: The Iran/Contra Story Continued," *Media Monitor* 1 (April 1987): 2.
33. Hess, *The Washington Reporters*, 99.
34. Alan P. Balutis, "Congress, the President and the Press," *Journalism Quarterly* 53 (Fall 1976): 509-515.
35. For a more detailed description of bureaucracy coverage, see Rivers, *The Other Government*, 50-68.
36. Martha Joynt Kumar and Michael Baruch Grossman, "Congress: The Best Beat in Town" (Paper delivered at the annual meeting of the American Political Science Association, Washington, D.C., 1986), 8.
37. Hess, *The Washington Reporters*, 104-105; and Michael J. Robinson and Kevin R. Appel, "Network News Coverage of Congress," *Political Science Quarterly* 94 (Fall 1979): 410-411.
38. Gregory C. Lisby, "Early Television on Public Watch: Kefauver and His Crime Investigation," *Journalism Quarterly* 62 (Summer 1985): 242.
39. Quoted in Steven V. Roberts, "Senators Squint into a Future Under TV's Gaze," *New York Times*, February 4, 1986.
40. Quoted in Dorothy Collin, "Senate Will Keep TV Plugged In," *Chicago Tribune*, July 30, 1986.
41. Stephen Frantzich, "Communication and Congress," in *The Communications Revolution in Politics*, ed. Gerald Benjamin (New York: The Academy of Political Science, 1982), 99.
42. Ibid., 100.

43. Warren Weaver, Jr., *Both Your Houses* (New York: Praeger, 1972), 12.
44. Blanchard, *Congress and the News Media*, 240. For a detailed content analysis of television coverage of Congress, see Robinson and Appel, "Network News Coverage of Congress," 407-418.
45. Blanchard, *Congress and the News Media*, 169-239.
46. Timothy E. Cook, "Show Horses in House Elections: The Advantages and Disadvantages of National Media Visibility," in *Campaigns in the News: Mass Media and Congressional Elections*, ed. Jan Pons Vermeer (New York: Greenwood Press, 1987), 161.
47. Timothy E. Cook, "House Members as National Newsmakers: The Effects of Televising Congress," *Legislative Studies Quarterly* 11 (Summer 1986): 203-226; Timothy E. Cook, "Newsmakers, Lawmakers and Leaders: Who Gets on the Network News from Congress?" (Paper delivered at the annual meeting of the American Political Science Association, Washington, D.C., 1984); and Stephen Hess, *The Ultimate Insiders: U.S. Senators and the National Media* (Washington, D.C.: Brookings, 1986).
48. Cook, "Show Horses," 163-166.
49. For descriptions of these publicity efforts, see Berkman and Kitch, *Politics in the Media Age*, 230; and Michael J. Robinson, "Three Faces of Congressional Media," in *The New Congress*, ed. Thomas E. Mann and Norman J. Ornstein (Washington, D.C.: American Enterprise Institute, 1981), 55-96.
50. Arthur Miller, Edie Goldenberg, and Lutz Erbring, "Type-Set Politics: Impact of Newspapers on Public Confidence," *American Political Science Review* 73 (March 1979): 70.
51. Daniel D. Polsby and Kim Degnan, "Institutions for Communications Policymaking: A Review," in *Communications for Tomorrow: Policy Perspectives for the 1980s*, ed. Glen O. Robinson (New York: Praeger, 1978), 501-514. See also Erwin G. Krasnow, Lawrence D. Longley, and Herbert A. Terry, *The Politics of Broadcast Regulation*, 3d ed. (New York: St. Martin's Press, 1982), 87-132.
52. Krasnow, Longley, and Terry, *The Politics of Broadcast Regulation*, 99.
53. Ernest Gellhorn, "The Role of Congress," in *Communications for Tomorrow*, ed. Robinson, 445-457.
54. For a full account of congressional investigations of television violence, see Willard D. Rowland, Jr., *Policy Uses of Communication Research* (Beverly Hills, Calif.: Sage, 1983).
55. Ben H. Bagdikian, "Congress and the Media: Partners in Propaganda," *Columbia Journalism Review* 12 (January-Febuary 1974): 3-10. Also see Lou Cannon's discussion of "the cozy coverage of Congress" in his *Reporting: An Inside View* (Sacramento, Calif.: California Journal Press, 1977).
56. Leslie D. Polk, John Eddy, and Ann Andre, "Use of Congressional Publicity in Wisconsin District," *Journalism Quarterly* 52 (Autumn 1975): 543-546.
57. Robinson, "Three Faces of Congressional Media."
58. Robinson and Appel, "Network News Coverage," 412. See also David L. Paletz and Robert M. Entman, *Media Power Politics* (New York: Free Press, 1981), 79-98.
59. 347 U.S. 483 (1954); and 369 U.S. 186 (1962).
60. *Engel v. Vitale*, 370 U.S. 421 (1962).
61. Chester A. Newland, "Press Coverage of the United States Supreme Court," *Western Political Quarterly* 17 (1964): 15-36. Also see Kenneth S. Devol, *Mass Media and the Supreme Court*, 2d ed. (New York: Hastings House, 1976).

62. David Ericson, "Newspaper Coverage of the Supreme Court: A Case Study," *Journalism Quarterly* 54 (Autumn 1977): 605-607. See also Michael E. Solimine, "Newsmagazine Coverage of the Supreme Court," *Journalism Quarterly* 57 (Winter 1980): 661-664.

63. David L. Grey, *The Supreme Court and the News Media* (Evanston, Ill.: Northwestern University Press, 1968). For additional examples of incorrect coverage, see Frank J. Sorauf, "Campaign Money and the Press: Three Soundings," *Political Science Quarterly* 102 (Spring 1987): 25-42.

64. Paletz and Entman, *Media Power Politics,* 106-109.

65. Robert E. Drechsel, *News Making in the Trial Courts* (New York: Longman, 1983), 19-22.

66. David Pritchard, "Homicide and Bargained Justice: The Agenda-Setting Effect of Crime News on Prosecutors," *Public Opinion Quarterly* 50 (Spring 1986): 143-159.

67. A detailed account of coverage of crime and justice system news is presented in Doris A. Graber, *Crime News and the Public* (New York: Praeger, 1980).

68. Susanna Barber, *News Cameras in the Courtroom: A Free Press-Fair Trial Debate* (Norwood, N.J.: Ablex, 1987), especially pp. 18-19.

69. Krasnow, Longley, and Terry, *The Politics of Broadcast Regulation,* 65-66.

70. Polsby and Degnan, "Institutions for Communications Policymaking," 513.

71. *McCulloch v. Maryland,* 4 Wheaton 316 (1819).

Readings

Denton, Robert E., and Dan F. Hahn. *Presidential Communication: Description and Analysis.* New York: Praeger, 1986.

Garay, Ronald. *Congressional Television: A Legislative History.* Westport, Conn.: Greenwood Press, 1984.

Hess, Stephen. *The Government/Press Connection.* Washington, D.C.: Brookings, 1984.

——. *The Ultimate Insiders: U.S. Senators in the National Media.* Washington, D.C.: Brookings, 1986.

——. *The Washington Reporters.* Washington, D.C.: Brookings, 1981.

Linsky, Martin. *Impact: How the Press Affects Federal Policymaking.* New York: Norton, 1986.

Morgan, David. *The Flacks of Washington: Government Information and the Public Agenda.* Westport, Conn.: Greenwood Press, 1986.

Surettte, Ray, ed. *Justice and the Media: Issues and Research.* Springfield, Ill.: Charles C Thomas, 1984.

Tebbel, John, and Sarah Miles Watts. *The Press and the Presidency: From George Washington to Ronald Reagan.* New York: Oxford University Press, 1985.

CHAPTER 8

The Media
as Policy Makers

In his autobiography Lincoln Steffens, who has been called "America's greatest reporter," tells how a history professor introduced him to an audience as "the first of the muckrakers." Steffens corrected the professor. "I had to answer first that I was not the original muckraker; the prophets of the Old Testament were ahead of me, and to make a big jump in time so were the writers, editors, and reporters (including myself) of the 1890s who were finding fault with 'things as they are' in the pre-muckraking period." [1]

Steffens was right. Public exposés of evil and corruption in high places have been common throughout recorded history. They rest on the assumption that exposure will shame the wrongdoers and lead to public condemnation of their deeds and possibly punishment. Ultimately, reforms may ensue.[2] Exposés have always been and will continue to be an important feature of social responsibility journalism in America. They are a major part of the deliberate manipulation of the political process mentioned in Chapter 1 as one of the media's chief functions.

In this chapter muckraking will be examined to show how it really works, with particular attention to the role played by public opinion. Agenda building, another widely used strategy for manipulating politics, will be examined in different situations, such as leadership crises, the development of science policy, and the support of interest group goals. Next we will assess the political impact of nationally broadcast factual and fictional documentaries on current political issues. Our study of manipulative journalism concludes with reflections on the responsibility of newspeople to refrain from questionable methods in their zeal to reform society.

Like other manifestations of the social responsibility ethic, manipulative journalism raises philosophical, ethical, and news policy questions. Do newspeople jeopardize important professional values when they try to shape the events that they report? Do they create a witch-hunting climate that intimidates officeholders and deters capable people from careers in politics?[3] If newspeople fail to objectively report the passing scene, do they sacrifice credibility? Where can media audiences turn for a reasonably unbiased view of the complexities of political life if media sources, like government officials, are partisans? Claims by newspeople that their political activities reflect the wishes of their audiences are questionable as long as the selection and activities of journalists are not subject to control by the publics that they claim to represent.

Despite the concerns it raises, the role of the journalist as political actor is currently popular. This is demonstrated by the many instances of outright collaboration between official policy makers and media personnel. It is also shown by the widespread practice of "leaking," where dissatisfied insiders, rather than attempting reforms on their own, enlist media support to gain their ends. Moreover, citizens routinely contact the media with problems concerning public affairs. In fact, just as the media have taken over many functions formerly performed by political parties during elections, so they have assumed many of the ombudsman, reform and law enforcement functions traditionally performed by other institutions in society. Whether this is the cause or consequence of the weakening of these other institutions remains a hotly debated question.

Manipulative Journalism in Perspective

The extent of newspeople's efforts to participate in policy making has fluctuated as philosophies of news making have changed. The turmoil of the 1960s, which raised the public's social consciousness, and the shift toward advocating a social responsibility ethic in journalism schools have once again raised manipulative journalism from a position of disdain to a position of high esteem. Approval is not unanimous, to be sure, but it is widespread, especially in elite media circles. Reporters and media institutions whose investigations have led to important social and political reforms frequently win prizes for high journalistic achievement. Given the prestige accorded to investigative journalists and the political succcesses attributed to them, it is no surprise that investigative units began to thrive in major print and electronic media institutions during the 1970s.

Independent investigative units that collaborate with media institutions have flourished as well. The nonprofit, foundation-subsidized

Center for Investigative Reporting, established in San Francisco in 1977, is an example. The center uses free-lance reporters who collectively conduct investigations and who can be hired by various media to undertake projects that cannot be readily handled internally. The Community Information Project in Los Angeles and the Better Government Association in Chicago are other institutions that do similar investigative work. There is also a national organization of investigative reporters and editors (IRE) that has been active in teaching its approaches to mainstream journalists.[4]

Collaboration between independent watchdog organizations and the media is mutually beneficial. It ensures that the investigations of interest to these institutions will be publicized, thereby increasing the chances for corrective action. Tapping into media resources also helps cover the costs of complex investigations that can run into hundreds of thousands of dollars apiece. This added financial support can be crucial. The media, in turn, gain collaborators who are skilled in investigating public issues and who often have excellent connections in government and in the community. The prestige and credibility of the organization may also enhance the credibility of a jointly issued report.

The substance and style of most investigative stories reflect three major objectives. The first is to produce exciting stories that will appeal to media audiences. Second, investigative reporters hope to gain plaudits from the journalism profession. Third, in addition to these routine journalistic goals, many reporters want to trigger political action or be part of it. Even when political consequences are not initially envisioned, most reporters feel highly gratified when their stories lead to actions that accord with their political and social preferences.

Sometimes the line between deliberate attempts to produce political changes and incidental sparking of reforms is too fine to distinguish. For example, when the media follow up on a report of a rash of deaths in nursing homes, and discover and describe deplorable conditions that led to these deaths, is this a case of muckraking designed to manipulate political events and bring about reform? Or does the idea that reform is needed arise naturally and purely incidentally from a routine news story? Was Steffens telling the truth when he claimed, "I did not intend to be a muckraker; I did not know that I was one till President Roosevelt picked the name out of Bunyan's *Pilgrim's Progress* and pinned it on us."[5] Could Steffens specialize in writing sensational exposés of corruption in state and local government and in private business for the sheer joy of delving into the muck, with no thought given to the major reforms that followed in the wake of some of his stories?

From the standpoint of the political reformer, it may not matter whether reform was an intended or unintended byproduct of investigative reporting. The distinction matters, however, to newspeople because

PUBLIC WATCHDOG

Reprinted by permission: Tribune Media Services.

it raises controversial issues about the proper role of journalism in American society. Journalists, even when they favor social responsibility journalism in the abstract, do not like to admit that they wrote their stories to produce social and political reforms.

Muckraking Models

How does investigative journalism lead to political action? There are three ways. Journalists may write stories about public policies in hopes of engendering a massive public reaction that will lead to widespread demands for political remedies. Alternatively, journalists may write stories to arouse political elites who are officeholders or who have influence with officeholders. These elites, eager to forestall public anger, then may attempt to resolve the problems, often even before the media report is actually published. Finally, action may be the result of direct collaboration between investigative journalists and public officeholders. They may coordinate news stories and supportive political activities to bring about desired reforms. We will trace the rate of success in each of these different types of situations.

The process can be pictured in the form of three models: the simple muckraking model, the leaping impact model, and the truncated muckraking model. Social scientists Harvey Molotch, David Protess, and Margaret Gordon, and their coworkers who developed these models, tested them in investigative situations entailing muckraking—sensational exposés of corruption usually involving high status individuals. The models also illustrate other types of manipulative journalism.[6]

The simple muckraking model begins when journalists investigate a serious societal problem that could be ameliorated through political action. The investigation leads to published news that stirs the public. Aroused public opinion then mobilizes policy makers who act to solve the problem. Schematically, the process usually looks as pictured below, although the sequence of the elements in the model may vary:

Journalistic investigation	→ Publication →	Public opinion →	Policy initiatives →	Policy consequences

When some elements in the model are skipped entirely, the leaping impact model is at work. For instance, following investigation and publication of the story, policy initiatives may be taken without prior public opinion pressure. Alternatively, a journalistic investigation may have policy consequences even without new initiatives in policy or publication of reports about the investigation. In the truncated muckraking model the muckraking sequence may be aborted at any point so that the investigation fails to lead to corrective policies. This occurs frequently and can happen in several ways. The investigation may not lead to published stories because the evidence is insufficient or too hot to handle. Published stories may not stir public opinion. An aroused public may not move public officials to act. Policy initiatives, even if they are not purely symbolic, still may not lead to any substantial correction of the problem.

Several examples of muckraking will illustrate these models. Most of the examples come from intensive studies of muckraking conducted by scholars who had arranged to be alerted to forthcoming media exposés. This permitted them to interview citizens and policy makers concerned with the issue under investigation, both before and after publication of the stories. The impact of the story could then be assessed far more accurately than is usually possible when stories come as a surprise and permit only ex post facto assessment. Actual changes in public policy also were monitored for a period of several months following the exposés. The journalists' motives and methods in conducting the investigations were judged as well.[7]

Simple Muckraking

A story about reform of a school for mentally retarded children in Staten Island, New York, illustrates simple muckraking: the media aroused the public, and the public then demanded and received action.

Television commentator Geraldo Rivera presented a seven-minute report about shocking conditions that he had observed during a visit to the Willowbrook State School. After a station near the school had shown the report, some seven hundred viewers called to express their concern. Shocked parents later gathered at the school and solicited promises of help from local public officials. The Staten Island Chapter of the Society for the Prevention of Cruelty to Children began hearings and asked the state and national government to investigate.[8] But the flurry of activity was short-lived and largely unproductive. Only minor reforms in the school's handling of children resulted from these investigations.

Such modest outcomes are typical in situations that reflect the simple muckraking model. Researchers rarely find solid evidence that media-aroused public opinion is a strong force for change. There are several reasons why. Many Americans are complacent or cynical about the political status quo. It is therefore difficult to spur them to take action on public problems, even those directly affecting them. For example, extensive efforts to arouse public concern about energy shortages and the need for conservation have proved largely futile.[9] Because most Americans' interests lie outside of politics, they ignore or assign little importance to investigative news stories, or forget them quickly, except when they are extraordinarily dramatic and point the finger at identifiable villains. Accordingly, politicians often feel safe in ignoring swells in public opinion, believing that they involve relatively few people and that they will soon subside when new issues capture the public's fancy.

On the other end of the interest spectrum, media investigative stories may be about an issue that is already a matter of great concern to the public. Although the investigative story confirms that concern, it does not push the public across the barrier of reluctance to press for political action. For example, a five-part newspaper series in the *Chicago Sun-Times* in 1982 on "Rape: Every Woman's Nightmare" dealt with the incidence and consequences of rape in the Chicago area. Interviews conducted prior to the series had shown that the public was already greatly concerned about the problem. The series maintained that concern, but it did little to spur new action to fight crime. An interesting, unexpected byproduct of the rape stories was heightened sensitivity of the newspaper staff to the problem. Following the series, *Sun-Times* stories on rape more than doubled in number, and coverage became more insightful.[10] Investigators rarely notice such unexpected consequences or much-delayed consequences. Hence reports about the effects of investigative stories often understate their impact.

Although it is difficult for the media to arouse public opinion, some investigative stories do. The Willowbrook State School case is an example. The elements that brought about its success included an emotional issue—the treatment of disabled children in the audience's locality; a flamboyant, well-known reporter who dramatized the story; and a local group of citizens directly and profoundly affected by the alleged misbehavior of public officials. When such a story captures people's interest, and they have little prior knowledge about the situation, they may learn much and become highly concerned. As we have noted, however, major corrective action remains unlikely.[11]

Leaping Impact Muckraking

A media exposé called "Arson for Profit" that was aired by ABC's "20/20" in 1979 exemplified the leaping impact model. The investigation indicated that extensive fire damage in Chicago's Uptown neighborhood resulted from arson planned by a group of real estate owners. The group would buy dilapidated buildings, insure them heavily, and then burn them down to collect the insurance. Following the exposé, government elites voiced concern but failed to act. Nevertheless, corrections occurred. The arson-for-profit perpetrators, fearing further public exposure, decided to retreat. In the month following the broadcast, fires declined by 27 percent in the area where arson for profit had flourished. It was the first decline in five years. Insurance payments for arson also dropped by more than 20 percent in the year following the arson stories. No other metropolitan area showed comparable drops. The Illinois legislature responded belatedly with very minor policy reforms. There were no criminal indictments of the parties implicated in the insurance fraud. This story exemplifies the leaping impact model because the leap was from publication directly to correction; elite arousal and, by and large, elite action and public opinion pressures were nonexistent.

The most common "leaping impact" situation takes place when newspeople and public officials openly collaborate. This "coalition journalism" may be initiated by media or government personnel, or it may arise by chance without prior formal contacts between media personnel and policy actors. Newspeople are very eager to involve government officials in investigative stories because this lends credibility and significance to their stories and increases the chances of substantial policy consequences. Although it may jeopardize the media's zealous pursuit of the watchdog role, coalition journalism gets results.

A good example of coalition journalism concerns the events following an NBC "Newsmagazine" story, "The Home Health Hustle," broadcast May 7, 1981, which exposed fraud and abuse in home health-care programs. Public opinion polls showed that the broadcast aroused the concerns of many viewers who previously were unaware of problems with these programs. But public opinion apparently was not instrumental in Congress's decision to introduce appropriate reform legislation. In the fashion of leaping impact models, the legislative results seemed to flow directly from collaboration between investigative reporters and members of the U.S. Senate that preceded airing of the story by several months.

Journalists had met with officials of the Senate's Permanent Subcommittee on Investigations to plan a series of hearings on home health-care fraud and to coordinate their broadcasts with the Senate's activities. The hearings were then announced during the broadcast. Subsequently, senators credited media personnel with major contributions to the investigation of home health-care fraud. However, it is uncertain to what degree the knowledge that television would feature the story spurred the senators to collaborate with the media. The combined investigative activities of the media and the Senate ultimately led to a number of proposals for corrective legislation. Still, in the end, the bills failed to pass. Aside from the effects of increased vigilance by public officials and home health-care consumers, there were no major changes that could be directly linked to the investigative stories.[12]

Similarly, when the rape series appeared in the *Chicago Sun-Times,* newspeople had already alerted policy makers. This permitted the policy makers to time announcements of previously planned measures, such as creation of a rape hotline, to coincide with the investigative series. When a story about unnecessary and illegal abortions in state clinics was about to break in Illinois, the governor immediately associated himself with the media investigators prior to publication. This made it possible to make reform proposals part of the original story. It also enhanced the governor's image as an effective leader.

Truncated Muckraking

The truncated muckraking model is well illustrated by the *Mirage* investigation, conducted in 1977 by the *Chicago Sun-Times* and CBS's "60 Minutes" program with the help of Chicago's Better Government Association, a civic watchdog organization. Hoping to demonstrate extensive graft in the city's regulatory agencies, the partners in the investigation opened a bar in Chicago, appropriately named the *Mirage.* The bar was wired to record transactions that might take place between its personnel and city officials. In a brief period of time, ample evidence of bribery and fraud was accumulated.[13]

After the story about the illegal transactions was published, public opinion polls recorded that many citizens were outraged. Nonetheless, they took no serious corrective action to prevent similar graft in the future. Schematically, the model ended with the arousal of public opinion, skipping elite arousal and action and final corrective activities. The failure to produce a correction does not necessarily mean that an official response never occurs. Symbolic responses are common, such as promises of reform by political leaders, or studies of the problem, including public hearings, but with no action follow-up. At other times policy makers may punish individual offenders but do nothing to correct the situation that is causing the problem.[14]

The Role of Public Opinion

Our examples of muckraking suggest that the major role attributed to public opinion in producing political action is greatly exaggerated. More often than not, the media fail to arouse the public, even when investigative stories are written to produce public excitement. When stories do agitate the public, little happens as a rule. Politicians and journalists have learned that public anger is short-lived. It can be safely ignored or channeled to support reform movements that are already under way. Corrective action is more likely to come when publicity-shy wrongdoers mend their ways, when the stories arouse elites, or when journalists and political elites have arranged to collaborate. It also helps when there are follow-ups on the story in different media and over a prolonged span of time.

Even though publicity rarely causes a tidal surge of public opinion, fear that it might do so makes the media more successful than other pressure groups in gaining their reform objectives. If public opinion is, in fact, largely irrelevant in generating political reforms, the media's claim that they are handmaiden to the democratic process becomes highly questionable. If the notion of an aroused public clamoring for reforms is an illusion, then are the media merely using the façade of public opinion support to enhance their already powerful position as a public interest pressure group?

Beyond Muckraking: Power Plays and Surrenders

Direct media intervention in the government process may take a number of forms other than muckraking. Three types of situations are usually involved: media power plays, media acting as surrogates for public officials, and media acting as mouthpieces for government officials or interest groups.

Least common are media power plays in which newspeople bully government officials into action by threatening to publicize stories that officials would prefer to conceal. During the Watergate investigations in the Nixon administration, a number of stories about political misdeeds were aborted when warnings by newspeople about prospective coverage brought about reforms. Similarly, Gary Hart dropped temporarily out of the presidential race in 1987 when the *Washington Post* threatened to publish new reports about his marital infidelities. In addition to overt threats, which are rare, implied or anticipated threats may have major political consequences. Politicians may act or refrain from acting because they know that newspeople could publish damaging information. Adverse publicity from influential columnists is especially feared.

Even less frequently, news personnel may act as surrogates for public officials by actively participating in an evolving situation, such as a prison riot or a diplomatic impasse. The solution, developed with the assistance of news personnel or at their initiative, may then significantly shape subsequent government action. Walter Cronkite's impact on relations between Egypt and Israel, discussed in Chapter 10, is a famous example of diplomacy conducted by journalists. More commonly, reporters often spark investigations of illegal activities by alerting law enforcement officials.

To prevent impending tragedies and solve existing cases, journalists have also become involved in broadcasts about kidnapped children and in "crime stopper" programs that feature reenactments or recountings of unsolved crimes. The programs use media stories, coupled with financial rewards, to elicit information from citizens that may help in solving the crime. They are featured in nearly five hundred communities in the United States and Canada and have helped to clear up thousands of felonies.[15] In fact, the Federal Bureau of Investigation credits such programs with facilitating the capture of up to 30 percent of the criminals on its Most Wanted list.[16]

A far more common form of interaction occurs when the media become a mouthpiece for government officials or interest groups, either because of belief in their causes or in return for attractive stories and other favors. This type of interaction often involves leaks. Government officials who are disgruntled with current policies or practices for personal, professional, or political reasons may leak information to sympathetic journalists to enlist their support. Journalists may cooperate and publish the allegations, or they may investigate the situation, often with the cooperation of the individuals who leaked the information. As we saw in Chapter 7, the political impact of leaks may be profound.

When newspeople and officials collaborate, the boundary between ordinary reporting and manipulative journalism can become blurred. It is difficult to tell when one merges into the other because a correct diagnosis requires establishing motivations. In many instances the available evidence strongly suggests that newspeople acted as political partisans who used their powers of publicity to foster preferred causes and to harm others. In other cases the main objective in publicizing leaked information is mercenary. Newspeople put their services at the command of anyone who promises to be a fertile source for future news or who can provide an attractive story, no matter what its merits may be. The television networks are particularly eager to obtain exciting scoops during "sweeps," the periods when audience ratings are measured.

Exploitation of the media by public officials and political interest groups as a tool to attain their political objectives is often quite obvious. The NBC television interview of an American hostage in Iran in the spring of 1979 is a good example. NBC broadcast an interview with Cpl. William Gallegos who had then been held hostage in the U.S. Embassy in Teheran for thirty-six days. CBS and ABC refused to interview Gallegos because his Iranian captors imposed restrictions on the interview. NBC agreed to the conditions, laying itself open to the charge of acting as a propaganda conduit for the Iranian militants who had seized the embassy. Most observers considered the controlled interviews as a ploy by the Iranians to gain access to American public opinion through the media. Rep. Robert Bauman of Maryland angrily suggested in Congress that NBC should be given "the Benedict Arnold award for broadcasting." NBC defended its broadcast, saying that it had produced greater understanding of the crisis. But the impression lingered that it had allowed itself to be used for the enemy's purposes and that this was improper and even disgraceful.

Although the media are often quite willing to publish a good story, even at the expense of fostering an undesirable cause, they are loathe to become unwitting government tools. In 1986, for example, officials of the Reagan administration were suspected of spreading false information about Libya in an attempt to forestall terrorist attacks. When rumors about the administration's deception surfaced, news executives expressed outrage. Roone Arledge, president of ABC News, epitomized the general reaction when he called it "despicable to tinker with the credibility of one of our most sacred and basic institutions, the press, for whatever reason." [17]

Agenda Building

In many instances the media manipulate the political scene by creating a climate for political action. This makes them major contributors to agenda building, the process whereby news stories influence how people perceive and evaluate issues and policies. Agenda building goes beyond agenda setting. The media set the public agenda when news stories rivet attention on a problem and make it seem important to many people. Media build the public agenda when they create a political climate that determines the likely thrust of public opinions.

Newspeople rarely stir up controversies when established elites agree on matters of public policy. The absence of reported conflict then makes it seem, often erroneously, that elites as well as the public approve the unchallenged policies. [18] But when an issue becomes a matter of controversy among political elites, the media frequently zero in on it. They "supply the context that . . . gives people reasons for taking sides and converts the problem into a serious political issue. In this sense the public agenda is not so much set by the media as built up through a cycle of media activity that transforms an elite issue into a public controversy." [19] The agenda building role of the media in policy making thus is symbiotic. The media are an essential part of the operation, but ultimate success hinges on major roles played by other political actors as well.

Molotch, Protess, and Gordon make this clear in the conclusion of their study of the role of investigative journalism in the Watergate affair. The resolution of the issue was not, as popularly believed, a triumph for unaided media power:

> We therefore disagree with those who would assign "credit" for the Nixon exposures to the media just as we would disagree with those who would assign it to the Congress. Nor should the credit go, in some acontextual, additive sense, to both of these sectors. Instead, the Watergate "correction" was the result of the ways in which news of the Nixon scandals fit the goals and strategic needs of important media and policy actors. All of these actors, each with some degree of "relative autonomy". . . , are part of an evolving "ecology of games," . . . part of a "dance" . . . in which actors have, by virtue of their differential skills and status positions, varying access to participate. Because they so continuously anticipate each other's moves, their activities are, as a matter of course, mutually constituted.[20]

Political Scandal

Sociologists Kurt and Gladys Lang reached similar conclusions. Their study of the role of the media in Watergate traces the precise part played by the media in this "ecology of games" in which the disparate interests of various political actors are blended to create and develop political scenarios. The Langs outlined the steps through which political agendas are usually constructed.[21] A look at the steps makes it clear that there is ample opportunity and often strong temptation for newspeople to guide agenda building deliberately.

Agenda building begins when newspeople decide to publish a particular story. In most instances this is a matter of free choice since few stories are so blatantly significant that omission is unthinkable. The second decision concerns the degree of attention to be given to the story. This is the point where ordinary agenda-setting activities can most readily turn into deliberate agenda building. If newspeople determine that a story should become prominent, they must feature it conspicuously and often enough to arouse the attention of the elite media, including national television, and the attention of political elites. The Watergate story, for instance, received extensive and sustained publicity in the *Washington Post* before it finally "caught on" and gained nationwide publicity.

Capturing national attention usually requires several other media-controlled steps. Issues must be put into a context that will interest media audiences. For instance, as long as the media put Watergate into the context of the 1972 presidential election, the story was discounted by media audiences as just another partisan squabble. Once the media were able to depict it as an issue of pervasive corruption and dishonesty at the highest levels of government, it generated widespread concern. Without this climate of public concern, severe penalties for the Watergate offenders, including the president, would never have been considered acceptable. In the course of putting issues into a conceptual framework, language becomes an important tool. When newspeople switched from writing and talking about the Watergate *caper* or the *bugging incident* and began to discuss the Watergate *scandal* and *tragedy,* what had been perceived as a fairly trivial incident became transformed into a very serious matter.

As the Langs noted, the particular sources that the media select to tell a story are important. Skewing inevitably takes place when newspeople tap one human mind, rather than another, for information and interpretation. In the case of major public policy issues, however, sources become symbols that indicate to media audiences whether a particular position is or is not meritorious. When the media featured prominent Republicans and members of the judiciary acknowledging the gravity of the issues at stake and the need for an investigation, Watergate became a political crisis justifying drastic action.

Scientific and Technological Innovations

Agenda building by the media is not limited to political scandals but includes many other types of issues. We will discuss two areas in which agenda building is of vast importance for American political life: science policy and social movements.

Government support and regulation of science operations have become highly controversial public policy issues in twentieth-century America.[22] The fate of nuclear energy in the United States provides a particularly interesting example because major shifts in public opinion have been recorded and can be compared with the thrust of media stories. Public opinion regarding the safety and desirability of nuclear energy dropped sharply before as well as after the Three Mile Island nuclear accident in 1979. While only 20 percent of Americans were opposed to locating a nuclear plant in their community in 1956, 56 percent were opposed in 1979. Since then opposition has risen. Sentiment for building more nuclear energy plants has dropped precipitously, and nuclear energy now is rated as the least preferred energy source.

Social scientists have attributed this loss of public support to perceptions among the general public, as well as portions of the scientific community, that scientists knowledgeable about nuclear power have lost faith in it. No one seemed to know for sure how this perception started and whether scientists were indeed disillusioned with nuclear power as an energy source. To find out, political scientists Stanley Rothman and S. Robert Lichter interviewed 72 nuclear specialists, 279 scientists who worked in nuclear-energy-related fields, and 741 scientists with no special ties to the nuclear industry.[23]

All of the nuclear experts wanted to continue nuclear development; 92 percent urged rapid rather than slow progress. Ninety-five percent of the experts from related fields also urged continued development; 70 percent favored rapid progress. Among scientists with no special ties to the nuclear industry, 10 percent wanted development halted. Ninety percent favored proceeding with nuclear development, albeit at a somewhat slower pace. Clearly, the widespread perceptions of science community opposition to developing nuclear energy were wrong. A replication of the study in 1985 in the United States and in 1986 in Germany confirmed these conclusions.[24]

A probe of the reasons for the faulty impression that most scientists opposed nuclear energy pointed to mass media stories. When pro- and antinuclear statements were counted in newspapers and television, antinuclear statements predominated. Although positive statements predominated slightly in the early 1970s, by 1976 negative articles outnumbered positive ones by a two-to-one margin.

The attitudes of journalists toward the issue of nuclear energy matched the tone of their stories. The vast majority of science writers, especially those working for elite media and television, objected to the use of nuclear energy. On a scale ranking support of nuclear energy from +9 (strong support) to −9 (strong opposition), nuclear experts ranked at +7.9 and scientists in related fields at +5.1. By contrast, science journalists at the *New York Times, Washington Post,* and the television networks ranked at +0.5. Rothman's and Lichter's figures for television reporters as a group were in minus territory at −1.9. Public television journalists were most strongly opposed with an average score of −3.3.

As Table 8-1 shows, a major factor in the predominantly unfavorable coverage was the choice of sources, particularly in the case of network television.[25] The small corps of reporters who specialize in science writing drew much of their information from enemies of nuclear development. For instance, television broadcasts between 1968 and 1979 quoted the Union of Concerned Scientists more than any other source. The union, an organization of antinuclear scientists, represented only a tiny fraction of the scientific community. Ralph Nader was the most widely quoted individual "nuclear expert" during the period in question. In the month following the Three Mile Island accident, pronuclear views were never featured prominently. Although the antinuclear views

Table 8-1 Source Orientation Regarding Nuclear Energy Stories, 1970-1983 (in percentages)

Source orientation	New York Times	Time, Newsweek, U.S. News & World Report	ABC, CBS, NBC
Pronuclear	9	17	11
Antinuclear	7	40	62
Neutral/balanced	84	43	27

Source: Adapted from Stanley Rothman and S. Robert Lichter, "Elite Ideology and Risk Perception in Nuclear Energy Policy," *American Political Science Review* 81 (June 1987): 393. Reprinted by permission.

Note: N = 486 for *New York Times,* drawn from 10 percent random sample; 213 for news magazines, drawn from full universe; and 582 from television networks, drawn from 50 percent sample.

of newspeople may have been the main reason for searching out and featuring compatible views expressed by scientists, other factors, many of them typical in news production, also played a part. Among them, the economies of news supply are very important. Journalists are more likely to select stories that are readily available to them with comparatively little effort. In the 1970s antinuclear information was more readily available in easy-to-use formats. This happened because most nuclear scientists did not publish their work in general circulation journals. The comparatively small number of scientists who frequently explained their views in lay terms in the popular literature were disproportionately inclined to oppose nuclear energy development.

When journalists who oppose nuclear development find that most stories published in general circulation sources support the views that they prefer, it is not surprising that they draw heavily on these sources. This allows them to develop an exciting theme—the danger of nuclear power and the inadequate safety measures of a major industry—and support it with views that can be designated as "expert." Relying on science articles in general circulation journals is far easier than delving into arcane scientific journals and making contact with scientific leaders who may be reluctant to supply the absolute statements of doom or salvation that make exciting headlines. In the words of David Paletz and Robert Entman, "When values are shared by source and press and probably readers too, there is no felt need on the part of reporters to seek countervailing information elsewhere." [26]

As yet no one has definitely proven that skewed selection of sources for nuclear energy stories accounts for the public's current hostility to nuclear energy. However, studies of public opinion polls on science issues show that extensive media coverage of scientific controversies is followed by increased public opposition to the highlighted technology, even when the coverage is not particularly hostile. When media coverage of the controversy diminishes, opposition diminishes as well. The public, it seems, opts against any technology when doubts are raised about its safety. It is especially sensitive to heavily negative safety reports. Political elites, in turn, are loathe to challenge scientific findings that the media have labeled as "expert" opinion or to take actions that may alarm the citizenry.[27]

Firm proof is also lacking that the current decline of the nuclear energy industry can be attributed in large part to this hostile opinion climate. But even without such proof, the evidence strongly suggests that the predominantly negative images of the nuclear industry featured in numerous media stories played a major part in undermining the growth of the industry.

The situation has been similar in other fields of science, including biomedical research.[28] Only a few scientists, distinguished by their controversial positions on public issues, are steady sources for news about new drugs, new medical procedures, and various aspects of genetic engineering. The rest of the scientific community has remained largely excluded, often by its own choice and sometimes because of its disdain for popularized stories. Similarly, only a few potentially risky technologies have been scrutinized by science reporters, with choices determined haphazardly or mirroring the interests of selected pressure groups. Many other science topics have been ignored and thereby kept off the public agenda, even though they address significant aspects of public health and safety.

Social Movements and Interest Groups

Just as the media regularly boost selected public policy issues, so too can they promote selected groups that are working for specific public causes. Whenever a group needs wide publicity to reach its goals, a decision by media personnel to grant or withhold publicity becomes crucial for the group's success. Many decisions about coverage are made without explicit political motivations to boost a movement or suppress it. But in some instances the sympathies of newspeople for particular causes guide their choices of news content in hopes of influencing the course of politics. This is what happened with Students for a Democratic Society (SDS), part of what came to be known in the 1960s as the "New Left." The story is particularly interesting because it demonstrates that attention from sympathetic newspeople may boomerang and produce unintended, highly destructive consequences.

SDS had received little media attention for its activities on American campuses until *New York Times* reporter Fred Powledge wrote a long, supportive story. It appeared in the *Times* on March 15, 1965, some five years after the birth of the movement.[29] Coverage by a national news medium amounted to symbolic recognition that student radicalism had become an important political issue. When SDS sponsored a Vietnam War protest march on Washington in the spring of 1965, the event received nationwide coverage. Major articles on the New Left appeared in national news magazines and in large circulation weeklies such as the *Saturday Evening Post* and the *New York Times Magazine.*

Although many newspeople sympathized with the gamut of left-liberal reforms advocated by SDS and knew that sensational publicity might be harmful, they decided, in line with media prescriptions for exciting stories, to focus on the movement's most radical leaders and goals. News stories pictured SDS as a single-issue group, dedicated to violent opposition to the Vietnam War, rather than emphasizing its concern with a broad array of issues ranging from civil rights to socialism and anti-imperialism.

This distorted image, besides misleading media audiences, also affected the self-perceptions of SDS members. Individuals singled out by the media as spokespersons for the organization became celebrities. With this new-found status, many no longer felt accountable to their rank and file. To maintain the flow of publicity that they deemed essential for their survival, SDS members stressed the radical left-wing elements in the organization that conformed to the media image. In turn, this attracted new Leninist and Maoist members who expected the organization to perform as pictured in the media. These new members took over the leadership of the organization and turned it away from its long-range reformist goals to short-range and violent antiwar activities.

Sociologist Todd Gitlin contends that the media's decision in 1965 to give wide publicity to SDS ultimately destroyed the movement and with it much of the power of the New Left. In his colorful metaphor, the media spotlight became a magnifying glass that burned everybody to a crisp. Media efforts to bestow legitimacy on the movement failed totally. As is true in other instances of agenda building, political forces other than the media contributed to the turn of events. Radicalization of the SDS movement was also enhanced by the Johnson administration's escalation of the Vietnam War and by the growing alienation from mainstream society that it produced among many Americans.[30]

Many critics of American media contend that the fate of SDS is typical for groups that challenge the established order. As Paletz and Entman argue,

> Organizations that accept establishment rules, and pursue incremental goals discretely, benefit from journalists' needs and practices. Groups whose methods violate convention, whose objectives require a significant alteration of the structure of power, usually find their radical activities

distorted or condemned, their radical analyses and proposals ignored or scorned. Any publicity they receive tends to isolate them from the mass of citizens, encouraging them to moderate their ways until they either fade from sight or shade into the establishment.[31]

Of course, many movements, interest groups, and lobbies have been helped by media coverage, as long as they did not deviate too far from mainstream values. The civil rights movement is a memorable case. Sympathetic nationwide coverage of freedom marches and of battles fought for civil rights in Little Rock, Arkansas; Selma, Alabama; and Oxford, Mississippi, helped ready lawmakers and the nation for passage of the Civil Rights Act in 1964. Support for consumer organizations and environmentalist groups constitutes another success story. Media publicity has legitimized these organizations in the eyes of the public and in the eyes of political elites.[32] Their activities now are covered regularly and favorably. Nader, the most prominent consumer advocate, has become a media celebrity and a respected, much-consulted guru. The concerns of consumer interest groups and of general public interest lobbies such as Common Cause have become the subject of legislation, implemented through newly created public agencies.

There seems to be a pattern in the role played by media on behalf of successful social movements. That is the conclusion of two West German scholars who analyzed how media coverage helped change German attitudes and laws dealing with conscientious objectors to military service.[33] Their study, which covered a fifteen-year period from 1961 to 1975, revealed that a few newspapers took the lead in supporting the cause of conscientious objectors. The rest of the media largely ignored the movement initially. Uncontested favorable publicity served to legitimize conscientious objectors and their demands and attracted new supporters. By the time the establishment press began to criticize the movement in the wake of protest activities by conscientious objectors, the movement had become so well accepted that its political demands could not be stopped. The struggle for acceptance of the movement had taken fifteen years, but it seemed much briefer because of sparse coverage by the mainstream press during the initial seven years. Protest actions finally aroused opposition forces and moved the struggle to the center of political attention.

The model illustrated by the case, which appears to be typical for successful social movements, involves four steps. Legitimation of the incipient movement begins with favorable coverage by a few sympathetic journalists. Undisputed media praise then attracts support for the movement among segments of the public. The third phase is reached when the growing movement becomes strong and legitimate enough to make political demands and engage in protest activities. At that time opposing voices are raised in the hitherto silent mainstream media. They come too late, however, to stop the success of the movement in the legislative arena and among important publics.

Low status organizations whose goals encompass routine human concerns are least likely to attract helpful publicity.[34] Political scientist Edie Goldenberg studied the attempts of four citizen groups in Massachusetts to attract newspaper coverage to the problems of welfare mothers, senior citizens, low-income tenants, and people deprived of fair treatment by the courts. Finding that these groups had little success, she concluded, "There is bias in the system that consistently favors some and neglects others." The favored groups are "haves," those who possess the resources to make and maintain contact with the press and to arrange their operations so that they complement the needs of the press. The unfavored ones are those "most in need of press attention in order to be heard forcefully in the political arena" yet "least able to command attention and ... least able to use effectively what few resources they do control in seeking and gaining press access." Goldenberg warns, "If intensely felt interests go unarticulated and therefore are unnoticed and unaffected by policy makers, one important aspect of rule of, for, and by the people is weakened." [35] In the eyes of social critics such as Goldenberg, a free press must be responsive to the needs of all segments of society.

Documentaries and Docudramas

To influence public policy, newspeople are not limited to straight news and feature stories. Fictional productions, such as docudramas shown to millions of viewers on prime-time national television, are used as well. Docudramas are especially compelling because they reconstruct events in highly dramatic, emotional ways. Unfortunately, the viewer cannot tell what part of the story is real and what part is dramatic frosting.[36]

The political goals of many documentaries and docudramas are obvious. As Oscar Gandy has pointed out, "Too frequently to be mere coincidence, serial dramas, or the made-for-television movies we describe as docudrama, have been aired simultaneously with the discussion of related issues in Congress." [37] An example of a widely publicized docudrama that coincided with related political events was "The Day After," a two-hour ABC dramatization of a nuclear attack on Kansas City and its aftermath. It was broadcast on Sunday, November 20, 1983, following an extensive prebroadcast advertising campaign that included an eight-page viewer's guide. The drama was replete with scenes of burnt bodies, faces with blinded eyes rotting from radiation sickness, smoldering rubble, and survivors reduced to preying on each other.

At the time of broadcast, nuclear weapons policy was in the limelight. The Reagan administration was attempting to gain support in the United States and in Europe for deploying American missiles in European NATO countries. Antinuclear groups at home and abroad were working feverishly to stop the deployment. The docudrama was aired a few days before the decision to place the missiles was to be approved by the West German legislature. Excerpts were made available to German television.

Supporters of missile deployment feared that the program would lead to massive public demonstrations designed to force a change in nuclear deployment policies. When the Reagan administration was invited to send a representative to participate in a postbroadcast discussion of the lessons of the docudrama, it showed its profound concern by sending Secretary of State George P. Shultz. Throughout the furor raised by the broadcast, ABC denied that the timing had been politically motivated. The November date was chosen, it claimed, to raise ABC's ratings during a "sweeps" month, when ratings would be reflected in advertising prices.

What, then, was the political impact of "The Day After," which was viewed by more than 100 million people in homes, schools, churches, and town halls?[38] It appears that the broadcast boosted the activities of antinuclear groups and engendered fears that "The Day After" might generate a defeatist attitude among Americans. But public opinion polls after the broadcast did not show massive shifts of public attitudes about nuclear missile policies. In Europe, where immediate drastic political consequences had been expected, the missiles were deployed without major obstacles.

A number of analysts ascribed the lack of impact to flaws in the docudrama, which left the reasons for the nuclear attack uncertain and failed to deal squarely with nuclear policy issues. Others felt that the public had gained knowledge and awareness from the film, but had learned to distance itself psychologically from fictional disasters. Therefore, the audience failed to empathize fully with the stricken residents of Kansas City.

Even though the apparent consequences of "The Day After" were less than expected, concern or hopes remain high that prime-time broadcasts and the associated media coverage and public discussions may have major political consequences in the long or short run.[39] This potential impact obligates a responsible press to take greater pains to present all sides of an issue and to be more accurate in its depiction, even in a fiction program. Critics of "The Day After" felt that the drama understated the likely consequences of an atomic attack. Moreover, the appropriate background for appraising various policy options was lacking. Viewers were not told that the possibility of negotiating a nuclear freeze was severely constricted by the unwillingness of other world powers with nuclear arsenals to reciprocate and to permit verification of compliance.

Methods: Fair and Foul

The fairness and accuracy of news presentations and the appropriateness of news-gathering techniques become important issues when one considers the media as potential actors in the political process. In recent years the media have frequently been accused of improper methods. Law suits filed against them have multiplied.

Confirming Prejudgments

A famous, $120 million libel suit illustrates concerns about the legitimacy of some media tactics. As discussed in Chapter 4, the suit was brought by Gen. William C. Westmoreland against CBS for statements made about him in a ninety-minute documentary on the Vietnam War called "The Uncounted Enemy: A Vietnam Deception." The principal message of the documentary was that the general, while commander of American forces in Vietnam, had deliberately manipulated information about the strength of Viet Cong troops before the 1968 Tet (or Vietnamese New Year) offensive. Allegedly, he was trying to show the president and Congress that American troops under his command were winning the war. The Viet Cong offensive demonstrated that the enemy's strength and tenacity had been badly underestimated.

The case is ideal for examining questionable media practices because the results of an internal CBS review of production methods were made public. The network's own investigation indicated that the producers of the documentary believed in Westmoreland's guilt from the very start and organized the production to support their preformed conclusions. According to the internal report, CBS personnel made eleven major errors while putting together the documentary. These included failing to adequately support the charge that a conspiracy was involved, choosing to interview mostly people who supported the program's overall conclusions, reshooting unsatisfactory testimony after allowing a witness to hear what others had said, and "coddling sympathetic witnesses." [40] The report, which was prepared by senior CBS producer Burton Benjamin prior to the Westmoreland suit, contained portions of unedited transcripts of interviews in which sources were apparently coached by interviewers. At times interviewers asked loaded questions such as whether the respondent agreed that there had been a "a full-fledged conspiracy to fake intelligence reporting." If respondents failed to agree, their remarks were omitted from the final broadcast. Materials that might have undermined the documentary's principal conclusions about General Westmoreland's activities ended up on the cutting room floor.

In the final documentary eight of the ten persons whose testimony was featured sided against Westmoreland. One of the two who did not,

Lt. Gen. Daniel Graham, was given a mere twenty-one seconds of air time, even though he had been the chief of the army's current intelligence and estimates division in Vietnam in the late 1960s. Overall, Westmoreland and his supporters spoke for only five minutes and fifty-nine seconds, while his accusers were given nineteen minutes and nineteen seconds, a ratio of better than three-to-one for the accusers.

Van Gordon Sauter, president of CBS News, acknowledged that CBS policies and standards had been violated during the making of the documentary, but he argued that these flaws did not undermine the editorial integrity of the broadcast. According to him, it was an accurate account of the distorted estimates of enemy strength by the American military in Vietnam.

After several years of legal sparring, Westmoreland dropped his libel suit. Despite extensive exploration, the substantive issues remain unsettled. The issues of media policy are clearer. There is little disagreement about the standards of fairness and accuracy that should be applied in broadcasts on important public issues. The standards by which CBS judged its own conduct make this apparent. But—and this is the disturbing aspect—these standards are breached all too often. Such breaches raise questions about the sense of responsibility of high-level media personnel. When important public matters are at stake, are the media, especially the influential electronic media, exercising sufficient care to make sure that the preconceptions of media personnel do not taint their stories and mislead media audiences?

With investigative journalism growing in popularity, the problem of inaccurate reports has mounted. In many instances reports have permanent economic, professional, and social consequences for the individuals and institutions whose story is told. In the Westmoreland case, for example, the reputation of a prominent general was at stake. In another case, one involving the Kaiser Aluminum and Chemical Corporation, business losses could run into millions of dollars. An investigative report had accused the company of knowingly selling dangerous household electrical wiring under false pretenses. A partially fictionalized documentary about the mass murder of black youths in Atlanta suggested that the killer might still be at large. It raised doubts about the fairness of the trial of the man convicted as the murderer. The broadcast prompted the mayor of Atlanta and civic leaders to launch a public information campaign to blunt the anticipated ill effects.[41]

The serious injuries inflicted when publicity is careless or biased have become a deep concern for civil libertarians. As Ira Glasser, executive director of the American Civil Liberties Union, has warned, "Justice by press release and summary political punishment are methods we should have by now learned to avoid." [42] The problem is made worse by the fact that rebuttals, if permitted at all by the networks, have been subject to their editorial control. Network representatives have argued that documentaries, unlike ordinary news, are edited productions so that uncensored rebuttals need not be permitted.[43]

Entrapment

Serious ethical issues are also raised when newspeople undertake undercover operations or bogus enterprises created to entrap potential and actual wrongdoers. The story told earlier about the *Mirage,* the tavern set up to elicit and record bribery by city officials, illustrates the practice. A far more massive crime trap was set by Canadian media to expose organized crime in North America. The investigation resulted in a three-and-a-half hour documentary broadcast by the Canadian Broadcasting Company (CBC) on March 27, 1979.

CBC reporters and agents who were planted inside organized crime circles used hidden microphones and cameras to obtain dramatic film footage of gangsters discussing their activities. In one instance a reporter arranged meetings with a woman suspected of helping gangsters to buy real estate in Atlantic City. The reporter pretended to represent a person in Italy who wished to export several million dollars from Italy to Canada. The money was then to be funneled into Atlantic City real estate under the guise that it belonged to legitimate Canadian investors. Through this initial contact, another meeting was set up between a disguised reporter, who had had previous experience as an informant for law enforcement agencies, and underworld dealers in illegal real estate. All of these meetings were taped, and some parts were filmed.[44]

Sting operations like these raise serious civil liberties issues even when they are conducted by regular law enforcement agencies, often under the watchful eyes of the courts.[45] The concerns about protecting the rights of suspects are even greater when the sleuths are acting without an official mandate and without supervision by a responsible public body. Quite aside from civil liberties issues, sting operations raise fundamental questions about the proper functions of the press. Should its watchdog role be carried to the point where it becomes a quasi-police force, tracking down selected offenders when a good story promises to be the likely reward?

Summary

In this chapter we examined direct involvement by journalists in the conduct of government. We began with an analysis of muckraking, comparing reality to a series of models of the process. The media's power to arouse public opinion with exposés of corruption is far less than is popularly believed. Even if the public becomes highly concerned, political action is not guaranteed. The belief that muckraking commonly produces reforms when journalists stir the public, and public opinion then pressures for political action, is wrong.

The most propitious road to reform is via direct liaisons between newspeople and government officials. When officials provide story leads in areas where they would like to produce action, or when newspeople can interest officials in taking action on issues that have come to the media's attention, successful political activities are apt to occur. On rare occasions the media are also able to produce action by using the club of potential unwanted publicity to force officials to act or by becoming participants in political negotiations.

The Watergate scandal illustrates how political action can emerge from the interplay of various social institutions. The media, through a series of agenda-building steps, created the climate in which it became possible to force the resignation of a president. Agenda-building examples from science policy and from the realm of interest group politics demonstrate the impact of the media on developments in these fields. The media serve as catalysts that precipitate the actions of other elements within the society. They make the course of events possible, but the ultimate outcome may defeat their political purposes because it is beyond their control.

The media's public policy-making roles influence American politics in general as well as the lives of many individuals and institutions. How sensitively and accurately they are performed therefore becomes a matter of concern. News gathering and news production can be substantially flawed, even when media institutions profess to believe in high standards. How often these standards are violated, and what the costs are to people caught in the net of inaccurate publicity, is a matter for conjecture.

One major cause lies at the heart of most instances when newspeople allow themselves to be used as mouthpieces for politicians and interest groups. That cause is the desire to produce exciting news stories. This is not surprising. Journalism requires telling stories that will attract audiences. That journalists are tempted to be good storytellers above all, even at the expense of other goals, should give pause to those who advocate that they should play the political game actively and regularly.

If one grants that newspeople should attempt to influence what gets on the crowded political agenda, one must ask whether their professional standards equip them to guide politics wisely and well. To put it another way: when issues are selected for attention, should their newsworthiness be the controlling factor? If the answer is "no," then the heavy hand of the media in policy making may be very dangerous.

Notes

1. Lincoln Steffens, *The Autobiography of Lincoln Steffens* (New York: Harcourt Brace, 1931), 357.
2. For a brief review of the history and tactics of muckraking, see William L. Rivers, *The Other Government: Power and the Washington Media* (New York: Universe Books, 1982), 119-143.
3. Suzanne Garment, "Political Imperfections: Scandal Time in Washington," *Public Opinion* 10 (May/June 1987): 10-12, 60.
4. David L. Protess, *Muckraking Matters: The Societal Impact of Investigative Reporting*, Institute for Modern Communications Research Monographs Series (Evanston, Ill.: Northwestern University, 1987), 13.
5. Steffens, *Autobiography*, 357.
6. Harvey L. Molotch, David L. Protess, and Margaret T. Gordon, "The Media-Policy Connection: Ecologies of News," in *Political Communication Research: Approaches, Studies, Assessments*, ed. David L. Paletz (Norwood, N.J.: Ablex, 1987), 26-48.
7. *Public Opinion Quarterly* has published reports on these investigations since 1983. Two recent articles are Donna R. Leff, David L. Protess, and Stephen C. Brooks, "Crusading Journalism: Changing Public Attitudes and Policy-Making Agendas," *Public Opinion Quarterly* 50 (Fall 1986): 300-315; and David L. Protess, Fay Lomax Cook, Thomas R. Curtin, Margaret T. Gordon, Donna R. Leff, Maxwell E. McCombs, and Peter Miller, "The Impact of Investigative Reporting on Public Opinion and Policymaking: Targeting Toxic Waste," *Public Opinion Quarterly* 51 (Summer 1987): 166-185.
8. Robert Muccigrosso, "Television and the Urban Crisis," in *Screen and Society*, ed. Frank J. Coppa (Chicago: Nelson-Hall, 1979), 44-45.
9. Chris T. Allen and Judith D. Weber, "How Presidential Media Use Affects Individuals' Beliefs about Conservation," *Journalism Quarterly* 60 (Spring 1983): 98-104, 196.
10. David L. Protess, Donna R. Leff, Stephen C. Brooks, and Margaret T. Gordon, "Uncovering Rape: The Watchdog Press and the Limits of Agenda Setting," *Public Opinion Quarterly* 49 (Spring 1985): 19-37.
11. Often the chief point of a program is simply to alert the public to a problem; immediate action may not be expected. For example, PBS officials filmed their documentary "Crisis at General Hospital," to make the public aware of the inequity of a two-tier health system in which people of means are served by excellent private hospitals, while the remainder of the population receives second-rate care in inferior public hospitals. Kenneth R. Clark, "Hospital Dilemma: The System Sends Poor Home to Die," *Chicago Tribune*, January 17, 1984.
12. Protess, *Muckraking Matters*, 29.
13. The full story is told in Zay N. Smith and Pamela Zekman, *The Mirage* (New York: Random House, 1979).
14. Protess, *Muckraking Matters*, 29.
15. Wayne King, "Houston Finds that Dramatizing Crime Does Pay," *New York Times*, January 23, 1984.
16. Michael Killian, "New FBI TV Series Will Seek Viewer Help in Nabbing Criminals," *Chicago Tribune*, February 5, 1988.
17. Robert D. McFadden, "News Executives Express Outrage," *New York Times*, October 3, 1986.

18. David L. Paletz and Robert M. Entman, *Media Power Politics* (New York: Free Press, 1981), 184. Also see David Weaver and Swanzy Nimley Elliott, "Who Sets the Agenda for the Media? A Study of Local Agenda-Building," *Journalism Quarterly* 62 (Spring 1985): 87-94; Jane Delano Brown, Carl R. Bybee, Stanley T. Weardon, and Dulcie Murdock, "Invisible Power: Newspaper News Sources and the Limits of Diversity," *Journalism Quarterly* 64 (Spring 1987): 45-54.

19. Gladys Engel Lang and Kurt Lang, *The Battle for Public Opinion: The President, the Press, and the Polls during Watergate* (New York: Columbia University Press, 1983), 58.

20. Molotch et al., "The Media-Policy Connection," 45, citing Peter Dreier, "The Position of the Press in the U.S. Power Structure," *Social Problems* 29 (February 1982): 298-310; Todd Gitlin, *The Whole World Is Watching: Media in the Making and Unmaking of the New Left* (Berkeley: University of California Press, 1980); Norton Long, "The Local Community as an Ecology of Games," *American Journal of Sociology* 64 (1958): 256; and Harvey L. Mototch, "Media and Movements," in *The Dynamics of Social Movement*, ed. Mayer Zeld and John D. McCarthy (Cambridge, Mass.: Winthrop, 1979), 71-93.

21. Lang and Lang, *The Battle for Public Opinion*, 59-60.

22. Oscar H. Gandy, *Beyond Agenda Setting: Information Subsidies and Public Policy* (Norwood, N.J.: Ablex, 1982), 149-162.

23. Stanley Rothman and S. Robert Lichter, "The Nuclear Energy Debate: Scientists, the Media and the Public," *Public Opinion* 5 (August/September 1982): 47-48.

24. Stanley Rothman and S. Robert Lichter, "Elite Ideology and Risk Perception in Nuclear Energy Policy," *American Political Science Review* 81 (June 1987): 383-404.

25. For a more general discussion of the problem of sources of science information, see Alan Mazur, "Media Coverage and Public Opinion on Scientific Controversies," *Journal of Communication* 31 (Spring 1981): 106-115; and Sharon S. Dunwoody, "The Science Writing Inner Club: A Communication Link Between Science and the Lay Public," *Science, Technology and Human Values* 5 (Fall 1980): 14-22.

26. Paletz and Entman, *Media Power Politics*, 144.

27. Patrick Leahy and Alan Mazur, "The Rise and Fall of Public Opposition in Specific Social Movements," *Social Studies of Science* 10 (1980): 191-205; and Mazur, "Media Coverage and Public Opinion."

28. For a symposium on science news, see *Journal of Communication* 31 (Spring 1981): 84-189.

29. Gitlin, *The Whole World*, 25-26.

30. For a model of the roles played by the media in fostering social movements, see Glenn G. Strodthoff, Robert P. Hawkins, and A. Clay Schoenfeld, "Media Roles in a Social Movement: A Model of Ideology Diffusion," *Journal of Communication* 35 (Spring 1985): 134-153. Also see Clarice N. Olien, George A. Donohue, and Philip J. Tichenor, "Media and Stages of Social Conflict," *Journalism Monographs* 90 (November 1984): 1-31.

31. Paletz and Entman, *Media Power Politics*, 146.

32. Gitlin, *The Whole World*, 284.

33. Hans Mathias Kepplinger and Michael Hachenberg, "Media and Conscientious Objection in the Federal Republic of Germany," in *Political Communication Research*, 108-128.

34. Paletz and Entman, *Media Power Politics*, 144.
35. Edie Goldenberg, *Making the Papers* (Lexington, Mass.: Heath, 1975), 146-148.
36. The potential impact of docudramas is discussed by William C. Adams, Allison Salzman, William Vantine, Leslie Suelter, Anne Baker, Lucille Bonvouloir, Barbara Brenner, Margaret Ely, Jean Feldman, and Ron Ziegel, "The Power of *The Right Stuff:* A Quasi-Experimental Field Test of the Docudrama Hypothesis," *Public Opinion Quarterly* 49 (Fall 1985): 330-339.
37. Gandy, *Beyond Agenda Setting*, 88.
38. Sally Bedell Smith, "Film on a Nuclear War Already Causing Wide Fallout of Partisan Activity," *New York Times*, November 23, 1983.
39. For a discussion of the subtle yet significant consequences that are often missed, see Stanley Feldman and Lee Sigelman, "The Political Impact of Prime-Time Television: 'The Day After,'" *Journal of Politics* 47 (May 1985): 556-578.
40. Richard Bernstein, "CBS Releases its Study of Vietnam Documentary," *New York Times*, April 27, 1983.
41. William E. Schmidt, "TV Movie on Atlanta Child Killings Stirs Debate and Casts Doubt on Guilt," *New York Times*, January 31, 1985.
42. Deirdre Carmody, "The Role of the Press in the U.S. Corruption Inquiry," *New York Times*, February 5, 1980.
43. For a typical case involving denial of the right to unedited rebuttal, see Sally Bedell, "ABC Backs Off Charge it Made Against Mobil," *New York Times*, June 22, 1982.
44. Andrew H. Malcolm, "TV Film Links to Mob in Toronto," *New York Times*, March 28, 1979.
45. Bennett L. Gershman, "Abscam, the Judiciary, and the Ethics of Government," *Yale Law Journal* 91 (July 1982): 1565 1591.

Readings

Gitlin, Todd. *The Whole World Is Watching: Media in the Making and Unmaking of the New Left*. Berkeley: University of California Press, 1980.
Lang, Gladys Engel, and Kurt Lang. *The Battle for Public Opinion: The President, the Press and the Polls During Watergate*. New York: Columbia University Press, 1983.
Leonard, Thomas G. *The Power of the Press: The Birth of American Political Reporting*. New York: Oxford University Press, 1986.
Linsky, Martin. *How the Press Affects Federal Policymaking: Six Case Studies*. New York: Norton, 1986.
Miller, Susan Heilmann. *Reporters and Congressmen: Living in Symbiosis*. Columbus, Ohio: Journalism Monograph Series No. 53, 1978.
Patterson, Margaret Jones, and Robert H. Russell. *Behind the Lines: Case Studies in Investigative Reporting*. New York: Columbia University Press, 1986.
Smith, Zay N., and Pamela Zekman. *The Mirage*. New York: Random House, 1979.
Steffens, Lincoln. *The Autobiography of Lincoln Steffens*. New York: Harcourt, Brace, 1931.

CHAPTER 9

Crisis Coverage

You awake at 4:00 a.m. Outside the civil defense sirens are screaming. What is wrong? Has it happened? Or is it about to strike? What are you supposed to do about this unknown menace? Almost instinctively you turn on your radio. Sounds of soft music. Just hearing them is reassuring. At least the radio is working. If there are things you must do immediately, the radio announcer will tell you. You wait for the music to stop, anxious to know what is happening. But you also hope it won't stop for a while—the longer it plays, the less chance that you're in real danger. They wouldn't play music if disaster were imminent.

Finally, the announcer breaks in. A tornado has been sighted nearby. "Take shelter," says the voice on the radio. "Keep away from windows. Stay indoors until the sirens stop. There will be further news bulletins at five-minute intervals." You heave a sigh of relief as you dress quickly, pick up your apartment keys and a small transistor radio, and head for the basement. Nothing has happened yet, and if it does, officials are obviously prepared to deal with the crisis. They already woke you, warned you about the potential menace to your life and property, told you how to protect yourself initially, and promised to shepherd you through the dangers of the hours to come.

The Nature of Crisis Conditions

This is just one small scenario of a periodic public crisis. Public crises are natural or manmade events that pose an immediate and serious threat to the lives and property or to the peace of mind of many citizens. Examples are assassinations of major public figures, terrorist attacks (particularly when hostages are taken), or major accidents, like train wrecks or spectacular fires. They trouble the public's peace of mind even when they threaten no personal harm to most observers. When such disasters happen, people expect to be informed and protected by the appropriate government agencies.

In times of crisis the media, particularly radio, become a vital arm of government. As usual, they select, shape, and report the news to people in and out of government. But, in addition, they provide government officials quick access to the public directly or indirectly through media personnel. These official messages keep endangered communities in touch with essential information and instructions. People are reassured and may be less likely to panic.

Because rapid transmission of information and commentary is most crucial in areas that are immediately and directly affected by the disaster, on-the-scene crisis coverage will be the focus of this chapter. However, many local problems have ramifications for remote areas. The coverage of a racial riot in Los Angeles may affect readers and viewers in Detroit or Chicago where conditions or situations may be similar. Publicity about airplane crashes or radiation leaks may influence the future of these industries throughout the country, not only at the disaster scene.

A dramatic example of the nationwide impact of a local event occurred in 1970 when four students were killed during an antiwar demonstration at Kent State University in Ohio. Wide publicity about the tragedy kindled protests on campuses from coast to coast. Classes stopped, students rallied, and thousands rushed to Washington to lobby against the Vietnam War and the Kent State slayings.

Besides its intrinsic importance, crisis coverage highlights major philosophical and policy issues that plague the government-media relationship. When the physical survival of ordinary citizens is at stake, their sensitivity to media publicity becomes heightened. The media's responsibility to serve public needs and the government's responsibility to control, direct, and even manipulate the flow of news for public purposes become for them issues of self-preservation. The Olympian view yields to a vision of danger at eyeball distance.

Four Crises

In this chapter we will examine media coverage of four crises: the assassination of President John F. Kennedy in Dallas, Texas, November 22, 1963; race riots in Winston-Salem, North Carolina, November 2-5, 1967; Israel's Yom Kippur War, October 6-28, 1973; and a series of natural and manmade disasters, including floods, storms, and potential radiation damage from a malfunctioning nuclear energy plant.

The Assassination of John F. Kennedy

The facts of the assassination of President Kennedy in the third year of his term are familiar. A young, vigorous president, who had created an aura of political freshness and idealism, was struck down by a sniper's bullets while traveling in an open limousine in a motorcade in Dallas. The president died in a hospital several hours after the attack. Initially, there was uncertainty about his physical condition. The extent and severity of his injuries were unknown. The exact procedures that would be followed in filling the presidential office without delay were unclear. Rumors mushroomed that the assassination was part of a larger plot by domestic or foreign political enemies of the president to kill prominent government officials. There were countless unanswered questions about the impact the disaster might have on American politics and policies. All these uncertainties compounded the grief and anger that touched millions of Americans in a very personal way.[1]

Racial Riots in North Carolina

In Winston-Salem in 1967, a black man was arrested on the street for drunkenness. He was taken to a local police station where a white policeman clubbed him for being unruly. Several days later the victim died of a fractured skull. Because this assault occurred during a period of racial unrest and mounting opposition to harsh police action, particularly against minority citizens, the police apparently tried to hush up the story. Nevertheless, rumors of the incident circulated in the black community, and a brief story appeared in one local newspaper. The National Association for the Advancement of Colored People (NAACP) planned a march to protest police brutality but was persuaded to cancel it for fear that it would provoke rioting.

After the victim's funeral, rioting began: rocks were thrown, windows were broken, small fires were started. Ultimately, five hundred people were involved, and the governor called out one thousand National Guard troops. There were rumors of bomb threats and looting and sniping. A curfew was then imposed, and the National Guard was supplied with ammunition, in case the situation got out of control. It did. Fighting lasted for four days. Fortunately, no one died, but more than one hundred people were injured, two hundred people were arrested, and there was $750,000 worth of property damage.[2]

The Yom Kippur War

The Yom Kippur War, or the War of Ramadan as the Arabs call it, began at 2:00 p.m. on October 6, 1973, when Egyptian and Syrian forces attacked Israeli troops along Israel's frontiers. Fighting was confined to the border regions, and there were no large-scale attacks on civilian populations. Although this was the fourth time in Israel's twenty-six-year history that the country found itself at war, the suddenness of the outbreak surprised most Israelis. There had been no political and little military warning of the attack, and hence few preparations had been made to cope with the initial crisis. On the day of the attack, people were busy with religious ceremonies of the Yom Kippur holiday, the most sacred day for members of the Jewish faith. Because of the holiday, the Israeli media were totally shut down.

The wailing of the air raid sirens at 2 p.m. jolted the nation back to worldly affairs. Radio and television immediately resumed broadcasting. Their first tasks were to summon military units, to broadcast civil defense instructions, and to inform an anxious public about ongoing events. In the days that followed, the media's initial responsibilities were expanded. New tasks included boosting the morale of the soldiers and the home front, directing propaganda broadcasts to the Arab world, and interpreting unfolding events so that the public could put them into perspective and understand and support government policies.[3] Officials censored stories that raised doubts about public policies.

Natural and Manmade Disasters

Disasters are akin in many ways to first strikes in war. In the case of floods, tornadoes, or chemical or radiation pollution, the physical impact of water, wind, or manmade substances suddenly threatens to wipe out lives and property and disrupt communication and transportation. People fear for their own welfare and that of their loved ones and communities.

Our analysis of disaster coverage is based on four floods and three storms in several cities and a threatened radiation calamity in March 1979 at the Three Mile Island nuclear plant near Harrisburg, Pennsylvania. In two of the floods, nearly the entire city was submerged in the wake of a hurricane; in the other two, flash floods wiped out part of the city. In the storm disasters, tornadoes destroyed major portions of towns in Georgia, Texas, and Iowa. Homes were leveled, burying people under the rubble. Telephone lines were broken; live electric wires threatened electrocution and fire. Streets became impassable even to rescue vehicles. Television stations, bereft of power, closed down.[4]

Unlike in the floods and storm disasters, in the Three Mile Island nuclear accident no actual destruction occurred. Nonetheless, news stories covering the dangers of radiation that might accompany a meltdown of an overheated nuclear reactor led to major disruptions in community life. More than 150,000 people fled the area. In the actual disasters, radio became the major source of emergency information. It is the most likely medium to have back-up power if regular power is disrupted, and, thanks to transistors, it is the most likely to be received by the public when electricity is unavailable.

Media Response and Role

During crises the public depends almost totally on the media for news that may be vital for its survival and for important messages from public and private authorities. The mass media are the only institutions equipped to collect this massive amount of information and disseminate it quickly. Therefore when people become aware of a crisis, they turn on their radios or television sets, often on a round-the-clock basis, to monitor developments.

Table 9-1 presents data on sources that people used for crisis information in three communities hit by recent disasters. The table demonstrates people's heavy reliance on electronic media and the comparatively small role played by interpersonal communication and direct experience. Community A, located on the Gulf Coast, had experienced numerous hurricanes. Communities B and C, in the Midwest, had suffered two tornadoes and two major floods, respectively. Community D had no experience with a major natural disaster. A sample of residents in each of these communities was asked, "From what sources have you obtained the greatest amount of information concerning natural disasters?" Several sources could be cited in response.[5] Respondents in the disaster-free control community were asked to speculate about what sources might be most useful.

The audience for crisis information is massive and loyal. In the days immediately after the Kennedy assassination, television sets everywhere

Table 9-1 Principal Sources of Disaster Information
(in percentage of responses)

Sources of information	Site A	Site B	Site C	Site D
Electronic media	66	59	75	75
Newspapers	24	20	40	64
Magazines	3	7	8	15
Nonfiction books	10	10	11	4
Other persons	17	12	14	9
Direct experience	37	32	20	6
Public education	9	6	5	—

Source: Dennis E. Wenger, "A Few Empirical Observations Concerning the Relationship Between the Mass Media and Disaster Knowledge: A Research Report," in *Disasters and the Mass Media: Proceedings of the Committee on Disasters and the Mass Media Workshop* (Washington, D.C.: National Academy of Sciences, 1980), 244. Reprinted by permission.

Note: Multiple answers were permitted. $N = 290$ for Site A, hurricane disasters; 281 for Site B, tornado disasters; 209 for Site C, flood disasters; and 341 for Site D, disaster-free control.

were turned on for nearly thirty-two hours of broadcasts about the unfolding events. In the United States alone, 51 million homes were tuned in. During the Yom Kippur War, the entire Israeli population used both radio and television. Sixty-eight percent of the population listened to radio all day long to catch the hourly news bulletins.

Besides information, the public looks to the media to explain and interpret the situation, since media personnel are often the first ones on the scene collecting reports and trying to fit them into a coherent story. Official investigations generally come much later. The media also guide the public to appropriate behavior during the crisis. They warn people to retreat to an air raid shelter, announce escape routes, describe purification of polluted food and water, and supply news of missing persons, or schedules to be maintained by schools and work places. Outside the immediate crisis area, news stories may mobilize relief operations.

Stages and Patterns of Coverage

Stage One. The typical scenario of crisis coverage has three stages. During the first stage, the crisis or disaster strikes or is announced as impending. Media people, officials, and onlookers rush to the scene. This immediately produces a flood of uncoordinated messages, largely transmitted over the airwaves. Radio and television stations interrupt regularly scheduled programs with bulletins announcing the crisis, or they may preempt the entire program for reports from the scene.

Minutes after the storm and flood disasters, stations that had survived the immediate impact of the catastrophe broadcast emergency messages. These stations rapidly became information collection centers. People would phone them with reports to be broadcast or call them for information. The most important broadcasts in the early hours of the disaster were messages describing what had happened, directing people to places where aid was available, summoning National Guard units and other security forces, and coordinating appeals for survival supplies, such as food, blankets, blood donations, and medical equipment.

In the early phase the number of news broadcasts rises steeply. During the Yom Kippur War, radio and television doubled broadcast time to a twenty-four hour schedule and replaced many regular programs with war-related news and interviews. News bulletins were issued hourly on radio and five times daily on television. After a major earthquake in 1964 ravaged Anchorage, Alaska, radio stations remained on the air continuously and asked people to stay tuned in for emergency messages.[6]

Once the initial announcements have been aired, many people who have heard the broadcast will relay the information to others by word of mouth, either in person or by telephone. This in turn stimulates those who have been alerted to tune in to subsequent broadcasts. For instance, when the news of the assassination of President Kennedy was first broadcast, a larger than average daytime audience heard it within minutes from the media because he was shot at noon when many people in the East and Midwest were listening to radio during lunch. Each person who heard the news told it to five or six other people on the average.[7] More than two-thirds of the American public—nearly 150 million people—received the news within one-half hour after the shooting. Similarly, on March 30, 1981, it took approximately ninety minutes to diffuse the news of the attempted assassination of President Ronald Reagan to 90 percent of the public. The average person then told three others.[8]

The striking characteristic of this first stage is the rapidity of the communication. Television and radio can focus the public's attention almost instantaneously on the developing situation. In many cases news about the crisis replaces most other stories. Whatever else happens in the world during the crisis period, regardless of its importance, may be totally blocked out.

At this early stage the media are the major source of information, even for public officials concerned with the crisis. Media reports serve to coordinate public activities. During the Anchorage earthquake, for example, the radio stations that were able to function became the focal point for coordinating information on casualties, property damage, and supplies so that officials could determine priorities for relief work. At a later stage direct communication among officials and other affected parties may supplement or even supersede media communication.

Next to reaching the disaster site, the chief problem for newspeople during the first stage is getting accurate information. Public officials and private citizens involved in the crisis may be reluctant to talk. Rumors abound. During the Yom Kippur War, stories about advance warning of the forthcoming attack, damage from the initial strike, and the preparedness of the Israeli army were garbled. During the Alaska earthquake, many buildings were evacuated unnecessarily because it was falsely reported that they had been condemned or were about to collapse. The number of dead and the extent of injuries were frequently exaggerated. In the case of the Kennedy assassination and the racial disturbances, there were intimations of conspiracies to commit more violence. Newspeople received many conflicting reports and lacked enough time to check their accuracy.

If highly technical matters are involved—as happens in explosions, structural failures, and radiation disasters, such as the Three Mile Island incident—it may be impossible to present a coherent story. Government officials, eager to allay the public's fears and prevent panic, usually minimize the dangers when communicating with newspeople. Reporters ordinarily lack the expertise to know when officials are concealing the truth. They cannot make sense out of baffling technical data nor simplify the information so that lay persons can comprehend it.[9] Imagine their puzzlement at one typical news conference when the Nuclear Regulatory Commission's chief spokesman, Harold Denton, attempted to correct a false report that the hydrogen bubble in the reactor was about to explode. Here is what Denton said:

> The oxygen generation rate that I was assuming yesterday when I was reporting on the potential detonation inside the vessel is, it now appears to have been, too conservative. There's an emerging consensus of technical opinion that the—for situations such as this where there's high oxygen overpressure in a vessel, that the oxygen evolution rate is very low, and our numbers for the rate of oxygen yesterday—I think I quoted a number on the order of 1 percent a day—is very, very conservative, and the actual rate is much lower than that.[10]

If you are baffled about what he meant, so were the reporters.

To provide continuous crisis coverage, television and radio stations must suddenly produce a steady stream of interesting crisis-related stories to fill many hours of broadcast time. The unrelenting pressure for fresh accounts often tempts media personnel to interview inexperienced eyewitnesses and commentators, who may lend a local touch without clarifying the situation. They also may report information that has not been adequately verified or that is atypical.[11] By focusing on the destruction of a tornado, for instance, the audience may be left with the wrong impression that the entire community is in ruins.[12] The pressure for news encourages reporters and public officials alike to speculate about what happened. At times they spin past prejudices into a web of scenarios that casts blame for the disaster or its aftermath on socially outcast groups. "Outsiders" in a community (ethnic minorities or political deviants, for example) often become the hapless scapegoats. The racial riots of the 1960s were routinely attributed to "outside agitators" who were depicted as common criminals, bereft of moral dignity and social consciousness. The Winston-Salem riots are a case in point.[13]

Stage Two. During the second stage, the media try to make sense of the situation. At this point enough time generally has elapsed so that the chief dimensions of the crisis have emerged. For instance, in a natural or manmade disaster, the full extent of the damage has been ascertained. Names of most victims and the degree of their injuries are known. Plans have been made for repairs and reconstruction. In the Kennedy assassination it became clear how the death occurred, even though the person or persons responsible for the crime were not yet known. Plans were made for the funeral ceremonies and for the transfer of power to the vice president.

In general, print media are able to do a more thorough job than radio and television in pulling together the various events and fitting them into a coherent story. Print media have larger staffs for investigation and more room to present background details that make the events understandable. For instance, in the hours and days following Kennedy's assassination, the *New York Times* probed into the motives for the assassination, the possibility of conspiracy, and the involvement of foreign agents—questions that the government's Warren Commission investigated only later and at a far slower pace.

During this second stage, governments and their critics may try to shape political fall-out from the disaster in ways that support their policy preferences. The 1986 nuclear disaster at Chernobyl in the Soviet Ukraine provides many examples. The explosion of the reactor forced the evacuation of ninety-five thousand people, left twenty-seven towns and villages uninhabitable, and produced fatal radiation sickness in hundreds of people.[14] Government sources in the United States and in the Soviet Union pictured the event as an aberration that happened because of a series of readily avoidable mistakes. The accident, they contended, should not undermine confidence in the safety of nuclear power plants. Antinuclear groups throughout the world tried to use the story to support the opposite point of view. By and large, their interpretation did not prevail.

Stage Three. The third stage overlaps with the other two. It involves attempts by media personnel to place the crisis into a larger, long-range perspective and to prepare people to cope with the aftermath. For instance, information on evacuation routes and ways to protect people and property may be updated. Steps toward restoration of normal conditions may be discussed. In wartime the third stage may involve broadcasting news, patriotic features, and action-adventure or comedy shows designed to relieve tensions and sustain morale. In the case of the Yom Kippur War, it also required structuring messages so that they would not give aid and comfort to the enemy, who could readily listen to broadcasts intended for Israeli consumption.

A concerted effort may have to be made to prevent panic. After the Anchorage earthquake the mayor and other city officials made frequent radio reports describing the damage and assuring people that the authorities had the situation under control. Similarly, following the assassination of Martin Luther King, Jr., in 1968, live camera facilities were set up to permit local mayors throughout the United States to communicate with their constituents. In Washington, D.C., for example, Mayor Walter Washington and other black leaders addressed the public repeatedly, urging people to stay calm. Network tributes to Dr. King were designed to stress peaceful behavior as a genuine tribute to the memory of the slain civil rights leader.

During the Three Mile Island incident, the federal government attempted to halt disquieting conflicting reports by centralizing news releases. All information furnished by government and plant officials about the disaster had to be cleared through a press center operated by the Nuclear Regulatory Commission near the site of the accident. Although officials of the damaged plant protested the censorship, they complied with President Jimmy Carter's order. Later a formal investigation of how forty-three newspapers and network evening newscasts reported the accident credited the media with providing balanced treatment in a highly confused and confusing situation.[15]

To reassure a shaken public after President Kennedy's assassination and to reorient Americans to the new administration, the media featured news about Lyndon B. Johnson's inauguration and assumption of presidential responsibilities. Immediately after Kennedy's death they made a special effort to inform the public concerning the whereabouts and activities of the new president and to convey the impression that the political life of the nation was continuing with only minor disruptions.

In the storm and flood disasters, after the initial relief activities had been organized, stations switched their emphasis to morale-building activities. The featured theme was that the community had shown its strength by coping heroically with the disaster and that it would now unite and rapidly build a better future. "Belmond is coming back," proclaimed the front page of the local newspaper in the Iowa town paralyzed by a tornado. "Belmond is looking ahead. It had received perhaps the cruelest blow ever dealt an Iowa town in the way of a natural catastrophe. But it is far from being beaten." [16]

Which medium—radio, television, or newspapers—performs best in crisis situations? Public opinion surveys from the Yom Kippur War provide some answers. More than half of the people who were interviewed about their media preferences said that radio had been best in providing initial information. Television was rated second best for information but best for interpreting events. As interpreter, radio ranked second, followed by interpersonal communication and newspaper coverage, in that order. Television also was called the best medium for tension release, followed by interpersonal communication. Only 5 percent of the respondents credited newspapers with providing relief from tension.

Less educated people relied more heavily on television and interpersonal communication for news and interpretation, while the better educated relied more on radio and newspapers. Less educated people also felt the highest levels of tension and found it most difficult to get relief. Without comparable information from other crisis situations, one can only guess that these reactions to crisis coverage by various media are probably representative of what occurs in similar crises in other countries.

Possible Effects of Coverage

Information about crisis situations, even if it is bad news, relieves disquieting uncertainty and calms people. The mere activity of watching or listening to familiar reporters and commentators reassures people and keeps them occupied. It gives them a sense of vicarious participation, of "doing something." To maintain this quieting effect, media personnel may avoid showing gruesome details of the crisis. For instance, photos of President Kennedy's injuries were not shown initially, although they were available. In the Three Mile Island accident, conjectures about possible effects of a nuclear explosion were avoided. To lessen the chance of panic, local media even rejected advertisements by merchants for "evacuation sales" and radiation detectors.

News stories may be able to reassure people that they do not bear their grief and fear alone. After seeing the same disaster pictures and listening to the same broadcasts, people can discuss the crisis with neighbors, friends, and coworkers who have shared their experiences. This gives the feeling of mutual support. Watching Kennedy's funeral on television and witnessing the grief of his young family made Americans feel that they were participating with millions of others in a national catharsis of grief. Many were able to cry to relieve their personal tensions.

If the news conveys the idea that the authorities are coping properly with the disaster, this, too, is reassuring. Scenes of a train or bus or plane crash become less frightening if the police, firefighters, ambulances, and medical personnel are on the scene. Watching the mayor or governor tour a disaster site provides further reassurance. Finally, directions about appropriate behavior may save lives and property and ensure that the stricken community continues to function.

The benefits of coverage are readily apparent in most but not all disasters. For instance, looting and rioting erupted or continued after the King assassination despite broadcasts intended to cool tensions. The broadcasts may have reduced the amount of violence, and television coverage may have restrained assaults by rioters or police, but we do not know for sure.

Negative Effects of Media Coverage

Media coverage also may have adverse effects. It is this possibility that raises serious questions about the responsibility of media personnel to consider the societal consequences of freedom to publish. The government's responsibility to prevent harm-producing coverage, possibly by strict censorship, also becomes a major political issue.

Careless or even carefully prepared news messages may so disturb people that they cannot act rationally. Once informed of a crisis, people may panic, endangering themselves and others. For instance, a precipitous mass exodus of frightened people during an impending flood or wind calamity may clog roads and overcrowd shelters; it may lead to injuries and death for those caught beyond the safety of their homes and work places. Pictures of violence may lead to a terrifying multiplication effect. Audiences frequently believe that the violent act is merely one of many. One house on fire or the sight of one victim's body may lead to visions of whole neighborhoods on fire and scores of victims killed. Police may be ordered to shoot lawbreakers on sight, and citizens may resort to excessive violence to protect themselves.

Statements provoking unwise reactions are more likely to be publicized in times of crisis because the exceptionally large demand for news and guidance reduces gatekeepers' vigilance. Pack journalism may run rampant when all available news is shared to provide as much coverage as possible. If mistakes are made by news sources or reporters, they appear in all the media. During the Kennedy assassination crisis, Dallas police made many incautious comments about Lee Harvey Oswald, Kennedy's accused slayer. The remarks were widely publicized and would have impaired Oswald's chances for a fair trial, had he lived. After the nuclear mishap at Three Mile Island, workers complained that erroneous media reports, based on conflicting assessments by government officials about the explosiveness of a hydrogen bubble, frightened their families into needless evacuation of the area and threatened the survival of the plant and their job security. Such consequences are commonplace as long as crisis news routinely dwells on worst-case scenarios without providing perspectives on their likelihood.[17]

Crisis and disaster news frequently attract crowds of citizens and reporters to the site, impeding rescue and security operations. News coverage of physical disasters routinely draws looters to the scene. When the media reported the deployment of antiterrorist commandos in 1985, after a Trans World airplane had been hijacked and hostages taken, the commandos lost the chance to surprise their targets.[18]

Media coverage also may incite or prolong rioting. For instance, during the racial riots in the Watts neighborhood of Los Angeles in 1965, police reported that the presence of television cameras seemed to escalate the violence. Rioters actually appeared to "perform" for the cameras. Publicizing even a few riot scenes may produce adverse results because people generally notice and remember acts of violence much more clearly than they do other aspects of riot coverage. When rioters in Detroit were asked what they had seen on television about race riots, 71 percent mentioned killings, shoot-outs, police brutality, arson, looting, rock throwing, fighting, screaming, and other violent acts. Yet President Lyndon B. Johnson's Special Advisory Commission on Civil Disorders (Kerner Commission) found that violent behavior constituted less than 5 percent of total television coverage of race riot incidents.[19]

Reprinted by permission: Tribune Media Services.

Media coverage of racial riots may let people know where police forces are deployed, permitting looters and arsonists to avoid those areas. Potential riot participants use news reports to learn where most of the action is so that they can join in the fray. In this manner the disturbance may be enlarged. During racial rioting in Detroit in 1967, live coverage of looting and shooting seemed to so arouse viewers that some who had never resorted to lawlessness took part in the violence.[20]

Wide publicity for heinous crimes (such as airline hijackings, poisoning of food supplies, or serial mass murders) may lead to "copycat crimes." Although rare, they spread terror and cause untold human suffering. This happened in the United States in 1982 after seven people were poisoned by cyanide-laced Tylenol tablets.[21]

Economic crises, too, can escalate as a result of media images. When prices on the financial markets plunged precipitously on October 19, 1987, media accounts used highly alarming language. *Panic, carnage, nightmare selling* were common descriptive terms. Moreover, the media frequently compared the crash to the 1929 stock market calamity and discussed the Great Depression that followed. Such gloomy news apparently fanned the growing panic and further weakened the markets.[22]

Planning Crisis Coverage

Because media play such a crucial role in keeping the polity going during crises, most media organizations have more or less formal plans to cope with crisis coverage problems. This is particularly true for electronic media. In one sample of seventy-two radio and television stations in twelve U.S. cities, 70 percent of the stations had plans for reporting natural disasters, and 73 percent had plans for reporting civil disturbances.[23] The plans generally were more detailed for natural disasters because needs are more predictable, and there is greater consensus about objectives. Nevertheless, much remains to be decided on the spur of the moment. Confusion inevitably reigns at the start of a crisis. After the Three Mile Island accident, for instance, it took three days before a communications center was established to coordinate the flow of messages.[24] In addition to media-sponsored plans, most stations are tied into the Federal Emergency Broadcasting System (EBS), a network for relaying news during a national emergency.

Crisis coverage planning has two aspects: preparing for the crisis and deciding how to present ongoing events. Plans to forestall crises are rare, probably because media focus on short-range happenings and predicting a crisis is difficult. Nonetheless, the media often have been blamed for neglecting preventive coverage. The Public's Right to Information Task Force of the President's Commission on the Accident at Three Mile Island blamed the Commonwealth Edison Company, the Nuclear Energy Commission, and the media for ignoring problems at the plant prior to the accident and for overemphasizing the safety of nuclear power.[25] In 1968 the Kerner Commission condemned the media for their silence about the plight of blacks in the United States. Ample early coverage, it claimed, might have prevented violence in the mid-1960s.

Most of the time it is difficult to argue the case for preventive coverage because there is disagreement about what social indicators herald a crisis. Besides, even if newspeople could accurately forecast an impending disaster, increased publicity might not prevent it. As we saw in Chapter 5, publicity does not necessarily produce behavioral changes, however easy and obviously beneficial they may be.

Coverage to prevent the government from involving the nation in dangerous hostilities, including war, raises several serious issues. We already have mentioned the willingness of major media to suppress advance publicity about the disastrous Bay of Pigs invasion in Cuba in 1961. Had the media published the story, the invasion might have been aborted. Alternatively, it might have taken place anyhow, but with greatly reduced chances for success and much heavier losses of human life. Would publication have been a patriotic or traitorous act? It is hard to tell.

In 1980 columnist Jack Anderson reported that an election-minded Carter administration was planning a military invasion of Iran to counteract the humiliation of the ongoing hostage crisis. The vast majority of papers that normally carry Anderson's column printed it. Most papers also printed government denials. One paper editorialized, "The reck-lessness of a politically motivated invasion would be far more dangerous than reckless journalism." [26] No major invasion ever took place. Wheth-er none was planned, contrary to Anderson's claim, or whether the column thwarted the plans was never clarified.

Natural Disasters. Rodney Kueneman and Joseph Wright, who examined the seventy-two radio and television stations' plans to cover natural disasters, found that the plans were generally predicated upon the assumption that people tend to panic and that coverage must be designed to forestall this. The management of 72 percent of the stations, particularly those that had previous experience with natural disasters, assumed that panic would occur. [27]

Preparation for predicted natural disasters may involve the publica-tion of news tracing the path of a storm or reporting geological studies that forecast the likelihood of earthquakes in an area. Official warnings and plans in case of disasters may be publicized along with information about protective measures that individuals can take. Stories that are graphic enough to arouse a lethargic population to prepare for the disas-ter, however, may cause panic or may be so scary that people shut them out of their minds. Such "ostrich" inclinations may explain why, despite frequent warnings about the danger of serious earthquakes in southern California, few residents have taken recommended precautions.

Civil Disorders. Interviewees at 83 percent of the stations in the Kueneman-Wright study assumed that broadcasts about civil distur-bances would produce a contagion effect so that more people would flock to the riot scene to commit violent acts. Broadcasters with previ-ous experience covering riots reported that "respected members of the community, who had jobs, who lived in pretty decent homes, joined the rioting and became looters and snipers because all of a sudden there was an unleashing of . . . hatred." [28] By contrast, social scientists who study disasters deny that panic and contagion occur frequently. [29] Whether or not they are correct, the important fact is that media personnel expect these reactions and act accordingly.

In Winston-Salem advance preparations for civil disturbances were made following race riots elsewhere. The 1965 riots in Watts had led many observers to conclude that rioting was started by outsiders who expected few penalties for law infractions. Therefore, the local papers in Winston-Salem, which were generally liberal on civil rights, decided to print stories pointing out that the city planned to treat rioters harshly. The preparatory stories also implied that rioters would most likely be outside agitators rather than local people. This type of publicity was intended to discourage would-be rioters by warning them that they faced stiff punishment. It also was intended to increase public support for harsh suppression of disturbances. If, as the mayor of Winston-Salem put it, rioting would be done by "thugs and hoodlums who see a chance to profit from looting," the local community would feel no sympathy for these offenders.

The Problem of News Suppression

In natural as well as manmade crises, suppressing news, either temporarily or permanently, raises major policy questions. How much coverage should be presented immediately, at the risk of telling an inaccurate story, spreading panic, and attracting bystanders and destructive participants, to the scene? What facts should be withheld initially or permanently? Eighty percent of the newspeople in the sample of radio and television stations mentioned earlier said that they would temporarily withhold information that might provoke troublesome reactions. Many would go further, indicating that they would withhold live coverage entirely, particularly in civil disturbances, because they believed that it would increase the intensity and duration of the crisis. Such a self-imposed blackout of live television and radio coverage occurred in Winston-Salem during the first day of rioting. The story was reported solely in the print media, making it less immediate and graphic. Similarly, in 1979 television networks avoided coverage of demonstrations involving Iranian students in the United States. It was feared that coverage would spur more disturbances, further straining tense U.S.-Iranian relations and endangering American citizens held hostage in Iran.

Some news outlets delay live coverage until officials have the situation under control. Others believe that suppression of live coverage will allow the spread of rumors that may be more inciting than judicious reporting of ongoing events. We do not know which of these views is most correct or how different circumstances affect reactions to media coverage of crises.

Deciding whether to suppress coverage becomes particularly difficult when a crisis involves terrorists, prison rioters, assassins of political leaders, or maniacal mass murderers who crave publicity. Granting exposure to them by live coverage glamorizes political violence and may encourage further outrages. "By transforming a killer into a celebrity, the press has not merely encouraged but perhaps driven him to strike again and may have stirred others brooding madly over their grievances to act." [30] As Rep. Edward Feighan, D-Ohio, pointed out after chairing congressional hearings on terrorism and the media, the television age poses new dilemmas for a responsible press. "Terrorism is a new form of symbolic warfare, and the television screen is the battlefield on which these wars will be fought in the future." [31]

Such accusations highlight the dilemma the press faces. Publicity does play into the hands of individuals willing to spread terror through indiscriminate killings and other abuses of the rights of fellow human beings. On the other hand, if the press fails to cover the terrorist acts, it can be accused of infringing on the public's right to know. It also forgoes publishing a dramatic event with wide audience appeal and substantial financial rewards. If the press follows the government's official line in describing terrorists and their motives, it becomes a government propaganda tool.[32] If it dwells on either the human strengths or the frightful human frailties of the violent actors, it will be accused of making saints out of villains or villains out of hapless victims of society's malfunctions.

Several rules for cautious reporting during crises have been widely adopted. For instance, television newspeople learned from filming the Watts uprising that they must keep their equipment inconspicuous. Consequently, when rioting broke out after the assassination of Martin Luther King, Jr., camera crews traveled to riot scenes in unmarked vehicles and kept camera equipment unobtrusive. They used available light rather than floodlights. The development of small videotape equipment that does not require floodlighting has helped immeasurably to keep coverage discreet.

Newspeople have also learned to avoid inflammatory details or language in their reports. For instance, editors in Winston-Salem instructed reporters in advance of the crisis to identify the troubled area precisely and to indicate that surrounding areas were quiet. This was intended to reduce the multiplication effect. Reporters were asked to keep details of the incident that led to the rioting to a minimum. Exaggerated language or unconfirmed reports of violence were to be avoided. The rule to follow was "When in doubt, leave out."

In the Winston-Salem case the media heeded these rules. The scope of rioting was minimized, for example, by reporting that "as the rioters moved through downtown last night, most of the city went about its business as usual. Many people probably never knew what was going on." [33] The riots were described as occurring "in connection with unrest created by the recent death," rather than *murder*, of a man "who died after injuries sustained when he resisted arrest and was hit," rather than *clubbed*, by a police officer. A detailed story of the incident was not published until several days after the rioting ended. Wire service copy, which was used in other cities, had said that the victim died "after he was blackjacked by a white policeman."

The Winston-Salem press largely avoided words such as *rioting mobs* or *murder* or racial designations. Photographs showed black and white law enforcement officials working together to quell the riots, assisted by both black and white citizens. They showed arrests of looters and confiscation of their loot. They did not predict future trouble or further threats nor run unconfirmed reports on dead and wounded and property damage. After the riots ended most newspeople and community leaders commended the press for handling the crisis as planned, with good results.

Nonetheless, muted coverage is problematic. It generally leads to presentation of the official story only and suppression of unofficial views. The perspectives of law enforcement officers, preoccupied with controlling crime, become paramount. In fact, stories are frequently cleared with the police before being published. As a result they stress peace-keeping aspects rather than the causes of violent behavior and the political and social changes that might prevent future violence.

In the Winston-Salem case the initial stories were not about blacks who supported the riots as a social protest against unfair treatment of their race by the white community. The media reports suppressed or failed to vent the feelings and ideas of militant black leaders. Instead, they concentrated on portraying blacks who supported the policies of the local governing elites. In the short run this helped keep the situation under control, but the long-run effects of carefully limited coverage are more troubling. In terrorist incidents or prison riots, failure to air the grievances of terrorists and prison inmates deprives them of a public forum for voicing their grievances. Their bottled up anger may lead to more violent explosions. Needed reforms may be aborted.

Some observers feel that muted reporting reduces the potential for arousing hatred and unbridgeable conflicts. Delayed coverage, they feel, can be more analytical and thus more likely to produce reforms. Others argue that the drama of an ongoing crisis raises public consciousness much better and faster than anything else. People will act to remedy injustice only if the situation is acute. If the heat of battle is already over, action may seem pointless. A permanent news blackout will make reforms highly unlikely. Those opposed to muted coverage or news suppression are willing to risk paying a very high price in lost lives, personal injuries, imprisonment, and property damage in hopes that immediate, complete coverage will shock the community to undertake basic social reforms. Most American political leaders, as well as most newspeople, have hitherto opted for muting violent conflict rather than bringing it to a head.

Finally, there is the unresolved philosophical question about the wisdom and propriety of news suppression in a free society. The true test of genuine press freedom does not come in times of calm. It comes in times of crisis when the costs of freedom may be dear, tempting government and media alike to impose silence. If a free press is a paramount value, then the die must be cast in favor of unrestrained crisis coverage, moderated only by the sense of responsibility of individual journalists.

Summary

In American political culture the normal feuds of politics are suspended when the nation is in danger. Although this unwritten rule is mentioned most often in connection with foreign policy, where "politics stops at the water's edge," it applies to the types of domestic crises discussed in this chapter. When life and property are endangered, when sudden death and terror reign, when well-known leaders are assassinated, or when the nation goes to war, people and their government pull together far more than in normal times. Although sensational media coverage has hindered government efforts to maintain calm in the past, the media today tend to abandon their adversarial role during crises. They become teammates of officialdom in attempts to restore public order, safety, and tranquility.

The media perform indispensable functions during crises: they diffuse vital information to the public and officials, interpret the meanings of events, and provide emotional support for troubled communities. Radio is particularly helpful in major disasters because its technical requirements are most adaptable to makeshift arrangements. It can broadcast without regular electric power supplies to people who have only a pocket transistor radio and are otherwise isolated.

Because the media play such a large part in public communication during crises, the manner in which they discharge their responsibilities has been of great concern to public officials and to the community at large. Information gaps, misinformation, and the dissemination of information that makes the effects of the crisis worse have led to demands that the information flow be controlled to better manage the crisis. Many media institutions have formal plans that temporarily set aside the usual criteria for publishing exciting news in the interest of calming the public.

Muted coverage, particularly during civil disturbances and incidents of political terrorism, may be unwise because it may drown out explicit and implicit messages about unmet societal needs. The need to plan for crisis coverage, however, is certain. Modern society faces crises of various sorts so frequently that policy makers in the media and in government would be remiss to make no plans for emergencies.

Notes

1. Wilbur Schramm, "Communications in Crisis," in *The Kennedy Assassination and the American Public: Social Communication in Crisis,* ed. Bradley S. Greenberg and Edwin B. Parker (Palo Alto, Calif.: Stanford University Press, 1965), 1-25.
2. David L. Paletz and Robert Dunn, "Press Coverage of Civil Disorder: A

Case Study of Winston-Salem, 1967," *Public Opinion Quarterly* 33 (Summer 1969): 329-345.

3. Tsiyona Peled and Elihu Katz, "Media Functions in Wartime: The Israel Home Front in October 1973," in *The Uses of Mass Communications: Current Perspectives on Gratifications Research,* ed. Jay G. Blumler and Elihu Katz (Beverly Hills, Calif.: Sage, 1974), 49-69.

4. The incidents are reported in Jerry J. Waxman, "Local Broadcast Gatekeeping During Natural Disasters," *Journalism Quarterly* 50 (Winter 1973): 751-758; and Russell R. Dynes, *Organized Behavior in Disaster* (Lexington, Mass.: Heath, 1970), 41-43, 88-89, 127-128.

5. Dennis E. Wenger, "A Few Empirical Observations Concerning the Relationship Between the Mass Media and Disaster Knowledge: A Research Report," in *Disaster and the Mass Media: Proceedings of the Committee on Disasters and the Mass Media Workshop* (Washington, D.C.: National Academy of Sciences, 1980), 242-244. For a discussion of news-gathering techniques during disasters, see Rahul Sood, Geoffrey Stockdale, and Everett M. Rogers, "How the News Media Operate in Natural Disasters," *Journal of Communication* 37 (Summer 1987): 27-41.

6. Daniel Yutzy, *Community Priorities at the Anchorage, Alaska Earthquake, 1964* (Columbus, Ohio: Ohio State University Disaster Research Center, 1969), 127.

7. Schramm, "Communication in Crisis," 1-25.

8. Walter Gantz, "The Diffusion of News About the Attempted Reagan Assassination," *Journal of Communication* 33 (Winter 1983): 56-65.

9. Mitchell Stephens and Nadyne G. Edison, "News Media Coverage of Issues During the Accident at Three-Mile Island," *Journalism Quarterly* 59 (Summer 1982): 199-204, 259.

10. Casey Bukro, "How Accurate Was Press About Three Mile Island?" *Chicago Tribune,* March 30, 1980.

11. T. Joseph Scanlon, "Media Coverage of Crises: Better than Reported, Worse than Necessary," *Journalism Quarterly* 55 (Spring 1978): 68-72.

12. Wenger, "A Few Empirical Observations," 252-253.

13. David L. Paletz and Robert M. Entman, *Media Power Politics* (New York: Free Press, 1981), 114-117.

14. Timothy W. Luke, "Chernobyl: The Packaging of Transnational Ecological Disaster," *Critical Studies in Mass Communication* 4 (December 1987): 357. See also Sharon M. Friedman, Carole M. Gorney, and Brenda P. Egolf, "Reporting on Radiation: A Content Analysis of Chernobyl Coverage," *Journal of Communication* 37 (Summer 1987): 58-79.

15. Deidre Carmody, "News Media Defended in Inquiry on Reports of Three Mile Island," *New York Times,* October 31, 1979; and Peter Sandman and Mary Paden, "At Three Mile Island," *Columbia Journalism Review* 17 (July/August 1979): 43-58.

16. Dynes, *Organized Behavior in Disaster,* 127-218.

17. Eleanor Singer and Phyllis Endreny, "Reporting Hazards: Their Benefits and Costs," *Journal of Communication* 37 (Summer 1987): 10-26.

18. Alex Jones, "U.S. Sees the Press Helping Hijackers," *New York Times,* June 20, 1985.

19. Benjamin D. Singer, "Mass Media and Communication Processes in the Detroit Riot of 1967," *Public Opinion Quarterly* 34 (Summer 1970): 238.

20. Ibid., 236-245.

21. For comparative analysis of the networks' television coverage of the case, see Dan Nimmo and James E. Combs, *Nightly Horrors: Crisis Coverage in*

Television Network News (Knoxville, Tenn.: The University of Tennessee Press, 1985), 179-198.

22. John Corry, "Network News Covers the Stock Market Frenzy," *New York Times,* October 21, 1987; and Alex Jones, "Caution in the Press: Was It Really a 'Crash'?" *New York Times,* October 21, 1987.
23. Rodney M. Kueneman and Joseph E. Wright, "News Policies of Broadcast Stations for Civil Disturbances and Disasters," *Journalism Quarterly* 52 (Winter 1975): 670-677.
24. David M. Rubin, "How the News Media Reported on Three Mile Island and Chernobyl," *Journal of Communication* 37 (Summer 1987): 47.
25. Sharon M. Friedman, "Blueprint for Breakdown: Three Mile Island and the Media Before the Accident," *Journal of Communication* 31 (Spring 1981): 116-128.
26. Douglas A. Anderson, "Handling of Controversial 'Merry-Go-Round' Columns," *Journalism Quarterly* 59 (Summer 1982): 295-298.
27. Kueneman and Wright, "News Policies," 671.
28. Ibid., 672.
29. See the report on the work of the Disaster Research Center at Ohio State University in E. L. Quarantelli and Russell R. Dynes, eds., "Organizational and Group Behavior in Disasters," *American Behavioral Scientist* 13 (January 1970): 325-456.
30. *New Yorker,* August 15, 1977, 21.
31. Edward F. Feighan, "After the Hostage Crisis, TV Focuses on Itself," *New York Times,* August 19, 1985.
32. Alex P. Schmid and Janny de Graaf, *Violence as Communication: Insurgent Terrorism and the Western News Media* (Beverly Hills, Calif.: Sage, 1982), 98. For an analysis of the symbiotic relationship of media and sources of crisis news, see Gadi Wolfsfeld, "Symbiosis of Press and Protest: An Exchange Analysis," *Journalism Quarterly* 61 (Autumn 1984): 550-555.
33. Quoted in Paletz and Dunn, "Press Coverage of Civil Disorder," 336.

Readings

Clarke, James W. *American Assassins: The Darker Side of Politics.* Princeton, N.J.: Princeton University Press, 1982.
Disasters and the Mass Media: Proceedings of the Committee on Disasters and the Mass Media Workshop. Washington, D.C.: National Academy of Sciences, 1980.
Greenberg, Bradley S., and Edwin B. Parker. *The Kennedy Assassination and the American Public: Social Communication in Crisis.* Palo Alto, Calif.: Stanford University Press, 1965.
Nimmo, Dan, and James E. Combs. *Nightly Horrors: Crisis Coverage in Television Network News.* Knoxville, Tenn.: University of Tennessee Press, 1985.
President's Commission on the Accident at Three Mile Island. *Report of the Public's Right to Information Task Force.* Washington, D.C.: U.S. Government Printing Office, October 1979.
Schmid, Alex P., and Janny de Graaf. *Violence as Communication: Insurgent Terrorism and the Western News Media.* Beverly Hills, Calif.: Sage, 1982.
Sood, Rahul, Everett M. Rogers, Geoffrey Stockdale, and Stephen Rafaeli. *Report on Government and Media Needs.* Washington, D.C.: Joint Information Center Project, Federal Emergency Management Agency, 1983.

CHAPTER 10

Foreign Affairs Coverage

On November 22, 1978, after eight years of acrimonious debate and many months of intensive negotiations in the United Nations Educational, Scientific and Cultural Organization (UNESCO), the United States and 145 other nations endorsed a Declaration on the Media. Article III, as is typical of public declarations, maps out huge responsibilities for the mass media. It states that "the mass media, by disseminating information on the aims, aspirations, cultures and needs of all people, contribute to eliminate ignorance and misunderstanding between peoples." The media also "make nationals of a country sensitive to the needs and desires of others," thereby ensuring "the respect of the rights and dignity of all nations, all peoples and all individuals." By drawing "attention to the great evils which afflict humanity, such as poverty, malnutrition and diseases," the media foster "the formulation by states of policies best able to promote the reduction of international tension and the peaceful and equitable settlement of international disputes." A tall order! Can, do and should American media fill it? How are they organized to do this job?

To throw light on such questions, we will discuss the overall significance that American media and American citizens assign to news about foreign countries. The types of foreign news most common in American media also will be examined. Foreign news gathering differs greatly from domestic reporting, so we will consider the qualifications of foreign correspondents and the unique problems they face. As a result of these problems, and because foreign news reflects American foreign policy interests and is designed to satisfy newsworthiness criteria, the American media often present a distorted world image. A number of examples and their consequences for U.S. foreign policy will be assessed. Finally, media performance will be evaluated in terms of UNESCO's high hopes for the press.

The Foreign News Slice in the News Pie

Newspeople commonly assume that the American public is highly ethnocentric, interested primarily in what goes on in the United States. Reports about the public's often astounding ignorance about foreign countries and foreign affairs lend credence to these assumptions. When asked, Americans themselves profess somewhat greater interest, professions unmatched by their news consumption habits.[1] When given a choice, they do not seek out foreign policy news. For example, when NBC News broadcast a prime-time, hour-long interview with Soviet leader Mikhail Gorbachev in December 1987, just prior to a U.S.-Soviet meeting designed to reduce the danger of war, only 15 percent of the national audience tuned in. Half of the viewers who at that time ordinarily watch NBC's entertainment programs switched to other networks. They preferred "Kate and Allie," "Frank's Place," and "The World's Greatest Stuntman" to listening to the leader of a superpower. Public opinion polls have repeatedly shown that two-thirds or more of the public is often unaware of important foreign news, even when the situation has received ample and prolonged coverage.

Although foreign news lacks attraction for many Americans, it receives a considerable amount of coverage, especially on network television. In noncrisis periods, foreign affairs stories average 11 percent of all stories in American newspapers and about 16 percent of the stories on national newscasts. Elite papers exceed these figures but not by much.[2] Compared with major domestic news stories, foreign news normally receives brief space and time and modest display. In addition, selection criteria are more rigorous. Foreign news must be more consequential, involve people of more exalted status, and entail more violence or disaster.[3] During crises, particularly prolonged ones that endanger American lives, coverage often doubles or even triples. Then foreign news may drown out most other news.

Although Americans' interest in foreign affairs is limited, it does ebb and flow with the shifting political currents. It was high during the Vietnam War, various Middle East crises in the 1970s and 1980s, and during President Richard Nixon's trip to China. It also peaked in 1979 when Iranian militants seized the U.S. Embassy in Teheran. It crested again in 1983 when the bombing of the U.S. Marine headquarters in Beirut, Lebanon, killed 241 American soldiers and later that year when U.S. troops landed on the tiny island of Grenada. The 1987 congressional hearings on U.S. weapons sales to Iran and on attempts to bargain for the release of hostages marked another high point in public attention to foreign policy. Even during periods when interest is at a low ebb, television has made more Americans than ever before aware of foreign news. It provides a "reality that lives on . . . in the memories of the millions who watched, rather than the few who were actually there." [4] Without television most people would have skipped such news if they encountered it in newspapers. Thus while exposure to foreign affairs information is massive, lack of interest still keeps learning at a relatively low level. [5]

When the spotlight shifts away from foreign news, the number of foreign correspondents usually declines. There were 637 accredited U.S. correspondents in South Vietnam in 1968. As American involvement in the war dwindled, the number dropped to 392 by 1970 and 295 by 1972. By mid-1974 only thirty-three remained. Even though this small corps of correspondents filed relatively few stories from Vietnam, editors often balked at running them in daily newscasts and papers because the public had presumably lost interest. When this happens, a spiral effect sets in. Presumed lack of interest leads to less coverage. Reduced coverage further lessens interest in foreign news. An upward spiral of domestic news takes up the slack. This pattern prevails in most of the country's newspapers and television newscasts whenever foreign crises subside.

Compared with average papers and newscasts, prestigious papers such as the *New York Times,* the *Washington Post,* and the *Los Angeles Times* provide fairly extensive, thorough, and steady foreign affairs coverage. The country's foreign policy elites, including government officials, depend heavily on these media, as a State Department official attests: "The first thing we do is read the newspaper—*the newspaper*—the *New York Times.* You can't work in the State Department without the *New York Times.*" [6] Members of the U.S. Congress, particularly those concerned with foreign affairs, and foreign officials in the United States have made similar comments. All feel that elite newspaper reports keep them informed faster and often better than their own official sources.

Making Foreign News

Although news making for domestic stories and for foreign stories differs substantially, there are many similarities. To make comparisons easier, our discussion of foreign news making will follow the organization of our discussion of domestic news making and news reporting in Chapter 3. First we will consider the gatekeepers—the corps of foreign correspondents who are the front-line echelon among gatherers of foreign affairs news. Then we will discuss in turn the setting for news selection, the criteria for choosing stories and the means of gathering them, the constraints on news production, and finally the effects of gatekeeping on foreign affairs coverage.

The Gatekeepers

Concentration of Control. A striking aspect of foreign news coverage is the extreme degree of concentration of the news-gathering process. Most foreign news for the American press is collected by only seven newspapers, the two wire services, and the three national television networks, along with an occasional story from syndicated columnists and news feature services. The papers are the *New York Times, Washington Post, Los Angeles Times, Baltimore Sun, Chicago Tribune, Wall Street Journal,* and *Christian Science Monitor.*[7] Most coverage comes from the wire services. They station reporters in nearly half of the countries of the world. North American and Western European countries are most likely to have resident reporters; Africa and the Eastern bloc are least likely to have them, a decidedly uneven distribution.[8] The wire services ferret out the stories that make up the pool from which other gatekeepers select complete reports or find leads to pursue stories more fully. Because wire service reporters work for a vast variety of clients throughout the world, their news must be bland so that it does not offend people whose views span a wide political spectrum. Wire service news therefore emphasizes fast and ample reports of ongoing events, not interpretation, which then falls to other foreign correspondents.

The stories gathered by this small corps of initial gatekeepers reach huge audiences. Newspaper syndicates, like the *New York Times* syndicate or the *Los Angeles Times-Washington Post* feature service, are able to frame foreign news for hundreds of papers in the United States and abroad.[9] Although subscribers generally use only a limited portion of the coverage made available by these sources, what they do use mirrors the story patterns and interpretation of the syndicates. For instance, when the *New York Times* labeled a 1958 Soviet note to Great Britain, France, and the United States as an "ultimatum," the American press followed the lead, even though the facts were questionable, and some papers had originally adopted more benign interpretations.[10] As Barry Rubin points out, "Once the main stories of the day have been identified and defined, the media can be like a stampeding herd, hard to turn toward a new interpretation of an issue." The stories chosen set the scene for follow-up stories. "The news of today sequels the news in the news of yesterday. Only a relatively small number of journalists are able or allowed to open up new areas of concern."[11] Stereotypes become fixed; countries and leaders whom gatekeepers depict as friendly or antagonistic to the United States may be characterized that way long after the reality has changed.

Surveillance of the Foreign Scene. In 1975, 676 full-time overseas correspondents served the American media, including 429 Americans and 247 foreigners. Six years earlier there had been 929 foreign correspondents, including 563 Americans and 366 foreigners. Between 1969 and 1975 the foreign correspondent corps declined by 27 percent.[12] Several reasons account for this. The winding down of the Vietnam War is one. The ability to dispatch correspondents quickly from an American home base to foreign countries is another. Air travel has made it possible for each American correspondent to reach and cover many more countries than ever before. But physical mobility is not matched by the psychic mobility that would allow reporters to feel at home in more countries. Nor is it accompanied by sudden spurts in knowledge that would permit reporters to cover a new area with insight.

High costs also have forced a steady decline in the number of foreign correspondents. In the 1980s it cost up to $200,000 a year to keep one correspondent abroad, a steep price considering the limited demand for foreign affairs stories. Because it is much cheaper, many papers use stringers instead of regular employees and rely on reports produced by local foreign news media. Stringers, usually citizens of the country from which they report, are paid for each story they produce.[13] At best, they may have keener insight into local problems than American reporters sent to the country. But, like the reports gleaned from local news media, they often fail to meet the news-gathering standards prized by American media, and they may be unable to tailor news stories to the needs of American audiences.[14]

U.S. correspondents abroad are unevenly distributed. More are stationed in friendly locations than in neutral or hostile ones. Table 10-1 depicts the regions in which American foreign correspondents were stationed in 1975, the latest year for which accurate figures are available. While numbers have fluctuated from year to year, the proportions have remained fairly constant for regional distributions as well as locations in particular countries. In 1975, for example, two-thirds of the Middle East correspondents were stationed in Israel and Lebanon. Correspondents accredited to Western Hemisphere countries served primarily in Canada, Brazil, and Argentina. Asian correspondents were concentrated in Hong Kong, Japan, and Australia. Africa was the most understaffed, with full-time reporters in only four countries. Their reports, however, were supplemented through news from Reuters and Agence France-Presse, the British and French news agencies respectively, which had more ample representation in Africa. With fewer foreign correspondents, the number of countries in which journalists were stationed narrowed as well. It dropped from sixty-four in 1972 to fifty-four in 1975.

What kinds of people are these journalists who select the foreign

Table 10-1   Distribution of Foreign Correspondents (in percentages)

Countries	American correspondents abroad	Foreign correspondents in United States
Western Europe	51	46
Central/East Asia	23	22
Latin America	15	10
Middle East/North Africa	8	6
Africa	5	1
Eastern Europe/USSR	3	5
Australia/New Zealand	2	3
Canada	1	3
Other/international agencies	—	4

Source: For U.S. data, John A. Lent, "Foreign News in American Media," *Journal of Communication* 27 (Winter 1977): 49; for foreign data, *Editor and Publisher International Yearbook,* 1987 (New York: Editor & Publisher, 1987), 46-56.

Note: Foreigners are listed by country of origin. Figures add to more than 100 percent because some correspondents cover more than one area. $N = 676$ for American correspondents abroad, 1,278 for foreign correspondents in the United States.

news for American elites and publics? What are their biases? And how do they compare with the correspondents who cover the United States for the benefit of foreign nationals?

A typical American journalist abroad is a white male in his forties, college educated, with more than ten years of reporting news under his belt. Many have remained at the same locations for several years, so that they are fully familiar with them.[15] As Table 10-2 shows, however, this does not necessarily mean language competence. More than 80 percent of American reporters stationed in Western Europe and Latin America read and speak the native languages fluently or with easy facility. But in Eastern Europe and Africa, these figures are cut in half. The poorest showing is in Central and East Asia, where only 9 percent of American reporters are able to read the intricate written characters, and only 18 percent can speak the languages well. Deficient reading skills hamper American reporters in local interviews and investigations. They must depend on translated newspaper reports and on handouts to the foreign press. This sharply curbs their effectiveness as reporters. In the Soviet Union, for instance, the translators are supplied and controlled by the Secret Service (KGB). Their presence during interviews is sure to dampen the free exchange of ideas that might otherwise take place.

Contacts with local people and personal ties that may supply good insights are also sparse. In Western Europe 33 percent of the correspon-

Table 10-2 Foreign Language Fluency of American Reporters (in percentages)

Fluency	Western Europe		Latin America		Asia		East Europe, Africa, Middle East	
	Read	*Speak*	*Read*	*Speak*	*Read*	*Speak*	*Read*	*Speak*
Native fluency	62	51	70	56	3	6	21	20
Easy facility	23	31	19	30	6	12	17	28
Partial	10	16	11	14	23	33	28	32
Slight	3	2	—	—	3	15	10	8
None	1	—	—	—	65	33	24	12

Source: Adapted from Leo Bogart, "The Overseas Newsman: A 1967 Profile Study," *Journalism Quarterly* 45 (Summer 1968): 300.

Note: N = 174. The question was: [If English is not the local language] "How familiar are you with the language spoken in the country in which you are stationed?"

dents say that most of their close friendships and social contacts are with nationals of the country. This is true for only 23 percent in Latin America, 16 percent in Eastern Europe, and 15 percent in Central and East Asia.[16] Although these figures double when more casual contacts are included, they still suggest that foreign correspondents are poorly integrated into the local setting.

By their own identification 54 percent of American foreign correspondents lean to the left in their politics, 32 percent are middle-roaders, and 14 percent lean to the right. These figures closely parallel those for staff people generally in prominent American news organizations (see Chapter 2). When the views of media people in prominent news organizations are compared with the views of business leaders, the gap is vast. For instance, on the question of whether American exploitation adds to Third World poverty, 55 percent of the media people said yes, compared with 22 percent of the business people.[17]

Table 10-3 shows how newspeople from various elite media answered this question. Political orientations among people affiliated with different news organizations obviously vary considerably. Reports on general trends mask these differences. For instance, the fact that an average of 49 percent of people in all the print media in the sample take the liberal stance (that is, agree that the United States adds to Third World poverty), compared with an average of 64 percent in the television media, masks the fact that *New York Times* personnel have a more liberal score than do CBS or NBC personnel.

Public relations agencies hired by foreign countries to promote

Table 10-3   Agree/Disagree on "U.S. Adds to Third World Poverty"
(in percentages)

Media institutions	Agree	Disagree
Print		
New York Times	61	39
Washington Post	61	39
Wall Street Journal	33	67
Newsweek	56	44
Time	35	65
U.S. News & World Report	28	72
Television		
ABC	64	36
CBS	45	55
NBC	57	43
PBS	83	17

Source: S. Robert Lichter, "America and the Third World: A Survey of Leading Media and Business Leaders," in *Television Coverage of International Affairs,* ed. William C. Adams (Norwood, N.J.: Ablex, 1982), 75. Reprinted by permission.

Note: N = 234. The statement was: "American economic exploitation has contributed to Third World poverty."

their images provide one very important, usually overlooked, source of news about foreign countries. Steadily growing numbers of countries are contracting for professional image management. By either stimulating or suppressing media coverage, public relations agencies can improve a country's media image. Presumably this then affects elite and mass opinion so that the country in question enjoys improved relations with American politicians and the American public.[18]

Surveillance of the American Scene. Altogether, 1,278 correspondents from foreign countries covered the United States in 1987. As Table 10-1 shows, most of them came from nations friendly to the United States. Just as Americans receive most news about friendly foreign countries, so most news about America goes to her friends.[19] The foreign journalists stationed in the United States represent various regions and countries unevenly. In 1987 the foreign press corps included five correspondents from black Africa. Israel was represented by twenty-seven correspondents, the Arab countries of the Middle East quadrupled their representation over the previous fifteen years to fifty-two. Taiwan in 1987 had eighteen registered correspondents, while the People's Republic of China, a newcomer to the foreign correspondent corps, had thirty-two. India was represented by nine newspeople, Pakistan by six. Canada's media sent forty-one, compared with nine from Mexico, the other next-door neighbor of the United States. With the exception of Argentina and Brazil, few Latin American countries had correspondents stationed in the United States.

Foreign reporters are an extremely well-educated group. Nine out of ten are university trained, and 22 percent have earned a doctorate. Seventy-eight percent are fluent English speakers, and a majority are fluent in a third language as well. In 1982 about half had advanced degrees, and 13 percent had Ph.D.s. On the average, they spoke three languages. Nevertheless, close contacts with Americans were limited. Only 7 percent said that their best and closest contacts were Americans. In political orientation, foreign newspeople covering the United States were further to the left than most American reporters. Seventy percent claimed to be left-leaning, 14 percent preferred a middle position, and 17 percent leaned to the right.[20]

It is difficult for foreign reporters to cover the whole United States adequately. Most correspondents are kept busy in Washington and New York. They rarely travel to other parts of the country, except to cover special events such as major sports competitions or presidential nominating conventions. Thus the impressions that foreigners receive about Americans' opinions and politics are largely the views of official Washington. The leftward orientation of most reporters from foreign countries produces a substantial amount of criticism of America's economic, military, and foreign aid policies and often makes the conduct of foreign relations rocky. Hostile coverage is only partially balanced by the influx of news from American media and government broadcasts, such as Voice of America or WORLDNET, a satellite program sponsored by the U.S. Information Service. WORLDNET enables reporters in foreign capitals to interview directly top administration officials.

The Setting for News Selection

Cultural Pressures. American correspondents abroad, like domestic journalists, must operate within the context of American politics and American political culture. Although their personal leanings may be to the left of the political spectrum, they aim for the middle ground in their stories because that is what their audiences presumably want. Keeping in touch with the American scene is deemed so important that news organizations bring their reporters back to the United States periodically to refresh their feel for what is going on at home.

Stories not only must reflect the American value structure, but they also must conform to established American stereotypes. Accordingly, stories by U.S. correspondents in Peru about the military government's reforms were rejected as lies because they contradicted the stereotype that military regimes support the status quo.[21] Similarly, the credibility of stories about the problems of Peruvian youth might be questioned unless these same problems were plaguing American youth.[22] On the other hand, U.S. correspondents abroad have greater leeway than their domestic counterparts to evaluate and interpret news because there is less likelihood that the domestic audience—ordinary citizens or powerful interest groups—will be offended.

Intra-organizational norms and pressures also influence news selection. The news is gathered by a small enough group of reporters so that personal contacts and cooperation are common. The wire services perform the initial gatekeeping tasks for most newspapers and electronic media. Elite papers then fashion the norms for presentation and interpretation that editors and reporters throughout the country adapt for their media.

Political Pressures. Overt and covert political pressures to publish or suppress news stories play a greater role in foreign news production than on the domestic scene. As guests in the countries from which they are reporting, foreign correspondents often must do their hosts' bidding. Many of these hosts are dictators who safeguard their political survival by ensuring supportive publicity for their regimes and squelching unfavorable coverage. Foreign correspondents, like native newspeople, are heavily censored. If foreign correspondents want to remain in the country, they must write dispatches acceptable to the authorities. Otherwise they face severe penalties—expulsion, confiscation of their notes and pictures, closure of transmission facilities, refusal of contact by public officials, and the like. This has led to a strange phenomenon: the most undemocratic countries often receive the least criticism while more open societies are freely reproached.

Censorship can take the form of denying visas to bar entry to the country or restrictions on travel within the country. Scores of countries have barred foreign reporters from entering or have expelled them after entry. Cambodia, Laos, Vietnam, Nicaragua, El Salvador, the Soviet Union, and the Union of South Africa provide vivid recent examples. Reporters from Soviet bloc countries are barred from travel in many parts of the United States and cannot attend State Department news briefings unless specifically authorized. When the Chinese city of Tangshan was destroyed by an earthquake on July 28, 1976, and more than 655,000 people were killed, reporters stationed in Peking, barely one hundred miles away, were denied permission for more than a year to visit the scene.[23] Britain kept foreign reporters away from the embattled Falkland Islands in 1983. Israel repeatedly has imposed tight censorship on coverage of its activities in Lebanon and in the occupied West Bank and Gaza Strip. During the Iran-Iraq hostilities in the early 1980s, reporters were permitted at the front only whenever the host country thought it had won an engagement. Large areas of Central America have been closed to reporters, making it almost impossible to adequately cover hostilities there. South Africa has made it illegal to quote "banned" people, describe prison conditions, or film protest demonstrations.[24] In the Soviet Union reporters who interview dissidents are harassed.

Bureaucratic hurdles abound. In Moscow television reporters depend on the Novosti Press Agency for camera crews and access to various sites. Cameras are made available only after the Foreign Ministry's Press Department approves a story proposal. Once a proposal has been filed, no deviations are allowed. Promised camera crews frequently arrive late or not at all. Pictures often are deliberately out of focus, and transmission equipment may be disconnected if events do not proceed as planned.

Reporters in some countries face physical danger. Not infrequently, they have been jailed, assaulted, and sometimes murdered. During the Nicaraguan revolution of 1979, a national guardsman, angry over American support of revolutionary forces, shot and killed an American television reporter. Several murders of newspeople in Lebanon in the 1980s have been attributed to Syrian authorities angered by stories these journalists wrote.[25] The Helsinki Accords of 1975, in which many countries promised free and safe access to each other's newspeople, have done little to improve the situation.

When countries previously closed to foreign journalists suddenly open their borders, the newcomers may be totally unprepared for insightful coverage. The opening of the People's Republic of China in 1972 is an example. Reporters arrived with President Richard Nixon and Secretary of State Henry Kissinger. During their short stay in China, the reporters dutifully shot those pictures that the Chinese allowed them to shoot and reported those stories that the Chinese arranged for them to report. The resulting coverage was a romanticized travelogue rather than solid political analysis.

Media Diplomacy. A recent development in foreign news production is "television diplomacy"—attempts by television correspondents in the United States and abroad to inject themselves directly into the political process and attempts by U.S. and foreign leaders to use television to further their causes. The Middle East situation presents a number of dramatic examples. CBS anchorman Walter Cronkite became a peacemaker on November 14, 1977, during a television satellite interview. At that time he drew from Egypt's president Anwar el Sadat a public promise to go to Jerusalem if this would further peace. In a separate interview Cronkite secured a pledge from Israeli prime minister Menachem Begin that he would personally welcome Sadat at Ben Gurion airport, should he come. With such mutual commitments, the scene was set for the historic meeting.

When Sadat arrived in Israel on November 19, anchorpersons from the three American networks were in his entourage. Among the welcoming crowds at the airport were an additional two thousand journalists from all over the globe. Again this was media diplomacy in the broadest sense. The event was covered live on American television and radio, giving the principals a chance to woo American audiences. In the weeks that followed, more than 30 million Americans and millions worldwide watched and judged the peacemaking process. Television alone devoted twenty-four hours of broadcasts to the spectacle, supplemented by radio and print news.

When Arab-Israeli peacemaking moved to the United States the following spring, media diplomacy continued. President Sadat, fully aware of the importance of courting the American public, made himself available for a television interview immediately after arrival for the 1978 Camp David meeting. The next day in his address to the National Press Club, he accused the Israelis of stalling the negotiations. Israel countered this propaganda move by promptly dispatching Foreign Minister Moshe Dayan on a ten-day speaking tour of major American cities to garner favorable publicity for the Israeli side.[26] The media reported it all with relish, proud of the role they had played in bringing about encounters between Israeli and Egyptian officials. Little thought was given to the political ramifications that ensue when foreign heads of state readily use the American press as their public relations tool.

The lessons learned by Sadat and Begin have not been lost on other world leaders. For instance, in 1979 Iran's revolutionary leader, Ayatollah Ruhollah Khomeini, rebuffed official emissaries from the United States who were sent to negotiate the release of the American embassy personnel held hostage by Iranian students. Khomeini preferred to discuss the situation with American television correspondents. A series of interviews was arranged. By requiring prior approval of questions, the Iranian government carefully controlled what was discussed. To ensure maximum exposure for the Ayatollah's views, Iranian leaders permitted an especially lengthy interview for the highly popular CBS program "60 Minutes." At the same time they assigned low priority to an interview to be aired on low-audience public television. The Iranian embassy also bought full-page advertisements in the *New York Times* and other American newspapers to acquaint the American public with Iran's version of the hostage story.

For their part, reporters used interviews with Iranian officials to suggest policies that might resolve the crisis and to elicit Iranian views and counterproposals. Placing these views before a worldwide audience made them part of the agenda of international politics. Media diplomacy facilitated negotiations that had broken down at the diplomatic level and generated a number of excellent proposals. Even when normal diplomatic relations exist, reporters often become part of the political process by publicizing interviews with political leaders in which the reporters determine and frame the issues to be discussed.

While media diplomacy is often helpful, it also is fraught with disadvantages and dangers. Government officials, who have far more foreign policy expertise than journalists, may be maneuvered into untenable positions. Foreign policy then may become incoherent and inexpert, with serious consequences for the nation. Another disadvantage of media diplomacy is that journalists may inadvertently provide a propaganda forum for foreign leaders. For example, lengthy interviews on American television in December 1987 enabled Soviet leader Mikhail Gorbachev to appeal to the 9 million Americans who watched him "The intended image was that of a man who poses no threat to American interests, a realist with whom one can do business, but a man who has no intention of being pushed around, especially on such domestic issues as human rights." [27]

Broadcasts about the U.S.-Soviet summit meeting constituted 60 percent of the news on the major networks between November 30 and December 10. Secretary Gorbachev's views received more airtime and more favorable commentary than did President Reagan's positions. Simultaneously, the media increased favorable commentary about an arms reduction treaty that was expected to ensue from the meetings of Reagan and Gorbachev. The influential *Washington Post*, which had split its coverage of the treaty evenly between supporters and opponents, gave comments by proponents a 12-to-1 edge in November and December.[28] Such extensive coverage was bound to affect the political climate in which the negotiations took place.

Economic Pressures. Economic considerations, like cultural and political factors, strongly influence foreign news selection. First, there is the usual pressure to present appealing stories that attract big audiences and keep the media profitable. This pressure is even more burdensome for foreign correspondents than for their domestic counterparts because their stories must be exceptionally good to attract large audiences. Second, there is the pressure to avoid or minimize huge production costs. Reporting events such as President Nixon's trip to China or Israel's Yom Kippur War cost each network in excess of $3 million per event. Leasing cables for news transmission is expensive and so is telephone communication. Satellite transmission is also costly, especially for short messages. Some stories therefore may be shut out because they cannot be transmitted cheaply, while others may be included merely because transmission is comparatively inexpensive and convenient.

DIPLOMACY IN THE 1980's

Reprinted by permission: Tribune Media Services.

Gathering the News: The Beat

The international beat system is quite similar to local beats. Originally, newspapers established their foreign news bureaus in major capitals of the world, primarily in Western Europe. From there correspondents covered entire countries rather than particular types of stories; London, Paris, Bonn, and Rome were the main news-gathering spots. In the wake of the Vietnam War, Saigon, Tokyo, Hong Kong, and other Far Eastern points became important news centers. China moved into focus with the opening of diplomatic relations in 1972.

The average newspaper bureau abroad has one or two correspondents, one or two film crews staffed by foreigners, perhaps a radio correspondent, and a few stringers. Correspondents from these bureaus jet to spots within easy flying range whenever big stories break. For local news they rely heavily on national news services that exist in two-thirds of the countries of the world. Countries without such services, and without satellite transmission facilities, are far less likely to receive coverage than countries that have them.

The major Western wire services and the three American television networks have overseas news bureaus in the main news centers of the world. However, for nonvisual news the networks rely heavily on wire and newspaper services. Seventy to 80 percent of foreign news copy read on the air comes directly from the wire services.[29] In this way "the major international news agencies and elite newspapers set the agenda for international affairs coverage by other media, including U.S. network television." [30]

The bulk of foreign affairs news for American media actually originates in Washington from various beats in the executive branch. The president's views tend to dominate whenever situations are controversial. However, the media put their imprint on the news by featuring confrontational and hard-line views.[31] At times foreign policy stories may be hard to get because officials are reluctant to talk whenever delicate negotiations or the prestige of the United States are at stake. A further common drawback to Washington stories is their lack of exciting pictures to dramatize them for television. Like domestic newspeople, foreign correspondents prefer to report predictable events, such as elections or summit conferences, so that coverage can be planned well in advance. The decision to film particular foreign stories abroad is usually made in the United States because the media's home offices consider themselves in closer touch with the interests of American audiences. Foreign bureaus do the actual filming.

Foreign news bestows unequal attention on various countries just as domestic news covers regions of the United States unequally. Neither is there any correlation between size of population and amount of coverage.[32] In general, beats cover America's closest political allies and major Communist countries. Specifically, this means England, France, West Germany, Italy, and the Soviet Union in Europe; Israel and Egypt in the Middle East; and, more recently, the People's Republic of China and Japan in the Far East. Africa and Latin America are lightly covered, except when Americans become concerned about humanitarian issues, like the treatment of blacks in the Union of South Africa, or civil strife involving charges of Communist influence, like the situation in Nicaragua in the 1980s. Asian coverage was light until the Vietnam War, when for several years it replaced stories from other parts of the world. Table 10-4 provides data on coverage of major regions of the world during two four-year periods, 1972-1975 and 1976-1979. It demonstrates the consistently heavy emphasis on Western Europe and the shifting focus of attention depending on the world's patterns of war and unrest.[33]

Criteria for Choosing Stories

Foreign like domestic news is selected primarily for audience appeal rather than for political significance. This means that stories must have an angle that interests Americans. Sociologist Herbert Gans, who exam-

Table 10-4   Network Coverage of Major Regions, 1972-1975 and
1976-1979 (in percentages)

Region	1972-1975	1976-1979
Eastern Europe and USSR	16	19
Western Europe	30	30
Middle East	20	30
Africa (Sub-Sahara)	2	13
South Asia	2	2
Southeast Asia and Pacific	34	9
East Asia	10	12
Latin America	7	14
Canada	2	4

Source: James F. Larson, "International Affairs Coverage on U.S. Evening Network
News, 1972-1979," in *Television Coverage of International Affairs,* ed. William C. Adams
(Norwood, N.J.: Ablex, 1982), 37. Reprinted by permission.

Note: Measured by the percentage of sampled stories in which one or more nations from
the region are mentioned. Percentages sum to more than 100 percent. $N = 2,680$ for 1972-
1975, 2,798 for 1976-1979.

ined foreign affairs news in television newscasts and in news magazines,
has identified seven subjects that are aired most often.[34] They include,
first, American activities in foreign countries, particularly when presidents and secretaries of state visit, and, second, events that affect
Americans directly in a major way (wars, oil embargoes, and other
problems that transcend national boundaries, like unemployment and
inflation).

A third area of interest concerns relations of the United States with
Communist countries. Internal political and military problems of these
countries are emphasized. Elections in non-Communist countries with
strong Communist parties, such as those in France and Italy, are also
part of the routine coverage of the "Communist menace." Fourth,
foreign elections in other parts of the world are covered if they involve a
change in the head of state. There also is a sentimental attachment for
following the major activities of European royalty.

The fifth subject area entails stories about dramatic political conflicts. Most wars, coups d'état, and revolutions are reported; protests, as
a rule, are covered only when they are violent. Left-wing coups receive
more attention than right-wing coups. Disasters, if they involve massive
loss of lives and destruction of property, are a sixth area of interest.
There is a rough calculus by which severity is measured: "10,000 deaths
in Nepal equals 100 deaths in Wales equals 10 deaths in West Virginia
equals one death next door." [35] In general, the more distant a nation, the
more frequently a newsworthy event must happen to be reported.

The seventh area of coverage involves the excesses of foreign dictators, particularly brutality against political dissidents (for example, the deeds of Uganda's former ruler Idi Amin and the leaders of Latin American death squads). Noticeably absent from American broadcasts and papers are stories about ordinary people and ordinary events abroad. These would be news to Americans, but, except for occasional special features, they are not *news* in the professional dictionary of journalists.

Foreign news stories also must have an appealing format. Emphasis on violence, conflict and disaster, timeliness or novelty, and familiarity of persons or situation are the major selection criteria. For instance, stories from Western Europe and other familiar areas are more likely to be published than stories from other parts of the world. When news from countries with unfamiliar cultures is published, the rule of "uncertainty absorption" comes into play. This unwritten rule requires that gatekeepers avoid foreign news of uncertain accuracy, coming from remote sources. Only plausible stories are acceptable, and they must be cast into a familiar framework, such as the battle against communism or the moral bankruptcy of military dictators.[36] Such biases make it very difficult to change images of culturally distant countries. Far-off parts of the world are rarely covered except when sensational events such as violence and disaster occur or there is negative news about top-level public officials.[37] Moreover, the high costs of covering news abroad force news organizations to limit the sites where they can maintain full-scale news operations.

The media's preference for news about current happenings has led to concentration on rapidly breaking stories in accessible places, regardless of their intrinsic importance. Long-range developments, such as programs to improve public health or reduce illiteracy or efforts to create new political parties, do not fill the bill if they lack a recent climax. Pressure for timeliness and novelty also fragments news presentation and usually precludes follow-through. This gives major events an unwarranted air of suddenness and unpredictability. They have neither a past nor a future—merely a brief presence in the parade of current events.

For example, when war-torn El Salvador held an election in March 1982, the press was there in full force, grinding out stories day after day. Coverage dwindled abruptly after the election, even though little had changed in El Salvador, and the Reagan administration continued to claim that the United States had important interests in that country. Most American media failed to explain the consequences of the election. When questioned about the exodus of newspeople, news executives said that other crises and events beckoned: the Falkland Islands War, fighting in Lebanon, and the foreign journeys of President Ronald Reagan and Pope John Paul II.[38]

At times coverage errs in the opposite direction. The story of Americans held hostage in Iran from November 4, 1979, to January 20, 1981, was vastly overcovered. Daily broadcasts featured dramatic visual scenes of young Americans held captive in a strange land, angry anti-American crowds, and anxious kinfolk at home. During the first six months of the crisis, nearly one-third of each nightly network newscast was devoted to the story.[39] With media attention riveted on developments in Iran, most other foreign news was slighted.

News Production Constraints

The problems of producing domestic news are magnified for foreign news making. Staffs are smaller, research facilities are more limited, language barriers are troublesome, and transmission difficulties may be enormous. Then, once the story finally reaches the audience, it may not be heard because of basic disinterest or ignorance of the setting in which it originated.

Production constraints are particularly severe for television news, which presents the bulk of foreign news to the average American. The quest for good pictures is often frustrated by restrictions on access or because facilities for taking and processing pictures are inadequate.[40] Pictures are especially important for foreign news because they bring unfamiliar sights, which might be hard to imagine, directly into viewers' homes. Starvation in India or Nicaragua, the lifestyles of primitive tribes in New Guinea or Australia, or street riots in Spain or Hungary are better understood if they can be visually experienced.

However, not even words and pictures combined can tell the whole story if the audience is unfamiliar with the setting in which the reported events are happening. Grisly street scenes of Israeli soldiers chasing and beating Palestinian protesters, rock-throwing youngsters confronted by armed Israelis, and overturned and burning vehicles created the image in 1988 of a brutal military and a country in the throes of an ugly civil war. These pictures profoundly affected the attitude of the American public, including the Congress, toward Israel. The sharp drop-off in affection resembled that suffered by Israel in the wake of reports about Israeli brutalities in Lebanon in the summer of 1982. Israeli pleas that the country's image was being distorted were of little avail. Most Americans were unaware that the riots were confined to a small section of the country. They failed to put Israeli reactions into the appropriate historical perspectives.[41] When gripping visuals constitute high drama, sans information, their impact can be overwhelming.

The need to keep news stories brief is particularly troubling for foreign correspondents because foreign news is often unintelligible without adequate background information or interpretation. Complexity therefore becomes a major enemy, and avoidance or oversimplification the defensive strategy. Stories must be written simply and logically even if the situation defies logic. Usually a single theme must be selected to epitomize the entire complex story.

The dominant theme of the Iran hostage stories was that innocent Americans were imprisoned by irrational anti-American terrorists—a gross oversimplification of a multifaceted situation. The complexities of Iran's internal politics received little attention because they could not be easily incorporated into a dramatic, visually appealing story. David Altheide, who studied coverage of the crisis, concluded that the reporting

> was consistent with criteria of production formats involving resolutions of practical concerns like accessibility, visual quality, drama and action, audience relevance, and encapsulation and thematic unity. The employment of these format considerations made newswork more predictable and manageable, but it also permitted the selection of themes resonant with cultural stereotypes and images already familiar to the journalists. In this way, cultural stereotypes, including political and ideological value judgments, found their way into news content.[42]

Effects of Gatekeeping

Foreign affairs coverage is ample, dramatic, and up to date, but it lacks depth and breadth, it stereotypes and oversimplifies, and it often distorts facts in the interest of timeliness. Accordingly, a twelve-year study of international terrorism stories led to the conclusion that "network coverage bore little relationship to actual patterns of occurrence. On the whole, the limitations of production and presentation, concerns over audience share, and the narrow focus of journalistic notions of professionalism result in coverage more notable for its erratic nature than for its systematic biases."[43] Officials and publics who rely on foreign affairs news may be misled, and faulty policies may ensue. The stories that preceded U.S. intervention in the Dominican Republic in 1965 are indicative of the dangers inherent in news practices today.

The Dominican Republic Case. When dispatches reached the United States in late April and early May 1965 that a military coup was in progress in the Dominican Republic, American correspondents were hastily sent to the scene. Upon arrival they were not allowed by Dominican Republic authorities to visit the cities and countryside because of the fighting. Instead, they received a briefing from the American ambassador based on secondhand information. Because of pressure to meet the earliest publication deadlines, stories were sent out before they could be verified. Since they had come from an authentic source—the American ambassador—no disclaimers were made.

The *Los Angeles Herald Examiner* reported on April 30 that Cuban Communists had arranged the insurrection and that the loss of life was horrifying. "There are about 2,000 casualties, and about half of them are dead. In one street alone, there were at least 90 people dead or dying. There are children dying on the streets with their stomachs ripped open, and nobody to bury their bodies. It is carnage. It is real civil war. The streets are almost literally running with blood." [44] One week later, on May 7, *Time* magazine still reported that "no one had an accurate count of casualties as frenzied knots of soldiers and civilians roamed the streets, shooting, looting and herding people to their execution. . . . The rebels executed at least 110 opponents, hacked the head off a police officer and carried it about as a trophy." *U.S. News & World Report* on May 10 spoke of victims being "dragged from their homes and shot down while angry mobs shouted, 'To the wall!' the same cry that marked mass executions in Cuba in the early days of Fidel Castro." [45]

On the basis of such reports, President Lyndon B. Johnson, with the approval of the Organization of American States, sent more than one thousand marines to the Dominican Republic to quell the rebellion, stop the bloodshed, and halt the march of communism. When the correspondents were finally allowed to visit the cities and countryside, they discovered that none of the horror stories that they had reported had been true. Instead of the more than one thousand bodies that, according to President Johnson, had made the intervention imperative, there were fewer than a dozen. There was neither looting nor display of severed heads. Only a small number of the forces seeking to overthrow the established government were Communists. But by that time it was too late to undo the severe political damage that the American intervention had done to the Dominican Republic and to the reputation of the United States.

The Lebanon Invasion. Similarly, Israel claimed that much of the news about Israel's invasion of Lebanon in 1982 was distorted because it came from biased sources that were not adequately verified by the networks. [46] NBC anchorman Roger Mudd said that ten thousand civilians had died, attributing the figure to the Lebanese Red Crescent, a Red Cross relief organization. Casting doubt on these figures, Israeli sources alleged that the brother of Yasir Arafat, the leader of the Palestine Liberation Organization (PLO), was the head of the Red Crescent at the time that organization released its figures. Israeli sources acknowledged 460 civilian deaths. NBC correspondent Jessica Savitch reported that fighting had left six hundred thousand civilians without food and other essential supplies, a figure larger than the total population of the area, according to Israeli sources. These sources claimed that twenty thousand civilians had been displaced.

Failure to present background information was another source of potentially serious misperceptions. NBC correspondents, for example, showed film of ruined buildings and described them as civilian targets. NBC failed to mention that the PLO frequently stored ammunition in houses in densely populated areas presumably to deter Israeli attacks. The tide of world public opinion might turn against Israel if it attacked these targets. This is precisely what happened.

Wars in the Television Age. Many politicians and other political observers now believe that fighting lengthy wars has become nearly impossible for democratic societies in the age of full-color, battle-front television. When battle scenes are broadcast nightly in gruesome color in the nation's living rooms, public support for wars vanishes. The political consequences can be vast. The ability of democratic societies to defend their interests and achieve their international goals may be diminished, especially compared with countries that are not subject to similar restraints. The depiction of Israel's invasion and siege of Beirut presents a case in point. In the wake of footage of human carnage, Israel lost measurable amounts of support from its closest allies. This loss reduced its ability to pursue the war and undermined its bargaining position.

In the Falkland Islands War between Great Britain and Argentina from April 2 to June 16, 1982, a Democratic nation and its authoritarian antagonist both resorted to the kind of censorship usually associated only with authoritarian regimes. Like the Russians in Afghanistan or the Syrians in Lebanon, the British and the Argentines curbed and delayed pictorial coverage of the war to reduce possibly adverse consequences at home. Similarly, no reporters were permitted to witness the first phases of the U.S. invasion of Grenada in 1983. At this point in time it is difficult to judge whether the one potentially beneficial consequence of television wars—the reduction in unwarranted armed conflict—has materialized to any degree, large or small.

Shortcomings and Distortions. Just like domestic news, foreign news neglects major social problems, particularly political and economic development issues. The reasons are readily apparent. Social problems are difficult to describe in brief stories, visual materials are often lacking, and changes come at a glacial pace. Some social problems are extremely complex; most reporters are ill equipped to understand let alone describe them. When they do describe them, the focus is on their dramatic negative aspects: shortages, famines, conflicts, and breakdowns. As Rafael Caldera, former president of Venezuela, told a press conference at the National Press Club in Washington, D.C., "the phrase 'no news is good news' has become 'good news is no news.'... Little or nothing is mentioned about literary or scientific achievements" in American media or "about social achievements and the defense against the dangers which threaten our peace and development." Instead, "only the most deplorable incidents, be they caused by nature or by man, receive prominent attention." [47] It is small consolation for such ruffled feelings that news selection criteria for Third World events are typical for news everywhere.[48]

Negative and conflictual news is more prevalent in the U.S. media than in the media of many other societies, especially those of the Communist world. Comparisons of news coverage in the United States and in Canada, a society that is culturally close to America, furnish examples. The rate of violence on Canadian television news is half the U.S. rate.[49] When the people of Quebec voted in 1980 on the question of separatism from Canada, the *Washington Post* warned that civil war might erupt. American papers featured stories about serious rioting by separatists in English sectors of Montreal. By contrast, the *Toronto Globe and Mail* buried a small story about minor unrest in Quebec in the back pages. The prospect of civil war was never mentioned and was characterized as "ludicrous" by knowledgeable observers.[50] During the Iranian hostage crisis, *New York Times* coverage was dominated by stereotypical portrayals of Moslems and by tales of violence. Substantially different, far more peaceful images emerged from reading the French paper *Le Monde.*[51]

By and large, Western news media feature more conflict than do media in authoritarian and totalitarian societies. In part this happens because government-controlled news organizations find it comparatively easy to shun dramatic negative news since government subsidies relieve them of the need to secure large audiences. Regardless of the reasons for the difference, the approach used by American news media draws attention to conflict rather than to peaceful settlement and makes much of the world outside of the United States seem chaotic. Although ordinary foreign news languishes in the back pages or is condensed into the briefest broadcast accounts, stories concerned with civil disorder and revolutions are featured prominently. Usually they are oversimplified and told from an American perspective that may be totally inappropriate. Instead of interpreting what the conflict means to the country and its people, the dominant concern ordinarily is whether the leaders are pro-West or pro-Communist and how this tilt will affect the international balance of power.

Distortions also plague domestic news coverage, but they are less deceptive because American audiences can see the situation more clearly; past experiences and socialization provide corrective lenses for viewing the domestic scene.[52] The foreign scene, by contrast, must be viewed without correction for myopia and astigmatism. Americans may be skeptical about the accuracy of the images, but they lack the means to judge the nature and degree of distortion.

Finally, the thrust of foreign news, like its domestic counterpart, provides support for government policies. Before the 1970s the media routinely accepted official designations of who America's friends and enemies were, and they interpreted their motives accordingly. Whenever relationships changed, media coverage mirrored the change. Editorials and news stories about India and the People's Republic of China provide many examples of shifting media appraisals that matched changes in official policy. In the post-Vietnam years support of the government's position, while less constant, has continued. For instance, a comparison of *New York Times* coverage of strife in Cambodia and East Timor and of elections in Nicaragua and El Salvador showed that "Communist-tainted" Cambodia and Nicaragua were judged unfavorably. By contrast, comparable events in East Timor and El Salvador, countries deemed friendly to the United States, were cast in a favorable light.[53] Because the president and executive branch have remained the prime sources of foreign affairs news, they can, most of the time, set the agenda of coverage and frame stories to reflect official perspectives.[54]

If the media are generally supportive of government policy, how can their adverse comments about the Vietnam War be explained? The answer is that the media emphasized the government's positions until many respected sources voiced their strong dissent. At that point the media continued to give the administration's views on the war the largest amount of coverage. They coupled it, however, with coverage of the growing dissent in America about the merits of Vietnam policies, giving ample attention to antiadministration voices and to antiwar demonstrations. Even when protest was featured, the media gave voice primarily to "respectable" dissenters, not to political and social outcasts.[55]

Support of the Status Quo. News emphasis stabilizes perceptions about the international status quo. Preoccupation with the developed powers reinforces many Americans' beliefs about the importance of these nations. Similarly, portrayal of less developed countries as incapable of managing their own internal affairs makes it easy to believe that they do not deserve higher status and the media attention that accompanies it.

Newspeople usually are willing to withhold news and commentary when publicity would severely complicate the government's management of foreign policy. For instance, the media refrained from sharply criticizing Iranian leaders during the 1979 hostage crisis to avoid angering them and suppressed information about America's breaking of Japanese military message codes during World War II. Both are examples in which major political interests were at stake. Likewise, news of delicate negotiations among foreign countries may be temporarily withheld to avoid rocking the boat before agreements are reached. This has happened when East and West Germans have been engaged in discussions about border crossings and when the Soviet Union has expressed willingness to negotiate arms limitations that it had previously refused to consider.[56]

The Unique Impact of Television

We have already mentioned that television has vastly broadened the American audience for foreign affairs coverage and that television anchors have repeatedly assumed roles formerly reserved for diplomats. But the medium has done even more.[57] With satellite transmission its audience has become global. Millions throughout the world, including government leaders, watched the 1987 hearings on U.S.-Iranian arms deals and coverage of the superpower summit meetings in 1987 and 1988. The fact that this international audience would be likely to react to these broadcasts constrained the behavior of the actors caught in the publicity glare. The political consequences were, no doubt, substantial.

Television changes the substance of important political events in ways that reduce the options of political leaders, as Zbigniew Brzezinski, President Carter's national security advisor, pointed out in a retrospective analysis of the Teheran hostage crisis:

> First, TV transforms essentially a political confrontation into a personal drama. The result is you cannot deal with it coldly in terms of the national interest but you must focus on the personal aspects. Secondly, as the confrontation becomes a personal drama, the bargaining capacity of the kidnappers is enhanced. Concentration on accommodation by the American government becomes more important. Thirdly, it humanizes the enemy. Therefore, you begin to make equations and equivalences, which dulls the sharpness of the possible response.[58]

One can argue that the influence of television in a hostage crisis is benign or that it is harmful. But few would argue with Brzezinski's claim that ample coverage alters the political situation.

Television may do three things in a crisis. First, it may dictate the national agenda by riveting public attention on the crisis to the exclusion of virtually all else. For example, during the stock market crisis of 1987, television slighted news about America's air attack on Iranian bases in the Persian Gulf and news about a domestic airline disaster. These would have been the top stories in calmer times. Second, televised crisis coverage may pressure the president to react hastily so that he does not appear weak and vacillating. As Lloyd Cutler, White House counsel to President Carter, put it: "If an ominous foreign event is featured on TV news, the President and his advisers feel bound to make a response in time for the next evening news program." [59] Third, television's impact on political elites and mass publics may narrow the president's freedom to bargain and maneuver. This happened during the Iranian hostage crisis. The Carter administration's poorly conducted hostage rescue mission has been attributed to pressures created by the prolonged television coverage of the hostages and publicized charges that President Carter was incompetent to resolve the situation.

Appraising Foreign News Making

Clearly, foreign news in the American press does not meet the high standards that UNESCO has set for it. It does not "eliminate ignorance and misunderstanding between peoples." It is too sparse for that and too unbalanced, focusing on the wealthier and more powerful countries. It assesses foreign countries largely in terms of U.S. interests, with little attempt to explain their culture and their concerns from their own perspective. It does not sensitize Americans to "the needs and desires of others" nor foster "respect of the rights and dignity of all nations." Rather, it reinforces Americans' preexisting assumptions and stereotypes. Major problems abroad, such as hunger, disease, and poverty, are ignored except when unusual disasters dramatize them temporarily.

These deficiencies must be assessed in light of the basic philosophy of news in a free society. As discussed in Chapter 1, American journalists by and large do not see themselves as extensions of the government, carrying out and keeping in tune with public policies. Although they may sympathize with UNESCO's goals, their first priority is to report exciting news to the American public. In a society that firmly believes in the independence of the press from government, this is a tolerable consequence.

Just as the press does not serve UNESCO's objectives, it fails to serve many objectives of the American government and many needs of the American public. Reporting of foreign news usually lacks a sense of history and a sense of the meaning of successive events. It therefore confuses the public. A good example is the widely believed story that China turned to communism because of failures of American foreign policy. This interpretation ignores the long-range forces that made revolution in China inevitable. It vastly exaggerates the power of the United States to change the course of Chinese politics. The news does not provide even sufficient information to permit most Americans to understand the rationale for major foreign policies such as support of the North Atlantic Treaty Organization (NATO) or the necessity for international economic cooperation.

Some stories, even those directly involving U.S. security, are ignored until events reach crisis proportions or until there is a precipitating incident. For instance, stories about the relative military strength of the United States and the Soviet Union did not receive prominent coverage until the Strategic Arms Limitation Treaty (SALT) negotiations in 1977. Before that time news was "so spotty and lopsided that it failed to provide the essential facts for understanding U.S. defense and military issues, the Soviet definition of détente, or the forward surge in Soviet military might." [60] *New York Times* correspondent James Reston put the problem this way:

> We are fascinated by events but not by the things that cause the events. We will send 500 correspondents to Vietnam after the war breaks out, and fill the front pages with their reports, meanwhile ignoring the rest of the world, but we will not send five reporters there when the danger of war is developing. [61]

Phil Foisie, the assistant managing editor of the *Washington Post,* adds, "We are surprised more often than we ought to be and need to be." [62] This leaves the country unprepared for twists and turns in foreign affairs that might have been foreseen.

As with domestic news, there is a continuous debate about whether the "right" foreign news issues have been covered in the proper way. Conservative critics complain about too much disparagement of U.S. activities to restrain communism abroad, too much sympathy for leftist regimes, and too little stress on military security. Liberal critics say the opposite. [63] Others point to distorted coverage during foreign policy crises that allegedly misled the American public and misdirected foreign policy. Debate about the adequacy of Vietnam War coverage has been especially heated. [64]

If one assumes that better information leads to better policies, then deficiencies in news coverage are grave. When President Carter complained that he was ill informed about unrest in Iran prior to the overthrow of the shah in 1979, he intimated that American policy making and public support for policies would have benefited from more accurate news. In this case the Central Intelligence Agency was blamed as well as the media, which perform what has been called a "massive overt intelligence operation." [65] Coverage of the Bay of Pigs invasion also raises questions about the chance for better policies if the media had told the story more fully and avoided ideological blinders. The media's stress on conflict—particularly on force as the solution for conflict and as a tool for conflict avoidance—contributes to feelings of insecurity.

Although the media are exceedingly important in providing the information base for policy information, their explicit input into foreign policy making is muted. When journalists give policy advice or criticize ongoing policies, their influence is generally weaker than the influence of formal government agencies. In fact, *New York Times* columnist James Reston claims that press advice has great influence on American foreign policy only when things are obviously going badly, as they did in the Vietnam War.[66] When policy failures are not readily apparent and the president alleges that all is going well, contrary media claims are not likely to be believed by officials and the mass public.

Impact on Public Opinion

Because most Americans lack interest and knowledge about foreign affairs, they are easily swayed by what they see and hear on television, their primary source of foreign news.[67] Television has spawned a new, impressionable public, highly susceptible to cues from the tube. Viewers are most readily influenced when stories reinforce stereotypes or challenge them convincingly, to the audience's surprise, and when they seem to relate to the lives of average Americans.[68] In the past, interest in foreign policy was largely confined to a newspaper-reliant elite whose education, interests, and experiences made them far more immune to media influence. Several decades ago "the public probably would never have heard of El Salvador, much less cared about it. Today the sheer volume of exposure to new information created by television assures a more involved public. Television has created a vast, inadvertent audience for news about foreign policy." [69]

Moreover, it has strengthened the president's hand when policies coincide with the tenor of news stories and limited the options when news and policies conflict. Public support for defense spending, for example, more than doubled between 1978 and 1980, jumping from 26 to 90 percent. Televised foreign news may well have been the explanation. It drove home the message that America's foes were gaining while the country was incapable of defending itself. The Iranian hostage crisis, the Soviet assault on Afghanistan, the upheaval in Poland, and the uncontrollable warfare in Central America were powerful scenes in this melodrama.[70]

As is true of most media effects, it is difficult to obtain convincing proof that public opinion about foreign countries mirrors the images media stories present. Nonetheless, available data suggest that it does. William C. Adams, on the basis of careful content analyses of television coverage of the Arab-Israeli conflict in the 1970s and 1980s, concluded that five important changes should have taken place in public opinion if it, indeed, reflected media coverage. Opinions should have become (1) more favorable to Egypt, (2) more sensitive to differences among Arab nations, (3) less favorable to Israel, (4) more sympathetic to Palestinians, and (5) slightly more pro-Arab overall. All of these changes occurred. Between 1976 and 1980 favorable opinion of Egypt rose by 25 percentage points, sizable differences in attitudes toward Arab countries developed, and opinions became more sympathetic to the Palestinians and more pro-Arab overall by 12 percentage points. By 1980 public sympathy for Israel had not yet dropped, in line with media coverage, but it began its downward trend shortly thereafter.[71]

Exporting News

Although the American public seems reasonably content with the foreign news it receives, Third World countries are unhappy with their coverage in the United States. Their disappointment about the world images presented to Americans is compounded by resentment that these images are exported to other countries throughout the globe. Eighty percent of the non-Communist world's political and economic news comes from only four huge American enterprises: the Associated Press (AP), United Press International (UPI), the *New York Times* News Service, and the *Los Angeles Times-Washington Post* News Service. Most of the remainder is produced by Britain's Reuters, France's Agence France-Presse, and Russia's Tass. Four countries thus dominate the world's news supply.[72]

This concentration has given rise to charges of media imperialism—the dependence of domestic media systems on dominant foreign media systems.[73] Dependence on foreign news resources is particularly galling for developing countries because they believe that the flow of news is primarily one way—into the developing world but not out of it. Western news purveyors slight Third World happenings and the information needs of people in developing nations. Foreign affairs journalism, according to these critics, should play an educational role in the Third World; it should inspire and mobilize people to work hard to develop their countries. Instead, it fosters cynicism and dejection over the way Third World leaders manage their problems. If press freedom leads to such results, it is a luxury developing countries cannot afford.

Third World critics also decry the corrupting effects of Western news and entertainment programs for Americans, other Westerners, and people of the Third World. Entertainment programs contain too much violence and too many sexually explicit episodes. They allegedly damage the cultural identity of poor nations, especially those that are vulnerable because colonialism has accustomed them to foreign values.[74] Imported news and entertainment offerings draw people away from their own heritage and create false expectations that it is easy to become rich. Third World people are tempted into materialism for the benefit of industrialists in the United States who are eager to sell their merchandise through television. Buyers of luxury goods then drain the Third World's resources.

Marxist interpretations of the motives and role of Western media are widely believed in the Third World. These interpretations seem quite plausible because the international news market is dominated by a few giant corporations headquartered in New York and other major Western cities. These organizations sell news, as well as more tangible goods, for profit. However, scientific proof is lacking that the Marxist interpretation of the causes and consequences of Western dominance of Third World news and media entertainment is correct. As we noted in Chapter 5, people do not automatically learn new ways of life from the media, even when offerings are designed to educate. Certain conditions must first be met to provide an appropriate context. Hence claims that exposure to Western news automatically indoctrinates the audience are false.[75]

Content analyses of Western media, including wire service news, show that many of the charges of deliberate discrimination against the Third World are either groundless or exaggerated.[76] The emphasis on problems and failures in the Third World, rather than successes, and lack of attention to many small nations appear to be natural consequences of applying to the Third World the same criteria used for the more developed portions of the globe. The consequences may differ, but the treatment is the same.[77] The media's emphasis on disasters and conflicts in the Third World reflects the reality that Third World countries are undergoing major social changes and therefore bear a disproportionate burden of pain and suffering.

Elite newspapers in America, in sharp contrast to smaller, less prominent papers throughout the country, pay considerable attention to Third World news.[78] In the *New York Times, Washington Post,* and *Christian Science Monitor,* for example, an average of 65 percent of foreign news coverage is devoted to the Third World. The Third World also fares well in the proportion of front-page stories, editorials, opinion-page articles, and letters to the editor.[79]

Early entry into the media business has given the major news producers an economic edge of size and scale that makes it well-nigh impossible for developing nations to set up viable competing enterprises.[80] The high cost of television programming and the comparatively low cost of purchasing foreign television entertainment—roughly one-tenth of the cost of original programming—also have discouraged Third World countries from creating their own television industries. Many developing countries still lack facilities for producing television shows. Those that do nonetheless import an average of more than half of their programs, particularly those shown in prime time.[81] In recent years local cultural programs have multiplied and are often exchanged among Third World nations. The Nairobi-based Program Exchange Center, for example, is a clearinghouse for circulating African cultural programs throughout the continent.[82]

Current structures and patterns of telecommunications give price advantages to large producers and consumers. News transmission rates are cheaper when volume is high, making it extremely costly for poor countries to send their messages out. It also costs more to transmit news from underdeveloped countries than vice versa. In fact, all the economies of scale benefit the rich and hurt the poor.

Because they are dissatisfied with the status quo and because they see news as a powerful political force, Third World countries have lobbied in UNESCO for placing strict controls on the influx of foreign news. It has been largely a dialogue of the deaf. The United States and other Western countries have strongly resisted these attempts, deeming them infringements of the right to a free press guaranteed by the Universal Declaration of Human Rights, which the United Nations approved in 1948. The trend toward controlled news in the developing world is making headway nonetheless. UNESCO has been involved in planning for a code of journalistic ethics that would define *responsible* reporting. It also has investigated ways to make journalism a government-licensed profession. The United States has withdrawn from UNESCO in the wake of these efforts.

Third World countries are also contesting the control of the United States and other Western powers over world radio and satellite facilities. In the past, scarce international frequencies were allocated on a first-come-first-served basis. The developed nations, including the United States, received the lion's share of the broadcast spectrum— nearly 90 percent and the bulk of satellite facilities. Third World nations want to change this. As they made clear at the World Administrative Radio Conference (WARC), which met in Geneva, Switzerland, in the fall of 1979, they want to divide the spectrum equally among all nations and bar radio and television satellite transmissions across national borders unless the receiving country has given permission. They are also demanding more control over satellites. The United States has resisted Third World demands, believing that nations with current capability to use advanced telecommunications facilities should control these facilities. Granting them to nations that cannot use them immediately, or even in the near future, seems to make little sense.

The United States is the world's foremost international broadcaster.[83] In the late 1970s U.S. agencies and several private American broadcasters were sending 2,534 program hours weekly throughout the world. (This compared with 1,998 hours sent by the Soviet Union.) International broadcast facilities are used to further important foreign policy objectives. The Voice of America (VOA) broadcasts, for example, are an integral part of the federal government's foreign information program, which is handled by the United States Information Agency (USIA). It broadcasts from more than one hundred short-wave transmitters in the United States and abroad. Programs are beamed in some forty languages and reach over 100 million listeners each week.[84] It also operates WORLDNET, the international satellite television network that transmits its programs globally and enables foreign news media to interview American officials directly. Additionally, VOA publishes fifteen magazines in eighteen languages.

VOA broadcasts portray American society and its problems and policies abroad and provide Western news to countries unlikely to receive it in any other way. VOA's largest service goes to the Soviet Union, to which it broadcasts 168 hours weekly in Russian, Ukrainian, Estonian, Latvian, Lithuanian, Armenian, Georgian, and Uzbek.[85] Other Eastern European countries receive eighty-seven hours of broadcasts. Radio Marti, added to VOA during the Reagan years, beams news to Cuba. It emphasizes developments in foreign areas where Cuban forces are active, such as Central America and Africa.[86] The international broadcast spectrum is also used for Radio Liberty (RL), which broadcasts foreign internal news, mainly to the Soviet Union; Radio Free Europe (RFE), which does the same for Poland, Czechoslovakia, Hungary, Romania, and Bulgaria; and RIAS, Radio in the American-Sector Berlin, which covers all of Berlin and East Germany.[87] Efforts by Third World nations to gain greater control over international broadcasts are viewed by American officials as threatening the foreign information programs of the United States and the image that the United States is trying to project.

Summary

The quality of U.S. foreign policy and the effectiveness of U.S. relations with other countries are crucial to the welfare of people throughout the world. Sound policy and relations require a solid information base. As this chapter has shown, the foreign affairs information base on which Americans depend leaves much to be desired. The causes are complex and cannot be changed readily. They involve the structure of the foreign correspondent corps, the sociopolitical setting in which correspondents must work, and the audiences to whose world views and tastes the news must cater.

Foreign correspondents are a well-trained, able group. But there are too few of them to cover the world. They work within a narrowly controlled organizational structure consisting of a handful of giant news-gathering institutions that supply the news and entertainment needs of the United States and much of the rest of the non-Communist world. If one distrusts giant information conglomerates that collect and shape the news for much of the world, the present situation is frightening.

Most Americans are reasonably well satisfied with the foreign news produced by these conglomerates. Many of the foreign clienteles, particularly political leaders in the Third World, are not. They complain that agents of monopoly capitalism are guilty of "electronic rape" of their people through decadent entertainment and Western political propaganda.

Foreign affairs news often must be produced under trying conditions. Strange locations and inadequate technological facilities can make a nightmare of the physical aspects of getting to the scene of the action, collecting information, and transmitting it. These technical difficulties are compounded by political difficulties. They include the reluctance of officials in the United States and abroad to commit themselves publicly on foreign affairs matters and the harassment of correspondents venturing into places where they are unwanted. Expulsion, imprisonment, and physical harm are common. With so much territory to cover and such limited personnel to cover it, newspeople frequently avoid areas where news is hard to get and devote their efforts instead to areas where public attitudes are supportive. This effectively removes many regions from media scrutiny and contributes to unevenness of news flow from various parts of the world.

How good is the foreign affairs news that reaches the United States and other clients of Western international news transmission facilities? The picture is mixed. Foreign correspondents must produce news that is at once timely, exciting, personalized, and brief yet understandable for an American audience that is not intensely interested in most events abroad. Given the problems of foreign affairs news production, correspondents dwell heavily on negative and sensational news. They write stories from an American perspective that follows the current administration's foreign policy assumptions and the American public's stereotyped views of the world. They primarily cover the most important countries, keeping America's national interests and policy objectives in mind. Despite these shortcomings, Americans can obtain a reasonably accurate view of salient political events abroad, particularly if they turn to several elite newspapers that generally give thorough exposure to controversial American foreign policies. However, these papers rarely challenge the merits of foreign policies.

In recent years television commentators occasionally have become active diplomats through interviews that set the stage for subsequent political developments. Aside from these adventures, media influence on foreign policy has been largely indirect, exercised primarily through surveillance activities, the power to choose what to report and what to omit, and the ability to interpret the meaning of events. There has been little investigative or adversary journalism except when foreign affairs were obviously going badly, as happened toward the end of the Vietnam War. Political controversy has largely stopped at the water's edge.

Notes

1. David H. Weaver and John B. Mauro, "Newspaper Readership Patterns," *Journalism Quarterly* 51 (Spring 1978), and David H. Weaver, *Recent Trends in Newspaper Readership Research,* Research Report No. 5 (Bloomington, Ind.: School of Journalism, Indiana University, June 23, 1978).

2. For comparative coverage figures see George Gerbner and George Marvanyi, "The Many Worlds of the World's Press," *Journal of Communication* 27 (Winter 1977): 55-56. The analysis was based on 1970 data. Also see S. M. Mazharul Haque, "Is U.S. Coverage of News in Third World Imbalanced?" *Journalism Quarterly* 60 (Fall 1983): 521-524.

3. Sophia Peterson, "International News Selection by the Elite Press: A Case Study," *Public Opinion Quarterly* 45 (Summer 1981): 143-163. The content of television network foreign news from 1972 to 1981 is discussed in James F. Larson, *Television's Window on the World* (Norwood, N.J.: Ablex, 1984). Also see Lynn Ludlow, "They Commute to the World: Changes in International News Reporting," *ETC* 44 (Spring 1987): 31-41.

4. Gladys Engel Lang and Kurt Lang, *Politics and Television Re-Viewed* (Beverly Hills, Calif.: Sage, 1984), 213.

5. Doris A. Graber, *Processing the News: How People Tame the Information Tide,* 2d ed. (New York: Longman, 1988), 104-107.

6. Bernard C. Cohen, *The Press and Foreign Policy* (Princeton, N.J.: Princeton University Press, 1963), 164-165.

7. Barry Rubin, "International News and the American Media," in *International News: Freedom Under Attack,* ed. Dante B. Fascell (Beverly Hills, Calif.: Sage, 1979), 187.

8. Larson, *Television's Window,* 171-178; and Ludlow, "They Commute to the World.'

9. William H. Read, "Multinational Media," *Foreign Policy* 18 (Spring 1975): 55-67.

10. J. Herbert Altschull, "Khrushchev and the Berlin 'Ultimatum': The Jackal Syndrome and the Cold War," *Journalism Quarterly* 54 (Fall 1977): 545-551.

11. Rubin, "International News," 214.

12. John A. Lent, "Foreign News in American Media," *Journal of Communication* 27 (Winter 1977): 46-50.

13. Rubin, "International News," 197-198. However, the fact that television news teams generally involve at least three people has produced some increases in the foreign correspondent corps.

14. Daniel Riffe, "International News Borrowing: A Trend Analysis," *Journalism Quarterly* 61 (Spring 1984): 142-148.

15. Leo Bogart, "The Overseas Newsman: A 1967 Profile Study," *Journalism Quarterly* 45 (Summer 1968): 293-306.

16. Ibid., 299.

17. S. Robert Lichter, "America and the Third World: A Survey of Leading Media and Business Leaders," in *Television Coverage of International Affairs,* ed. William C. Adams (Norwood, N.J.: Ablex, 1982), 71. The data were collected in the fall of 1979 and winter of 1980.

18. Jarol B. Manheim and Robert B. Albritton, "Changing National Images: International Public Relations and Media Agenda-Setting," *American Political Science Review* 78 (September 1984): 641-657; and Robert B. Albritton and Jarol B. Manheim, "Public Relations Efforts for the Third

World: Images in the News," *Journal of Communication* 35 (Spring 1985): 43-59.

19. Shailendra Ghorpade, "Foreign Correspondents Cover Washington for World," *Journalism Quarterly* 61 (Autumn 1984): 667-671; and *Editor and Publisher International Yearbook, 1987* (New York: Editor & Publisher, 1987), 46-56. As Table 10-1 shows, the countries most heavily covered by the United States send the most reporters to the United States.

20. Ghorpade, "Foreign Correspondents," 667.

21. Peterson, "International News Selection," 159.

22. Robert M. Batscha, *Foreign Affairs News and the Broadcast Journalist* (New York: Praeger, 1975), 156.

23. Sean Kelly, "Access Denied: The Politics of Press Censorship," in *International News*, 249.

24. See Anne-Marie O'Connor, "Dateline: Honduras; Subject: the Contras," *Columbia Journalism Review* 26 (May/June 1987): 38-41; and John Grogan and Charles Riddle, "South Africa's Press in the Eighties: Darkness Descends," 39 *Gazette* (1986): 3-16.

25. John Kifner, "Reporter's Notebook: Fear is Part of Job in Beirut," *New York Times*, February 22, 1982.

26. Bob Wiedrich, "Sadat Has Invented a New Diplomacy," *Chicago Tribune*, February 9, 1978.

27. Bill Keller, "The Image: Moscow Goal," *New York Times*, December 1, 1987.

28. The Center for Media and Public Affairs, *Media Monitor* 1 (December 1987): 5-6.

29. Batscha, *Foreign Affairs News*, 122.

30. James F. Larson, "International Affairs Coverage on U.S. Network Television," *Journal of Communication* 29 (Spring 1979): 147.

31. For examples, see Montague Kern, Patricia W. Levering, and Ralph B. Levering, *The Kennedy Crises: The Press, the Presidency, and Foreign Policy* (Chapel Hill: University of North Carolina Press, 1984). Also see Daniel C. Hallin, "The Media, the War in Vietnam and Political Support: A Critique of the Thesis of an Oppositional Media," *Journal of Politics* 46 (February 1984): 2-24.

32. For example, only five out of eighteen countries in equatorial and lower Africa receive substantial coverage. See Jeff Charles, Larry Shore, and Rusty Todd, "The New York Times Coverage of Equatorial and Lower Africa," *Journal of Communication* 29 (Spring 1979): 151.

33. James F. Larson, "International Affairs Coverage on U.S. Evening Network News, 1972-1979," in *Television Coverage of International Affairs*, 37.

34. Herbert J. Gans, *Deciding What's News: A Study of CBS Evening News, NBC Nightly News, Newsweek and Time* (New York: Pantheon Books, 1979), 30-36. See also Peterson, "International News Selection," 144-149; and Johan Galtung and Mari H. Ruge, "The Structure of Foreign News," *Journal of Peace Research* 2 (1965): 64-91.

35. Edwin Diamond, *The Tin Kazoo: Television, Politics, and the News* (Cambridge, Mass.: The MIT Press, 1975), 94.

36. Susan Welch, "The American Press and Indochina, 1950-1956," in *Communication in International Politics*, ed. Richard L. Merritt (Urbana, Ill.: University of Illinois Press, 1972), 227-228; and Daniel C. Hallin, "Hegemony: The American News Media from Vietnam to El Salvador: A Study of Ideological Change and Its Limits," in *Political Communication Research:*

Approaches, Studies, Assessments, ed. David L. Paletz (Norwood, N.J.: Ablex, 1987), 17.

37. Galtung and Ruge, in "The Structure of Foreign News," have developed a much quoted scheme for rating the newsworthiness of various types of foreign affairs events. See also Elinar Ostgaard, "Factors Influencing the Flow of News," *Journal of Peace Research* 2 (1965): 39-63.

38. Jonathan Friendly, "El Salvador Overlooked as Most of Press Turns to Other Crises," *New York Times,* July 10, 1982.

39. William Adams and Phillip Heyl, "From Cairo to Kabul with the Networks, 1972-1980," in *Television Coverage of the Middle East,* ed. William C. Adams (Norwood, N.J.: Ablex, 1981), 26.

40. Rubin, "International News," 227.

41. Francis X. Clines, "In U.S. TV, Israelis Find an Unflattering Mirror," *New York Times,* February 1, 1988; and John Kifner, "Israeli Officials Object to U.S. News Coverage of Riots," *New York Times,* December 29, 1987.

42. David L. Altheide, "Impact of Format and Ideology on TV News Coverage of Iran," *Journalism Quarterly* 62 (Summer 1985): 351.

43. Michael X. Delli Carpini and Bruce A. Williams, "Television and Terrorism: Patterns of Presentation and Occurrence, 1969 to 1980," *Western Political Quarterly* 40 (March 1987): 45-64.

44. Paul Bethel, "Anarchy in Domingo: City Without Food, Water, Medicine in Civil War," in *Mass Media and the Mass Man,* ed. Alan Casty (New York: Holt, Rinehart and Winston, 1968), 218.

45. Theodore Draper, "Contaminated News of the Dominican Republic," in *Mass Media and the Mass Man,* 212-214.

46. John Corry, "TV: View of NBC Coverage of Lebanon Invasion," *New York Times,* February 18, 1984.

47. Fernando Reyes Matta, "The Latin American Concept of News," *Journal of Communication* 29 (Spring 1979): 169.

48. Gary D. Gaddy and Enoch Tanjong, "Earthquake Coverage by the Western Press," *Journal of Communication* 36 (Spring 1986): 105-112. For a conflicting analysis, see William C. Adams, "Whose Lives Count?: TV Coverage of Natural Disasters," *Journal of Communication* 36 (Spring 1986): 113-122.

49. Benjamin D. Singer, "Violence, Protest, and War in Television News: The U.S. and Canada Compared," *Public Opinion Quarterly* 34 (Winter 1970-71): 611-616; and Chris J. Scheer and Sam W. Eiler, "A Comparison of Canadian and American Network Television News," *Journal of Broadcasting* 16 (Spring 1972): 156-164.

50. James P. Winter, Pirouz Shoar Ghaffari, and Vernone M. Sparkes, "How Major U.S. Dailies Covered Quebec Separatism Referendum," *Journalism Quarterly* 59 (Winter 1982): 608.

51. Edward W. Said, *Covering Islam: How the Media and the Experts Determine How We See the Rest of the World* (New York: Pantheon Books, 1981), chap. 2.

52. Hanna Adoni and S. Mane, "Media and the Social Construction of Reality: Toward an Integration of Theory and Research," *Communication Research* 11 (July 1984): 323-340.

53. Edward S. Herman, "Diversity of News: 'Marginalizing' the Opposition," *Journal of Communication* 35 (Fall 1985): 135-146.

54. Lent, "Foreign News in American Media." See also Jyotika Ramaprasad and Daniel Riffe, "Effect of U.S.-India Relations on *New York Times*

Coverage," *Journalism Quarterly* 64 (Summer/Autumn 1987): 537-543; Hallin, "Hegemony"; and David Altheide, "Media Hegemony: A Failure of Perspective," *Public Opinion Quarterly* 48 (Summer 1984): 476-490.

55. Robert M. Entman and David L. Paletz, "The War in Southeast Asia: Tunnel Vision on Television," in *Television Coverage of International Affairs*, 181-201; and Hallin, "The Media."

56. W. Phillips Davison, "Diplomatic Reporting: Rules of the Game," *Journal of Communication* 25 (Autumn 1975): 138-146.

57. The discussion that follows is based on James F. Larson, "Television and U.S. Foreign Policy: The Case of the Iran Hostage Crisis," *Journal of Communication* 36 (Autumn 1986): 108-130; and Joseph Fromm, "TV: Does It Box in President in a Crisis?" *U.S. News and World Report*, July 15, 1985, 23-24.

58. John Corry, "The Intrusion of Television in the Hostage Crisis," *New York Times*, June 26, 1985.

59. Ibid.

60. Ernest LeFever, *T.V. and National Defense* (Chicago: Institute for American Strategy, 1974), 139.

61. James Reston, *Sketches in the Sand* (New York: Knopf, 1967), 195.

62. Rubin, "International News," 216.

63. Thomas M. McNulty, "Vietnam Specials: Policy and Content," *Journal of Communication* 25 (August 1975): 173-180. See also Ernest W. LeFever, "CBS and National Defense," *Journal of Communication* 25 (Autumn 1975): 181-185.

64. Peter Braestrup, *Big Story: How the American Press and Television Reported and Interpreted the Crisis of Tet 1968 in Vietnam and Washington* (Garden City, N.J.: Anchor Press/Doubleday, 1978).

65. Rubin, "International News," 193.

66. Ibid., 182.

67. The influence of television on the perception of unfamiliar issues is discussed in Shanto Iyengar and Donald Kinder, *News that Matters: Television and American Opinion* (Chicago: University of Chicago Press, 1987).

68. William C. Adams, "Mass Media and Public Opinion About Foreign Affairs: A Typology of News Dynamics," *Political Communication and Persuasion* 4 (1987): 263-278.

69. William Schneider, "Bang-Bang Television: The New Superpower," *Public Opinion* 5 (April/May 1982): 13-14.

70. Larson, "International Affairs Coverage," 34-35.

71. Adams and Heyl, "From Cairo to Kabul," 16, 19-22.

72. Mustapha Masmoudi, "The New World Information Order," *Journal of Communication* 29 (Spring 1979): 172-185. For an explanation of how international news services function, see Jonathan Fenby, *The International News Services* (New York: Schocken Books, 1986).

73. For a discussion of media imperialism, see Herbert I. Schiller, *Communication and Cultural Domination* (White Plains, N.Y.: International Arts and Science Press, 1976); and René Jean Ravault, "International Information: Bullet or Boomerang?" in *Political Communication Research: Approaches, Studies, Assessments*, ed. David L. Paletz (Norwood, N.J.: Ablex, 1987), 245-265.

74. The impact of foreign television is assessed in Alexis S. Tan, Sarrina Li, and Charles Simpson, "American TV and Social Stereotypes of Americans in Taiwan and Mexico," *Journalism Quarterly* 63 (Winter 1986): 809-814.

75. Ravault, "International Information"; and Glen Fisher, *American Communication in a Global Society* (Norwood, N.J.: Ablex, 1987), 15-18.

76. W. James Potter, "News from Three Worlds in Prestige U.S. Newspapers," *Journalism Quarterly* 64 (Spring 1987): 73-79.

77. Wilbur Schramm and L. Erwin Atwood, *Circulation of News in the Third World: A Study of Asia* (Hong Kong: Chinese University Press, 1981); and David H. Weaver and G. Cleveland Wilhoit, "Foreign News Coverage in Two U.S. Wire Services," *Journal of Communication* 31 (Spring 1981): 55-63. For a contrary view, see Daniel Riffe and Eugene F. Shaw, "Conflict and Consonance: Coverage of Third World in Two U.S. Papers," *Journalism Quarterly* 59 (Winter 1982): 617-626.

78. Coverage by smaller media is discussed in G. Cleveland Wilhoit and David Weaver, "Foreign News Coverage in Two U.S. Wire Services: An Update," *Journal of Communication* 33 (Spring 1983): 132-148.

79. Haque, "Is U.S. Coverage of News in Third World Imbalanced?" 523-524. Some confusion in dividing stories by country of origin has arisen from the fact that many Third World stories are transmitted through communications centers, such as London or New York. For example, most news from Latin America is relayed via New York. See Leonard R. Sussman, "Information Control as an International Issue," in *The Communications Revolution in Politics,* ed. Gerald Benjamin (New York: The Academy of Political Science, 1982), 183.

80. Boyd-Barrett, "Media Imperialism," 130.

81. Elihu Katz, "Cultural Continuity and Change: The Role of Mass Media," in *Communications Policy for National Development,* ed. Majid Teheranian, Farhad Hakemzadeh, and Marcello L. Vidale (London: Routledge & Kegan Paul, 1977), 133. Price-conscious television stations in the developed world are equally heavy importers of American television entertainment shows. For examples, see Henry Giniger, "J. R. Ewing and Captain Furillo in Paris," *New York Times,* November 21, 1987.

82. David Crary, "Don't Look for 'Nairobi Vice'," *Chicago Tribune,* December 11, 1986.

83. Kelly, "Access Denied," 255.

84. Glen Fisher, *American Communication in a Global Society* (Norwood, N.J.: Ablex, 1987), 139.

85. David M. Abshire, "A New Dimension of Western Diplomacy," 40. Also see Allen C. Hansen, *USIA: Public Diplomacy in the Computer Age* (New York: Praeger, 1984).

86. Fisher, *American Communication,* 141.

87. Sig Mickelson, *America's Other Voice: The Story of Radio Free Europe and Radio Liberty* (New York: Praeger, 1983).

Readings

Adams, William C. *Television Coverage of International Affairs.* Norwood, N.J.: Ablex, 1982.
——. *Television Coverage of the Middle East.* Norwood, N.J.: Ablex, 1981.
Fisher, Glen. *American Communication in a Global Society.* Norwood, N.J.: Ablex, 1987.

Hallin, Daniel C. *The 'Uncensored War': The Media and Vietnam.* New York: Oxford University Press, 1986.

Kern, Montague, Patricia Levering, and Ralph B. Levering. *The Kennedy Crises: The Press, the Presidency, and Foreign Policy.* Chapel Hill: University of North Carolina Press, 1983.

McPhail, Thomas L. *Electronic Colonialism: The Future of International Broadcasting and Communication.* 2d ed. Beverly Hills, Calif.: Sage, 1987.

Pollock, John Crothers. *The Politics of Crisis Reporting: Learning to Be a Foreign Correspondent.* New York: Praeger, 1981.

Rice, Michael, with Jonathan Carr, Henri Pierre, Jan Reifenberg, and Pierre Salinger. *Reporting U.S.-European Relations: Four Nations, Four Newspapers.* New York: Pergamon, 1982.

Stevenson, Robert L., and Donald Lewis Shaw, eds. *Foreign News and the New World Information Order.* Ames: Iowa State University Press, 1984.

CHAPTER 11

Trends in Media Policy

In Shakespeare's *Julius Caesar* Brutus urges his fellow conspirators to act while the time is ripe:

> There is a tide in the affairs of men
> Which, taken at the flood, leads on to fortune;
> Omitted, all the voyage of their life
> Is bound in shallows and in miseries.
> On such a full sea are we now afloat;
> And we must take the current when it serves
> Or lose our ventures.[1]

Communications policy has been standing on just such a threshold in the waning years of the twentieth century. New technologies call for a rethinking of established policy directions, but old policy concepts linger and make the future hostage to the past. Thus far, attempts to take control of the tides of change have faltered, diminishing the chance to reap the full benefits made possible by the communications revolution.

Both the forces pushing for new communications policies and the obstacles that lie in the way will be discussed in this chapter. We will explore some of the areas of disenchantment with mass media performance that have fueled demands for reform and the steps taken by dissatisfied communicators and audiences to improve and supplement the existing information supply. The potential impact of major new technologies on politics and policy alternatives will be examined. Finally, we will peer into the murky crystal ball to try to discern the shape of future communications policies that will guide the interaction between the mass media and the American political system in the twenty-first century.

Dissatisfaction with the Media

The 1960s and 1970s were decades of political disenchantment in the United States. Many people became dissatisfied with political institutions and blamed them for the ills of society. Vocal protesters have always been vastly outnumbered by the "silent majorities" whose silence is interpreted as approval of the political system or resignation to its unavoidable shortcomings. But even the silent have often felt that the times were out of joint, if only because of the increase in publicly voiced dissent.

The media, particularly television, have been frequent targets of protest. Although recent polls give high marks to newspapers and television, more than one hundred thousand complaints about television are registered annually at the Washington Broadcast Bureau of the Federal Communications Commission (FCC).[2] Most complaints concern the display of obscenity, excessive crime and violence, infringement of equal time and fairness provisions, the treatment of racial and religious matters, and the substance and amount of advertising.

Besides the formal complaints lodged with the FCC, a host of less formal criticisms have been made as well. Media critics call television a vast intellectual wasteland. They chide the networks for greedy pandering to mass audiences and blame shallow programming and cheap appeals to human emotions on the desire to secure high ratings that will raise advertising income. They complain about the scant criticism of American society and politics and the sizable support for the status quo. Similar complaints are voiced about print media. Newspapers are accused of superficial coverage, catering to their financial benefactors, and all-too-frequent mean-spirited excursions into sensationalism and sleaze. The press, says *Chicago Tribune* columnist Bill Granger, has become judge, jury, and executioner—the pitbull of politics.[3]

Media orientations toward politics have been criticized as both too liberal and too conservative. Sniping from the left about the media's subservience to the establishment and insensitivity to the concerns of the politically powerless and economically deprived has been balanced by criticism from the middle and the right. Conservatives accuse the media of demeaning the status of American business and labor and of respected professions such as medicine and law. The media, they argue, are unduly romantic about the woes and virtues of the poor, the disadvantaged, and the racially different. In the process the media allegedly undermine national security and hurt the nation's prestige at home and abroad. The media also have been accused by liberals and conservatives alike of invading individual privacy and impairing the fairness of the judicial process.

The gist of the charges is that the media do not serve "the public interest" and that they fail to nourish a viable democratic political order. These elusive concepts are always measured by political yard-sticks of disputed accuracy and validity. What is important to an understanding of media policy making is the response to perceived media deficiencies. How do dissatisfied Americans cope with shortcomings in their information supply? Coping strategies can be grouped into three types: (1) various forms of informal criticism, expressed regularly and sporadically; (2) the establishment and use of formal criticism mechanisms; and (3) the use of alternative media.

Informal Criticism

Informal criticism has come from within the journalism profession as well as from the general public. Specialized journals that frequently review media performance, such as the *Columbia Journalism Review* or the *Washington Journalism Review,* publish criticism by media professionals. Many review journals have been short-lived because they could not maintain enough subscribers to pay their expenses. The degree of influence wielded by such journals is a matter of opinion. Within narrow circles, professional reputations may be affected. But the circulation of these reviews is so limited, and the pocketbook effects of adverse criticism are so negligible, that their pressure on the industry to alter journalistic practices is likely to be small.

More robust and probably more influential vehicles of criticism are critical essays by media commentators for television networks and high-circulation newspapers and news magazines. Columnists such as Les Brown, reporters such as John Corry, and TV hosts such as Ted Koppel have become familiar gadflies of the news business and the journalism profession. Their work supplements the efforts of many academic experts who have written critical appraisals of the mass media in recent years. Authors David Altheide, Norman Isaacs, Tom Goldstein, Edwin Diamond, Ben Stein, and Herbert Schiller belong in this group.[4] The media also routinely are scanned critically, if informally, at professional conventions of social scientists and journalists. Special workshops, such as the annual Aspen Conference on Communications and Society, have focused narrowly on specific problems of the media and have publicized reform proposals.

Informal criticism has also come from various public interest groups. In many cases these have been institutions organized for other purposes, such as the national Parent and Teacher Association or the American Medical Association. Special media action groups have voiced their concerns publicly. The National Citizens Committee for Broadcasting and the Children's Television Workshop, discussed more fully in Chapter 2, are examples. Complaints by public interest and media action groups, like most other forms of informal criticism, have been largely ineffectual. The critics may disturb the news profession momentarily, but they rarely induce a change in media policies.

Formal Criticism

Formal protests about media performance can be lodged with the FCC, the government agency charged with supervision of the electronic media. As mentioned earlier, the FCC's Broadcast Bureau in Washington accepts citizen complaints. Interested parties also have a chance to present their perspectives on media policy at FCC hearings. The commission holds such hearings before granting broadcast licenses or when licenses have been challenged. They provide opportunities to counter the pressures brought by the media industry and balance the pro-industry biases that public regulatory bodies often develop.

Formal avenues for criticism and policy suggestions by the public are beneficial. However, a number of serious problems have diminished their usefulness. Most fundamental and least solvable is the problem of making sure that the complaints and suggestions thus aired represent community beliefs. Advocates of mainstream positions are often conspicuously silent. The laudable desire to hear and heed dissenters may lead to inadequate concern about the merits of their claims, to the detriment of more general public interests.

A few examples of vociferous protests will illustrate the problem of determining what constitutes the "voice of the people." Some of these protests were ignored; others were heeded. The mini-series "Holocaust" that dramatized Nazi atrocities was loudly opposed by a variety of groups claiming that it generated anti-German feelings and hatred between Jews and gentiles. Yet it was widely acclaimed by many critics and attracted between 38 and 48 million viewers nightly. Similarly, between 30 and 40 million people watched each episode of the "Godfather" I and II series about Mafia ventures. Most of these viewers considered the program worthwhile. Yet thousands of Italian-Americans denounced the show and complained through various public channels that it slandered Italians. Stories about abortion, homosexuality, drug addiction, the activities of religious cults, or the successful ventures of discredited politicians have often been suppressed or toned down because of the flood of protests they might invite.

Lack of money can be a major barrier to challenging industry representatives effectively in an FCC hearing or before a court of law. In the past, protest groups have had to rely on their limited resources, except when the broadcast industry has voluntarily shouldered their legal fees. Because payments in such cases are available only for legal costs, protest groups have been encouraged to sue rather than try to negotiate settlements. It has been suggested that the FCC should pay the expenses of protest groups. Since Congress is unlikely to allocate special funds for this purpose, the commission, which is short on money, is unlikely to implement this suggestion.

In general, lawsuits involving claims about harmful television programming have failed. A widely publicized example is the trial of Ronny Zamora, a teen-ager who was convicted by a Florida court for murdering an eighty-three-year-old woman. His parents sued the three networks for negligent programming, claiming that television shows had incited and taught their son how to murder. The suit was dismissed by a federal judge who ruled that the media had not been negligent.[5] In 1978 a California court likewise dismissed a negligence suit against NBC brought by the parents of a young rape victim. The rape had mimicked a scene from the movie "Born Innocent," which had been shown on television four days earlier.[6]

To enhance public influence on communications policy, there have been proposals to place ombudsmen—formal advocates of the public's interests—in various bodies that deal with communications policy. Alternatively, a central ombudsman office has been proposed to assist public interest groups and individuals in preparing and presenting their complaints and suggestions. Thus far, these proposals have not been implemented. However, nearly two dozen newspapers have set up ombudsmen facilities to permit readers to challenge news policies.[7] Readers' concerns and ombudsmen's activities are regularly reported by the papers.

Media Councils

Elected or appointed bodies that hear and investigate complaints about mass media output—"media councils"—are another avenue for channeling criticism. These councils then publicize their findings, using the power of publicity to correct undesirable media practices. Generally, media councils lack power to enforce their recommendations. Media councils have been used in Great Britain and in some midwestern and western states and cities in this country.

Controversy over the merits of media councils came to a head in the United States in 1973 when a private research organization, the Twentieth Century Fund, created a task force to look into the establishment of an independent, private National News Council. The council would monitor national news sources: wire services, the weekly news magazines, and the national newspaper syndicates. As proposed by the task force, it was "to receive, to examine, and to report on complaints concerning the accuracy and fairness of news reporting in the United States, as well as to initiate studies and report on issues involving the freedom of the press." [8] With members drawn from the public and the journalism profession, the council was intended as a forum for independent appraisals of the fairness and representativeness of media performance. Its findings were to be released to the public in reports and press releases. But, aside from the power of publicity, there would be no means to enforce the council's recommendations.

The press has strongly opposed media councils, even though they have earned substantial respect and approval in Britain and the United States and even though they appear to have enhanced media credibility and reduced the frequency of libel suits.[9] Major U.S. media rejected the Twentieth Century Fund proposals for a National News Council by a two-to-one margin. The council, they feared, would impair editorial independence by publicizing its appraisals of the merits of ongoing news policies. Newspeople claimed that such a watchdog organization was unnecessary because they were serving the public well. Despite media opposition, however, a National News Council was set up in 1973. Several news organizations gave space to its activities and reports, but it never became a major force in arbitrating questions of media ethics. It finally was dissolved in 1984.[10]

Alternative Media

Hundreds of specialized media address information needs neglected or poorly served by the regular media. Many concentrate in whole or in part on political commentary. The *New Republic, Mother Jones,* the *National Review,* and, at times, the *New Yorker* are examples. Moreover, recent simple and cheap technologies enable interest groups to publish and distribute their own magazines, newsletters, and audio and video tapes on controversial political issues. Antinuclear and environmental groups, for example, have created and distributed tapes either for individual use or for broadcast.[11] Supporters of candidates for political office have done the same.

Numerous professional and trade journals are devoted to a multitude of human interests such as religion, sports, fine and popular arts, automobiles, stamp collecting, and bird watching. If audiences numbering into thousands and even millions of people constitute a "mass," these are, by definition, mass media. Modern means of distributing information bridge the distances that physically separate these mass audiences who share specialized interests. The demand for targeted information has increased in recent years; witness the mushrooming of magazines such as *Psychology Today, Sports Illustrated,* or the even more focused *Ski, Photography,* and *Car and Driver.* Currently, more than ten thousand magazines are published in the United States.[12] Their popularity led to the demise of broadly oriented magazines such as *Look, Life,* and the *Saturday Evening Post,* which lost advertising revenues to these competitors.

Alternative media also have developed in the newspaper field. A large foreign language press in the United States serves various ethnic and nationality groups. In 1987, 372 foreign language newspapers were published in thirty-nine languages. Another 148 papers, most of them weeklies, catered to the needs of black audiences. Religious groups, too, publish their own newspapers. For example, there were 117 Jewish papers in the United States in 1987.[13] Local community newspapers, published daily, every other day, or once a week, present community news.[14] The metropolitan press does not have space for such news, which would be of little interest to most of its readers. Instead, it often targets special news supplements to specific neighborhoods within cities.

Radio stations in many American cities service specialized groups, and a few cities have specialized television outlets. An average of four hundred radio stations cater almost exclusively to ethnic groups, especially blacks and Hispanics. Other stations, including a number of television stations, provide periodic programming for ethnic groups and other specialized audiences. The lush growth of specialized media serves as a partial antidote to the concentrated ownership of general mass media (see Chapter 2). The potential role of cable television, yet another means for serving particular community interests, will be discussed more fully later in this chapter.

For many people the term *alternative media* conjures up visions of the politically radical, iconoclastic, and counterculture newspapers that were plentiful in the late 1960s and early 1970s. Many Americans, particularly youth and minorities, opposed the positions taken on the Vietnam War and other issues by the regular media. Dissenters therefore created the *underground press.* The name was applied because these media carried on the flagrant opposition to government policy that is often forbidden in other countries, where such media must hide from the police. Underground actually was a misnomer for the American media of protest because they were allowed to operate quite openly. But it gave them an aura of fighting the establishment at great personal risk.

The *Seed*, the *East Village Other*, the *Berkeley Barb*, the *Rat*, *The Great Speckled Bird*, and other underground publications went beyond rejecting the current political establishment. They also rejected the values and culture of American mainstream society. In this they differed from social responsibility journalism that supports basic American values and attacks only their violations. Politically, the underground media were generally left-wing in orientation: Communist, Socialist, or Anarchist. They attracted attention by being totally subjective and visually and verbally shocking. Profanity, pictures of sexual activities, and pornographic cartoons and drawings abounded because these underground journalists felt that their attacks on American society must be sensational to succeed.

The rise of the underground press demonstrates that mass media can still be started and operated with modest means. The media of the

1960s were financed mostly through sales advertising for things like counterculture records, music productions, X-rated movies, and classified advertisements requesting services such as sex partners, nude models, or hallucinogenic drugs. Staffs were paid meager salaries or no salaries at all.[15] The counterculture papers concentrated on features rather than regular news stories. They assigned their limited personnel only to stories that they planned to use, rather than covering a full series of regular beats. For daily news and some features they relied on the Underground Press Service (UPS), Liberation News Service (LNS), and other news service cooperatives.

To beat the high cost of printing, the underground media used inexpensive offset processes. As soon as papers were ready, they were peddled on street corners near university campuses. There were no set numbers of issues per year, no regular publication schedules, no business staffs or circulation departments. At the height of underground press popularity, readership was estimated at 10 million, with most issues used by several people.

Underground media in the 1960s were not limited to the comparatively unregulated print realm. They also flourished in the regulated broadcast field. Underground radio stations featured mostly rock music and disc jockeys who commented on society, sexual matters, the drug culture, and other counterculture interests. The FCC rarely interfered with their unconventional activities, except when they flouted the law too brazenly. For instance, when a Texas rock station tipped off the local drug community about a drug raid planned by police, there was an investigation into the sources from which the station had received the advance information.

The mushrooming of protest media in the 1960s and 1970s—at one time there were nearly one thousand underground newspapers and four hundred counterculture radio stations—attests to the vitality and flexibility of the mass media system.[16] The abrupt decline of underground media with the end of the Vietnam War—there are only a handful left, and most of them either have turned middle-class or have become predominantly pornographic—also shows that the system is able to prune its unneeded branches when the demand ends.[17]

The tolerance of the government for underground media demonstrates that government control over media content, however offensive, has had a light touch. Few countries equal and none exceeds the freedom to express radical viewpoints enjoyed by American media. In fact, some of the causes pressed by underground news sources ultimately became part of the mainstream of politics. In the end waning public support rather than official censorship led to the steep decline in this genre of journalism. Neither technical nor legal barriers block a revival, should social or political conditions provide enough incentives.

The Impact of New Technologies

Marshall McLuhan, the television guru of the 1960s, predicted that the world would become a global village where humanity would share a global culture via television.[18] His vision of shared audio-visual news and entertainment has largely come to pass, but reality is far richer than even McLuhan imagined. The vast amounts of diverse information produced by new technologies permit people to create their own, individualized information diet. The new age of personalized mass media has arrived.

This store of information that is readily available to media audiences has grown by leaps and bounds.[19] Small as well as large communities share in this bounty, reducing the dangers of local monopoly control over information and opening up hitherto closed communication ghettos. Computers, communication satellites, wired broadcasts, laser fiber optics, very high-speed integrated circuits, and other new technologies provide a virtually unlimited array of channels for electronic transmission of news and entertainment. Even newspapers can be printed and transmitted electronically. Cable television systems now in operation, or in the planning stage, project that they will offer broadcasts from twenty to one hundred separate channels. The vast number of radio and television programs available from satellites can be received by television stations over the air or through cable channels. Individual consumers can tap directly into these offerings through backyard satellite dishes. Space for various types of electronic transmissions, including television, can be rented by public and private parties from the satellites' owners. Stations can even use satellites to supply other stations with live videos of stories that the station has covered locally. These offerings reduce dependence on current network programming and vastly expand television programming options.

Video recorders, video tapes, and video discs store electronic fare, allowing people to watch what they want when they want it. Annoying commercials can be readily deleted. By 1988 nearly 40 million of America's 88 million households had at least one video recorder, a phenomenal growth spurt over a decade. Pay cable and pay-over-the-air television provide special entertainment or special interest programs at moderate costs. People pay solely for those programs they choose to watch. For instance, students can enroll in television courses that are available only to those who have paid for the course. Similarly, medical information can be relayed through cable to doctors throughout the country, as can programs on crime fighting for police personnel or opera performances for opera buffs. This is akin to the services presently rendered by specialized journals and magazines with national circulations.

When programs are interactive, participants can communicate di-

rectly with each other, just like they would if they met in person. In fact, two-way channels on cable television have become commonplace. Viewers can interact with others while watching the same programs. Two-way communication technologies using radio, telephones, and computers have improved steadily. They have been useful in integrating outlying areas with social service systems in more populated centers. In Alaska and northern Canada, for example, these technologies deliver educational and health services and give people a greater voice in government.[20]

   Thanks to the new technologies the mass media business has made noteworthy advances on three fronts: news gathering, news processing, and news dissemination.[21] Access to computer data bases and satellites has put an enormous store of usable information within reach of average newspeople wherever they may be. Even foreign countries kept off limits by hostile rulers can be explored by satellites, as can remote areas of the globe and even the private retreats of powerful elites. The ability to search data bases electronically for specific bits of information and to combine these data in a variety of ways opens up countless new possibilities for creating news stories. When it comes to distribution, the array of available channels for immediate or delayed transmission has multiplied far beyond the range deemed possible a scant twenty-five years ago.

Several serious problems created by the new technologies will require thoughtful new policies. But the FCC and Congress thus far have done little beyond preliminary discussions and studies. They have not tackled the crucial issue of standardization of technologies so that investments in equipment and training can be kept moderate. If systems remain largely incompatible, consumers (including the news media) will be able to use only a small portion of the new information riches. Safeguarding individual privacy also presents major hurdles. Today computers can assemble scattered bits of information in seconds to derive a comprehensive portrait of an individual's past. Unless individual privacy becomes more fully protected, the computer age could well turn into an Orwellian nightmare of living in glass cages exposed to instant public scrutiny.

Similarly, the new information-gathering techniques will make it far more difficult to protect national security information from prying eyes. Congress and the courts will be hard put to strike a sound balance between a free press and a secure society. All this is happening at a time when the ease of disseminating information through private or public channels may make responsible journalism more difficult than ever before.

Barriers to Development

A look at technology may tell us what is possible rather than indicate what is likely to happen, particularly in the short run. A number of political barriers block the full development of new mass communication technologies. Above all, the usual bureaucratic barriers must be surmounted. Many new developments never get off the ground because bureaucracies impose too many regulations to guard against abuses. Unrealistically high standards are frequently prescribed, raising costs beyond economically feasible levels. State and local rules, piled on top of federal regulations, complicate the picture even further. Not only do they add more requirements, but rules issued by various jurisdictions often conflict. Every major technological revolution—and the information transmission revolution is major—has brought about economic and political dislocations. Such massive changes are fought by those whose knowledge and equipment will be made obsolete by them. Communications technologies involve large investments so that their sudden obsolescence becomes a crushing financial blow.

Some of the new mass media offerings endanger current jobs. For instance, round-the-clock cable educational programs, structured like regular classrooms, threaten teachers' jobs. Medical programs that teach people better medical self-care methods may be unwelcome competition for the health professions. Televised programs featuring outstanding practitioners and facilities may establish standards for professional performance that average institutions cannot meet.

Early entrants in a technological field also develop a squatter's mentality about rights they have acquired, such as the right to use certain broadcast frequencies or particular technologies. Newcomers, on the other hand, are eager to reallocate facilities in line with their special interests. They want to mandate the use of more advanced technologies, even before they can guarantee that a market for these technologies and services will develop. This could wipe out proven interests in favor of new claimants whose prospects for success are uncertain. Obstacles also arise because competing new technologies benefit various groups unevenly. Power struggles, which may be prolonged, are fiercest before the status quo is determined. Meanwhile, technology continues its advance, raising new problems that further delay the green light for implementing new systems.

The Emergence of Cable Television

Cable television's rocky history in the United States illustrates the problems posed by technical innovations. It also illustrates the many political decisions that must be made to fit a new information technology into the existing legislative and administrative structure. Technological progress marches on relentlessly. The costly cable technology may be outmoded before it reaches maturity. Cheaper technologies, such as those using direct broadcasting satellites to receiver dishes on earth or transmitting television over telephone wires, may be the wave of the future.

When cable television first became available in 1949, established broadcasters viewed it as a serious threat. They feared that the availability of numerous television channels would lead to a large menu of programs similar to the variety then offered by radio shows. This would splinter television audiences. Smaller audiences would mean smaller advertising revenues and smaller profits for existing stations. In turn, this might mean poorer programming because reduced revenue would necessitate curtailment of expenditures. Television networks were also concerned that cable operators would pirate, rather than buy, their signals and broadcast the programs they had produced at high cost. When satellite technology evolved, fears mounted. The networks might be destroyed entirely if stations could pick up programs directly from satellites and broadcast them nationwide via cable television.

The initial response of the FCC to cable technology was typical of regulatory agencies. The commission, prodded by established interests, protected the status quo with regulations that prevented the newcomers from harming these interests. These regulations sharply limited the types of programs that cable television stations could broadcast when they competed with established network services. Consequently, the growth of the cable industry was stunted.

Cable industry groups ultimately persuaded public officials that cable technology was needed because it could reach people in locations inaccessible to regular television signals. The idea of breaking the near monopoly enjoyed by the networks over broadcasting also became attractive. So did the possibility of opening up many new channels for broadcasting to groups hitherto shut out by a limited spectrum. By 1972 these pressures were sufficiently strong to convince the FCC to ease its regulations on the types of programs that cable television could broadcast. The cable system had a new lease on life. However, in what is also a typical move when new technologies arise, the FCC imposed a number of very costly regulations to force cable television to serve public needs that had never been met in the past. A minimum of twenty channels was required, including outlets for the general public, educational institutions, and local governments. There were also requirements for two-way capabilities and for carrying signals of local broadcasters.

When these rules also turned out to be too burdensome to allow rapid development of cable television, they were eased in 1976. Service requirements imposed on the new industry were loosened further after successful legal challenges by cable operators who questioned the propriety of regulating cable television as if it were using scarce airwaves when cable transmission channels were plentiful.[22] In 1979 the FCC issued a lengthy research report on the economic impact of cable broadcasting. It concluded—erroneously as it turned out—that cable was only a minor economic threat to the established television industry and that it did not endanger the industry's "ability to perform in the public interest." In the wake of these findings, the federal shackles were removed from the industry, one by one.[23] With the passage of the Cable Communications Policy Act of 1984, deregulation was complete.[24] The act deregulated rates and made renewal of cable franchises nearly automatic in areas with ready access to over-the-air television—roughly 90 percent of the cabled areas.

Meanwhile, the resistance of the established industries to this new competition had gradually softened. In fact, a number of them, heeding the old adage "If you can't lick 'em, join 'em," invested heavily in cable facilities, once the FCC eased controls regarding crossownership and admission of the networks to the cable market. Figure 11-1 illustrates the rapid explosion of the cable industry in the 1970s and 1980s. By 1988 more than half of the nation's television households were linked to cable systems, and network television had lost nearly 20 percent of its prime-television audience.

Figure 11-1   The Cable TV Explosion

Year	Penetration Rate (percent of households with cable)	Cable Subscribers (in thousands)
1965	3.3	1,760
1970	7.5	4,498
1975	13.3	9,197
1980	22.6	17,671
1981	28.3	23,219
1982	35.0	29,341
1983	40.5	33,794
1984	43.7	37,291
1985	45.3	38,700
1986	47.4	41,000
1987	50.5	44,188

Source: Compiled from "Cable Household Penetration," Multichannel News, December 7, 1987, and Cabletelevision Advertising Bureau data, 1986.

Today the old-line media enterprises see cable largely as a new delivery system for the news and entertainment programs that they already produce. Nine satellites orbit the earth carrying programs from more than fifty cable channels to the 7,800 cable systems in the United States.[25] Table 11-1 shows the media industry's heavy investment in the new technology and the consolidation of ownership in the industry. In fact, by 1985 the fifty systems analyzed in Table 11-1 served 60 percent of the nation's cable television audience. The top ten in the group served 43 percent. Some analysts predicted that the top twenty-five companies would control 80 percent of the subscribers by 1990. Small independent companies were rapidly vanishing from the market.[26] If present trends continue, including the escalation of costs for entering the cable business and surviving the initial years, oligopoly may become the dominant cable pattern.

The FCC's willingness to let old-line media buy cable systems contrasts sharply with its nearly total prohibition of telephone company activity in the cable field. Telephone companies are allowed to serve only remote areas that cable cannot profitably reach. Should the tele-

Table 11-1   Ownership of Top Fifty Cable Systems

Category of owner	Number of systems	Percentage of systems	Percentage of cable homes
Broadcasters	23	46	30
Newspaper/magazine publishers	17	34	25
Film producers and distributors	6	12	9
Independents	19	38	25
Other	3	6	5

Source: Adapted from Herbert H. Howard, "An Update on Cable TV Ownership: 1985," *Journalism Quarterly* 63 (Winter 1986): 709. Reprinted by permission of the Association for Education in Journalism and Mass Communication, publishers of *Journalism Quarterly.*

Note: Includes only the fifty largest multiple-system organizations. Totals exceed N of 50 and 100 percent because many owners do business in more than one category. Ownership may be full or partial.

phone companies receive permission to freely enter the cable business, the estimates for growth of the cable audience will rise sharply because existing telephone wiring could then be adapted. Fears that AT&T, the giant telephone enterprise, might monopolize the cable scene led to its initial exclusion from the cable market.[27] The court-ordered break-up of the company in 1984 has lessened that fear.

FCC rules and the opposition of the established industries have not been the only hurdles faced by the cable industry. There are numerous local political hurdles as well. Laying of cables requires permission from local authorities. To avoid undue duplication of facilities, franchises must be granted. Usually these go to a single company only. The franchising process has been highly political, in terms of both the selection of a particular company and the determination of the conditions of the franchise. Many small enterprises have been squeezed out because they have been unable to pay the costs of bidding for a contract, to grease the wheels of politics, or to finance initial red-ink years. Like most public utility companies, the survivors enjoy monopoly status within the cable field.

In the absence of national rules, local franchising policies have been diverse.[28] Franchisers and franchisees must agree on the time to be allowed for constructing the system and the life of the franchise (usually fifteen years). They also must agree on requirements regarding public service and open-access channels and service for outlying areas where costs will exceed profits temporarily or permanently. Service to rural areas may pose insurmountable economic problems, particularly in the western plains and the Rocky Mountain states. Alternatives to cable, such as microwave relays, satellite broadcasts, or transmission over telephone wires, may have to be considered. Difficult decisions have to be made in choosing appropriate government agencies to supervise the execution of cable contracts and to ensure that programming serves the public interest. Finally, major controversies need to be settled regarding the nature of the fee structure and the manner in which government exacts its tribute.

Regulatory Options

Governments have several policy options for dealing with cable and other emerging communication systems. First, they can play a hands-off, laissez-faire role, allowing the system to develop as its private owners please.[29] This is the policy advocated in various proposals to revise the Communications Act of 1934. The precedent for this policy is the traditional stance of government toward the print media. If one believes that government should regulate information supply only when transmission channels are scarce, as happened with early radio and television, then it makes sense to leave cable television unregulated. When electronic broadcast outlets are plentiful, market forces presumably come into play so that necessary services will be supplied in a far more flexible way than is possible when government regulations intervene. The only restraints that may be needed are safeguards to protect national security and maintain social norms and privacy.

Second, cable television and other systems can be treated as common carriers, like the telephone or rail and bus lines. In the case of cable, the rationale is that it is a vital resource for the transmission of information that should be available to everyone wishing to send messages. Common carrier status makes transmission facilities available to everyone on a first-come, first-served basis. The owners of cable facilities would not broadcast their own programs as is common now. Instead they would lease their channels to various broadcasters for fees regulated by government. Such open access would obviate current complaints that cable operators selectively exclude certain programs.

The FCC and various local governments like the common carrier concept. It has been adopted for dealing with communications satellites. But the U.S. Supreme Court decided in 1979 that cable could not be considered a common carrier. An Arkansas operator, Midwest Video Company, therefore could not be required by federal regulations to provide public access channels.[30] The ruling pleased the cable industry because it preserved its control over policy making. However, the ruling does not bar state and local authorities from imposing common carrier status on the industry.

Congress, too, has repeatedly imposed some common carrier features on the industry. In the mid-1960s, for instance, it ordered cable systems to carry all local stations so that cable customers would receive programs broadcast by local over-the-air services. The industry brought suit and won judgments in 1985 and again in 1987 that the "must carry rule" violated the First Amendment rights of cable companies.[31] The victory for cable systems was a defeat for champions of broad rights of public access to the media. Now their right of access to the cable audience depends on the good will of cable system operators.

The government has a third option. It can confer public trustee status on communication enterprises. Owners of cable facilities, for example, would have full responsibility for programming, but they would be required to meet certain public service obligations. These might include adherence to equal time provisions and limitations on materials unsuitable for children or offensive to community standards of morality. They might also encompass rules about access to cable to ensure availability of public and government channels, including facilities to broadcast public education, public safety, and medical and social service information.

The rationale for conferring trustee status on broadcasters has been twofold. In the past the scarcity argument has been powerful, but it has lost validity. The other argument for trustee status is that television is a highly influential medium. It should be regulated to make sure that valuable programs are broadcast and harmful ones avoided and that certain canons of fairness are observed. This is a powerful argument with strong support in much of the world. It is the argument that Third World nations have made so persuasively, as discussed in the previous chapter. But it is not the primary argument on which the American system was built, and it is incompatible with the First Amendment.

Paying the Piper

Whether cable television and other new technologies are treated like any private enterprise, like a common carrier, or like a trustee, their costs have to be paid. There are three possibilities for financing, each with different policy consequences: advertiser support, audience payments, and government subsidies.

Like television at present, cable services can be sustained by advertisers. This requires programming that has mass appeal. Such programming is bound to share the strengths and weaknesses of current over-the-air television. Sponsor influence may increase in the cable age because competition for sponsors becomes keener when channels multiply. Many stations, particularly those with small audiences, may even find it difficult to attract enough sponsors to pay for their operations.

While advertising revenues have been growing, cable television continues to rely heavily on audience payments. These have generally taken the form of a monthly service charge for the facilities, to which an installation charge has often been added. Special additional programming may be available for a flat monthly rate or on a per program basis. The average yearly cost in 1988 was $275 per household. Service charge financing has been quite popular in many foreign countries. In the United States, however, it initially met with resistance because good services are available throughout the United States free of charge.

By the mid-1980s much of the initial resistance to paying for television had been overcome. Half of America's households had been cabled, and many were paying for special programs in addition to their standard monthly fees. Although a number of programming services had succumbed to competition and some new cable ventures were in financial difficulties, the industry as a whole was thriving. Some of its services, like live coverage of major news happenings, provided by Cable News Network (CNN), had become highly influential. These largely unedited broadcasts supplied up-to-the-minute information to government officials, lobbyists, and to other news professionals.[32] Moreover, the worst fears of old-line broadcasting entrepreneurs had not materialized. The number of viewers dropped measurably but not catastrophically. The networks were ailing financially, but competition from the new media was not the only reason (see Chapter 2). As had been the case with past innovations, the new media had not mortally wounded their predecessors.

A major social drawback of service charges for cable broadcasts is that poor families who most need many of the specialized programs are least able to pay. Middle-income families who already enjoy many social advantages benefit most. The information resources made available to them through cable programs enhance their status, leaving lower class people farther behind.[33] This problem could be reduced through government subsidies paid to the cable industry on a basis similar to financing public television, or through government subsidies paid to the poor. The latter system seems preferable to avoid making cable financially dependent on the government, thereby endangering cablecasters' freedom of action.

The Shape of the Future

Regulation versus Deregulation

New communications technologies require a complete rethinking of the scope and purposes of federal regulation of broadcast media. The Communications Act of 1934 was passed because transmission facilities were scarce; Congress wanted to make certain that the limited number of franchises served broad public interests and were parceled out equitably. Fifty years later the basic regulatory framework remains intact although its ostensible raison d'être has largely vanished. Despite mushrooming broadcast outlets, total deregulation and reliance on traditional

First Amendment values are still distant goals. Dissatisfaction with the services supplied by private entrepreneurs has fueled opposition to deregulation. The wave of mergers in the 1980s, which placed most established and emerging networks under the control of big corporations, rekindled fears that the media might become the mouthpieces of special interests, and that financial returns would be their programming lodestar. Plummeting revenues and sharp cuts in news division staffs heightened these fears.

At the international level pressures also are mounting for increasing government control and responsibility for media performance. This is happening at a time when the lines between unregulated print and regulated electronic media are blurring. The price of progress in electronic transmission of printed news may be the loss of freedom from government regulation. To prevent this, Sen. Bob Packwood of Oregon introduced a constitutional amendment in 1982 to explicitly extend First Amendment rights to the electronic media. Congressional opposition has thus far blocked its passage.

A great challenge faces broadcast policy makers when it comes to media regulation. They can yield to domestic and international pressures and make government the arbiter of what is good and safe news and entertainment for the public, or they can leave that role in private hands, at the mercy of nonelected media tycoons. Given these alternatives, this author casts her vote for the latter option, believing with Thomas Jefferson that "error of opinion may be tolerated where reason is left free to combat it." [34]

Two-Way Communication and Televotes

Another important area of public concern is two-way electronic communication. This feature of the communications revolution has been hailed as the gateway to genuine direct democracy, especially at the local level. In the future public business presumably can be conducted in front of the television set. Citizens can watch the proceedings of legislative bodies and cast votes of approval or disapproval.

Pilot projects already have been conducted in the United States and abroad.[35] In San Jose, California, for example, school board meetings were televised. All sides of controversial school issues were aired, and the televised discussion was supplemented by newspaper articles. The public was then given a chance to vote on policy suggestions through two-way cable or through ballots printed in the local newspapers. Unfortunately, participation was uneven. In San Jose, as in most of the other "televote" projects, the bulk of votes came from middle-class people. Most lower-class people did not participate.

Another problem has been the reluctance of public officials to implement policies supported by televotes. There are several reasons.

On the national level, electronic voting raises important constitutional issues. The United States is a representative democracy that holds elections at regular intervals. Between elections, officials make decisions they consider to be in the public interest. The Constitution did not provide for direct democracy governed by a series of plebiscites. Hence direct democracy may be unconstitutional. Quite aside from legal questions, the merits of direct democracy at various government levels in the United States remain highly controversial. Widespread adoption of electronic plebiscites, with or without extensive prior information campaigns, is therefore unlikely in the foreseeable future.

The possibility of using the two-way circuitry for educational programs, particularly those that would improve the status of disadvantaged groups, is less controversial. Again the major obstacle, beyond funding and making the technology available, is motivating people to use it. Both successes and failures have been recorded in initial experiments.

Spartanburg, South Carolina, for example, experimented with cablecasts of high school subjects to permit adults to earn high school diplomas without leaving home. Sixty-two percent of the adults in the area lacked a high school diploma. The fifteen-week program made use of interactive technology; students used an eight-button terminal to answer the teacher's questions and ask for help with problems. For people who took the course, results were as good as those obtained from actual classroom attendance. But the program had to be discontinued because too few people were enrolled to keep the per-pupil cost within reasonable limits.[36]

By contrast, a program geared to senior citizens in Reading, Pennsylvania, became very popular. The program linked three senior citizen centers and connected them to public schools, the city council, and other public places. Whenever the centers were hooked up with a public facility, such as a city council session, questions asked of city council members, and their answers, could be heard and viewed in all the centers. Participants in the three centers could also interact with each other. All programs were produced and conducted by senior citizens. Potentially shut-in and shut-out adults were thus reintegrated into the community. They became more aware of their mutual problems and problems of the community at large. The community benefited from hearing senior citizens' views about public policies.[37]

Two-way cable has offered a variety of programs to general audiences, but they have been less popular than expected. Warner Amex Cable Communications's QUBE system, which served 350,000 viewers in Columbus (Ohio), Cincinnati, Pittsburgh, Dallas, Houston, and St. Louis suburbs, rarely attained more than 2 percent participation for its interactive programs. These included talent contests, astrology shows, exercise classes, interactive games, football games, town meetings, and public hearings involving federal agencies. In the course of a month, cumulatively about one-quarter of QUBE subscribers chose to participate in some form of two-way programming. Game shows with a chance to win prizes and public policy questions attained the highest response rates. In 1984 QUBE two-way services were sharply curtailed. The reasons for the disappointing results of the six-year program may have been the audience's reluctance to participate, unattractive program formats, and technical difficulties in responding when several viewers were watching one television set.[38]

Fragmentation of the Broadcast Audience

The multitude of cable channels and the even broader options created by video tape technology have prompted fears that the national political consensus will become fragmented. Specialized television fare in news and entertainment could diminish attention to politics and splinter the national consensus that is supported by national media.[39] As discussed in Chapter 5, nationwide dissemination of similar news has fostered shared political socialization. When news becomes fragmented, people are likely to be socialized in disparate ways. If political programming becomes available only on channels dedicated to politics, will people choose to watch it? Will government leaders be able to convey their messages to the public? A music fan, tuned in to an all-music station, may watch music programs only; a black or Hispanic person may tune in only to stations concerned with black and Hispanic affairs. Many citizens thus may become prisoners of their special interests and may miss out on happenings in the broader culture.

On the positive side of the ledger, specialization raises the possibility of a better fit between audience needs and public messages. Government programs may operate more successfully, given ampler opportunities for one- and two-way communication with selected audiences. The electoral chances of minority candidates and parties may improve with increased ability to target their messages to selected audiences. The possibilities for change are staggering, but too undefined as yet to hazard predictions.

Fears that fragmentation of the broadcast audience will lead to political fragmentation are not shared by everyone, of course. Many people point out that the national consensus was not ruptured when alternative media were used in the past. They argue that fragmented interests create the demand for fragmented media rather than the reverse. If there is political and social consensus, people will seek out information pertaining to the larger community. Even if the new media increase fragmentation, many people do not find this objectionable, believing that pluralism is preferable to the traditional melting-pot ideals.

Media pluralism may herald more local programming. As mentioned earlier, most local governments are eager to use cable channels to broadcast local political news. Local school systems and police and fire departments have also sought access to cable to air their concerns. If publicity means power, the new communications media may enhance the power of local institutions, possibly at the expense of national ones. The two-way capacity often makes programming attractive to local audiences even when it lacks the polish of professional programs. The new communications media therefore may allow local organizations to reach much larger constituencies than was hitherto possible. By 1987 more than forty thousand hours of community programming was broadcast each week on community access channels. No audience figures were available, but they probably were modest considering the mixed quality of the broadcasts.

While the possibilities for strengthening local communities through increased publicity are good, cable television along with satellite technology also can deflect interest away from the local scene and produce global villages of like-minded people. National cable television networks, such as the Cable News Network owned by Atlanta-based Turner Communications, or the Colorado-based Tele-Communications, Inc., which owns over six hundred cable outlets, are examples of movement in this direction.[40]

Public Television

Yet another issue brought to the fore by the coming age of broadcast plenty is the fate of public television. As discussed in Chapter 2, public television was organized to provide an alternative to the typical programming available on the commercial networks. It also was intended to be an outlet for programs geared to minorities. These are the very services that cable television presumably will perform on a commercial basis. Since public television has always depended on public subsidies, and its audiences, except for children's programs, have been quite limited, pressures to abandon it may become strong.

Of course, the hitch in this argument is the presumption that the mushrooming commercial television enterprises will be willing and able to fill the niche occupied by the public broadcasting system. A glance at any weekly television schedule raises serious doubts. Most of the new outlets provide clones of the offerings that are familiar from network television.[41] Sophisticated cultural and educational programming is scarce and has not been commercially viable because audiences have remained small. The difficulty of keeping the public broadcasting system solvent may spell its death knell, nonetheless. The European practice of funding public broadcasting principally through consumer fees has never been considered a realistic option in the United States.

The Consequences of Change

The concerns outlined thus far are undoubtedly not the only ones ahead. Many others will require decisions that go far beyond solving technical issues. The direction of communications policy is at stake and with it the tone and possibly the direction of American politics generally. John M. Eger, a former director of the White House Office of Telecommunications Policy, has remarked that this is indeed a time of decision."For as we are moving into a future rich in innovation and in social change, we are also moving into a storm center of new world problems." The new technologies are "a force for change throughout the world that simply will not be stopped, no matter how it is resisted." And then he asks, "Are we ready for the consequences of this change? Are we prepared to consider the profound social, legal, economic, and political effects of technology around the world?" [42]

Currently, the answer is "no." In the communications field the structure for policy making at all government levels is fragmented and ill-suited to deal with the existing problems, to say nothing of those that must be anticipated.[43] Policies are improvised when pressures become strong, yielding in a crazy-quilt pattern to various industry concerns, to public interest groups, to domestic or foreign policy considerations, to the pleas of engineers and lawyers, and to the suggestions of political scientists and economists. Narrow issues are addressed, but the full scope of the situation is ignored.[44]

Neither Congress nor the executive branch is willing to enter this thicket of controversy when so many other battles must be fought. It is not likely that policy leadership will emerge. "Muddling through," the watchword for the 1970s and 1980s, is likely to be the watchword for the 1990s as well.

Summary

Many people are dissatisfied with the performance of the mass media, especially television. Through media councils and other channels the public can air its dissatisfaction, but criticism usually has had limited success in changing media content. To fill the gaps left by the major mass media, many alternative media have been created. These media are organized either to serve demographically distinct populations or to cater to particular substantive concerns or political orientations.

Among alternative media the underground press is especially interesting. During the 1960s it demonstrated that the government will tolerate a journalism that attacks major domestic and foreign policies, even in wartime. The mushrooming of underground print and broadcast media during the Vietnam War era also showed that, in a business dominated by giants, small enterprises can operate successfully on a shoestring. The limited demand by the general public for published radical dissent, however, makes it difficult to sustain such publications over long periods of time.

In this chapter we also explored the social and political consequences of technological advances in mass media and outlined the areas where new public policies are needed. We briefly described some of the new electronic tools and sketched their capabilities in bringing about the age of broadcast plenty and of two-way communication. Their impact on life and politics in the United States could be enormous. Two-way circuitry has been hailed as the gateway to genuine direct democracy and as a great educational tool. However, electronic plebiscites are as yet too controversial to be adopted widely. Fragmentation of the broadcast audience has raised fears of political fragmentation and breakdown of the national political consensus that has been deemed essential for successful democratic government.

Various changes in regulatory policy will be required to integrate the new media technologies into the existing mass media regulatory structure. More importantly, major policy changes could arrive, almost unannounced, if the political impact of new technologies is not considered and guided carefully. By using electronic transmission facilities, the print media could be subject to the same government regulations as electronic media. A bastion of freedom might fall. The forces favoring greater government control of media content are strong at a time when most types of media use some form of electronic transmission. Whether the mass media are regulated more tightly or given freer rein, deliberate choice rather than drift should be the basis for the decisions. In that choice the perceptive comment of the *Washington Post*'s Alan Barth should be remembered: "If you want a watchdog to warn you of intruders you must put up with a certain amount of mistaken barking." [45]

Notes

1. *Julius Caesar,* act 4, scene 3, line 218.
2. David Gergen, "The Message to the Media," *Public Opinion* 7 (April/May 1984): 5-8; Andrew Randolph, "What Credibility Problem?" *Editor & Publisher,* vol. 119, January 18, 1986, 12-13; Michael Robinson, "Pressing Opinion," *Public Opinion* 9 (September/October 1986): 56-59; and Philip Meyer, "Credibility: And Now the Good News," *Presstime* 7 (June 1985): 26-27.
3. Bill Granger, "Sleazy Does It: Decency and Fair Play Take a Holiday in the New-New Journalism," *Chicago Tribune Magazine,* January 3, 1988, 4. Also see Norman E. Isaacs, *Untended Gates: The Mismanaged Press* (New York: Columbia University Press, 1986).

4. David Altheide, *Creating Reality: How TV News Distorts Events* (Beverly Hills, Calif: Sage, 1976); Isaacs, *Untended Gates;* Tom Goldstein, *The News at Any Cost: How Journalists Compromise Their Ethics to Shape the News* (New York: Simon and Schuster, 1985); Edwin Diamond, *The Tin Kazoo: Television, Politics, and the News* (Boston: MIT Press, 1975); Ben Stein, *The View from Sunset Boulevard* (New York: Basic Books, 1979); and Herbert Schiller, *Mass Communication and American Empire* (New York: Augustus M. Kelly, 1969).

5. *Zamora et al. v. Columbia Broadcasting System et al.*, 480 F. Supp. 199 (S. D. Fla. 1979). See also Robert E. Drechsel, "Media Tort Liability for Physical Harm," *Journalism Quarterly* 64 (Spring 1987): 99-105; and Juliet Lusbough Dee, "Media Accountability for Real-Life Violence: A Case of Negligence or Free Speech?" *Journal of Communication* 37 (Spring 1987): 106-138.

6. *Olivia N. (a minor) v. National Broadcasting Company,* 74 Cal. App. 3d 383 (1978), 126 Cal. App. 3d 488 (1981).

7. Donald T. Mogavero, "The American Press Ombudsman," *Journalism Quarterly* 59 (Winter 1982): 548-553, 580.

8. "Press Council Stirs Debate," *Chicago Journalism Review* 6 (April 1973): 20.

9. Ronald Farrar, "News Councils and Libel Actions," *Journalism Quarterly* 63 (Autumn 1986): 509-516.

10. Jonathan Friendly, "National News Council Will Dissolve," *New York Times,* March 23, 1984. Media critic Norman Isaacs has proposed ombudsmen as the best alternative to news councils. See Isaacs, *Untended Gates,* 132-146.

11. Erik Barnouw, "Historical Survey of Communications Breakthroughs," in *The Communications Revolution in Politics,* ed. Gerald Benjamin (New York: The Academy of Political Science, 1982), 20.

12. Ray Eldon Hiebert, Donald F. Ungurait, and Thomas W. Bohn, *Mass Media V: An Introduction to Modern Communication* (New York: Longman, 1988), 73.

13. *Gale Directory of Publications* (Princeton, N.J.: Gale Research Company, 1987), 1168-1182; Leo W. Jeffres and K. Kyoon Hur, "The Forgotten Media Consumer: The American Ethnic," *Journalism Quarterly* 57 (Spring 1980): 1017; Roland E. Worseley, *The Black Press, U.S.A.* (Ames, Iowa: Iowa State University Press, 1971); and Henry La Brie III, ed., *Perspectives of the Black Press: 1974* (Kennebunkport, Maine: Mercer House Press, 1974).

14. Morris Janowitz, *The Community Press in an Urban Setting; The Social Elements of Urbanism,* 3d ed. (Chicago: University of Chicago Press, 1980).

15. John W. Johnstone, Edward J. Slawski, and William W. Bowman, *The Newspeople* (Urbana, Ill.: University of Illinois Press, 1976), 157-179.

16. They are described more fully in Johnstone, Slawski, and Bowman, *The Newspeople,* 157-181; Laurence Leamer, *The Paper Revolutionaries: The Rise of the Underground Press* (New York: Simon and Schuster, 1972); and Jack A. Nelson,"The Underground Press," in *Readings in Mass Communication,* ed. Michael C. Emery and Ted Curtis Smythe (Dubuque, Iowa: W. C. Brown Co., 1972), 212-226.

17. Dan Wakefield, "Up From the Underground," *New York Times Magazine,* February 15, 1976, 15.

18. Marshall McLuhan, *Understanding Media: The Extensions of Man* (New York: McGraw-Hill, 1964); and Marshall McLuhan and Quentin Fiore, *The*

Medium Is the Message: An Inventory of Effects (New York: Bantam Books, 1967).

19. Ithiel de Sola Pool, *Technologies of Freedom* (Cambridge, Mass.: Harvard University Press, 1983), 152-156; and Sally Bedell Smith, "New Technologies Alter Viewing Habits," *New York Times,* October 9, 1985.

20. Heather E. Hudson, "Implications for Development Communications," *Journal of Communication* 29 (Winter 1979): 179-186.

21. U.S. Congress, Office of Technology Assessment, *Science, Technology, and the First Amendment,* OTA-CIT-369 (Washington, D.C.: U.S. Government Printing Office, 1988), 1-33.

22. *Home Box Office, Inc. v. FCC,* 567 F. 2d 9, D.C. Circuit (1977); cert. denied, 434 U.S. 829 (1977); *FCC v. Midwest Video Corp.,* 440 U.S. 689 (1979).

23. Pay television had been freed from federal controls in 1977. Remaining federal controls were dropped by 1979. Benjamin M. Compaine, Christopher H. Sterling, Thomas Guback, and J. Kendrick Noble, Jr., *Who Owns the Media? Concentration and Ownership in the Mass Communications Industry,* 2d ed. (White Plains, N.Y.: Knowledge Industry Publications, 1982), 381, 407.

24. "Cable TV," *Consumer Reports* 52 (September 1987): 547-554.

25. Ibid., 548.

26. Herbert H. Howard, "An Update on Cable TV Ownership: 1985," *Journalism Quarterly* 63 (Winter 1986): 706-709; and "Cable-TV Companies Fine-Tune Mergers to Boost Size, Profits," *Chicago Tribune,* March 13, 1988.

27. Compaine et al., *Who Owns the Media?* 390-393.

28. FCC regulations prevail over conflicting state regulations. *Capital Cities Cable v. Crisp,* 104 U.S. 2694 (1984). Federal law may preempt state laws. See William E. Hanks and Stephen E. Coran, "Federal Preemption of Obscenity Law Applied to Cable Television," *Journalism Quarterly* 63 (Spring 1986): 43-47.

29. Benno C. Schmidt, Jr., "Pluralistic Programming and Regulation of Mass Communication Media," in *Communication for Tomorrow: Policy Perspectives for the 1980s,* ed. Glen O. Robinson (New York: Praeger, 1978), 214.

30. *FCC v. Midwest Video Corp.,* 440 U.S. 689 (1979).

31. "Cable TV," *Consumer Reports,* 555.

32. Andrew Rosenthal, "Watching Cable News Network Grow," *New York Times,* December 16, 1987.

33. George A. Donohue, Phillip J. Tichenor, and Clarice N. Olien, "Mass Media and the Knowledge Gap: A Hypothesis Reconsidered," *Communication Research* 2 (1975): 3-23.

34. First inaugural address, March 4, 1801. See Andrew A. Lipscomb, ed. *The Writings of Thomas Jefferson,* vol. 3 (Washington: Thomas Jefferson Memorial Association, 1905), 319.

35. Richard Hollander, *Video Democracy: The Vote-From-Home Revolution* (Mt. Airy, Md.: Lomond, 1985).

36. William A. Lucas, "Telecommunications Technologies and Services," in *Communication for Tomorrow,* 248.

37. See Red Burns and Lynne Elton, "Reading, Pa.: Programming for the Future"; Eileen Connell, "Reading, Pa.: Training Local People"; and Mitchell L. Moss, "Reading, Pa.: Research on Community Uses," all in *Journal of Communication* 28 (Spring 1978): 148-167.

38. Sally Bedell Smith, "Two-Way Cable TV Falters," *New York Times,* March 28, 1984.

39. James G. Webster, "Audience Behavior in the New Media Environment," *Journal of Communication* 36 (Summer 1986): 77-91.
40. Use of cable television is compared with use of other media in Gerald L. Grotta and Doug Newsom, "How Does Cable Television in the Home Relate to Other Media Use Patterns?" *Journalism Quarterly* 59 (Winter 1982): 588-591, 609. Also see "Cable TV," *Consumer Reports.*
41. The reasons for this situation are explained by David Waterman, "The Failure of Cultural Programming on Cable TV: An Economic Interpretation," *Journal of Communication* 36 (Summer 1986): 92-107.
42. John M. Eger, "A Time of Decision," *Journal of Communication* 29 (Winter 1979): 204-207.
43. Lucas, "Telecommunications Technologies and Services," 248.
44. Ithiel de Sola Pool, "The Problems of WARC," *Journal of Communication* 29 (Winter 1979): 187-196.
45. Alan Barth, "If the Press Didn't Tell Us, Who Would?" (Chicago: Sigma Delta Chi, 1987).

Readings

Altschull, J. Herbert. *Agents of Power: The News Media in Human Affairs.* New York: Longman, 1984.
Arterton, F. Christopher. *Teledemocracy: Can Technology Protect Democracy?* Beverly Hills, Calif.: Sage, 1987.
Bennett, W. Lance. *News: The Politics of Illusion.* 2d ed. New York: Longman, 1988.
Isaacs, Norman E. *Untended Gates: The Mismanaged Press.* New York: Columbia University Press, 1986.
Kessler, Lauren. *The Dissident Press: Alternative Journalism in American History.* Beverly Hills, Calif.: Sage, 1984.
Pool, Ithiel de Sola. *Technologies of Freedom.* Cambridge, Mass.: Harvard University Press, 1983.
Rogers, Everett M. *Communication Technology: The New Media in Society.* New York: Free Press, 1986.
Wilson, Clint C., and Felix Gutierrez. *Minorities and Mass Media: Diversity and the End of Mass Communication.* Beverly Hills, Calif.: Sage, 1985.
Wolfson, Lewis W. *The Untapped Power of the Press: Explaining Government to the People.* New York: Praeger, 1985.

INDEX

ABC (American Broadcasting Company). *See* Capital Cities/ABC

ACT. *See* Action for Children's Television

Abortion, media and, 10

Access to information. *See* Information

Access to media. *See* Media, access to

Accuracy in Media (AIM), 58

ACLU. *See* American Civil Liberties Union

Action for Children's Television (ACT), 58

Adams, William C., 353

Adults. *See also* Attitudes; Behavior; Learning
  media influence on
    attitudes/behavior, 3 5, 10 11, 31 32n.27, 147-159, 167-182, 188n.53, 289-292
    political socialization, 152-155, 167, 168, 169-175, 182-183, 208
    voting, media effects on, 13-14, 15, 224-227

Advertising
  access to media, 122
  cable television, 381-382
  censorship, 139-140
  children's programs, 121
  cigarette, 139-140
  political, 195-196, 203
  programming, effects on, 57-58, 81-82, 121
  public broadcasting, 39-40, 55
  public service, 180-182
  truth in, 117

Agence France-Presse wire service (French), 251, 331

Agenda-setting theory in media use, 163-164

Agnew, Spiro, 244

AIM. *See* Accuracy in Media

Alabama Education Television Network, 120

Alternative media, 370-372

Altheide, David, 345

American Broadcasting Company Network (ABC). *See* Capital Cities/ABC

American Civil Liberties Union (ACLU), 298

American Newspaper Publishers Association (ANPA), 56

American Research Bureau (ARB), 105n.3

"Amerika," 58

Amin, Idi, 343

Anchorage, Alaska, earthquake coverage, 310, 311, 313

Anderson, Jack, 318-319

Anderson, John, 202, 212, 215, 217, 218, 220

Annenberg School of Communications, 168

ANPA. *See* American Newspaper Publishers Association

Antenne Deux (France), 39

Antitrust regulations, 48, 51, 70n.18

AP. *See* Wire/press services companies

Apple, R.W., Jr., 2, 198

Arafat, Yasir, 346

ARB. *See* American Research Bureau

Arledge, Roone, 287

"Arson for Profit," 283

Askew, Reubin, 204
Aspen Conference on Communications and Society, 367
Associated Press. *See* Wire/press services
Attitudes. *See also* Learning
    media impact on, 3-5, 10-11, 31-32n.27, 147-159, 167-175, 179-182, 188n.53
    television impact on, 56, 226, 239
Audiences
    demographic variables, 156-158
    media-audience interaction, 164-166
    program selection, 159-164

Babbitt, Bruce, 97
Bagdikian, Ben, 91, 265
Baker, Howard, 1980 campaign, 220
Baker v. Carr, 266, 267
Banzhaff v. Federal Communications Commission, 117
Barron, Jerome, 119
Barth, Alan, 388
Bauman, Robert, 287
BBC. *See* British Broadcasting Corporation
Begin, Menachem, 337-338
Behavior
    adults, socially undesirable behavior, 178
    children, crime and violent behavior, 176-178
    media influence on, 168, 175-176, 179-182
    voting, 225-227
Bell, Griffin, 241
Benjamin, Burton, 297
Bennet, W. Lance, 10-11
Better Business Bureau, 57
Better Government Association, 279
Bias
    election coverage, 206, 209-212
    foreign news, 333-334, 347-349
    political, 102-103
Biden, Joseph, 200, 219
Blumler, Jay, 9
Bogart, Leo, 157
Boorstin, Daniel, 8
Bork, Robert H., 241, 244
"Born Innocent," 369
Boston Globe, 231n.37
The Boys on the Bus, 208

Braestrup, Peter, 80
Branzburg v. Hayes, 123, 124, 141
British Broadcasting Corporation (BBC), 36, 39
Broadcasting, 56
Brokaw, Tom, 2, 48, 49, 79
Brown, Jerry, 1980 campaign, 205
Brown, Les, 367
Brown v. Board of Education, 266
Brzezinski, Zbigniew, 17, 18, 350
Burger, Warren E., 266
"The Burning Bed," 147
Bush, George, 218, 219
    1980 campaign, 220
Business community
    Freedom of Information Act and, 130
    influence on media, 36-38, 48
    information relating to, 126-127, 130
    ownership of media, 41-44
    small business vs. big business control, 48-50
Byrd, Robert, 258
Byrne, Jane, 210, 211, 213

Cable News Network (CNN), 382
Cable Satellite Public Affairs Network (C-SPAN), 205, 250, 258
Cable television. *See also* Television
    capabilities, 373, 378
    financing, 381-382
    government coverage, 250, 258
    history, 376-377
    local control, 381
    ownership patterns, 52, 379
    programming, 56, 386
    proposed deregulation, 382-383
    QUBE, 384-385
    regulations, 56, 264, 378-381
    as specialized medium, 385
Caddell, Pat, 248
Caldera, Rafael, 347-348
Camp David meetings, 123, 240, 338
Campaigns. *See* Elections
Canadian Broadcasting Company (CBC), 299
Candidates, political. *See* Elections
Capital Cities/ABC
    Iran hostage crisis coverage, 287
    media ownership, 44, 45-46
    proposed merger with ITT, 249
Carswell, G. Harrold, 241

Carter, Jimmy
  briefing book incident, 20
  Camp David meetings, 123, 240, 338
  control of information, 314
  debates, 115, 200
  Iran, 201, 318, 350-351, 352
  issue positions, 217, 218
  media, use of, 198-199, 249, 250, 251
  media coverage, 198-199, 200-201,
    202, 205, 206, 213-214, 215, 216,
    243
  neutron bomb issue, 17-18
  1980 campaign, 220, 227
  1976 campaign, 223, 226-227, 248
  People's Republic of China, 248
Cartoons, violence in, 177
CAW. *See* Citizens for the American
  Way
CBC. *See* Canadian Broadcasting
  Company
CBS. *See* Columbia Broadcasting
  System
CBTV. *See* Coalition for Better
  Television
Censorship. *See also* News, suppres-
  sion; Obscenity; *Pentagon Papers;*
  Pornography
  advertising, 139-140
  Bay of Pigs, 24, 245, 247, 248-249,
    318, 352
  courts, 133-135, 139
  editorial, 65
  foreign correspondents, 336-337,
    347
  judicial, 268-269
  pressure groups, 57-58
  pretrial publicity, 133
  protective, 139-140
  security, 128, 129, 314, 315-316
  Three Mile Island incident, 314
  Third World, 356
Center for Investigative Reporting,
  278-279
Challenger explosion, 172
Chernobyl disaster, 313
Chicago Sun Times, 207-208, 211,
  282, 284
Chicago Tribune
  ownership of, 42
  political influence, 200
  reporting, 6, 75-76, 207-208, 211,
    213
  wire service, 47

Child, Marquis, 202
Children
  crime and violence in media, 176-
    178
  political socialization, 150-152
  television programming, 40, 121
Christian Crusade, 118
Christian Science Monitor, 97
  Third World coverage, 355
Citizens for the American Way, 58
Civil Rights Act of 1964, 294
Civil rights movement, 8, 294
Clark, Tom, 268
Classified information, government
  control and, 28
CNN. *See* Cable News Network
Coalition for Better Television
  (CBTV), 58
Cognitive balance theory of media
  use, 161
Coldevin, Gary, 151-152
Columbia Broadcasting System
  (CBS), 45-46, 70n.23, 236, 241, 287
  Vietnam War documentary, 297-
    299
Columbia Journalism Review, 367
Commercials, 117-118, 195-196
Common Cause, 294
Communications Act of 1934, 51, 55,
  56, 263, 380, 382
  reform proposals, 118-119
  Section 315, 114, 118-119
Communications policy, 262-264.
  See also individual presidents
Communist systems. *See also* Soviet
  Union; Totalitarian governments
  media control, 22, 23
  media coverage, 342
Community Information Project, 279
Competition
  media, 27, 47
  print vs. electronic media, 55, 119
  television industry, 52
Conflict in media. *See also* News,
  selection
  effects of, 98
Congress, U.S.
  communications policy, 262-264
  media coverage, 236, 254-260, 263
  media functions, 260-261
  media relations, 261-262, 265
  presidential coverage, compared
    with, 254-256, 260, 261

reelection, media effect on, 265
reporting of, 259-260
television coverage, 250, 254, 257-259
Congressional Quarterly, 259
Congressional Record, 258
Conscientious objectors, 294
Constitution
  electronic voting and, 384
  First Amendment, 27, 69n.3, 112, 123, 271
Control of media, private. *See also*
  Business community; Lobbies
  conflict of interest, 36
  Federal Communications Commission (FCC) regulations, 47, 50-55
  foundations and, 39-40
  government control, compared to, 37-38
  market size, 44-47
  media personnel, 59-65
  profit considerations, 36-37
Control of media, public. *See also*
  Ownership of media; Regulation of media
  authoritarian control, 21, 22-23, 25, 26-27
  background, 20-21, 35-38, 41
  methods, 25-29
  nonauthoritarian control, 21-22, 23-26, 27-29
  objectives, 25
  public broadcasting system, 39-41
  United States, 38-41
Controversy, coverage of, 99
Cook, Fred J., 118
Corporation for Public Broadcasting (CPB), 39, 69n.9
Courts. *See* Judiciary; Legal issues
Cox Broadcasting Corporation, 44
CPB. *See* Corporation for Public Broadcasting
Crane, Philip, 1980 campaign, 220
Crime. *See also* Legal issues
  copycat, 317
  exposure to, in media, 178, 190n.78
  investigative reporting and, 286
  news reporting, 84, 85, 89, 98, 188n.56, 268, 321-322
  publication restrictions, 139
"Crisis at General Hospital," 301n.11
Crisis coverage
  effects of, 315-317

media response/role, 309-314, 317-320
media suppression, 320-322
public crises, 305-308
Cronkite, Walter, 80, 235, 240
  Egypt-Israel relations, 286, 337-338
Crouse, Timothy, 208
C-SPAN. *See* Cable Satellite Public Affairs Network
Cultural Indicators project, 168
Cuomo, Mario, 97
Cutler, Lloyd, 350

Daley, Richard J., 97, 248
Daley, Richard M., 126, 210, 213
Daly, Steve, 194
Davis, Dennis, 169
"The Day After," 16, 82, 147, 295-296
Deaver, Michael, 144n.42
Debates
  coverage of, 75-76, 155
  effects of, 200
  equal time rule, 115
Declaration on the Media (United Nations), 327, 351
Defender, 207-208, 211
Degnan, Kim, 270
DeLorean, John, 133
Democratic governments, media control in, 29, 36
Demographic variables
  audiences, 156-158
  media personnel, 60-61, 66, 80
  media use and socialization, 156-158
  news, 61-65
Denton, Harold, 312
Deregulation
  background, 55-56
  Van Deerlin plan, 55
Dervin, Brenda, 157
Detroit, racial riots, 316-317
Detroit News
  Supreme Court coverage, 267
  television stations, 52
Documentaries/docudramas, 295
Dole, Robert, 103, 220, 258
Dominican Republic, coup in, 345-346
Dow Jones, 45
Dukakis, Michael, 219
DuPont, Peter, 204
Durham Morning Herald, 236

East coast press, 66. *See also* Press corps
EBS. *See* Emergency Broadcasting System
Edelman, Murray, 10-11, 172
Eger, John M., 387
Egyptian-Israeli relations, 337-338, 353-354
Eisenhower, Dwight, 200, 238
Elections. *See also* Voting
  adequacy of coverage, 219-221
  bias in coverage, 206, 209-212
  costs, 203-204
  equal time provision, 113-115
  issues, 215-221, 232n.48
  media coverage of, 206-221, 233n.61
  media effects on, 193-228
  "medialities," 218-219
  models of coverage, 209
  primaries, 198, 199, 204, 220, 221
  research on, 194-196, 227-228
Electronic media. *See also* Radio; Television
  access to, 114, 119-123, 141
  broadcast rights, 120
  commercials, 117-118
  controversial material, 115, 116-117
  crisis planning, 318-319
  judicial proceedings, 269
  presidential access to, 120-121
  print media, compared with, 119, 148-149, 214, 215, 218, 225, 241-242, 312-313, 314
  social change through, 181-182
  U.S. broadcasting, 356
Electronic transmission. *See* Transmission, electronic
Electronic voting, 383-384
El Salvador, election coverage, 343
Emergency Broadcasting System (EBS), 318
Engle v. Vitale, 267, 268
Entertainment
  media function, 185n.20
  news selection criterion, 96-97, 174-175
Entman, Robert, 291, 293-294
Entrapment, 299. *See also* Investigative journalism
Epton, Bernard, 210
Ervin, Sam, 257

Equal time/space, 113-116, 120
Establishment. *See* Political establishment
Ethics in journalism, 57, 138
Evans, Timothy, 193-194
Evers, Medgar, 157
Executive branch. *See also* Government; Government information, Presidents
  congressional coverage compared with, 254-256, 260, 261
  effect of media on, 238-241
  foreign affairs coverage and, 255, 341
  media functions and, 237-238, 260
  media relations with, 238-241, 243-251
Executive privilege, 130
Exit polling, 226

"Face the Nation," 253
Fairness doctrine, 114, 119, 141
  fair treatment rules, 55, 115-118
Falkland Islands war, British censorship in, 336, 347
Falwell, Jerry, 133
Farber, Myron, 136
FCC. *See* Federal Communications Commission
Federal Communications Commission (FCC). *See also* Licensing
  advertising, 121
  complaints to, 366, 368-369
  debates, 115
  deregulation, 55-56
  investigation of, 263-264
  Johnson, Nicholas, 58
  lobbies and, 58-59, 269
  policies, 50-51, 53, 264, 269-270, 368-369
  pornography, 139
  programming, 46, 53-55, 121
  public broadcasting, 40
  regulations, 44-45, 47, 51-55, 263-264, 269-270
  rulings, appeals of, 269-270
  station ownership, 44-45, 47
  underground media, 372
Federal Trade Commission, truth in advertising, 117
Feighan, Edward, 320
Finkbine, Sherri, 10

First Amendment, 27, 69n.3, 112-
113, 123, 125, 135, 136, 140, 141-
142, 226, 269
  cable television and, 381, 383
Foisie, Phil, 352
Ford, Gerald, 17, 115, 132, 202, 223, 246
Foreign affairs news
  correspondents, 329-334, 357
  Dominican Republic case, 345-346
  evaluation of, 351-353, 358
  gatekeeping, 345-349
  international beat system, 340-341
  Iran hostage crisis, 349
  Israeli-Palestinian conflict, 344
  Lebanon invasion, 346-347
  news selection, 335-337, 341-344
  pressures on reporting, 335-337
  production constraints, 344-345, 358
  public opinion and, 353-354
  television and, 350-351, 358
  Third World complaints, 354-358,
    363n.79
  U.S. coverage of, 328-329
  U.S. foreign policy and, 337-339,
    349-350, 351-353, 357
  U.S. newspapers, 330
  wire services, 330, 340-341
Fourth estate, 112, 123
France, television in, 35
Franchising, 26
Frankfurter, Felix, 134, 267
Freedom of Information Act of 1966
  access to business information,
    126-127, 130
  access to government documents,
    125, 143n.27
  1986 amendment, 125
  1974 amendment, 125
Freedom of the press. *See also* Censorship; Control of media, public;
  First Amendment; News, suppression
  access to information, right of,
    123-130
  access to media, right of, 112-123,
    119-123, 141
  commercial messages, 117-118
  electronic media, 114-119, 269
  libel and, 111
  media councils, 369-370
  political role, 29
  print media, 113-114, 118-119
Fulbright, J. William, 254

Gag orders, 134-135. *See also* Individual rights
Galbraith, John Kenneth, 272n.5
Gallegos, William, 287
Gannett newspaper chain, 45
Gans, Herbert, 94, 341-342
Gatekeeping. *See also* Foreign af-
  fairs news
  effects, 78, 80, 94-102, 345-349
  evaluation of, 103-104, 105
  foreign news, 329-334, 345-349
  gatekeepers, 77-80, 91-92, 120
  production constraints, 91-93
  story selection, 78-86, 89, 91-92
GE. *See* General Electric Company
General Electric Company (GE), 42,
  43, 45-46
General Motors, 57
Gerbner, George, 80, 154-155
Germany, conscientious objectors, 294
Gertz v. Robert Welch, 137
Ginsburg, Douglas, 241
Gitlin, Todd, 293
Glasnost, media control and, 22
Glasser, Ira, 298
Glenn, John, 199, 202, 203
"Godfather I, II," 368
Goldenberg, Edie, 295
Goldwater, Barry, 118
"Good Morning, America," 253
Gorbachev, Mikhail, 247, 328, 339
Gordon, Margaret, 281, 288
Government. *See also* Executive
  branch; Congress, U.S.; Political
  establishment; Public officials; Su-
  preme Court, U.S.
  coverage of, 236-237, 270-271
  media relationship to, 235-236,
    270-271
Government control of media. *See*
  Control of media, public
Graham, Daniel, 298
Granger, Bill, 366
Gratification theory of media use, 159-160
Greenberg, Bradley, 157
Grenada invasion
  censorship, 347
  media access, 124
  media coverage, 248

Hagerty, James, 238
Haig, Alexander, 103
Halberstam, David, 240, 247

Hargis, Billy James, 118
Hart, Gary, 11, 199, 200, 203, 219, 285
Hartman, David, 159-160
Hatfield, Mark, 17
Haynsworth, Clement F., 241
Head Start programs, 241
Health campaigns, 182
Hebert, Elsie, 125
Helsinki Accords of 1975, 337
Hess, Stephen, 255
"Heterophily," 180
Hijacking, 316. *See also* Terrorism
Hollings, Ernest, 204
Holmes, Oliver Wendell, 140
"Holocaust," 368
"Homophily," 180
"Housewife syndrome," 180
Hustler v. Falwell, 133, 138

Individual rights
  access to information, 123-130
  access to media, 112-123
  fair trial, 133-135, 143n.40, 144n.42
  media personnel, 140
  privacy, 131-133
  public versus private rights, 132-133, 137-138
  publish, 141
  reputation, 137-138
Informants, shield laws and, 135-137
Information. *See also* Censorship; Control of media; News suppression
  business, 126-127, 130
  executive privilege, 130
  Freedom of Information Act, 125-127, 130, 143n.27
  government documents, 125-130
  Grenada invasion, 124
  media access to, 26, 28, 123-130, 138-139, 140, 245, 311-312
  national security, 127-129, 138-139, 245
  new technologies and, 373-376
  public right to, 112-123
  sources, 78-79, 101-102, 135-137, 289, 291, 309, 310
  Supreme Court and, 123-124
Insurance Institute for Highway Safety, 180
Investigative journalism. *See also* Crisis coverage; Muckraking
  agenda building, 287-295

  collaboration with media institutions, 278-279
  collaboration with public officials, 283, 284, 286, 287-288, 300
  collaboration with watchdog organizations, 279
  effectiveness of, 282-283
  fairness and methods, 278, 297-299
  generating political action, 280-285
  objectives, 278, 279-280
  political scandal, 288-289
  science policy and, 289-292
  shield laws, 135-137
  social movements and, 289, 292-295
Iran
  hostage affair, 201, 318, 320, 338-339, 344, 345
  Iran-contra affair, 1-3, 173, 255
  Iran-Iraq hostilities, 222, 336
  Khomeini, Ruhollah, 338
Israel
  invasion of Lebanon, 336, 346-347
  relations with Egypt, 337-338, 353-354
  relations with Palestinians, 344
  Yom Kippur War, 309, 310, 311, 313, 314

Jackal syndrome. *See* Pack journalism
Jackson, Henry, 198
Jackson, Jesse, 8, 194, 202, 219
Jackson, Robert H. 134
Jarvis, Howard, 112
Jennings, Peter, 49-50, 79
Johnson, Lyndon, 80, 200-201, 240, 261, 314, 346
Johnson, Nicholas, 58
Journalists. *See also* Media personnel
  "backgrounders," 252-253
  debates, 155
  demographics, 60-61, 66, 80
  editorial choice, 9-11, 64, 81
  elections and, 193-228
  foreign affairs reporting, 330-335
  investigative, 278-280, 286. *See also* Investigative journalism
  pack journalism, 48, 208-209, 316
  political orientation, 62-65, 80-81, 208

reporting, 78-82, 132, 134, 209,
    252, 259-260, 266-268, 272n.5,
    291, 312, 321-322, 335-337, 343
responsibilities of, 315, 322, 323
role models, 23, 24-25, 29, 32n.43,
    67, 72n.70, 102, 278
shield laws, 135-137
Judiciary
    censorship by, 268-269
    communications law and, 269-270
    media coverage of, 237, 265-266
    media coverage, effects of, 266-268
Justice, Department of, 249

Kaiser Aluminum and Chemical
    Corporation, 298
Keeter, Scott, 170-171
Kefauver, Estes, 257, 258
Kemp, Jack, 97
Kennedy, Edward
    campaign issues, 217
    media image, 200
    1980 campaign, 220
    public opinion polls, 202
Kennedy, John F.
    assassination of, 5, 85-86, 157, 309,
        311, 312, 314, 315
    Bay of Pigs, 245, 247, 248-249, 318,
        352
    debates, 115, 200
    media coverage, 243
    use of media, 237, 241, 246, 247
Kennedy, Robert, assassination of, 157
Kerner Commission, 316, 318
Khomeini, Ruhollah, 338
King, Martin Luther, 8, 157, 313,
    315, 321
Kissinger, Henry, 252
Knight-Ridder newspaper chain, 45
Koppel, Ted, 367
KTTL-FM, 140
Kueneman, Rodney, 319

LaFollette, Robert, 212
Lambeth, Edmund, 57
Lang, Kurt and Gladys, 288, 289
Lasswell, Harold, 5
Le Monde, 348
League of Women Voters, debates, 115
Learning
    campaign coverage, 222-225, 227-
        228
    deterrents to, 173-175

effects, attitudes, 167-176
effects, behavior, 176-182
measurement of, 167-169
processes, 164-166
theories, 14-15
Third World and, 354-355
Lebanon, 336, 337, 346-347
Legal issues, 111-142, 369
Lerner, Daniel, 179
Lenin, Nikolai, 23
Libel laws, 137-138
Liberation News Service (LNS), 372
Libertarian philosophy, 21-22, 24, 67
Licensing
    deregulation and, 55
    lotteries, 53-54
    performance control, 53-54
    regulation and, 51-53, 114, 368
    renewal, 52-53, 58, 119, 121, 140
Libel Defense Resource Center, 111
Lichter, S. Robert, 290
Life, 200, 370
Lippmann, Walter, 165
LNS. See Liberation News Service
Lobbies
    access rights and, 122
    citizen groups, 58-59
    FCC and, 58-59, 269
    industry, 56-57
    media, 269
    public interest, 294
Local news
    congressional coverage and, 255,
        260-261
    story selection criteria, 86, 97,
        107n.23
Local Program Network (LPN), 246
Local programming
    cable television and, 386
    audience preference for, 86
    regulations, 54-55
Loeb, William, 212
Look, 370
Los Angeles Herald Examiner, 345-346
Los Angeles Times
    election coverage, 200, 212
    foreign affairs coverage, 329
    newspaper survey, 109n.55
    political survey, 63
    wire service, 47
LPN. See Local Program Network
Luce, Henry, 200, 247
Lucey, Pat, 215, 218

McClure, Jessica, 222
McClure, Robert, 195
McCormick, Robert, 200
McLuhan, Marshall, 6, 86, 373
Magruder, Jeb Stuart, 246
Mainstreaming, 155. *See also* Socialization, political
Malcolm X, 157
Manchester Union Leader, 212
Manipulative journalism. *See* Investigative journalism; Muckraking
Markets, media, 44-47
Marshall, John, 271
Matthews, Chris, 257
Media, access to
  advertising, 122
  electronic media, 114, 119-123, 141
  president's, 120-121
  print, 122-123, 141
  right of, 112-123, 141
Media control. *See* Control of media;
  Regulation of media
Media distortion
  foreign affairs, 327-328, 345-350, 352
  news, 174, 241-242, 243
  political process, 197-200
Media effects. *See also* Attitudes;
  Behavior
  attitude and behavior consequences, 3-5, 10-11, 12, 31-32n.27, 188n.53
  in government, 257-259
  measurement of, 12-16
  of neutron bomb story, 16-19
  political consequences, 3-5, 9, 10-11, 12-20, 29, 193-228, 238-241, 353-354
  role models, 23, 24-25, 29, 32n.43, 67, 102
  Third World complaints, 354-357
Media functions, 4, 5-12, 24-25, 42, 180, 211-212. *See also* Crisis coverage; Publicity
Media personnel. *See also* Journalists; names of specific media personnel
  control of media by, 59-60, 242
  demographics, 60-61, 66, 80
  goals and tactics, 242-243, 262
  organizational factors, 65-67
  relationship with Congress, 262
  relationship with executive branch, 243-251

responsibilities of, 315, 322, 323, 327, 351, 356
Media policy, trends in
  alternative media, 370-372
  councils, 369-370
  dissatisfaction with media, 366-369
  ombudsmen, 369
Media use patterns, 3-4, 37, 40. *See also* Multimedia combinations
"Meet the Press," 253
Mencken, H.L., 82
Meyrowitz, Joshua, 167
Miami Herald, 11, 113
Miami Herald Publishing Company v. Tornillo, 113-114
Mirage investigation, Chicago, 284-285, 299
Modernization
  media effects on, 179-182
  psychological barriers to, 179-181
Molotch, Harvey, 281, 288
Mondale, Walter, 155, 199, 200, 203, 210, 217, 218
Monopoly control, 26
Morison, Samuel Loring, 129
Mother Jones, 370
Muckraking, 12, 277. *See also* Investigative journalism
  models, 280-285, 301n.11
  public opinion, role of, 285
Mudd, Roger, 346
Multimedia combinations. *See also* Radio; Television
  WHDH-TV, 52-53
  regulation, 44-45, 47, 52-53
Murdoch, Rupert, 67
Mutual Broadcast System, 246

NAB. *See* National Association of Broadcasters
Nader, Ralph, 58, 112, 290, 294
National Association of Broadcasters (NAB), 56-57
National Black Media Coalition (NBMC), 58
National Broadcasting Company (NBC), 287
  "Born Innocent," 369
  Iran hostage crisis coverage, 287
  Lebanon coverage, 346-347
National Citizens' Committee for Broadcasting (NCCB), 58

National Highway Traffic Safety Administration, 181
National issues, agenda, 30n.12
National Latino Media Coalition (NLMC), 58
National News Council, 369-370
National Public Radio (NPR), 39
National Review, 370
National security issues
  Iran hostage crisis, 129, 318-319
  media access and, 127-129, 138-139, 245
National Telecommunications and Information Administration, 249
NBC. *See* National Broadcasting Company
NBMC. *See* National Black Media Coalition
NCCB. *See* National Citizens' Committee for Broadcasting
Nebraska Press Association v. Stuart, 134
Networks
  foreign affairs coverage, 338, 340-341, 342, 345
  mergers, 52
  radio, 46, 47
  regulations, 70n.23
  television, 45-46, 47
  White House press corps, 250
Neutron bomb issue, 16-19
New England Journal of Medicine, 120
New Republic, 370
New York Daily News, 243
New York Sun, 85
New York Times
  access to, 121-122
  Bay of Pigs coverage, 24
  election coverage, 220, 231n.36, 231n.37
  foreign affairs news, 237, 329, 330, 349
  Iran hostage crisis, 348
  Kennedy assassination, 313
  leadership role, 48
  Pentagon Papers, 128-129
  presidential coverage, 236
  public opinion polls, 201-202
  SDS story, 292-294
  shield law, 136
  Supreme Court coverage, 267
  Third World coverage, 355
  wire service, 47

New York Times Company, ownership, 44
New York Times v. Sullivan, 137
New York Times Co. v. United States, 128
New Yorker, 370
Newhouse newspaper chain, 45
News. *See also* Foreign affairs news; Gatekeeping; News making; Newspapers
  access to, 26
  agenda building, 287-295, 300
  agenda setting, 163-164, 288
  analysis, 195, 236
  broadcast rights, 120
  comprehension, 171
  costs of, 49-50, 203, 331, 339, 355-356, 372
  demographics and, 61-65
  diversity of, 53-54, 268, 328
  gathering, 86-90, 103, 291, 340-341
  general characteristics, 96-102
  negative/conflictual, 348
  production constraints, 91-94, 104-105
  selection, 80-86, 91-92, 94-102, 104, 106n.22, 108n.42, 113, 205-206, 214, 335-337, 339
  space allocation, 91, 93, 107n.23
  suppression, 320-322, 334. *See also* Censorship
News, release of
  "backgrounders," 252
  leaks, 253-254, 278, 286
  news briefings, 251, 259
  news conferences, 251-252
  press galleries, 261
  press releases, 248, 251, 259, 265
  radio spots, 251
News magazines
  "The Home Health Hustle," 283-284
  news selection, 92-93
News making. *See also* Gatekeeping; News
  crime, 268
  evaluation of, 102-104, 105, 300
  economic issues, 216-217, 232n.48, 255,
  foreign affairs, 97, 216-217, 232n.48, 255, 323
  gatekeeping in, 77-80, 94-102, 105, 259

government, 235-271, 268, 300
  methods of, 297-299
  models of, 76-77
  social problems, 216-217, 232n.48,
    268, 347-348
Newspaper coverage. *See also* Print
  media; names of individual newspapers
  controversy, 99
  crisis, 313, 314, 315. *See also* Crisis
    coverage
  election, 217, 221, 222-223,
    231n.36. *See also* Elections
Newspapers. *See also* Print
  media
  electronic printing/transmission,
    373, 388
  foreign language, 371
  ombudsmen, 369
  ownership patterns, 45-47, 48
  permits, 26
  production constraints, 91-94, 104-
    105
  readership, 148, 156-158, 353
  regulations, 51
  statistics, 42, 45, 70n.29
Newsweek, 198
Newsworthiness, definition of, 205
Nields, John W., Jr., 2
Nielsen, A.C., rating service, 105n.3
"Nightline," 253
Nixon, Richard M. *See also* Watergate
  access to government information,
    127
  China trip coverage, 337
  communications policy, 116, 249
  credibility, 12, 166, 167
  media relations, 26
  1972 election coverage, 195
  1960 TV debates, 115, 200
  use of media, 41, 195, 240
NLMC. *See* National Latino Media
  Coalition
North, Oliver L., 1, 2, 30n.3
Novosti Press Agency (Soviet), 337
NPR. *See* National Public Radio
Nuclear energy
  attitudes toward, 289-292
  Chernobyl disaster, 313
  coverage of, 290-292
  Three Mile Island, 241, 311, 313,
    315, 316, 318, 289-290

Obscenity
  government control and, 28
  restriction of publication, 139
Office of Management and Budget,
  249
Office of Media Liaison, 249-250
Office of Telecommunications Policy, 249
Ombudsmen, 369
Onassis, Jacqueline Kennedy, 132
Oswald, Lee Harvey, 316
Ownership of media. *See also* Control of media, public
  private control, 36
  public control, 36, 38-39
  semipublic control, 39-41
Ownership of media, private. *See
  also* Control of media, private
  business configurations, 41-44
  competition, 47, 52, 55
  newspaper, 45
  regulations, 47, 51-53
  television, 45-46

Pack journalism, 48, 208-209, 316
Packwood, Bob, 383
Palestine Liberation Organization
  (PLO), 346
Paletz, David, 291, 293-294
Palmer, Kyle, 200
Pastore, John, 264
Patterson, Thomas, 195, 220
PBS. *See* Public Broadcasting Service
Pell v. Procunier, 124
Pentagon Papers, 128-129, 138
"People Like Us," 241
Pettit, Tom, 198
Philadelphia Inquirer, 258
Piaget, Jean, 152
Plissner, Martin, 243
PLO. *See* Palestine Liberation Orga-
  nization
Political elites
  coverage of, 81, 94-95
  media impact on, 19-20, 225, 238,
    280, 283, 287-288, 291, 350-351
Political establishment
  anti-establishment behavior, 100
  media effect on, 197
  party influence, 197
  support for, 100-102
Political parties. *See* Political estab-
  lishment

Political process. *See also* Elections;
  Voting
    manipulation of, 12, 277-300
    media effect on, 166, 224, 238-241
    media support for, 7
Polsby, Daniel, 270
Pornography
    exposure to, 178
    restrictions on publication, 139
Powell, Jody, 215
Powledge, Fred, 292-293
Presidential Commission on Obscen-
  ity and Pornography, 139, 178
Presidential debates, 115, 155, 200.
  See also names individual candi-
  dates
Presidential elections. *See also* Elec-
  tions; names of individual candi-
  dates
    length of, 199
    media coverage of, 207, 212-213,
      215-218, 220, 222-224, 231n.36
    media effect on, 197-206, 214-215,
      224, 228
Presidents. *See also* Executive
  branch; Government; Media, access
  to; names of individual presidents;
  Press corps; White House Press
  Corps
    media coverage, 236, 241-242, 254-
      256
    media functions for, 237-238, 323
    relationship with media, 243-251,
      253
    use of media, 247-250, 251-252
Press corps
    Eastern/Washington, 246, 248,
      250-251, 259
    foreign, 334-335
    Supreme Court, 266, 267
    U.S. foreign correspondents, 329,
      330-334, 340
    White House, 250-251
Press releases, 248, 251, 259, 265. *See
  also* News, release of; Wire/press
  services
    Agence France-Presse (French),
      251, 331
    Associated Press (AP), 46-47
    foreign affairs coverage and, 340-
      341
    Liberation News Service (LNS),
      372

Reuters (British), 251, 331
    Underground Press Service (UPS),
      372
    United Press International (UPI),
      46-47
    White House press corps, 250-251
Primaries. *See* Elections
Print media. *See also* Newspapers
    access to, 122-123, 141
    electronic media, compared with,
      119, 148-149, 214, 215, 218, 225,
      241-242, 312-313, 314
    electronic transmission, 373, 388
    freedom of, 113-114, 118-119
    presidential coverage, 242
Prior restraint, 28, 128
Privacy Protection Act of 1980, 136
Procter and Gamble, 57
Programming
    advertising and, 57-58, 81-82, 121
    cable television, 56, 386
    children's, 40, 121
    FCC and, 46, 53-55, 121
    general, 39-41, 58, 81-82, 87, 158-
      159
    harmful, 369
    local, 54-55, 86, 386
    public broadcasting, 39-41
    public service, 54, 180-181
The Progressive, 128
Protess, David, 281, 288
Psychic mobility, 179
Public broadcasting
    deregulation and, 55
    financing of, 39-40, 41, 55
    programming, 39-41,
    Public Broadcasting Service
      (PBS), 39
    satellite distribution systems, 40
Public Broadcasting Act of 1967, 39
Public Broadcasting Service (PBS),
  39
Public officials, coverage of, 236
Public opinion
    arousal, 281, 282, 299-300
    foreign affairs coverage and, 353-
      354
    media, influence on, 285, 299
Public opinion polls
    exit polling, 226
    foreign affairs, 328
    image-making, 198, 201-202, 203
    role of, 196, 199, 291

Public records, access to, 125-130
Public service programming, 54, 180-181
Public Telecommunications Act of 1978, 39
Public television, impact of cable television on, 386
Publicity
  access to media through, 122
  congressional, 261, 262
  effects of, 101, 112, 261, 285, 292, 293-294
  granting of, 4, 8, 112-113, 122
  lack of, 7, 8, 244-245, 260
  Supreme Court, 266
  terrorism and, 320-321
  threat of, 4, 5-7, 241, 285-286, 300
  violence as, 99

Race riots, 312, 316-317, 319
Racial discrimination
  coverage of, 216, 240
  employment, 58
  programming, 58
  Marxist interpretations of, 164
Radio
  crisis coverage, 314, 323
  deregulation, 55-56
  Mutual Broadcast System, 246
  National Public Radio, 39
  networks, 46, 47
  ownership patterns, 44-47, 51-52
  specialized, 371
  stations, 70n.17
  statistics, 39, 42
  U.S. control of, 356
  World Administrative Radio Conference, 356
Radio Free Europe, 357
Radio Liberty, 357
"Rape: Every Woman's Nightmare," 282, 284
Rather, Dan, 48, 49-50, 79
Rating services, 105n.3
Reagan, Ronald
  budget proposals, 254
  campaigns, 195, 202, 203, 210, 213-215, 217, 218, 219, 220, 226
  Carter briefing book, 20
  Corporation for Public Broadcasting, 69n.9

debates, 115, 155, 200
  executive privilege, 130
  Iran-contra investigations, 1
  media, use of, 246, 254, 287
  public broadcasting, 40
  reaction to "The Day After," 296
  Reaganomics, 116-117
  Saturday radio broadcast, 246
  social programs, 241
  Supreme Court nominees, 241
  trip to Bitburg, Germany, 242
  trip to Europe, 236
  trip to Iceland, 247
Rebuttal, right of, 114, 118, 141
Red Lion Broadcasting Co. v. FCC, 118, 119
Reform. *See* Investigative journalism; Muckraking
Regulation of media
  deregulation, 55-56
  Council of Better Business Bureaus, 57
  Federal Communications Commission, 44-45, 47, 51-55, 263-264, 269-270
  manipulation of, 118
  National Association of Broadcasters, 56-57
Reporters. *See* Journalists; Media personnel
Reston, James, 352-353
Reuters wire service (British), 251, 331
Richmond Newspapers v. Virginia, 135
Rights. *See* Individual rights
Rivera, Geraldo, 282
Robertson, Pat, 219
Robinson, John, 169
Robinson, Michael, 219, 265
Rockwell, George Lincoln, 157
Roosevelt, Franklin Delano, 202
Roosevelt, Theodore, 12, 252
Rothman, Stanley, 290
Rubin Barry, 330

Sadat, Anwar el, 337-338
SALT. *See* Strategic Arms Limitation Treaty
Satellites
  foreign news, 335, 350
  impact of, 250
  U.S. control of, 356

Satellite distribution systems, 40
Saturday Evening Post, 293, 370
Sauter, Van Gordon, 298
Savitch, Jessica, 346
Sawyer, Eugene, 193-194
Saxbe v. Washington Post Co., 124
Scandal, political, 288-289
Schorr, Daniel, 137, 144n.55
Schwartz, Tony, 174
SDS. *See* Students for a Democratic
  Society
Sears Roebuck, 57
Sedition laws, 26-27, 28
Selective exposure theory of media
  use, 160-163
Shepherd v. Florida, 133-134
Sheppard v. Maxwell, 133-134
Shield laws, 135-137
Sigal, Leon, 87, 227
Sipple, Oliver, 132
"60 Minutes," 138, 173, 284, 338
Small, William, 59
Social problems
  adoption of change, 181-182
  coverage, 97, 99-100, 179-181, 347-
    348
Social responsibility philosophy, 22,
  24-25
Socialization, political. *See also*
  Learning
  adult, 152-155, 167, 168, 169-175,
    182-183, 208
  cable television and, 385
  childhood, 150-152, 167-168
  demographic factors, 156-158
  definition, 150, 164-165
  manipulation of media for, 183
  selectivity and, 161-162
Solomon, Douglas S., 182
Sources, 78-79, 101-102
  crisis information, 309, 310
  nuclear energy, 289, 291
  shield laws and, 135-137
Soviet Union, media control in, 22,
  23
Spartanburg, South Carolina, high
  school project, 384
Special Advisory Commission on
  Civil Disorders (Kerner Commission), 316, 318
Stahl, Leslie, 203, 205
Steffens, Lincoln, 277, 279
Sting operations, 299

Strategic Arms Limitation Treaty
  (SALT), 352
Stringers, 331
Stock market crash of October 1987,
  219, 222, 317, 350
Students for a Democratic Society
  (SDS), 292-293
Subsidies, 26
Sullivan rule, 137
Summit Meeting, 339
Supreme Court, U.S.
  cable television, 380
  gag orders, 134-135
  libel laws, 137-138
  media access to, 123-124, 268-269
  media coverage, 236, 266-268
  media relations, 267-268
  newsworthiness of, 266
  obscenity, 139
  Pentagon Papers, 129
  privacy protection, 136
  shield laws, 135-136
  review of FCC rulings, 269-270
Surgeon General's Advisory Committee on Television and Social Behavior, 264

Taylor, Maxwell, 247
Technology. *See also* Cable television; Satellites
  development of, 375-376
  impact of, 373-375
  two-way communications, 383-385
Television. *See also* Cable television;
  Electronic media; Regulation of
  media
  audience interaction, 14, 164-166
  attitudes and behavior, effects on,
    56, 226, 239. *See also* Attitudes;
    Behavior
  control, 56-57. *See also* Regulation
    of media
  deregulation, 55-56
  learning, effects on, 148-149, 155,
    174-175, 184n.4
  networks and cable TV, 45-46, 47
  news selection, 47, 48-49, 53, 87,
    89, 93, 104. *See also* News
  production constraints, 91-94, 104-
    105
  program selection, 159-164
  programming, 39-41, 87, 158-159
  public vs. commercial, 40

ratings, 161
reporting, 93
time spent watching, 150-151, 152,
   184n.7
Television coverage
   committee hearings, 257-258
   Congress, 254, 258-259
   crises, 314, 320, 350-351
   debates, 75-76, 155, 200. *See also*
      individual participants
   documentaries, 295
   election issues, 231n.36
   foreign affairs, 353
   Iran-contra affair, 1-3, 173, 350
   Israeli-Egyptian peace efforts,
      337-338
   judicial proceedings, 237, 265-266
   presidential campaigns, 193-228
   presidents, 239-241, 254, 353
   Supreme Court, 269
   terrorism, 320
   Vietnam War. *See* Vietnam War
Television diplomacy, 358
   Walter Cronkite, 337-338
Television stations. *See also* Cable
   television
   licensing, 52-54
   ownership patterns, 39, 45-47, 51-53
   profitability, 52
Terrorism, 320-321
Third World, 354-357
Three Mile Island nuclear accident
   coverage of, 241, 311, 313, 315, 316,
      318
   public opinion and nuclear power,
      289-290
Three Sites Project, 169, 172
Time, 198, 200, 213, 346
Times Mirror Company, 45
"Today," 17, 253
Tofani, Loretta, 136
Toronto Globe and Mail, 348
Totalitarian governments, media
   control in, 27, 29
Transmission
   direct and mediated, 241-242
   electronic, 373, 388
   facilities and federal regulation,
      51-55
Treason laws, media control and, 26-
   27, 28
Tribune Company newspaper chain,
   45, 70n.14

Truman, Harry S., 202, 241, 257
Turner, Ted, 52
Twentieth Century Fund, 369-370
"20/20," 283

Udall, Morris, 198
Underground press, 371-372
Underground Press Service (UPS), 372
UNESCO. *See* United Nations Edu-
   cational, Scientific and Cultural
   Organization
Union of Concerned Scientists, 290
United Church of Christ, Office of
   Communication, 58
United Nations Educational, Scien-
   tific and Cultural Organization
   authoritarian media control, 22
   Declaration on the Media, 327, 351
   Third World countries and, 356
United Press International (UPI).
   See Wire/press services
United States
   broadcasting, 356
   foreign correspondents, 330-334
   foreign coverage of, 334-335
   role of media, 24
United States Information Agency
   (USIA), 356
Universal Declaration of Human
   Rights of 1948, 356
UPI. *See* Wire/press services
UPS. *See* Underground press service
USIA. *See* United States Informa-
   tion Agency
U.S. News & World Report, 346

VanDeerlin, Lionel, 55
Vietnam War
   CBS documentary and William
      Westmoreland, 136, 297-299
   foreign news coverage, 349
   Lyndon Johnson and, 201
   media coverage, 15-16, 83-84, 239-240
   media interpretations of, 80
   Pentagon Papers, 128-129, 138
   protests, 293
Violence in media. *See also* News
   effects of, 98-99
Voice of America, 38, 335, 356-357
Voting. *See also* Elections
   media effects on, 13-14, 15, 225-
      227
   knowledge base for, 224-225

Walker, Dan, 120
Wall Street Journal, 122
Wallace, George, 212
Walters, Barbara, 49-50
War, coverage of, 342, 347
WARC. *See* World Administrative
  Radio Conference
Washington, Harold, 193, 210, 213
Washington, Walter, 313
Washington Journalism Review, 367
Washington Post
  Carter briefing book story, 20
  election coverage, 212, 231n.37
  foreign affairs coverage, 329
  neutron bomb story, 16-19
  Pentagon Papers, 128-129
  Quebec separation from Canada,
    348
  Richard Nixon and, 26
  Summit Meeting, 339
  television stations, 52
  Third World coverage, 355
  Vietnam War, 80
Watergate. *See also* Nixon, Richard M.
  effects of, 300
  media and, 240, 246, 285, 288-289
Watts riots, 319, 321
Weaver, David H., 60
Weinberger, Caspar, 252-253
Westmoreland, William, 136, 297-
  298
WHDH-TV, 52-53
White, Byron R., 136, 141
White, Theodore, 20
White House Office of Media Liai-
  son, 249

White House Office of Telecom-
  munications Policy, 249
White House Office of the Press Sec-
  retary, 249-250
White House Press Corps, 250-251.
  See also Press Corps
Wilhoit, G. Cleveland, 60
Willowbrook State School, 282-283
"The Winds of War," 173
Winston-Salem, North Carolina, ra-
  cial riots, 319-320, 321-322
Wire/press services
  Agence France-Presse (French),
    251, 331
  Associated Press (AP), 46-47
  foreign affairs coverage and, 330,
    340-341
  Liberation News Service (LNS), 372
  Reuters (British), 251, 331
  Underground Press Service (UPS),
    372
  United Press International (UPI),
    46-47
  White House press corps, 250-251
Women, media personnel, 61
World Administrative Radio Confer-
  ence (WARC), 356
WORLDNET, 335, 357
Wright, Joseph, 319

Yom Kippur War, coverage of, 309,
  310, 311, 313, 314

Zamora, Ronny, 369
Zemel v. Rusk, 123
Zukin, Cliff, 170-171